ALEXANDER OF APHRODISIAS

On the Soul Part 1

ALEXANDER OF APHRODISIAS

On the Soul

Part 1
Soul as Form of the Body,
Parts of the Soul,
Nourishment, and Perception

Translated with an Introduction
and Commentary by Victor Caston

B L O O M S B U R Y
LONDON • NEW DELHI • NEW YORK • SYDNEY

Bloomsbury Academic
An imprint of Bloomsbury Publishing Plc

50 Bedford Square	1385 Broadway
London	New York
WC1B 3DP	NY 10018
UK	USA

www.bloomsbury.com

Bloomsbury is a registered trade mark of Bloomsbury Publishing Plc

First published in 2012
Paperback edition first published 2014

© 2012 by Victor Caston

Victor Caston has asserted his right under the Copyright, Designs and Patents Act, 1988,
to be identified as Author of this work.

British Library Cataloguing-in-Publication Data
A catalogue record for this book is available from the British Library.

ISBN HB: 978-1-7809-3024-4
PB: 978-1-4725-5798-8
ePDF: 978-1-4725-0172-1

Library of Congress Cataloging-in-Publication Data
A catalog record for this book is available from the Library of Congress.

Acknowledgements

The present translations have been made possible by generous and imaginative
funding from the following sources: the National Endowment for the
Humanities, Division of Research Programs, an independent federal agency
of the USA; the Leverhulme Trust; the British Academy; the Jowett Copyright
Trustees; the Royal Society (UK); Centro Internazionale A. Beltrame
di Storia dello Spazio e del Tempo (Padua); Mario Mignucci; Liverpool
University; the Leventis Foundation; the Arts and Humanities Research
Council; Gresham College; the Esmée Fairbairn Charitable Trust; the Henry
Brown Trust; Mr and Mrs N. Egon; the Netherlands Organisation for Scientific
Research (NWO/GW); the Ashdown Trust; Dr Victoria Solomonides, the
Cultural Attaché of the Greek Embassy in London. The editor wishes to
thank John Thorp, James Wilberding, Michael Griffin, Donald Russell and
William Charlton for their comments, Sebastian Gertz for preparing the
volume for press, and Deborah Blake at Bristol Classical Press, who has been
the publisher responsible for every volume since the first.

Typeset by Ray Davies

Contents

In memoriam
Robert W. Sharples
1949-2010

Acknowledgements

As a graduate student in London in 1985-7, I had the good fortune to study Alexander of Aphrodisias with Bob Sharples. I met with him weekly to read Alexander's *On the Soul* and discuss the text's finer points, while attending the university lectures he offered on Post-Aristotelian philosophy with my supervisor Richard Sorabji and the many seminars they organised at the old Institute for Classical Studies on Gordon Square. It was an exciting time to be in the UK working on ancient philosophy. The turn to Hellenistic philosophy was still relatively new, Long and Sedley's collection had just been published, and the project to translate all the commentators on Aristotle was just getting under way. They were wonderful years.

In retrospect, I had no idea just how fortunate I was. No one in the twentieth century did more to advance the study of the Peripatetics after Aristotle, from Theophrastus to Alexander. His scholarship was exemplary, not merely for its erudition, which was remarkable, or for its range and sheer quantity, which was impressive, but above all for his critical judgement. He was unusually alive to the openness of texts to multiple interpretations and the recalcitrance of counterevidence: short of decisive refutation, which he took to be rare, one always had to acknowledge the possibility of alternative readings, and he was ingenious at devising ways in which they might be defended against even his own favoured view. In others, these might merely have been methodological scruples. But in Bob they were also a natural expression of his own characteristic modesty and his charity towards others. As a teacher, he was unfailingly generous and supportive. Bob immediately read any draft you gave him and returned it with copious, thoughtful comments and acute criticisms, often within just a day or two. I could not have studied Alexander with anyone better.

Like many others, I was greatly saddened to hear of Bob's illness and untimely demise, and he passed away while this volume was still in preparation. Both it and the second volume are dedicated to his memory.

I would also like to thank several other people who were crucial in bringing this volume to term, above all the editor of the series, Richard Sorabji, who has my deepest gratitude for his detailed and invaluable comments, his unwavering encouragement, and (not least) his patience and trust. Thanks are also due to Ian McCready-Flora, who served as my research assistant in the summer of 2009, and to Michael Griffin, the editorial assistant through most of the project. Both made excellent contributions, which I have tried to acknowledge in the notes. Sebastian Gertz, the editorial assistant who saw the project through to its final stages, also has my thanks for his yeoman's service with all the corrections and changes. I am grateful as well to the students in my graduate seminar at the University of Michigan in the winter term of 2009, who worked through an earlier draft of the entire translation, and to the participants in a mini-conference on the present volume at the Humboldt-Universität in Berlin in March 2011, especially my commentators Jakub Krajczynski, George Karamanolis, and Miira Tuominen. I learned a great deal from both groups, who helped save me from quite a few errors. In addition, I owe a great debt to Ian Crystal for his Herculean efforts to assemble the index locorum. Such tools are invaluable for making a scholarly work useful, and they rarely get the thanks they deserve.

Finally, I would like to record my greatest debt of all, to my wife, Ruth, for her love and support, and for all the joy that she and my two daughters, Eva and Sarah, have brought me. Without them, I could not have accomplished any of the things I have.

Introduction

Alexander of Aphrodisias, easily one of the greatest commentators on Aristotle – later Greek commentators sometimes refer to him as 'the Commentator' (*ho exêgêtês*) on Aristotle[1] or even as a 'new' or 'second Aristotle'[2] – is also one of the foremost Aristotelians in the tradition, alongside Thomas Aquinas and Ibn Rushd, a philosopher in his own right, who developed a profound and systematic synthesis of Aristotle's views that was to have lasting influence.

Life and works

We know little of Alexander's life, apart from the fact that he came from Aphrodisias, a city in Caria (a region in the southwest of modern day Turkey), and that sometime between 198 and 209 CE he was appointed by the emperors Septimus Severus and Antoninus Caracalla to a chair in Aristotelian philosophy in Athens, one of four chairs established for each of the major schools of philosophy by Marcus Aurelius in 176.[3] It has often been assumed that Alexander is referring to this appointment in the dedication of his treatise *On Fate*.[4] But recently this has been confirmed by an inscription from Aphrodisias, which Alexander had dedicated to his father, who was also named Alexander and was a philosopher as well (perhaps even the author of *On Fevers* and the collections of medical problems attributed to an 'Alexander of Aphrodisias'). The inscription gives the full name of the younger Alexander (that is, the commentator) as Titus Aurelius Alexandros.[5] We also know that he studied with Sosigenes and Herminus (who had been one of Galen's teachers as well).[6] Based on these facts, we can infer that Alexander was born sometime between 140 and 165.[7]

Apart from commentaries on Aristotle's works, Alexander also wrote philosophical treatises, articulating and defending in his own voice an Aristotelian point of view.[8] The present work, *On the Soul*, is one of the few surviving treatises, along with one on determinism and freedom of choice (*On Fate*) and another on material composition (*On Mixture*). Alexander also wrote a commentary on Aristotle's *On the Soul*. But the commentary is now lost and survives only in isolated quotations.[9] The present treatise is sometimes mistakenly referred to as a commentary, because of its faithfulness to both the sequence of topics and the doctrines put forward in Aristotle's *On the Soul*. But the purpose of the two types of work is nonetheless different: a commentary seeks to elucidate a text; a treatise seeks to defend the truth. Unlike his commentaries, Alexander's treatise *On the Soul* does not focus on Aristotle's statements line-by-line or puzzle about manuscript readings and alternative interpretations. Instead, he simply presents the view itself, elaborated and argued for in the way he sees best, referring to Aristotle's text only at intervals for added emphasis and authority.[10] That Alexander's treatise agrees so extensively with Aristotle's *On the Soul*, in both its organisation as well as in doctrine, is just a sign of how much he thinks Aristotle got right. As Alexander explains in the opening pages of his *On the Soul*, he reveres Aristotle because there is *more* truth (*alêthesteras*) in his views than in others, and so will have achieved his aim if he elaborates and defends them well (2,4-9).[11] But that obviously permits him divergences, modifications, and revisions, as well as elaborations and further developments.

The organisation and aims of the treatise

The most obvious similarity between Aristotle's *On the Soul* and Alexander's is the sequence of topics, as just mentioned. But in fact the overlap is only partial. Alexander only follows the same order as Aristotle from 27,1, where Alexander picks up Aristotle's ascent through the powers of living things, starting with his general remarks about these powers in *On the Soul* 2.3; and their discussions remain more or less parallel until the end of Alexander's treatise, where he adds an appendix on the *hêgemonikon* or governing part of the soul and its location in the body (94,7-100,17). Because of this extensive correspondence, much of Alexander's treatise can be consulted as if it were a continuous commentary on Aristotle *On the Soul* 2.3-3.13, even though that is not its form or express purpose.

The first twenty-six pages of Alexander's treatise, on the other hand – a full quarter of the work as a whole – do not correspond directly to any major section of Aristotle's *On the Soul*. In these pages Alexander explores the Aristotelian notion of form in order to ground and explain Aristotle's central claim that the soul is the form of the body. This section naturally has many points of contact with the earlier parts of Aristotle's treatise. But they are limited to a few key passages or doctrines. Otherwise, the course of discussion is very much Alexander's own.

This superficial difference in organisation points to more significant underlying differences in both method and objectives. Aristotle approaches the subject dialectically, in his characteristic fashion. He begins by surveying the 'reputable views' (*endoxa*) that have been held on the topic, to see where there are disagreements as well as consensus, and then teases out various 'puzzles' (*aporiai*), which set the agenda for his subsequent discussion. His aim is to recover what is right in each position in a way that also shows how to resolve the difficulties they face, and he later refers back to these disagreements at various points in the treatise to show

how his own theory provides a more adequate solution. Aristotle thus actively engages the earlier history of the subject for the entire first book of *On the Soul*. He begins his own positive exposition in earnest only in the second book, which opens with his definition of the soul as the form of the body.

In contrast, Alexander's approach is not dialectical, but systematic. His aim is to elaborate the conceptual framework necessary for understanding Aristotle's theory, above all the metaphysical foundations on which the whole theory rests – something which Aristotle does only in the most cursory way in his *On the Soul*. If the soul is best understood as the form of the living body, then we first need to grasp the distinction between matter and form, and reflect on its implications, before we can appreciate how it can account for the psychological functions investigated in the remainder of the treatise. What Alexander offers is a masterful synthesis of Aristotle's views, drawn from across the corpus, to which he adds extensive supporting arguments and distinctions. It is both insightful and illuminating. It is also controversial. Although many contemporary philosophers will find it extremely attractive, someone like Paul Moraux (1942), working in the midst of the neo-Thomist revival, clearly felt it was threatening and had to be answered in the most forceful terms.[12] But there can be no doubt that it is an Aristotelian vision of real power and profundity.

There is a second respect in which Alexander's approach differs. Understandably, he is not concerned so much with Aristotle's predecessors as with his own contemporaries and rivals. For Alexander, unlike Aristotle, Aristotelianism is already an established position, and Alexander's aim is to show that it is still very much a live option, indeed the best. He consciously positions himself midway between the dualism of Middle Platonists like Atticus (late second century CE) and the materialism of the Stoics, undoubtedly still the most dominant philosophical force of his day. It is hard for us not to focus on the sharpened polemical character of Alexander's arguments and the ways in which he is or is not fair. But we should not overlook the more important underlying fact that for Alexander exegesis is not an antiquarian or historical exercise, but a philosophical one.

Naturalism

Alexander makes his opposition to Platonism clear in the opening pages of the treatise, even though he does not refer to it by name. At 2,17 he uses a phrase from Plato's *Phaedo* to mark the fundamental difference in orientation. In the original passage, Socrates diagnoses Simmias' doubts and fears about the fate of the soul: Simmias is at a loss because he cannot reconcile his belief that (i) the soul is a balance or 'harmony' of bodily powers, and so something that will dissipate at death, with his conviction that (ii) the soul is something 'more divine and more noble than the body' (*kai theioteron kai kallion on tou sômatos*, 91C-D; cf. 94E). Between these two options, Socrates' allegiance to the second is never in doubt, and he goes on to argue at length against the first view that the soul is in any way a function of the body. In contrast, Alexander challenges the underlying dilemma. On his view, the soul is *both* something worthy of our greatest admiration *and* something that is entirely natural and indeed mortal. We will cease to find this puzzling, he says, once we appreciate how wondrous the workings of nature are. By grasping how nature works in general and how the soul is a part of nature, we will come to find both halves of this conjunction completely convincing (2,10-25).

Alexander gestures briefly in this passage at biological marvels: he mentions the structure of our bodies, the regulation of our inner organs, and the ways in which they are adapted to our external limbs and their functions. But this is not something he examines in any detail in this treatise or, for that matter, in any of the extant works. What he focuses on instead is more basic and metaphysical. On the Aristotelian view, the soul is the form of the body and so, Alexander argues, the relation between the two will be essentially the same as in other natural objects: in this respect, the same basic principles apply to both living and non-living things. Such things obviously differ from each other in their specific characteristics, powers, and activities. But this does not mark a fundamental metaphysical difference. It is due rather to *physical* differences in their material composition and organisation. Greater complexity in the powers of things is to be explained by a corresponding complexity in their underlying matter (8,5-17).

For Alexander, then, the distinction between matter and form is only the beginning. We also need to consider the specific differences between various forms and the corresponding differences in their underlying matter. Alexander proceeds to survey the whole of nature, starting with the four elements and rising through inanimate substances, plants, animals, and finally humans (8,17-11,13).[13] At each stage of this *scala naturae*, there is a dramatic increase in the variety of species of natural substances, their distinctive abilities, and their behaviour. In fact, he argues, the increase in complexity from one broad echelon to the next is strictly proportional: the extent to which plants surpass inanimate substances in their variety and powers is as great as the extent to which animals surpass plants (10,12-17). Once we have considered the whole of nature in this way and seen how the powers of natural substances are a function of their underlying material constitution, he urges, we will no longer be astonished at the powers of animals and humans: any 'natural piety' they evoke in us will be the same as what we feel before the equally amazing, though simpler, powers of natural substances at lower levels, right down to the elements themselves (11,5-13). There is no fundamental discontinuity here that would require a different kind of explanation than we use for other natural substances. What we marvel at here pervades the whole of nature.

To emphasise the general applicability of these underlying principles, Alexander repeatedly explains characteristics of the soul by reference to what holds for forms even in the simplest case, of the elements, such as the lightness of fire and the heaviness of earth.[14] His point is *not* that the elements have a soul or that the soul of living things can be reduced to combinations of the elements or their features, but rather that many of the conclusions he draws about the soul follow simply *from its being a form*, and so are strictly analogous to characteristics that belong to the forms of other things, including those which are inanimate or even elemental. The features that distinguish the animate from the inanimate are, in contrast, the subject of the more detailed discussions that constitute most of the subsequent treatise.

Form and matter

The basic framework for Alexander's discussion rests on his understanding of form and matter. He introduces the distinction by considering artefacts like statues, where the components are more evident to us (2,25-3,13), before proceeding to the more fundamental case of natural objects (3,13-21). We can draw a further division that will prove pivotal, though, within the class of natural objects, between simple and compound bodies (3,22-8). All natural objects are bodies, and all bodies are composed of matter and form. But some natural bodies – namely, compound bodies – are composed from other *bodies*, whereas simple bodies are not. Evidently the underlying matter in these two cases is quite different. Since the matter of compound bodies consists of other bodies, they will have a matter and form of their own; and if they are also compound bodies, then their matter in turn will be bodies and so composed of matter and form again; and this will continue so long as the underlying matter consists of compound bodies. There is obviously potential here for great complexity in the constitution of bodies. Understanding how the properties of the underlying bodies contribute to the properties of the compound will be crucial for the material account of any natural substance.

Simple bodies like the four elements, in contrast, lack this complexity. They provide the base case: though themselves composed of matter and form, their matter is not a body and so not composed of anything further. Alexander here develops the classic conception of prime matter (3,28-4,20), or what he calls 'matter in the fundamental sense' (*kuriôs hulê*). Since prime matter is not itself a body, it does not contain within itself any intrinsic form or quality of its own. He defines it, in fact, as what is 'amorphous, formless, and shapeless', a formulation used by both earlier Aristotelians and Stoics, and whose phrasing traces back to Plato and Aristotle.[15] But although prime matter lacks any intrinsic quality *of its own*, it nevertheless cannot exist apart from *some* form or quality. Consequently, it can be separated from form only in thought (6,17-19); it cannot exist 'by itself on its own' (*autên huphestanai kath' hautên*, 4,8-18.20-1; cf. 18,2-7). Apart from a few brief reports in the doxographic tradition, Alexander's discussion is the first full elaboration of the idea. It is still hotly debated whether this is part of Aristotle's own conception of matter.[16]

At least as important, though, is Alexander's conception of form. As Alexander points out, the forms of natural bodies are even less independent than matter. For while prime matter cannot exist on its own, the matter of compound bodies can, since they are composed from bodies and bodies are precisely what can exist on their own. The forms of natural bodies, in contrast, can never exist on their own, but must always exist in some matter (4,20-5,2; see also 4,8-9; 5,21-2; 17,11-12). Here again we see claims that will later become orthodox stated much more fully and directly than in Aristotle. And while Alexander does not press the point, his emphasis on the dependence of form has significant ramifications in context. For if, as he will later make clear, the soul is a form of a natural body, then the soul cannot exist on its own, but must be inseparable from the body (17,9-15).

Less well appreciated are Alexander's innovations about forms. In setting out his notion, he emphasises that forms are something non-bodily (*asômata*, 5,18-6,2; 7,9-14). He clearly intends a sharp contrast with the Stoics, who also hold there are two basic principles or *arkhai* of things, one of which is qualityless matter and the other the divine *logos* that pervades and shapes all things, giving them their distinctive qualities. On the Stoic view, however, both principles are *bodies*.[17] But what precisely does Alexander mean when he says that form is non-bodily? He is not claiming that forms can exist separately from bodies, as we have just seen. Nor is he making a point about the irreducibility of form to matter, though he surely is committed to this (17,17-18). Given the fundamental distinction between form and matter, it is trivially true that forms are immaterial. But this cannot be his point in the present context, since he also thinks that *prime matter* is non-bodily, even though it is surely material. The contrast again is with the Stoic doctrine of principles. Alexander will later argue that since forms are not bodies, they are never composite (17,15-18,10), something that is not true of matter in general, apart from prime matter. But this does not seem to be the motivation for the view we are now considering so much as an elaboration or consequence of it.

Alexander's point is more subtle and profound. It is best understood as turning on the metaphysics of *causality*. The Stoics characterise their two principles in explicitly causal terms: one principle acts, the other is acted upon, and together their interaction results in the constitution of ordinary objects (see n. 17 above). But on the Stoic view only bodies can act or be acted upon.[18] Hence, the principles of bodies must themselves be bodies (see n. 17 above). Alexander rejects this model of causality. Only bodies can affect one another in this way. But the principles of bodies do not themselves affect anything. Rather, bodies act and are acted upon *in virtue of their forms* (7,9-13; cf. 6,21-3; 31,10-25). Forms are thus *causally relevant* – indeed, they are precisely what grounds or explains a body's ability to act or be acted upon in a certain way. But they are not themselves the *agents* or *subjects* of change. Alexander is not making a point about materialism or reduction, but about ontology. A form is not a body itself, but something that *belongs* to a body. Today we take for granted a distinction between bodies and the properties of bodies; it hardly needs saying that properties are not themselves bodies. But it was a relatively new point at the time. Although the basis for it is certainly in Aristotle, he never states it so fully and explicitly. Alexander is one of the first to develop the point at length.[19] To say that forms are non-bodily, then, is simply to make a distinction about which ontological category they belong to. It does not compromise or qualify his materialism in any way.

Alexander uses this conception of form to explain some of Aristotle's more distinctive claims about the soul. The first is that the soul cannot itself undergo change (*akinêton*): it does not move, grow in size, or undergo any kind of alteration or modification in its own right.[20] The composite substance to which the soul belongs is what in fact undergoes any changes ascribed to the soul, not the soul itself. The soul undergoes these changes only vicariously, in so far as it is an essential part of something that does properly undergo change – as Aristotle and Alexander standardly put it, the soul undergoes these changes only 'extrinsically' (*kata sumbebêkos*). Alexander's point, however, is that this is not peculiar to souls, but something that holds of causal powers, dispositions, and forms quite generally. None of them undergoes change itself, but rather the things that bear them do and they do so in virtue of having these dispositions or powers. The only things that can properly undergo change are things that exist separately on their own (21,22-22,23).

Alexander further uses this view to explain a second, closely related doctrine. Because the soul does not undergo any modification itself, it is not the *subject* of psychological states properly speaking (23,6-24). As Aristotle says in what has come to be known as 'the celebrated Rylean passage', *DA* 1.4, 408a34-b18, the soul no more perceives or thinks than it builds or weaves; to think that it does is, in effect, to make a category mistake. It is more accurate to say that a living being does these things *with* or *in virtue of* its soul. Alexander emphasises again that this does not hold merely for the soul, but for *all* powers and dispositions generally. The heaviness of earth does not travel downwards by using earth; rather earth moves downward in virtue of its weight (23,24-24,4).

For this reason, Alexander firmly rejects the suggestion that the soul might be a homunculus, like the pilot of a ship, a possibility Aristotle mentions in passing as still unsettled at *DA* 2.1, 413a8-10. If the soul were like a pilot, Alexander argues, it would be separable from the living body, and possibly even a composite itself. But if the soul is a form or disposition of the living body, and so its completion (*entelekheia*) and culmination (*teleiotês*), as Alexander maintains, then the soul is inseparable from it. It is nothing but the ability of a living thing to function as such, in the ways characteristic of its kind. It would therefore be better to compare the soul to the *art* of piloting, to the principles that govern the operations and well-functioning of the ship. If the comparison with a pilot is merely a vivid way of making this point, through a kind of synecdoche, it is harmless. But if the comparison essentially involves an inner person who uses and guides the ship, then it is to be rejected, whether the soul is taken to be incorporeal, as the Platonists would maintain, or corporeal, as the Stoics and other materialists would (15,10-26; 20,26-21,21; cf. 14,4-5; 79,19-20). All such dualisms face a serious mind-body problem, according to Alexander: once we have granted their premise that the soul and the body are separate from each other and different in nature (*kekhôrismena te allêlôn onta kai tas phuseis diapheronta*), it is no longer clear how the two could ever constitute a unity (21,16-21).

On the Aristotelian view, in contrast, the soul and the body are not separable in this way. They are both aspects of the living thing that cannot exist apart from it or from each other. The way in which the soul is present in (*en*) the body, and so the way in which the living thing is constituted from (*ek*) them both, cannot be reduced to any other kind of presence or composition: to that extent, the relation between the soul and the body is *sui generis* (11,14-12,7; 14,24-15,5). But since it is just the relation between form and matter, it is also a commonplace relation, found in all composites, animate or inanimate, and is not invoked because of any special peculiarity of the soul or mind. The Aristotelian solution to the mind-body problem is thus not *ad hoc*, but a principled application of a broader metaphysical strategy.

Finally, Alexander's conception of form explains a distinctive feature of his approach. On his view, the forms of natural substances, and hence souls, are ultimately to be understood as *causal powers* or *dispositions*. Forms are the features of substances that enable them to do or undergo the activities characteristic of their kind – in Aristotelian terminology, a form just is the ability to perform one's specific function or *ergon*. Aristotelians in the last forty years have taken this approach to be pivotal and placed great emphasis on it. But the first person to make this central is Alexander. A striking feature of his treatise, as a quick glance at the Greek-English Index will show, is how prevalent the word *dunamis* or 'power' is – much more so, in fact, than *energeia* or 'activity', which one might otherwise have assumed would be more important, given the ontological and definitional priority Aristotle assigns it in the *Metaphysics*. But there is no substantive or doctrinal difference here, only one of emphasis. A power must inevitably be defined as the power to perform or undergo a certain activity, just as this activity can in turn be understood as its culmination and fulfilment. Both Aristotle and Alexander stress, moreover, that the soul and its faculties are to be identified with the *first* attainment or completion (*entelekheia*) of a living body: they are the features a living thing *actually* has that *enable* it to act or behave in certain characteristic ways. Actually performing these activities represents a further, *second* attainment or completion, which need not be taking place in order for a thing to be alive or endowed with the relevant psychological faculties.

This approach has even broader ramifications. If the forms of *all* natural substances are first attainments or completions, as Alexander seems to believe, then the metaphysics of natural substances in general is best pursued in terms of the causal powers or dispositions they possess, in virtue of which they perform their distinctive activities. Such an approach is, in a broad but important sense, a *functionalist* one: to be a certain kind of thing is to be capable of performing specific activities, and its form is just what enables it to do this.[21] The basis of this view, again, is clearly in Aristotle. But Alexander's conception of form as a causal power is the first fully explicit articulation of it.

Supervenience and emergentism

The claim that different kinds of substance differ in form, then, is to be spelled out in terms of the different causal powers each has: these powers are what makes each the kind of thing it is.

Such differences are not adventitious, moreover: they do not float freely on top of the underlying matter. A given body cannot take on just any form. It can only take on those for which it is *appropriate* as matter – it must be *suitable* for the kinds of activity characteristic of that form. This functional constraint on matter, of what sort of matter must be present *if* a given type of form is to be realised, is what Aristotle calls 'conditional necessity'.[22] The same constraint applies directly to souls and bodies, and it was the failure to appreciate this, in both Aristotle's and Alexander's opinion, that led Pythagoreans to their mistaken doctrine of metempsychosis: a human soul cannot employ the body of a sea slug any more than the principles of carpentry govern the playing of a musical instrument like an oboe.[23] It is not just that the activities of souls presuppose *some* bodily activity or other and so must be embodied (12,7-13,8). Their activities require bodies of a specific sort, suited to carrying them out.

Aristotle further thinks, more strongly, that each type of body has a distinct form of its own; and in context it is clear that this principle is meant to apply directly to bodies and souls (*DA* 1.3, 407b23-4). Alexander is even more explicit. Which type of soul a living thing has is a 'consequence' of the kind of body it has (*epi têi toutôn poiai sustasei epêkolouthêsan hai diaphoroi psukhai*), so that they 'covary' with one another (*summetaballousin de allêlois*); more generally, which type of soul a living thing has 'follows' on the kind of temperament or blend of its body (*têi poiai krasei tou sômatos kai hê tês psukhês hepetai diaphora*, *Mant.* 104,27-34). In the contemporary technical sense of the term, then, souls *supervene* on bodies:[24] the same type of body must have the same type of soul; hence, any difference in the type of soul that living things have implies a corresponding difference in the type of body.[25]

Now, it might be objected that the 'supervenience' of souls on bodies is in one sense trivial: *living* bodies, *eo ipso*, necessarily have a soul. It even seems built into Aristotle's definition: the soul, he says, is the form of a 'natural body that through its power has life' (*sômatos phusikou dunamei zôên ekhontos*, *DA* 2.1, 412a27-8), that is, it is the form of something which can perform the activities distinctive of living things and is thus alive; the soul simply is that ability or set of abilities in virtue of which the living thing is alive. A body, therefore, which is incapable of performing these functions is not the sort of thing a soul *can* belong to (412b25-6). We might say that the dead body lying over there is a man, but only through a kind of courtesy, or as Aristotle says, by 'homonymy' (412b17-413a3). It is not a man in the primary sense, of something which is living, breathing, capable of walking, talking, engaging in meaningful interactions, and experiencing a broad range of phenomena. A corpse is a man only in the sense that it *was* a man in this primary sense. But then the soul, as Alexander rightly points out, is not an 'accident' or extrinsic feature (*sumbebêkos*) of the relevant kind of body, something that this body might have or lack, while otherwise remaining the same (14,24-15,5).[26] On Aristotle's view, then, the organic body of a living thing is *essentially* ensouled: it is by its nature alive, with functioning organs, and so *must* have a soul – it is *animate* in the full, etymological sense of the word. It would be trivial to claim that souls supervene on bodies of this sort. Wherever there is a living body, there must *eo ipso* be a soul as well. Different types of soul, moreover, might also plausibly be thought to covary with different types of body, when this is understood in terms of the fully functioning, organic bodies of different types of living thing.

Alexander is willing to go a good deal further than this objection allows, however. The soul, in his view, is a power and form that supervenes (*epiginomenon*) on the particular mixture of underlying bodies, which are blended together in some specific proportion (25,2-3).[27] The underlying matter here is not the organic body, but the various bodies and materials that go into its make-up, comparable to the separate ingredients that make up the famous *tetrapharmakon* or 'four-fold drug' (24,23-25,2), a potent cocktail mixed from otherwise ordinary ingredients (according to LSJ, wax, tallow, pitch and resin). At one point, in fact, he even seems willing to regard the relevant underlying bodies as extending down to the level of 'simple bodies', that is, down to the four elements that ultimately constitute the body (26,21-2). If we want to explain the vast differences between different types of souls – say, of animals, which can perceive and move in various ways, and plants, which can only nourish themselves, grow and reproduce – we will need to refer to the number and kinds of underlying bodies, and how they are blended and joined together (10,14-19). The material composition of a living substance is thus an 'origin and principle' (*arkhê*) in the following sense: differences in forms follow from and supervene on differences in the underlying matter (10,24-6), where these are understood in terms of ingredients that can exist and be described *independently* of the living substance they come to form. Supervenience, moreover, is not a phenomenon peculiar to souls and bodies, but something which holds for all natural bodies. In order to adequately explain the tremendous diversity of forms and causal powers throughout nature, we must refer to the underlying diversity in the materials that constitute these different bodies (8,13-25). Forms supervene on matter quite generally, then: there cannot be a difference in the former without some corresponding difference in the latter.[28] The combination of underlying bodies is therefore a *sufficient condition* for the corresponding form that supervenes upon it.[29]

Attributing such a position to Alexander sometimes meets with resistance because it is thought to imply a form of reductive materialism or at the very least a rejection of Aristotle's commitment to the explanatory priority of form, the view that his preferred explanations refer in the first instance to form rather than matter and so are fundamentally 'from the top down'. But in fact neither consequence follows. Alexander is clear on this point. He straightforwardly rejects reduction. The blend (*krasis*) or mixture (*mixis*) of underlying bodies can itself be said to be a kind of 'harmony' or tuning (*harmonia*), in line with a tradition reaching back at least as far as Plato's *Phaedo*, to a view put forward by the Pythagorean Simmias (85E-86C).[30] Whenever the constituents of the body possess a harmony of the right sort, there will also be a corresponding kind of soul, which cannot exist apart from it. But, Alexander insists, even if we grant this much, the soul should *not be identified* with this harmony; rather, it is a power that *follows from* this harmony (24,18-23; 25,3-9; together with the note on 5,5-6). This distinction might seem overly nuanced. But it is a direct and principled response to the views of his predecessors. An earlier Peripatetic, the famous editor of Aristotle's works, Andronicus of Rhodes (first century BCE), had said the soul was *either* a blend of underlying bodies *or* the power that followed upon them; and Galen of Pergamum (second century CE) criticised Andronicus for not just coming right out and identifying it with the blend. But from Alexander's point of view, Galen picked the wrong disjunct.[31] Souls and their causal powers do follow from mixtures of certain sorts. But these powers do not belong to any of the ingredients in their own right. They are distinctive, new powers that *emerge* from this combination of material factors – literally, they are 'born' or 'begotten upon' them (*epigennasthai*).[32]

Once again, this is not something peculiar to the soul or mind. As Alexander's survey of the *scala naturae* is intended to show (8,17-11,13), it occurs throughout nature, starting with the elements. Just as the causal power of being buoyant or light emerges from the elemental qualities of being hot and dry, from which it is distinct (5,5-6), so new causal powers arise at each successive level, with the increasing complexity of the material constitution in compound bodies (8,8-10; 11,11-13). These bodies are capable of behaviour quite unlike that of the materials that make them up, which cannot be explained as the result of merely aggregating their powers or their effects. But distinct causal powers mark off distinct kinds of things and so a difference in form. Each new level of complexity therefore involves formal differences that cannot be identified with or reduced to the levels underlying it as matter. The primary causal explanation of behaviour distinctive of a certain level will thus always be 'from the top,' in terms of the higher-level form that emerges, even if the lower underlying levels determine *which* form emerges. And even there the role of form is still paramount. Higher-level forms emerge only in compound bodies, where the constituent materials are themselves bodies and so have form and matter of their own;[33] and it is these lower-level *forms* which contribute something (*suntelousês ti*) to the higher-level form that stands in common over them (*to epi pasin koinon eidos*). It is for this reason that Alexander describes the higher-level form as 'in a sense a form of forms and a culmination of culminations' (*eidos pôs eidôn ... kai teleiotês tis teleiotêtôn*, 8,10-13). All explanation of difference, then, is ultimately in terms of form: higher-level forms explain the distinctive behaviour of a substance, while the lower-level forms of the constituent materials are responsible (*aitia*) for which higher-level form emerges (10,17-19).

This 'layered model of reality', as Jaegwon Kim has described it, is a form of non-reductive materialism which bears a striking resemblance to nineteenth- and twentieth-century emergentism, both in motivation and in scope.[34] It likewise holds that even though natural substances are exhaustively constituted from material elements, their behaviour is not governed solely by the powers and laws that characterise the lower levels. At each new level, there are new orderly patterns of behaviour, which must be explained in their own terms by the principles governing that level. This is evident already at the lowest levels, in the gap that emerges between the basic properties of the physical elements and the more complex laws that govern chemical combinations and interactions. On this view, the phenomena of life and mind are not exceptions to a general rule, but rather one layer of complexity among many.

Parts of the soul

Since the soul is to be understood functionally, in terms of the causal powers that set living things apart from inanimate things, it should come as no surprise that Alexander devotes the remainder of his treatise, much as Aristotle does, to an examination of the individual powers that distinguish souls from other forms.

Alexander follows Aristotle in the division and order of powers, as well in their underlying rationale. Their criterion is essentially *taxonomic*: given how these powers are distributed across living things, it is evident that some can exist without others and are therefore distinct. In this way, it can be shown empirically that there are three basic clusters of causal powers, corresponding to three kingdoms of living things, which together form a kind of hierarchy. At the bottom are basic vital functions like nutrition, growth, and reproduction, which are the only vital powers that plants have (29,1-10); next come the powers of perception and movement, which distinguish animals (29,10-22); and last the powers of reason and thought, which only humans have, at least among mortals (29,22-30,6).[35]

But in the hierarchy of living things, there is also an important overlap in the distribution of powers, with each successive echelon incorporating the powers of the earlier ones: thus, animals have the basic vital powers in addition to the perceptual ones, and humans have all three kinds. Different powers of the soul are typically joined together in a given type of living thing, then, and cannot be prised apart, even when there are distinct sets of organs subserving them (37,4-38,11). The distinct powers within a living thing thus come to possess a certain unity and integrity, even when they can be found separately in other species (29,26-30,6; cf. 30,6-17).

The serial order of souls and the accumulation of powers within them has methodological ramifications. The only powers common to every type of soul are the most rudimentary vital ones. Why not define life and souls in general in terms of these common powers? If we were to, the resulting definition would not make clear how or why the soul finds its fullest expression and culmination in humans, who possess all of the powers distinctive of souls. On the other hand, were we to use this highest realisation to define the soul in general, we would exclude each of the lower kinds of soul, even though they are complete in their kind. The only way to proceed, then, is through an investigation of the individual powers which are shared piecemeal between the different kinds of living thing (16,18-17,1; 28,13-29,1).[36]

Alexander also makes explicit an underlying premiss of this general approach, namely, that the soul consists in a *finite plurality* of powers, and offers systematic arguments in its favour. He rejects monistic approaches to the soul – he mentions Democritus, but surely the Stoics are in his crosshairs here[37] – on the grounds that monists cannot account for psychological conflict, as Plato argued in *Republic* IV (27,1-8); more importantly, such approaches make nonsense of the essential connection between the organs and structure of a living being and the kinds of powers it possesses by nature, that is, between its matter and form (27,8-28,2). At the other extreme, though, we cannot imagine that souls have an infinite number of powers, since living bodies have a finite number of organs and so can only engage in a finite number of different types of activity (28,3-13). Our approach should accordingly take account of the organs and structure of the body, as well as how the activities of living things are distributed over time and across species. The ability to nourish oneself and to reproduce are distinct, not just conceptually, but in terms of the organs involved and their maturation at different stages in the development of an individual living thing (35,9-22). But we also know that there are no species which naturally have one of these basic abilities and not the other, so that both must belong to the same general power of soul (29,1-3; 32,15-22). The principle of individuation here is thus relatively coarse-grained. This makes it reasonable to think of *faculties* here rather than just abilities, which might be more finely individuated.

Nourishing and reproducing oneself

Alexander offers a very full and valuable discussion of nourishment, growth, and reproduction, with many important details (31,7-37,3). In the interests of space, I will simply mention a few of the noteworthy ones. To nourish itself, a living thing must take in food from the environment and transform it, assimilating it to the materials that make up its own body, so that it can grow by accretion. In this respect, Alexander's account conforms to Aristotle's general model of causal interaction: what is initially unlike becomes like through the action of the agent on the patient, in this case through the action of the living thing on the nourishment (33,13-28). Alexander attempts to go further, though, by showing how nourishing oneself differs from other cases where something is enlarged through the assimilation of contraries. But in the end, he cannot do it without reference to the soul: nourishment occurs only where the agent of growth is animate (33,28-34,26).

Alexander further develops Aristotle's views of reproduction as well. Although nourishment and growth are ways of preserving and sustaining oneself (35,13-16), the production of another thing like oneself is not. But it bears a certain similarity: it is the closest a mortal being can come to immortality, namely, by preserving the species to which one belongs (36,6-9; 32,11-15). The foetus has a soul like its parent, though it does not completely manifest these powers until the relevant organs for carrying out their respective activities have developed, apart from the activity of nourishing itself (36,22-37). Although the foetus engages in this most basic activity from very early on under its own power (*ex hautou*, 36,27), it nevertheless receives its nourishment from the mother. Because of this, Alexander argues, the foetus can 'not yet be said to be an animal or alive simply as such and on [its] own', but is instead a part of the mother (38,4-8).

Perceiving

Alexander devotes almost all of the remaining treatise (38,12-92,14), nearly half of the treatise as a whole, to the powers of cognition, that is, to perceiving in general, the individual senses, the common sense, representation (*phantasia*), and understanding (*nous*), with an interlude on desire and action (73,14-80,15). The present volume contains only the first sections of this, concerning perception in general, perceptible objects, and sight. Again, in the interest of space, I will highlight only some of Alexander's more distinctive contributions here.

Alexander begins his discussion of perception by emphasising what it has in common with nourishing oneself. Like nourishing, perception also consists in a causal interaction in which the agent makes the patient like itself through a kind of alteration or change in quality (38,21-39,6; 39,14-18). But in this case it is the external, perceptible object that is the agent: the animal becomes like part of the world, rather than transforming part of the world into itself. Alexander explains this teleologically, by appealing to the utility of perception. In order to survive and thrive, an animal must be able to avoid threats and pursue opportunities, and it detects these by perception (39,9-10).

What the senses undergo in perceiving is not, however, the same sort of change or alteration that food undergoes when it is digested. The latter cases involves a transformation and change of form in the patient: as the food becomes assimilated to the body, it loses some of its previous causal powers. The senses, in contrast, do not lose their ability to perceive when they perceive, as Aristotle makes clear in *On the Soul* 2.5; on the contrary, perceiving is just the *realisation* of this ability. Alexander always marks this difference with a qualification: perceiving is 'a kind of ' (*tis*) change, alteration, or modification, or only 'in a way' (*pôs*). But at the same he also insists that perceiving occurs 'through' (*dia*) a change, alteration, or modification of the sense organs (39,1-2) in the primary and literal sense of these words.[38] In terms of recent debates over Aristotle's theory of perception, Alexander rejects 'spiritualism' without embracing full-out 'literalism': he insists that perception requires *some kind* of literal change of the sense organs, without *identifying* perceiving with that change.[39] In making these distinctions, interestingly, he does not directly employ Aristotle's claim that in perception the sense receives the form 'without the matter' (*aneu tês hulês*), though he also describes perception in these terms (39,13-14).

Alexander develops these basic doctrines into a systematic causal theory. On his view, when any of the five peripheral sense organs is stimulated, it 'relays' (*diadidonai*) this change to a central organ of perception (39,18-21), which he identifies with the heart, where perception actually occurs (39,21-40,3). In the cases of the three distance senses – sight, hearing, and smell – there is a further link earlier in the chain: perceptible objects affect our senses only by first affecting an external medium which relays or transmits this message (*diakoneisthai*) to the peripheral organs.[40] The basis for this view can be found in various remarks scattered throughout Aristotle's corpus (although his view about where perceiving occurs is less than clear). But Alexander gives them added prominence and coherence, by synthesising them into a unified whole and placing them at the forefront of the theory.

Perceptibles and error

Like Aristotle, Alexander divides perceptible objects into those which are perceptible intrinsically (*kath' hauta*) and those which are perceptible extrinsically (*kata sumbebêkos*); the former are divided again into those which are intrinsically perceptible to one sense exclusively (*idia*) and those which are common to or shared by several senses (*koina*). But Alexander also corrects or modifies the characterisation of each of these groups, sometimes significantly.

In the case of extrinsic perceptibles, Alexander states clearly something some commentators have assumed, but Aristotle never explicitly says, namely, that they are 'not perceptible at bottom' (*oude aisthêta tên arkhên*; 41,9), but are perceptible solely in virtue of another quality which is intrinsically perceptible, to which the perceptible in question is extrinsically related (41,6-10). On this view, extrinsic perceptibles are not *strictly* perceptible at all, but in effect only by homonymy. Aristotle, in contrast, appears to classify them in his division as genuine perceptibles, even if they are not perceptible in the primary or *fundamental* sense (*kuriôs*, 418a24-5) that exclusive perceptibles are.[41]

In the case of common perceptibles, like shape, number, or change, Alexander claims that they need only be able to affect *more than one* sense, rather than all of them, as Aristotle incautiously states.[42] This modification has the added benefit of making the subdivision between exclusive and common perceptibles dichotomous. He also remarks that the two kinds of intrinsic perceptible are 'interwoven' (*sumpeplegmena*) with one another (83,17-22) and so jointly affect the peripheral organs (65,11-16); the effect of the common perceptibles is then relayed to the central organ (41,4-5). But unlike exclusive perceptibles, the common perceptibles are not perceived by the power to perceive colours, for example, or odours. They are perceived only by the common power of perception, which Alexander calls the 'common sense' (65,10-11.16-21).

Perhaps the most striking change, though, is in Alexander's characterisation of intrinsic perceptibles exclusive to a single sense. In *On the Soul* 2.6, among other texts, Aristotle claimed that it was *impossible* for the senses to be mistaken about the exclusive perceptibles themselves, though they might be in error about where they were located or which objects had them.[43] But in one passage, Aristotle qualifies this by allowing that the perception of such perceptibles is either true 'or involves the least amount of falsehood' (*DA* 3.3, 428b18-19). Alexander seems to temporise even further when he maintains only that the perception of exclusive perceptibles is 'the *most* true' and even then only when a number of conditions are satisfied (41,13-15). He holds that such perception is veridical only in *natural* or *normal* conditions, of which he lists five: (i) the condition of the organ, (ii) the direction in which the object lies, (iii) its distance from the sense, (iv) the condition of the medium, and (v) the absence of interference (41,13-42,3). When one or more of these conditions is not met, he claims, perceptual error is likely to occur.[44] This discussion comes as part of a more general characterisation of perceptual error: it occurs whenever the change in the sense deviates from the quality in the object which gives rise to the perception and so fails to correspond to it.[45]

Seeing, light, and colours

Alexander begins his discussion of sight by considering the types of objects perceptible exclusively to it, which includes not only colours, which can be seen in the light, but also phosphorescent objects, which can be seen in the dark (42,4-7; 43,16-18).[46] Thus neither sight nor what can be seen are *defined* in terms of colour: colour is just one of the things that can *produce* it. Its role, like that of phosphorescent objects, is causal. Colours are what can produce the sorts of changes in an illuminated, transparent medium that in turn can affect an animal's eyes in such a way as to produce sight (42,5-11; 43,11-44,2). Although we do not in general see this effect on the medium itself, Alexander thinks that in some circumstances we can. He gives a long list of cases where the air surrounding an object is as though tinged (*hôsper khrônnumena*) with its colour or that of a facing object (42,11-19).

To see a colour, the intervening medium of air or water must not only be transparent, it must also be illuminated. Like Aristotle, Alexander holds that light is not a body that travels through the medium. But in Alexander's view, it is also not a condition or modification of the medium which the medium takes on in the way that matter receives a form or quality (42,19-22). The medium does not itself undergo any alteration or modification in its qualities when it is illuminated, but rather a relational change – what some have called a 'mere Cambridge change' – due to the presence of fire or something similar in the medium (42,22-43,4; 43,8-11; 45,2-5).[47] Unlike other changes, illumination occurs instantaneously without duration (*akhronôs*), even across vast distances (43,11): it occurs immediately, as soon as fire or some other illuminant is present in the medium and ceases as soon as it is removed (42,22-43,1).

When the medium is illuminated in this way, it realises fully its nature as something transparent – something, literally, *through* which an object *appears* (*diaphanes*).[48] It is this power which allows it to relay the colours of objects to sight and so function as a medium. But interestingly this is not what makes them 'see-through' (*diopton*). On the Aristotelian view, *all* bodies have some degree of transparency in them (44,20-1), even if they are not see-through at all; and in bodies with definite boundaries or surfaces of their own, the transparency in them is responsible for their colour (44,18-23; 46,12-14), different colours being due to the admixture of opaque materials like earth (44,5-45,10). It is when a transparent material lacks a definite boundary of its own, like air or the sea, and is shaped instead by the bodies around it, that the material lacks a colour of its own and is transparent in the fullest sense of being 'see-through' (44,23-44,5; 46,7-11).[49] Light is *like* a colour of these transparent bodies (44,16; 45,1; though compare 45,17-19). But in the end, light no more constitutes their own proper colour than does their being tinged by surrounding bodies.

In the remainder of the treatise, which can be found in the next volume, Alexander continues his examination of the individual senses – hearing, smell, taste, and touch – and the common sense. He then goes on to consider other abilities animals possess, such as representation, desire, and striving, as part of the soul capable of perception, before turning finally to the understanding, which in the sublunary realm can only be found in humans.

Notes

1. Although this claim is generally accepted (Zeller 1923, 817-18 esp. 818 n. 1; Thillet 1984, liii esp. n. 2; Sharples 1987, 1179 esp. n. 23), it has more recently been contested by Barnes *et al.*, who argue that this and similar phrases are 'not honorific titles – they are ordinary referring expressions', much as we might use 'the author' at the end of a book review, without meaning 'The Author *par excellence*' (1991, 4 n. 28). The objection is clever and has some merit. But it is not borne out by the evidence as a whole.

There are a few cases in philosophical commentaries where *ho exêgêtês* is used anaphorically to pick up a prior mention of Alexander or some other commentator in context. This is most obvious where a contrast is being drawn between the commentator and the author commented on: thus Simplicius contrasts what Aristotle says with what his commentator Alexander says (*in Phys.* 1170,1-2.13) and Proclus contrasts Plato and Porphyry in the same way (*in Tim.* 1.322.4-7); similarly, Olympiodorus contrasts the commentator Alexander with 'the great philosopher' Ammonius (*in Meteor.* 263,20-1). There are also a few cases of anaphora without any contrast being made: thus, Simpl. *in Phys.* 313,30 appears to be referring back to Alexander at 312,1 and 1176,32 refers back to him at 1175,13; similarly, 213,34 refers back either to Alexander at 213,23 or Syrianus at 213,24. The greatest number by far occur in the Platonic commentaries of Damascius: he sometimes refers to Syrianus simply as 'the commentator' (*in Phaed.* I §§ 222, 235, 236, 243) and even more frequently to Proclus (*in Parm.* §§ 312, 394, 421; *in Phileb.* §§ 133, 200, 242; *in Phaed.* I §§ 297, 405; II 14, 25, 88, 89, 100, 110, 128, 129, 132, 145, 147; on Damascius' various forms of reference for these authors, see e.g. Westerink 1959, xvii). Philoponus similarly refers to both Taurus and, more commonly, Proclus as 'the commentator on Plato' (*de Aet. Mundi* 311,18; 482,22; 520,25; 521,3; 524,14; 553,9).

But this sort of case is the exception rather than the rule. In virtually all of the passages in the commentaries on Aristotle where the singular *ho exêgêtês* is used to refer to a specific individual, it is as part of an epithet *of Alexander* specifically (e.g. 'Alexander the commentator', 'Alexander the commentator on Aristotle', 'the Aphrodisian commentator'): Them. *in DA* 120,18; Syr. *in Metaph.* 53,12; 100,6-7; 122,11-12; 195,12 (Syrianus uses *ho hupomnêmatistês* instead of *exêgêtês* in all but the second passage); Ascl. *in Metaph.* 93,18; 245,26-7; Ammon. *in de Int.* 13,19; 39,14; 100,20; 202,4; Simpl. *in DC* 121,12; 700,9; *in Phys.* 707,33-4; *in DA*, 52,28; Philop. *in An. Pr.* 126,20-1; *in GC* 62,17-18; 82,12-13; 214,23; 226,17-18; *de Aet. Mundi* 48,10; 191,19-20; Michael, *in EN V* 584,3. (I am grateful to Michael Griffin for discussion on some of these passages.) In all of these cases, the phrase 'the commentator' is a mark of distinction: it is not used in the commentaries on Aristotle for any other commentator, except once, for an unnamed commentator distinguished from Alexander at Olymp. *in Meteor.* 273,27-8. This honorific use is confirmed by other epithets used for Alexander. Simplicius refers to him as 'the most authoritative commentator on Aristotle' (*tou gnêsiôtatou tôn Aristotelous exêgêtôn, in Phys.* 258,16-17; *ton gnêsiôteron*, 80,15-16) as well as 'the most industrious' of them (*ho philoponôtatos, in Phys.* 795,34-5). Syrianus calls him 'the most industrious' as well (*in Metaph.* 54,12-13).

Someone might conceivably object that the epithet 'the commentator' is only used to distinguish him from other Alexander's, such as Alexander 'the Great' (*ho megas*), as he is in a late discussion of homonymy (Michael *in EN IX-X* 4,17). But there is no reason to think that there is any danger of confusing these or any other Alexanders in these contexts generally; and even if there were, it is always possible (and indeed common) to use place names to distinguish such homonyms. It is noteworthy, then, that Alexander of Aphrodisias is virtually the only one who receives the epithet 'the commentator'.

2. Syrianus *in Metaph.* 100,6; David [Elias], *in Categ.* 128,12-13. The first passage praises a commentator on Aristotle as the 'new' or 'more recent Aristotle' (*ho neôteros Aristotelês*), but does not identify him further by name, though he mentions 'the Aphrodisian commentator' at 100,4 and 10. (On the use of the comparative, see Thillet 1984, xxix, cf. xxvii n. 1.) The second passage speaks explicitly of the 'instructor' Alexander, who 'by right is himself like a second Aristotle' (*edei gar auton hoion deuteron onta Aristotelên*). Zeller took the reference in both passages to be to Alexander of Aphrodisias (1923, 805-8 n. 2 at 807). This was contested by Moraux 1967, 177-82, although he is forced to emend both texts in crucial ways. For a convincing and detailed response, see Thillet 1984, xix-xxxi.

3. Philostratus *VS* 566; Lucian, *Eunuch* 2-3; cf. Dio Cassius 72.31. For more detail, see esp. Oliver 1970, 80-91; Lynch 1972, 170; Todd 1976, 6-7; Oliver 1977, 166; Glucker 1978, 146-53; Oliver 1981, 216-17, 221-5 (including his critique of Dillon [1977] 1996, 233); Hahn 1989, 126-8; and most recently Watts 2006, 33-5. Oliver 1981, 224 emphasises that we do not know the subsequent fate of the chairs after Marcus Aurelius' death; cf. also Lynch 1972, 177, though contrast Watts 2006, 34-5. On the mention of *two* Peripatetics in Lucian, see Lynch 1972, 171; Glucker 1978, 148-50; Hahn 1989, 126-7 n. 30. Thillet speculates (1984, lxxviii esp. n. 2) that *On Fate* was dedicated in response to a *promotion* (164,14) in the Peripatetic section of the faculty at the 'University of Athens'. But it need only be a reference to Alexander's initial appointment to the imperial chair of Aristotelian philosophy, which does not presuppose a university or a faculty, as the work of Lynch and Glucker has persuasively shown.

4. For the dedication, see *Fat.* 1, 164,1-3.13-15, although see Sharples' commentary (1983, 125 ad loc.) on Caracalla's antipathy to Aristotelians. Alexander's failure to mention Gaeta in his dedication suggests that the treatise must have been composed before the latter's becoming Augustus in 209: see Todd 1976 1 n. 3; Thillet 1984, vii-viii n. 3, cf. lxxv; and Sharples 2005a, 47, though Barnes et al. (1991, 1 n. 1) regard this as 'reasonable, but not perhaps absolutely mandatory'.

5. For the inscription, see Chaniotis 2004a, 388-9 (inscription no. 4, with photo) and 2004b. For an extensive discussion of its implications, see Sharples 2005a (including the identification of the title *diadokhos* with the imperial chair, at 52-3; and the possible attribution of works to Alexander's father, 53-6).

6. For the evidence on his teachers, see Sharples 1990, 86-9; 2005a, 49-50; also Thillet 1984, viii-xxxii. On Sosigenes himself, see Moraux 1984, 335-60 and on Herminus, 361-98. Moraux's further conjecture (1967) that Aristotle of Mytilene was also one of Alexander's teachers is, despite its influence, highly questionable: against it, see Thillet 1984, xi-xxi and Opsomer and Sharples 2000 passim (with further references on the question at 256 n. 30).

7. For extensive, critical discussion, see Sharples 2005a, 50-2.

8. For a comprehensive survey of Alexander's works and the secondary literature on them, see Sharples' invaluable survey (1987), 1182-99.

9. Alexander refers to his commentary (*hupomnêma*) on *On the Soul* at *Quaest.* 1.11a, 21,18; 1.11b, 22,26; Philoponus expressly speaks of Alexander's own *On the Soul* as a distinct treatise (*idion biblion*) at *in DA* 159,18-19. For further discussion, with references, see Sharples 1987, 1186, paragraph (g); Moraux 2001, 317-53. Moraux argues that the treatise makes use of formulations from the commentary, which it expands on and elaborates, and is therefore later than the commentary (2001, 338). For a collection of the fragments on the understanding (*nous*), see Moraux 1942, 203-21.

10. A similar difference can be observed in Aquinas' treatises and commentaries: even though his commentaries clearly reflect his overall outlook, their immediate purpose is to explain Aristotle's text and this constrains what he is willing to mention or devote his energies to, in contrast with his own systematic works.

11. All references to Alexander's *On the Soul* are to the Berlin Academy edition of Alexander's *Scripta minora* in the *Supplementum Aristotelicum*, vol. 2 part 1, edited by Ivo Bruns (1887).

12. Moraux's sympathies are plain, despite his protests against those who consider Alexander's solutions *only* in comparison with Thomas', since he still takes Thomism to be the ultimate criterion (1942, xxii-xxiii). His frequent denunciations of Alexander's materialism – of how it is 'fundamentally anti-Aristotelian', a view which 'could not be more foreign' to Aristotle's theories (31, 33, 39, 42, 44, 48) and harbours 'heresies' (172, 173), with a 'monstrous' and 'genuine contradiction' at its core (11, 34, 44, 48, 167, 168-9, 173) – reveal just how much is at stake for someone with Moraux's allegiances.

13. Alexander explicitly restricts his scope in this treatise to the sublunary realm, where substances come to be and perish, and so excludes from consideration the souls of the divine movers of the heavenly spheres and the Prime Mover (28,26-8; cf. 1,2).

14. 9,14-25; 11,5-13; 20,19-22; 22,4-12.15-23; 23,24-24,4; cf. 5,4-18; 13,22-14,3.

15. For detailed references, see the note on 3,28-4,4.

16. For references, again see the note on 3,28-4,4.

17. D.L. 7.134 = *SVF* 2.299 = LS 44B 3, retaining the MSS reading – see LS 1.274, 2.266; this is confirmed by Alex. *Mixt.* 225,3-5 = *SVF* 2.310.

18. For references, see the end of the note on 7,9-13.

19. For references, see the note on 7,9-13.

20. In one sense, the soul also does not come to be or perish either, since Aristotle denies that there is coming to be or perishing of forms in general (*Metaph.* 7.8, 1033b5-8). But in a broader sense, he allows it, since the form or essence is 'what *comes to be* in another thing' (*ho en alloi gignetai*, 1033b7); that is, there is a moment when there is something with a given form, where there had not been before, and there is another later moment when there is not any longer (7.15, 1039b23-7; 8.3, 1043b14-16; cf. 6.3, 1027a29-30; 8.5, 1044b21-2; 12.3, 1070a15-17). For a good discussion of this nuance, see Frede and Patzig 1988, 2.136-7. Aristotle is even willing in fact to speak about the form 'supervening on' the matter (*epigignesthai*) in these cases, although not in the technical sense of the term that we will see in Alexander (1035a12; 1036a31, b6; cf. 1035a5). Alexander in any case speaks of the soul both as 'coming to be' in this broader sense (see *e.g. DA* 24,3-4 below) and as 'supervening' on matter (10,25; 24,19; 25,2; 26,22), while also being openly committed to the orthodox denial of forms' coming to be in the narrower sense (ap. Simpl. *in de Cael.* 578,32-579,2). For more extended discussion, see Accattino 1995, 198-200.

21. Functionalism in this broad sense, concerning the nature and power of *substances*, does not imply functionalism in the narrower sense used in contemporary philosophy of mind, which defines mental *states* in terms of their inputs, outputs, and causal role with respect to other mental states, although the two senses are obviously compatible with one another. There are good reasons, however, to think that Aristotle is a functionalist only in the broad sense outlined above, and not in the narrow sense: see my 2006, 320-2.

22. *PA* 1.1, 639b21-30, 642a1-13; *Phys.* 2.9 passim.

23. Aristotle, *DA* 1.3, 407b13-27; cf. 2.2, 414a22-5; Alexander *DA* 27,15-28,2.

For more on metempsychosis, including Alexander's critique, see note to 27,15-28,2 below.

24. For more on this technical notion, with references to the contemporary literature, see my 1997, 313-14. For discussion of the authenticity of *Mant.* 104, see the end of n. 92 on 10,24-6.

25. The converse, it is important to note, need *not* hold: for all that has been said here, it might be possible for there to be a difference *in bodies* without a corresponding difference in souls, in which case the same soul might be found in different types of body, so long as each was suitable, a possibility contemporary philosophers refer to as 'multiple realisability'. But this just shows that the present claim about supervenience is distinct from the earlier one, which is meant to rule out metempsychosis.

26. For further references, see the note on 14,24-15,1 below. In spite of these clear denials, Moraux 1942 claims that Alexander is nonetheless committed to this view and so in contradiction both with himself and Aristotle (xix, 42-4; cf. 9-10).

27. For Alexander's use of 'supervene' (*epiginesthai*) and further references, see the note on 25,2 below.

28. Quite generally, but *not* universally: even leaving aside questions about forms that exist apart from matter, it is clear that the most basic elemental forms – the four elemental qualities of hot, cold, wet, and dry – do *not* supervene on prime matter, since each of these different forms can belong *to the same underlying substratum*. But this is not surprising either, since prime matter has no qualities or differences of its own and so no form essential to it. Apart from this base case, though, *all other* natural forms – the forms, that is, of compound bodies – *will* supervene on their underlying matter. See note on 10,17-19 below.

29. For further discussion, see the note on 10,24-6 below.

30. For more on this conception of the soul and the ensuing debate, see my 1997.

31. For references, see the note on 25,2-4 below.

32. For Alexander's use of 'emerge' (*epigennasthai*) and further references, see the note on 5,5-6 below.

33. Emergence does not occur in simple bodies, because their underlying matter is prime matter. Since prime matter is compatible with all of the elemental qualities, none of them supervene on it: being completely without form, it does not determine which elemental qualities will be instantiated. See n. 28 above.

34. Kim 1993, 337-9; McLaughlin 1992 passim.

35. Alexander explicitly excludes divine beings from consideration in this treatise, on the grounds that if they can be said to have a soul at all, it is only by homonymy: see 28,25-9 below with corresponding note.

36. Alexander would likely fault a disjunctive characterisation of the soul – as that which, e.g., enables a living thing to nourish itself *or* perceive *or* think – for equally failing to capture the sense in which the highest soul constitutes the fullest and most complete expression of soul powers.

37. See note on 27,6-7 below.

38. For discussion and references, see (3) in the note on 38,21-39,2 below.

39. For a brief summary of this debate, see my 2006, 328-30; and at greater length in my 2005.

40. For the terminology of 'relaying' and 'transmitting' see the notes on 39,18-21 and 41,1-3 respectively.

41. Alexander may not always take such a hard line: for discussion of a possible alternative in *Quaest.* 3.8, see the final paragraph of the note on 41,8-10 below.

42. *DA* 2.6, 418a10-11, a18-19, though he seems to recognise the difficulty at *Sens.* 4, 442b4-7.

43. For the many references, see the note on 41,13-42,3 below.

Introduction

44. Similar lists are reported by various sceptics and are sometimes associated with the Stoics' epistemology. But whether they are its ultimate source or, as I think more likely, the Academic Carneades, or possibly even Aristotelian sources, cannot be determined from our evidence. For references, see the last paragraph of the note on 41,13-42,3 below.

45. For further discussion of perceptual error and the correspondence principle presupposed, see the note on 41,10-13.

46. We might be tempted to regard the appearance of phosphorescent objects equally as colours. But Alexander's point is that their appearance in the dark is different from their actual colour: an object's own colour is the way it looks in the light.

47. On mere Cambridge changes, see (2) in the note on 38,21-39,2.

48. For this etymology, see 43,5-8 below, along with the note for further references.

49. Alexander discusses transparent solids like glass, horn, and mica, which have definite boundaries of their own, in other treatises: for references and discussion, see the note on 42,7-8 below. For Aristotle's view, see Sorabji 2004*b*, 131.

Note

Text and editions. The text used for this translation is from Ivo Bruns'
Berlin Academy edition of Alexander of Aphrodisias' *Scripta minora*, in
the *Supplementum Aristotelicum*, vol. II, part 1 (Berlin: G. Reimer, 1897).
Any changes are flagged by an asterisk in the translation and noted
separately in the Textual Emendations.

The division of Alexander's *On the Soul* into two 'parts' does not correspond to a division in our manuscripts or editions, but was made purely
because of the exigencies of publication.

All references to Alexander's other works, as well as that of the other
Greek commentators on Aristotle, are to the Berlin Academy's *Commentaria in Aristotelem Graeca* (1882-1909).

A key to the abbreviations for other ancient texts can be found in the
Index of Passages at the end of the volume, along with the name of the
editor, where more than one edition is commonly in use.

Translation. Translating Alexander into readable English presents certain challenges. He is, if you will, one of the first authors to write in
academic German: he is given to frequent *Schachtelsätze* and long series
of subordinate clauses (in which he occasionally gets lost himself). Worse,
he standardly conditionalises his formal arguments into a single sentence
that includes not only the many premisses, but also their individual
elaborations and justifications. Preserving these syntactical features of his
treatise would serve little purpose. In many cases, it is possible to break
his sentences into smaller units without affecting their underlying logical
relations.

To make the structure of Alexander's inferences even clearer, though, I
have taken the liberty of using the modern typographical convention of
nested paragraphs with identifying numbers or letters for the different
premisses or senses of a term being distinguished. This is not in fact a
great departure from Alexander, since he sometimes uses numbers himself to distinguish different conditions and claims (e.g. 22,27-23,3;
41,15-42,2). I have also sought to be as consistent as possible in rendering
his terminology, so that it is easier to see how much more natural his
inferences and assumptions might seem as originally framed. (Variations
in the translation of each term are recorded in the Greek-English Index at
the end of each volume.) In quite a few cases, I have also avoided custom-

ary translations, where another rendering would bring out etymological connections to other terms or invigorate an otherwise arid and abstract construction. Instead of translating *teleiôsis* as 'perfection' and *entelekheia* as 'actuality', for example, I have rendered them as 'culmination' and 'completion' respectively, to bring out their connections with the underlying notion of a *telos* or end. Similarly, instead of translating *aisthêtikê dunamis* as 'the perceptive faculty' or 'potentiality', I have used 'the power for perceiving' to bring out the emphasis Aristotle and Alexander both place on the corresponding activity. The unfamiliarity of these translations (and in some cases inelegance) will undoubtedly rub some readers the wrong way. But my hope is that they will make Alexander's positions and arguments seem less arcane or obscure.

Commentary. In line with the principles of the series, my notes have two primary aims: (i) to make philosophical sense of the arguments in the main text and (ii) to provide the necessary background to understand them by supplying the references to Alexander's predecessors and contemporaries – to Aristotle above all, but also various Stoics, Platonists and Peripatetics – and cross-references to Alexander's own works. Unfortunately, I have had to limit myself severely with regard to the secondary literature: to have included them more fully would have swollen the size of the volumes unduly. The two main exceptions I have allowed myself are recent commentaries on the treatise, a superb one in Italian by Accattino and Donini (= AD) as well as a French one by Bergeron and Dufour (= BD), as they are directly on the treatise itself and unlikely to be widely known or available to English readers. Although I cite them most often to mark our disagreements, I have learned immensely from them both.

Abbreviations

Abbreviations of ancient works can be found in the Index of Passages Cited. The abbreviations below are for modern reference works.

AD = Paolo Accattino and Pier Luigi Donini. 1996. *Alessandro di Afrodisia: L'anima*. Traduzione, introduzione e commento. (= Biblioteca Universale Laterza, v. 447.) Rome: Laterza.

BD = Martin Bergeron and Richard Dufour. 2008. *Alexandre d'Aphrodise: De l'âme*. Texte grec introduit, traduit et annoté. Paris: Librairie Philosophique J. Vrin.

DK = Hermann Diels and Walther Kranz (Hrsg.). [1903] 1951. *Die Fragmente der Vorsokratiker*. Griechisch und Deutsch. 6. Auflage. 3 Bände. Berlin: Weidmann, 1951.

Dox. Gr. = Diels, Hermann. 1879. *Doxographi Graeci*. Collegit, recensuit, prolegomenis indicibusque instruxit. Berlin: G. Reimer.

LS = A.A. Long and D.N. Sedley (eds). *The Hellenistic Philosophers*. 2 vols. Cambridge: Cambridge University Press, 1987.

SVF = von Arnim, Hans Friedrich August. 1903-24. *Stoicorum Veterum Fragmenta*. 4 vols. Leipzig: B.G. Teubner.

Textual Emendations

The following list contains the emendations to Bruns' text which are followed in the translation (marked there by an *).

5,7	Retaining the MSS's *autou* instead of Bruns' *hautou*.
6,7	Retaining the MSS's *autous* instead of Bruns' *hautous*.
6,11	Accepting AD's correction of the MSS's *te* to *ge*.
6,23	Supplying <*pur*> a second time, just after *pur*, following the Hebrew translation.
7,20	Retaining the MSS's *autou* instead of Bruns' *hautou*.
14,1	Accepting Bruns' suggestion <*en*> *toi loipôi*.
14,8	Correcting the MSS's *kekhôristo* to *ekekhôristo*.
14,24	Reading *diapheron* instead of the MSS's *diaphorôn* or *diapherôn* (or Bruns' emendation, *diaphoron*).
15,6	Keeping the MSS's *autou* instead of Bruns' *hautou*.
16,1	Omitting *hên kai teleiotêta kai entelekheian ethos Aristotelei legein* with Bruns.
16,13	Accepting Bruns' suggestion to correct the MSS's *dunamenou* to *dunamenon*.
18,1	Accepting Bruns' emendation, *to einai*, instead of the MSS's *to eidos*.
18,2	Retaining *autês* with the MSS instead of Bruns' *hautês*.
18,10	Reading *tou sômatos* with the Hebrew translation instead of *tôn tou sômatos merôn* with the MSS.
19,5	Accepting Usener's conjecture *tôi*, with *einai* understood, instead of the MSS's *to*.
20,9	Accepting Bruns' emendation of *hautou* and *hautôi* (twice) for *autou* and *autôi* (twice).
20,22-3	Accepting AD's emendation *tên psukhên hôs eidos* instead of Bruns' *tên hôs psukhên eidos*.
21,1	Emending the text to read *all' ê holôs* rather than the MSS's *all' ei holôs* or Bruns' more drastic *all' oud' hôs*.
22,18	Accepting Bruns' emendation *hautên* for the MSS's *autên*.
22,27	Omitting *kai*, following the Hebrew translation.
27,9	Omitting Bruns' insertion of *zôia*.
28,5	Accepting Bruns' suggestion that we read *esesthai*, with the Hebrew translation, rather than the MSS's *legesthai*.

30,2	Retaining the MSS's *dunameôn* instead of Bruns' *dunamenôn*.
31,14	Accepting Bruns' *hautôi* instead of the MSS's *autôi*.
33,14	Accepting Bruns' deletion of *trophê legetai*.
34,4	Inserting *huph'* before *hôn*, with AD.
34,5	Retaining the MSS's *tauta*, instead of Usener's emendation *tanantia*, printed by Bruns.
34,21	Accepting Bruns' *tode* instead of the MSS's *to de*, and inserting <*ê tode*> afterwards with AD.
35,4	Reading *khôris toutou*, following AD's suggestion, instead of the MSS's *khôris tautês*.
35,24	Accepting Victorius' correction of the MSS's *phusikês* to *phutikês* (printed by Bruns).
36,5	Retaining the MSS's *autou* instead of Bruns' *hautou*.
36,17	Accepting Bruns' emendation of *hautôi* for *autôi*, and his suggestion that we read *homoion poiousa* for the MSS's *homoiousa*.
37,14	Accepting Bruns' suggestion that we read *oude* instead of the MSS's *oute*.
38,5	Accepting Bruns' emendation of *pherousês* for *trephousês*, in line with the Hebrew translation.
39,5	Omitting the first *kai* with AD.
39,21	Reading *ep'* with AD rather than the MSS's *eit'* (acute) or Bruns *eit'* (circumflex).
40,5	Omitting Bruns' addition of *phutikês* before *tês psukhês*.
40,19	Accepting Bruns' correction of the MSS's *homoiôs ei* to *homoiôsei*, in line with the Hebrew translation.
40,21	Reading the neuter *idia*, rather than the plural *idiai* (MS V, Bruns) or the feminine *idia* (MS a). Cf. 41,3.
41,6	Inserting *ha* following the first *aisthêta*, with AD, instead of Bruns' suggested insertion <*ta kath' hauta ouk aisthêta, ha*> at the same point, following the Hebrew translation.
41,10	Accepting Bruns' emendation of *hêi* for the MSS's *ê*.
44,8	Accepting Bruns' emendation of *hupo*, following the Hebrew translation, instead of the MSS's *auto*.
45,3	Accepting Bruns' suggestion that we read the singular *auto*, rather than the plural *auta* in the MSS.
45,23	Accepting Bruns' emendation of *monon* for the MSS' *monôn*.
	Accepting Bruns' emendation of *sômata* for the MSS' *khrômata*.
46,11	Retaining the MSS' *horiston* instead of Bruns' emendation of *ahoriston* (following the Hebrew translation).

Alexander of Aphrodisias
On the Soul

Part I: Soul as Form of the Body,
Parts of the Soul, Nourishment,
and Perception

Translation

My aim is to speak about the soul that belongs to a body subject to coming-to-be and perishing:[1] to say what its essence (*ousia*)[2] is and what its powers are, how many powers there are, and what their difference is from one another.[3] For given that

1. a person ought, before all else, to obey what the gods com-   5
mand;
2. 'Know Thyself' is commanded and decreed by the Pythian god,[4]

and so not merely by a god, but one who is believed to foreknow the future[5] and who proclaims and declares that

3. each person, through knowledge of himself,[6] will achieve the life in accordance with nature;[7]

but

4. self-knowledge consists in the knowledge of that in virtue of   2,1
which [each person] is himself;
5. a human is a human in virtue of the soul;

it follows necessarily that

6. any person who intends to obey the god and live the life in accordance with his nature must first analyse the soul and know just what it is.[8]

Just as I have great reverence for Aristotle's works on other subjects, since I find more truth in the views passed down from him than in   5
what others have claimed, I regard what he states in his theory of the soul in the same way as well. I will therefore have fulfilled my aim if I can set out his claims about the soul as clearly as possible and offer suitable arguments to show how each of them is well formulated.[9]

What is the soul's essence?[10]   10

Anyone who is going to examine in detail what is said about the soul and reach agreement on characterisations of its essence must first appreciate the extraordinary magnificence of nature, before all else. For once we have learned just what sort of thing nature is and have been persuaded that its workings are more incredible than any marvel produced by art,[11] we will more easily be convinced by what

15   is going to be said about the soul.[12] For the view that its powers and
activities cannot easily be harmonised with what is said about it,
because they are 'more divine and greater than any bodily power',[13]
is no reason to get mired in puzzles about the soul. Hence, those who
do not wish to go against sensible claims about the soul ought first to
20   look at the construction of the body that has the soul and to investigate the regulation of its inner parts and then afterwards the grace-
ful agreement of the external parts with them.[14] For after studying
these, it will no longer seem so incredible that the soul, which has
within it so many origins and principles of change (*arkhai*),[15] is
25   something that also belongs to this body, which is constructed so
incredibly and magnificently.

Now those who have made it their business to analyse such things
find the following, more than anything else, to be true and evident:
that every bodily, perceptible substance (*ousia*) is a compound of both
3,1   (*i*) some underlying thing, which we call 'matter', and (*ii*) a nature
that shapes and gives definition to this matter, to which we give the
name 'form'.[16] Anyone who looks at the products of various arts will
see clearly that this is how things are. Whichever artefact one
5   chooses, one finds something in it which is underlying matter and
something which is form: bronze, stone, wood, wax, or whatever is
shaped by art is an underlying subject, while that in it which is
produced by the artisan is form. For the statue's matter is bronze or
stone (if the statue happens to be made from one of these), while its
form is a particular kind of shape and particular kind of contour,[17]
10   which is what the art produces and indeed is art. For anything
artfully produced in the underlying matter by someone who possesses the art is art.[18] The body that is naturally suited to receive the
art, but which does not [already] have what is produced in it by art
as part of its own definition, is the art's matter.[19]

Just as each body constituted and formed by art exhibits this
duality, the same duality can be found even before that in natural
15   bodies, that is, bodies which have been formed naturally, since art
imitates nature, not nature art.[20] In each natural body as well, then,
there is something that is underlying matter and something in [the
matter] that is form. Thus, in the case of bronze, either water or the
vaporous emission is matter (on the assumption that all metals that
can be melted have moisture as their matter);[21] while its form is a
20   certain type of consistency and solidity.[22] So just as art is the form
produced in something by art, nature is likewise the form produced
in things formed naturally.[23]

There is a difference between natural bodies, however. For some
of them are simple, while others are compound.[24] The underlying
matter of compound bodies is also a natural body, composed out of
25   matter and form, since every natural body is a compound of these.[25]
Simple bodies, in contrast, do not have a further compound underly-

ing them, since in that case [a simple body] would be compound too. But if what underlies them is not a compound, then it is not a body either, given that every body is a compound of matter and form. What underlies simple bodies and serves as their matter, then, is going to be a kind of nature that is simple and separate from form, and which 4,1 by its own definition is 'amorphous, formless, and shapeless'. Because it is formless and said to be so, that which rids it of the aforementioned lack, by having come to be in it, is given the name 'form'. The former sort of nature is what one would call 'matter in the fundamental sense'.[26] For the underlying subject in compound bodies – that is, 5 their matter – is not matter simply as such,[27] because it is conjoined with a form and there is something further which in turn is its matter. But in bodies where the underlying subject is simple, their matter is matter in the fundamental sense and simply as such, which cannot exist on its own[28] (because anything that does [have matter and exists on its own] is a compound body, as was stated earlier).[29] As it is always found together with some form, it is separated from it 10 in thought alone, being related to the forms of simple bodies in the way that wax is related to shapes.[30] For any [piece of] wax one conceives of is necessarily conjoined with a shape, since it is impossible to conceive of wax which is shapeless. Yet to be wax is not to be conjoined with some particular shape, for if a determinate shape were included in its essence, then [wax] that was not conjoined with 15 this shape, but some other one, would no longer be wax. Matter in the fundamental sense is related to the forms of the simple natural bodies in just the same way. For it cannot exist separate from any of them, and yet to be [matter of this kind] does not consist in being conjoined with any of them either. For then it would not be simple and non-bodily, nor could it be the matter of some other simple body, since it would perish with the loss of its own form.[31] 20

It is not only matter of this sort that cannot exist by itself just on its own, but the form that comes to be in it too. In fact, this is true of form even more than it is true of matter.[32] For in the case of matter, even though matter in the fundamental sense cannot exist on its own, the matter in compound bodies, conceived as proximate [matter],[33] is not matter simply as such, but the matter of some specific thing (*tode ti*),[34] and it *does* exist on its own. The matter in artefacts is certainly 25 of this sort. In contrast, none of the forms that come to be in matter is ever able to exist on its own, whether it belongs to a simple body or to a compound one. Thus the forms produced by the arts in various underlying matters are inseparable from them, even though these 5,1 [matters] are capable of existing separate from the [forms].[35]

Now, a form produced by art is not a substance (*ousia*),[36] since art is not [a substance] either; for this sort of form is also art, as was said earlier.[37] But a form produced naturally is a substance, because nature is in fact a substance and this sort of form is a nature.[38] In the

5   case of fire, which is a simple, natural body, heat and dryness, as well
as[39] the lightness that emerges from them and above them,[40] are its
form, while what underlies these is its matter, which by its nature*
is not any of these, but is receptive of them and their contraries
equally.[41] (It is because of this nature that the transformations of the
simple bodies into one another occur.[42]) While neither of these [sc.
either its form or its matter] is a body, what is composed out of them
10   is by that very fact a body and fire, for it possesses a principle of
upwards motion – namely, lightness – from its nature and substance
(taken as form). This lightness, as fire's form and nature, does not
itself undergo change. For how could lightness ever undergo change
itself just on its own, when it belongs to something else and is not just
on its own? For lightness is a power of the body that has it; but no
15   power is separable from what it empowers.[43] For this reason, even
though it does not undergo change on its own, it is responsible[44] in
the body which has it for the change that arises from this body, and
it is in virtue of this that the body which has it is said to change,
because[45] undergoing change belongs to the body on account of and
in virtue of lightness, which is its power and nature.

      Neither of the simple body's basic components, then, is a body. For
20   the matter [of a simple body] is not a body either,[46] since every body
is tangible[47] and conjoined with a contrariety of some sort, whereas
the matter [of a simple body] lies beyond every tangible quality and
contrariety;[48] and a body is existent, whereas matter needs form in
order to be.[49] For the same reason, form is not a body either, because
6,1   it is incapable of being on its own, since it is inseparable from the
matter, as has been shown.[50]

      Each of these, on the other hand, is a substance. For a natural form
is a substance, just as matter is,[51] since the parts of a substance are
substances; or better still, it is because each of them is a substance
that what is composed out of both is also a substance and a single
5   nature of some kind.[52] This is unlike artefacts, which are substances
in virtue of the underlying matter and qualities in virtue of their
forms.[53]

      Those who are puzzled as to how it is possible for a body to come
from non-bodily items[54] would not be puzzled if they knew them* and
so were to appreciate that anything that comes to be a specific thing[55]
comes to be from something that is not that thing, as hot comes from
not hot, but cold does not come from cold or white from something of
10   the same sort.[56] For even if something else hot is responsible for the
particular thing that becomes hot becoming so, nevertheless the very
thing* that becomes hot becomes hot from [having been] not hot. For
something that is already [hot] does not become [hot]. Consequently,
even if someone were to accept body's coming into being, he would
have to say that it comes to be from what is not body.[57] But given that,
as we claim,

1. body does not come to be simply as such[58]

since there is always body, if the universe is in fact eternal and incapable of either coming to be or perishing;[59] and   15

2. the coming into being of some particular body, that is, of any body, is from something which is not that particular body,

it follows that

3. the coming into being of some particular body is not from what is not a body simply as such after all.

For just as we separate matter from form in thought and in account, even though it is not actually separable – for though it is separable from this particular form, it is inseparable from form simply as such, just as wax is inseparable from shape[60] – in the same way the coming   20 into being of body as body is something that likewise occurs only in thought and in account.[61]

Although fire and each of the other [simple] bodies is in possession of just what it is from both the underlying matter and the form in it, [each of them] is just what it is in virtue of form.[62] For fire is fire* in virtue of form, and earth is earth in virtue of the same thing [viz., form]; and the same argument applies to water and air as well. For   25 each of them is just what it is said to be in virtue of form, since

1. each of them is a specific thing in virtue of its difference from the rest
2. each has this difference from the rest in virtue of its own form

since the underlying matter in all of them is the same.[63] Therefore,

3. each of these is just what it is in virtue of form.

And if

4. that in virtue of which each thing is just what it is, is its   30 culmination[64]

since the culmination of something that comes to be is the stage at which it, having come to be, ceases coming to be, as it has already   7,1 come to be and developed completely, and it ceases coming to be whenever it has come to be fully in its form,[65] then it would make sense to say

5. each body's culmination is in its form.[66]

Yet if

1. each thing formed by art and, even prior to that, each thing   5 formed naturally is just what it is in virtue of its form
2. [the form] is the culmination of each,

then it is true, by conversion,[67] that

> 3. that in virtue of which every compound of matter and form has its being is its form and culmination.

Bodies act and are modified in virtue of non-bodily items

Not only does what each thing is come from its form, as do its
10 differences from other beings, but the differences between bodies with regard to acting and being modified also come about in virtue of forms. For when bodies act or are modified in so far as they are bodies, they act or are modified in a particular way due to the form, since eah of these also is in virtue of the difference in forms. So it makes sense to claim that bodies act and are modified in virtue of non-bodily items.[68]

15   In natural bodies where the underlying subject is simple – that is, [where the underlying subject is] matter in the fundamental sense, which underlies the simple, basic bodies that in turn are elements of other bodies – both the form and nature of these [simple bodies] will be simple as well. Because of this, their nature will be responsible for just a single simple change. For if nature is an origin and principle of change, then a simple nature will be the origin and principle of a simple motion, and [the motion] will be simple and
20 single in the fundamental sense. Hence, some of these will be moved exclusively upwards or exclusively downwards in virtue of their* nature.[69]

With other [bodies], in contrast, where the proximate subject is no longer simple, but already a kind of body and compound – for every body is compound in this way[70] – the form in these cases will be more complex and more advanced as well,[71] as will their nature. This, too, makes sense. For the form in the underlying matter also makes a
8,1 contribution to the form of [the compound body],[72] and all the more so if there is not just one body underlying it [but many], as is necessarily the case with natural compound bodies. For the underlying subject is not a single simple body in any of them, since the natural transformation of a single simple body is into another simple
5 body.[73] Consequently, if there is to be a compound natural body, over and above the simple bodies, then it must have several simple bodies as its underlying subjects, where the number is one corresponding to the difference between the forms in them. This is the reason why things of this sort are compound bodies. The [body], then, which has many differing forms conjoined with matter as its underlying sub-
10 jects, has a nature and form that is of necessity more complex and more advanced, since each nature in the bodies underlying it makes a contribution to the form that stands over them all and is common

to them.[74] For this sort of form is in a way a form of forms and a kind of culmination of culminations.[75]

For this reason, we should also not be surprised by the difference amongst forms in natural bodies, since we plainly find what is responsible for their diversity in the underlying subjects. For it makes sense that the number of forms in the bodies underlying them, together with their distinctive mixture,[76] should bear responsibility for such great diversity.[77] For even when there is just a single underlying subject that does not contribute to any difference in things composed out of it – for the matter [in question] is of this sort[78] – the pairing of dryness or moisture with the heat or coldness in it is responsible for a very great difference in the things composed out of it, such that one pair of them comes to be fire, another air, another earth, and another water, and one comes to be heavy and another light, and others possess each of these in a derivative sense. Given all this, how could it fail to make sense that bodies produced from a certain sort of mixture and blend of all of them will differ enormously from the others, in both their forms and their powers for change?[79]

Consider, then, how immensely trees and plants, which are all natural compound bodies, differ from simple bodies in their powers for change. The [simple bodies] have an origin and principle within themselves for just a single, simple motion, while each [tree and plant] has within itself the origin and principle of being nourished and of motion in all directions by growing; in addition, each of them also has a power of producing something like itself.[80] Although plants have all these features in common, they further differ thoroughly from each other in form because they are different in matter and in the mixture and blend of the matter underlying them.[81] For trees are the most distinct from each other, much more than even vegetables, which are plants too, as well as natural, compound bodies. But among [vegetables], too, we see yet again the greatest difference from one another, and nothing else is responsible for this other than what was just mentioned. This sort of form and this sort of culmination is already the first power of the soul. For if every living thing is alive in virtue of a soul,[82] and plants are alive – since to nourish oneself and grow is to be alive – then plants will have a soul and their form will be a soul.[83] For just as with simple bodies, the form corresponds not to the activity that issues from the power, but to the power from which the activity issues. For the nature of earth does not consist in being moved downwards, since it is no less earth when it remains stationary. Rather, [the nature of earth] is the power from which its being moved downwards issues, namely, heaviness. Each [of these] is a culmination too: both heaviness, since it is a form, and the activity that occurs in virtue of it, since the activities that issue from dispositions and powers are their culminations. In cases where both occur, the culmination that corresponds to the disposition and power

15

20

25

9,1

5

10

15

20

is first and exists prior in time to the activity that occurs in virtue of
it.[84] The same holds for compound bodies too. So if forms are not the
activities issuing from powers, but the powers instead, which, be-
25   cause they exist prior to the activities issuing from them, are first and
come before them, the first culmination of plants will also be a form
and a soul.
10,1   Now, once this has been agreed to and granted, I do not think
anyone will dispute that an animal is likewise a natural, compound
body, composed of soul and body. If, as a body, it gets its being from
them, and every body is a compound of matter and form,[85] then
clearly one of them will be the animal's matter and the other its form.
5   But from what has been said about plants, it is clear that the soul is
the form, although this was not intelligible from what had been
demonstrated at the beginning of our discussion. For it was granted
that that in virtue of which each thing has its being is its form and
culmination.[86] What it is to be an animal belongs to an animal in
virtue of a particular kind of soul, namely, the one for perceiving,
10   since it is due to this that an animal is an animal and differs from
everything else that is not an animal.[87] In an animal, therefore, the soul
is a form of the body, since the forms in all bodies are forms of the
underlying matter in them, where its soul, as a form, is more advanced
than the [soul] in plants to the same extent that the soul in them is
[more advanced] than the forms in the simple, primary bodies.[88]
15   The differences between souls for perceiving preserve the same
proportion again in relation to each other that the forms of simple
bodies have to the soul of plants and that the soul of plants in turn
has to the soul for perceiving.[89] What is responsible for the proportional difference between them is the difference in the bodies
underlying them, as regards their number and the particular kind of
blend, mixture, and formation.[90] And that makes sense. For if 'the
20   beginning (*arkhê*) is not just half, but the largest part of the whole',[91]
then it makes sense that a difference in the origins (*kata tas arkhas*),
even if small, can be responsible for a great difference. This is obvious
from the forks in roads too. For a small disparity between them is
often responsible for travel to places a great distance from each other.
But the proximate matter of each thing that comes to be is also an
origin. So it makes sense that the difference in forms that supervene
25   on differences in the proximate matter follows from them. For not all
matter can receive the same culmination.[92]
So in things at the ground level, which do not yet have a body
underlying them, the form is simpler too; whereas in things in which
a compound body with distinctive parts useful for different activities
11,1   underlies them, the form is conjoined with many powers, since it is a
form and culmination of a complex and organic body.[93] For just this
reason, then, the soul is a form of this sort of body.[94] The soul that
has a simpler organic body is simpler, while the soul comprising

many powers is more advanced and its underlying body, of which this
particular sort of soul is a form, is more complex and more organic. 5
If someone on first hearing thinks it incredible that the soul is this
sort of body's form and nature,[95] just as lightness is fire's [form and
nature],[96] but then looks at the distinction between the bodies that
have these forms and sees how unspeakably greater the construction
of animate bodies is than that of simple bodies, he would no longer 10
think those who speak in this way are saying anything incredible, since
it is not incredible, but makes the most sense of all, to say that the
proportion that the bodies underlying the forms have to one another is
the same as the one that their forms preserve to each other.[97]

The demonstration that the soul is a form

That the soul is a form can be shown as follows. It is agreed that

   1. an animal[98] is composed out of soul and body. 15

But

   2. something is said to be 'composed out of things'[99] either
     a. in the way that [something] is composed out of parts that
     are preserved in the whole and the sort of things into which
     it is also divided,

as when we say that a house is composed out of bricks;[100] or

     b. in the way that something blended is composed out of
     things,

like honey water,[101] for we say that this is [composed] out of water
and honey, but that honey water is no longer something that is
divided into these, due to the fact that neither of them is preserved
or still retains its nature after blending;[102] or 20

     c. in the way that [something] is composed out of matter and
     form,

as we say that a statue is composed out of bronze and a shape.[103] But
if being 'composed out of things' is said in these ways, then

   3. an animal should be composed out of soul and body in one of 12,1
   these ways.

But

   4. it cannot be in the first way (*a*),

since that would then be a juxtaposition of soul and body, so that the 5
body would no longer be animate throughout;[104] and if so, then the
soul would contribute not to the character of the animal, but rather
to its size.[105] But

5. it cannot be in the second way (*b*) either,

since it is not the case that the animal comes to be when the soul and the body perish, as happens when things come to be from a blend of things.[106] The only option left, then, is to say that

6. an animal is composed of soul and body (*c*) as matter and form.

One might also learn that the soul is a form of the body, and not a substance itself just on its own (*autê kath' hautên*),[107] from its activi-
10   ties. For no soul activity can occur apart from a bodily change,[108] just as there could not be motion from natural tendencies either,[109] since the body engages in these activities in virtue of the power within it. For being nourished, growing, and generating another like oneself occur in virtue of a soul power, but the changes belong to the body. Moreover, an animal perceives through the perceptual organs, which
15   are bodies, and desires themselves plainly occur when a certain body undergoes change.[110] For appetites, passions, and rage occur in animals in this way; in fear as well there is an alteration and contraction of the body. Representation[111] also occurs through a body, if at any rate it depends on perception in activity, as will be shown.[112] No one
20   would deny that in striving,[113] too, what undergoes change is a body. Even thinking (*phronein*), if it does not occur without representation, would itself be something that occurs through a body too.[114] If it is not possible to conceive of any activity of soul apart from a bodily change, then clearly [the soul] is something that belongs to the body and is inseparable from it. For if it were separate it would be superfluous, since it would not be able to engage in any of its own activities on its own.[115] It is evident, then, that [the soul] is the form of the body and
25   that the changes in virtue of it come about in virtue of the body's
13,1 aptitudes.[116] For on some occasions, when there are strong, external factors responsible, which are capable of setting in motion anger, fear, appetite, or some other affect like this, we are either not affected in any way at all or only superficially and to a small extent; whereas on other occasions when [external factors] are minor or incidental, we
5   overflow with affects, whenever the body is excited and primed and predisposed towards the affect, either due to a shortage or abundance or combination of certain humours. For we become angry more easily when there is an excess of bile, and often we are afraid or upset in circumstances because our body is thus disposed in a certain way.[117]

'In something' [is said] in how many ways?

One could show that the soul is a form of the body in the following
10   way as well. Everyone agrees that the soul is *in* the animal's body. But even though 'being in something' is said in many ways,[118] the

statement 'the soul is in a certain body' cannot be meant in any other way. For something can be said to be 'in something' either

> *a*. in the way that a species (*eidos*) is in a genus

as, for example, human is in animal; or

> *b*. in the way that a genus is in [its] species

as animal is in winged and footed and aquatic, since the being of the genus that is divided into species is in the species that come from the genus and are contradistinguished from one another. Or   15

> *c*. in the way that a part is in a whole

as a hand is in a body; or

> *d*. in the way that the whole is in its parts,

since the whole body of a human being is said to be in the head, neck, trunk, and other parts from which the whole body is made up. One thing is also in another

> *e*. in the way that something is in a vessel or in a place,

as we say, for example, that Dion is in the marketplace or wine is in   20
the jug. Further,

> *f*. characteristics which belong to things extrinsically (*ta sumbebêkota*) are also said to be in them,

as white is said to be in the white body, and

> *g*. things that are blended are said to be in the blend made from them,

just as honey and wine are in the honeyed wine.[119] But in addition to all of the ways just mentioned, something is also said to be in something

> *h*. in the way that a form (*eidos*) is in matter.

For that in virtue of which something that is composed from others itself has being is [in] the rest* in the way that a form is in matter.   14,1
This is how a particular kind of shape is in a statue, which is composed from bronze and shape, and how heaviness is in earth, which is composed from matter and [heaviness].[120]

Now, while 'in something' is said in these ways – since a pilot will be in the ship in one of the ways just mentioned[121] – the soul is not in   5
the body (*c*) in the way that a part of [the body] is in it. For in that case it would be a body, since part of a body is a body, and it would contribute to the animal's size, not its character.[122] Moreover, not all of the body would be animate, but each of them would be separated* from the other, unless a body can pass and extend through a body

10   (something not at all easy to conceive).[123] Nor is the soul (*d*) a kind of
     whole, where the parts of the body are parts of the soul, so that the
     soul would be [in them] in the way that the whole is in its parts.[124]

         Nor is the soul in the body (*a*) in the way that a species is in a
     genus, since the body in which the soul is present is not the genus of
     the soul. For each of these is one in number, whereas genera and
     species are common and universal; and further the soul would be a
15   body.[125] But the soul is also not in the body (*b*) in the way that a genus
     is in its species, for the reason mentioned above[126] and because if the
     soul were said to be the genus of the body, every body would be a soul,
     just as every human is an animal.[127]

         Nor is the body (*e*) a place for the soul either. For in that case the
     soul would be a body, since anything that on its own is in a place is a
     body,[128] and further the body will be a place, since the body will thus
20   be either an empty extension or the boundary of the container (as
     these are the views concerning place).[129] Moreover, what is in a place
     contributes nothing towards the place's being a particular sort of
     thing, but the animate body gets its differences with respect to other
     bodies from the soul.[130] Nor is [the body] like a vessel. For a vessel is
     also a place for that which is in it, differing* from place only in that
     it is carried along with the things that are in it.[131]

25   Nor is the soul in the body (*f*) in the way that an extrinsic
15,1 characteristic is in an underlying subject. For the soul is a substance
     and can receive contraries. But no extrinsic characteristic is a sub-
     stance.[132] Moreover, what is in some underlying subject is not
     responsible for the being of what underlies it, since what underlies it
     can also exist separately from it, whereas the organic body in which
5   the soul is present gets what it is to be organic from the soul.[133]

         Nor again is the soul in the body (*g*) in the way that the ingredients
     from which something is blended are in the blend. For none of the
     things that are in something in this way still retains its nature, as
     neither wine nor honey are preserved in honeyed wine;[134] whereas
     the soul and the body both persist in the animal. Moreover, every
     blend is [a blend] of bodies, so that the soul in that case would be a
     body too.[135]

10   Nor can the soul be in the body in the way that a pilot is in a ship.[136]
     For if one conceived of the pilot (1) as the art of piloting, then the soul
     would be in the body in the way that a disposition and form is in
     matter, since dispositions are in the things of which they are dispo-
     sitions in this way, since they are both non-bodily and inseparable
     from the things which they are in.[137] If, on the other hand, one
     conceived [of the pilot] (2) as the pilot himself that possesses this
15   disposition, then the soul will be a body (since the pilot is endowed
     with a body),[138] and it will be in some circumscribed part of the body
     in the way that [something is] in a place, and not all of the body will
     be responsive to itself or have an accompanying awareness, since not

all of it will have soul.[139] In addition, the soul in that case would move the body by force and so, being this sort of thing once it had become separated from the body, it would be able to enter into it again, with the result that the same body would sometimes be animate and sometimes not. If it were such a thing, what would be responsible for the soul's entering the body and how would it enter? What would be responsible for its staying?[140] And even before that, what would its essence and nature be? If the soul is like a pilot, rather than the art of piloting, it will also be composed itself from matter and some form. [But then] this form would be the soul, since what it is to be a soul comes from the same thing that what it is to be a pilot comes from. For each thing has what it is to be just the [sort of] thing it is in virtue of its form, and the pilot gets what it is to be a pilot from the form, not the matter.[141]

20

25

If the soul cannot be in the body in any of the ways just mentioned, the only option left is that the [soul] is in the [body] in the way that a form is, since each thing's form is that in virtue of which it is just what it is, and it is in virtue of the soul that the animal is an animal.[142] Now, given that

16,1

1. the soul* is a form

as has been shown;[143] and

2. [it is] an enmattered form[144]

since it is [the form] of a body, and a natural body at that – for it is not artificial, like the body of a statue is – a natural body which is not simple, like the body of fire, but compound and organic;[145] and it has further been shown that

3. the form is a culmination of that of which it is a form;[146]

5

and it is characteristic for Aristotle to say that

4. the culmination is a completion (*entelekheia*),[147]

since it is responsible for the fact that the object to which it belongs is complete (*en tôi telei*), it makes sense, then, that he offered this sort of characterisation:

5. [the soul] is a 'first completion'.[148]

For there are two kinds of completion, (*a*) one which is a disposition and power and (*b*) another which is the activity issuing from that power, and of these the power is first and the culmination corre- sponding to it is the form.[149] [The soul] is a completion, then, that is,

10

6. it is 'the first [completion] of a natural, organic body'.[150]

For an organic body is one that has many different parts able to subserve the soul powers.[151] Hence, [Aristotle] says that the organic body 'has life by its power',[152] using the phrase 'has life by its power'

for 'is able to actively live'.* For something that already possesses an
15   advanced soul can do and undergo many things in virtue of it: [it can]
be nourished, grow, reproduce, perceive, desire, think, speak, act, be
healthy, be ill. For things are no less animate even when they are not
in activity, but still capable of it. The qualification 'as a power' makes
clear that [the soul] is the first completion.[153]

This is in fact the essence (*ousia*) of the soul.[154] For it comprehends
under a single characterisation many souls that are not the same in
form as each other and yet also stand in a certain order with respect
20   to one another, such that one of them is less advanced and first, while
the next is more advanced than it, because it has some other power
in addition to these; and then a third [type of soul], which in addition
17,1 to these powers has certain other powers yet again.[155] When things
are related to each other in this way, their general characterisation
(*koinos logos*) cannot be perspicuous for the following reason. On the
one hand, their definition has to be attributed to all of them. On the
other hand, none of the more advanced ones among them can be fully
5   expressed in such a characterisation, since then the less advanced
ones would no longer be comprehended under the definition. Hence,
the general characterisation of the soul is simpler and more general
[than a definition], since it does not make reference to any of the
[powers] thought above all to be soul powers. For this sort of characterisation is based on something that belongs to all these things in
common (*koinôs*).[156]

The soul is inseparable from the body whose soul it is

If the soul is a form, as has been shown,[157] then necessarily

10   *i*. it is inseparable from the body whose soul it is
ii. it is non-bodily
iii. it is incapable of undergoing change on its own[158]

since every form is of this sort. For a body is a composite that exists
on its own,[159] but a form is [a form] of something else – since this is
the sort of thing a completion and a culmination are – and cannot be
without that of which it is [the form], just as a limit cannot be apart
from that of which it is the limit. The soul, therefore, cannot be
15   separated and exist on its own.[160] But then it is not a body either.[161]

A form, furthermore, cannot be a body along the lines of those who
claim, like the Stoics, that every body is either matter or composed
from matter.[162] For form is not matter, since the latter is qualityless,
while the former is a kind of quality.[163] But it is not composed from
matter either. For if the form were composed from matter and
form,[164] then in the first place, what is different from the composite
will be the same as it;[165] and in the second place, this will continue to
20   infinity, since this [second] form will be composed from matter and

form, and that form in turn will require matter and form again. For
if someone were to claim that a form is composed in this way from
matter and form, but not from some further form, because it has [its]   18,1
being* together with matter,[166] then matter on their view would not
be qualityless, as its definition states, since it requires some form or
quality in order to be. But if they claim that matter is qualityless,
even though it is incapable of existing separate from a quality, on the
grounds that the quality is not included in its own nature, then by   5
the same argument the form and quality ought to be separate from
matter as well, even though their existence is conjoined with matter,
since the matter is not contained in their own nature.[167] Furthermore, how can absurdity be avoided if someone claims that the
matter, when it receives the form and the quality, also receives some
matter in addition? For that is what they must say if they claim that
the form and the quality are an enmattered body.[168]   10
    It is a mark of confusion to maintain that since

    1. the parts of a body are necessarily bodies*

just as the parts of a surface, a line, or a time are surfaces, lines, and
times, respectively; and

    2. the form and the matter are parts of an animal

therefore

    3. [each is] also a body.[169]

For [form and matter] are not parts of the body in such a way that   15
the body can be carved into them. For the parts of the body into which
it is carved contribute to the body's size and continue to exist after
they are carved.[170] Form and matter are not parts of the body in this
way, but in the way that bronze and its contours are parts of the
statue. Dividing up the statue does not result in them, as it does into
a head, trunk, and legs. But the composite is composed from them as   20
parts, even though not in the same way.[171] For the shape of the statue
is a part, though not in a way that contributes something to its size
– it contributes to its character instead – and not as something that
can persist in separation from the matter.[172] For the division of the
body and other continuous objects mentioned above[173] results in parts
that have a size and persist after the division. For this reason, [the   25
shape and the bronze] are not parts of body simply as such, but of the
particular sort of body of which they are a part, and they are that in
virtue of which [the body] is of that particular sort, even though they
are not a body [themselves].[174]
    The following argument does not show anything either. It main-
tains that

    1. anything whose part is a body is itself a body

2. the sense that is part of the soul is a body

so therefore

3. the soul is a body.[175]

19,1 For if one conceives of the sense as the perceptual organ, what is
conceived *is* a body, but not a part of the soul; whereas if one
conceives of it as the power for perceiving, then it is a part of the soul,
but will *not* be what is conceived as a body.[176] For if the soul is a body,
and a body not in the way that matter is, it will be composed from
5 matter and form, given that every body other than matter* is such
on their view.[177] But if so, then the soul will in fact be the form in that
body. For if what underlies [that body] is a body and so a specific
thing capable of existing on its own – since it is either breath
(*pneuma*) or something else which is not animate – then that which,
when added to this persisting body, makes it animate from some-
10 thing inanimate would be the soul on their view.[178] For one cannot
claim that breath comes to be a soul by adding a quality to the breath.
For if adding the quality to breath produced an essential transformation in the breath, one could claim that breath is transformed into
soul. But if it remains breath after adding the quality, then the
15 breath would not be a soul nor would the quality added to it make it
a soul, since the breath's essence is not transformed; rather [the
quality] is just an extrinsic characteristic of breath. For no natural
body can convert from one nature to some other without having been
transformed essentially. The nature of soul and breath are different.[179] One surely cannot claim that breath is a genus of soul, since it
20 has existence on its own. For no genus is such as to exist on its own.[180]

The soul is not one of the simple bodies

Those who claim[181] that the soul is a form of the body, but make it one
of the underlying bodies in the animal, such as fire or air or some
other body, fail to realise that they are making part of the matter a
form of the remaining matter. But this is absurd. For the nature of
25 form and matter is different, as has been shown,[182] since one is an
underlying subject, while the other is in it; and one is shaped, while
the other is that in virtue of which it is shaped. As a consequence,
those who make such claims will have to say that fire or air is a
culmination of the other three bodies and that it comes into being
from their mixture, since that is the sort of thing a culmination is.[183]
But then it would no longer be a simple body, since whatever comes
30 into being from the mixture of several bodies is not simple, and there
would not be four simple bodies. One of the four bodies cannot come
to be from the mixture of the others either, given that it is necessary
for something constituted from a mixture to exhibit all the powers of

the ingredients from which it has been mixed. For mixture differs from perishing in that mixed ingredients do not perish entirely. But it is impossible to maintain that moisture and coldness are present in fire or that dryness and coldness are in air.[184] (Of the four [simple bodies], moreover, which one specifically would be a form of the other three, rather than another?)[185] The only powers in the animal, furthermore, would be those that belonged to the body which had been produced from the blend of the others: if what had been produced was fire, the powers would be heat and dryness, and if it was some other [body], they would be its powers, since this is what had been produced from them. If, on the other hand, the powers of the other bodies were to persist in the animal no less than its powers,[186] then it could not have been produced from them and so would not be a form. But if not, then it is not a soul either.[187] 35

20,1

5

If, furthermore, the soul is one of the [simple bodies], then either not all of the animal will be animate or, alternatively, a body will extend through a body.[188] But what view could be more absurd than that? For how can a body, which is filled with itself and does not have any empty space inside it, receive another body into itself which is similarly filled with itself?* For if something which is full of itself is to receive something else, which again is likewise full of itself, then nothing will prevent it from receiving another yet again and still another: since it was no less full on its own than it is now having received something else into itself, it will not be prevented from receiving a second thing, and thus nothing will prevent the largest body from coming to be in the smallest. Yet how is it not absurd to say that a place that has been filled up by a certain body is able to receive another body while staying the same, since the body that filled it remains in it and has not changed place? We have, however, spoken about the absurdity of this theory elsewhere at length.[189] 10

15

Those who speak in this way, moreover, do not preserve the analogy between the form in an animal and the forms of simple bodies and the forms of artefacts. For heaviness is not this sort of form, nor is lightness or shape.[190] 20

If one were to say, moreover, that the soul, understood as a form,* is one of the simple bodies, on the grounds that it is the form, and not the composite, which informs the matter, then it should be the form of this body – namely, lightness, or the heat and dryness conjoined with it, or a form of one of the simple bodies – which is a soul on the view of those who speak in this way.[191] 25

Those who say that the animal's soul is a form, but a form in the way a substance is, which is separable by itself just on its own as the pilot of the ship is, on the grounds that the pilot is also a form and culmination of the ship, do not speak correctly either. For the pilot is not the ship's form or its culmination, since [a ship] is still a ship even without the pilot.[192] Or rather* the pilot might be said to be a form of 21,1 the activity of the ship, since the activity, as [the activity] of a ship, comes about in the ship in virtue of the particular shape which is its form and the pilot contributes something to the activity. But the soul is a form of the animal in so far as it is an animal, and it is not animate only when it engages in activity. It is just because of this that

5 the soul is the first completion [of the body].[193] That the soul is not [the form] of an animal in the way that the pilot is a form of a ship is clear from the fact that the ship persists, even when the pilot is gone, whereas the animal is no longer an animal once the soul is gone. Hence, the soul bears more of an analogy to the shape of the ship instead. For the ship has its being in virtue of this, just as the animal

10 does in virtue of its soul.[194] The pilot, moreover, is not present throughout the entire ship, but animal's entire body is animate.[195] In addition, if the soul were in the body in this way, it would also be possible for it to re-enter the body again after having been separated. For what will there be to keep the soul within the body, if it is this sort of thing?[196] The body, furthermore, will not be moved in virtue of

15 its own nature; hence it will be moved contrary to nature. But every forced change contrary to nature in fact occurs due to meeting bodily resistance, so that by this argument the soul would again be a body.[197]

In general, it would also make sense to ask those who say that the soul is a form of the body in this way, just what joins and holds the two of them together, given that they are separate from one another and differ in their natures, so that what is composed from them is

20 and remains a single thing? For it is difficult to find something responsible for the unity of such things, both when they first come together and after they have come together.[198]

The soul itself just on its own is unchangeable

Since the soul is a form of the body of the sort discussed above,[199] and such a form is inseparable from the body, it will also perish along with the body (as much of it, at any rate, as is a form of a perishable body).[200] But in that case the soul will also be incapable of undergoing

25 change on its own. For not everything that is responsible for a change in something necessarily undergoes change itself.[201]

Anything which is detached and separated from the things it changes and which changes them through bodily contact necessarily undergoes change itself when it effects change. For things that push,

22,1 pull, spin, or carry something are in fact responsible for the change in the things changed by them because they themselves undergo change in this way.[202]

In contrast, where the powers and dispositions of what undergoes change are responsible for change of some sort in the things that possess them, not only do they not need to undergo change themselves in order to produce change, they cannot. For it is impossible

for something to undergo change on its own if it is not separable on 5
its own. But dispositions, powers, and the forms of bodies quite
generally (which, it has been shown, include the soul) are all like
that.[203] For heaviness is responsible for earth's downward motion and
can produce change in this direction in it without undergoing change
on its own. For how could heaviness be changed on its own, if it is a
form and a nature of the body which posseses it? In the same way,
the soul of animals has responsibility for all the changes that belong 10
to [the animal] as an animal, since it is in virtue of the soul that an
animal has the power to be changed in this way. It changes the body
in this way without undergoing change itself just on its own.[204]

That having been said, the soul does undergo change jointly with
the body undergoing change and is changed extrinsically, something
that necessarily holds for any form that resides in and accompanies
the body of which it is the form, because it is inseparable from it.[205] 15
In fact, whenever the form is properly responsible for the body's
change, although the form primarily changes the body on that occasion, it also changes itself extrinsically, since it undergoes jointly
with the body the change it produces in it. For heaviness changes
itself extrinsically,* whenever it is responsible for the downward
motion of the body that has it. The soul too, then, will change itself 20
extrinsically whenever the animal that possesses it is changed in
virtue of it. For although it will also undergo change extrinsically
when the animal changes place due to some other cause, it would be
changed by itself only in the case where the change comes about in
virtue of itself.[206]

Further, if [others] say that the soul undergoes change precisely
because it produces change,[207] then it should also be said to be at rest 25
whenever it is responsible for the body's rest. For what kind of
arbitrariness would it be if the soul produces change by undergoing
change itself, yet does not also bring the body to rest by being at rest?
But if it did, then change would no longer belong in the essence of the
soul.[208] For if* (*i*) its proper function is exhibited more during rest 23,1
than in change, then (*ii*) being at rest will more properly and more
naturally belong to the soul. But the first, (*i*), is in fact the case, since
the most proper function of the soul, understanding, occurs more
through the soul's being at rest than by its undergoing change.[209] For
this reason, understanding occurs more in old age than in youth, and
more in the sober than in the drunk, and more when the body is at 5
rest than in motion.[210] Being at rest, therefore, naturally belongs to
[the soul] more than undergoing change does.

Accordingly, it is more truthful to say, not that the soul undergoes
change or that it is at rest in its own right, but that the animal does
each of these things in virtue of the soul. For just as we do not say
that the soul walks or sees or hears, but that the human being does
in virtue of the soul,[211] so too with all the other activities and changes 10

in which one engages as something animate and as a human, it is not the soul which engages in activity and undergoes change,[212] even though we are often tempted to [say this] because the body that undergoes change in activities of this sort is not as discernible to us as it is [in other cases].[213] But even in these cases, an animal and a human engage in activity in virtue of the soul, in virtue of which [a

15 human] possesses what it is to be human. For a human feels pleasure and feels pain, becomes angry and is afraid, loves and hates, learns and understands, recollects and remembers in virtue of the soul, since [a human] is able to do these things because it has this kind of form and this kind of culmination.[214] For just as a wrestler wrestles in virtue of the disposition for wrestling, but the disposition for

20 wrestling does not itself wrestle; and the oboist plays oboe in virtue of the disposition for playing the oboe, but the disposition for playing oboe does not play the oboe;[215] and the weaver weaves but the disposition for weaving does not weave; so one should suppose that the same holds likewise for those activities which things possessing a soul engage in in virtue of being animate.[216] For in none of these cases does the soul in its own right engage in a vital activity; rather that which possesses the soul does so in virtue of it.

25 The view that these particular activities belong to the soul because it uses the body as an organ is simply not true. For this case is like that of other powers and dispositions. No power or disposition engages in activity by using that of which it is a disposition. Rather, it is the other way around: the things that possess the powers and dispositions engage in activity in virtue of these powers and dispositions.[217] For heaviness is not carried downwards by making use of

30
24,1 earth, of which it is a power. Rather, earth is carried downwards in virtue of heaviness, which is its power and form, its culmination and completion. The same holds for the soul as well, since it is likewise a power and form and completion of the body that has it, as it comes into being from a certain mixture and blend of the primary bodies, as has been shown.[218]

5 What engages in activity related to the soul is that in which the governing part of the soul is found,[219] since that is what is initially animate in its own right;[220] and it uses the organic parts of the body for the activities related to the soul.[221] For the organs animals use for activities related to the soul are congenital parts of the body, not

10 separate parts as in the case of the arts.[222] For sinews, hands, feet, and perceptual organs are body parts of this kind. A sense organ, for example, is a part of the organic body for awareness of a perceptible.

The soul is an origin and principle for animate things and something that is responsible in so far as it is productive of the vital changes in them. But it is also responsible in the way that a form is, as has been shown,[223] and in addition as a 'that for which', that is, in

15 the way that an end is [responsible], given that for things that have

a soul [the soul] is an end and a culmination, while the things that lead to the end are for the end.[224] For everything produced naturally is produced for something, namely, the end in it.[225]

The soul is not a harmony

One should not assume that people who claim that

1. the soul is a form that supervenes on a particular sort of mixture and blend of the bodies underlying it   20

[also] claim that

2. the soul is a harmony.[226]

For suppose that the soul cannot be separate from this sort of blend and mixture; it does not thereby follow that it is the same as the soul. For the soul is not a particular kind of blend of bodies – which is what a harmony is – but a power that emerges above a particular kind of blend,[227] analogous to the powers of medicinal drugs, which are assembled from a blend of many [ingredients]. For in their case too, the mixture, composition, and proportion of drugs – such that one of   25 them, it might turn out, is 2:1, another 1:2, and another 3:2 – bear some analogy to a harmony. The power, however, which emerges from the blend of drugs exhibiting this harmony and proportion is not likewise a harmony too. For while the harmony is the proportion and composition of the mixed ingredients, the ointment's power is not the   25,1 proportion by which the ingredients are mixed.[228]

    The soul is also of this sort. For the soul is the power and form that supervenes[229] on the blend of bodies in a particular proportion, not the proportion or composition of the blend.[230] For it would make more sense for someone to say that health is a harmony than to say that   5 the soul is, since the former comes closer to a harmony than the soul does. For health is a balance of various things, where this balance is just a composition and mixture of certain things in a certain proportion.[231] The soul, in contrast, is not a balance, but the power [that supervenes] on the balance: it cannot be without this balance, but is not [the same as] it.[232]

    'Harmony' is said in two ways.[233] It is said in one way of the composition of bodies. For when [bodies] are composed so as not to   10 admit anything similar between them, they are said to 'be in harmony' and a composition of this kind is said to be a 'harmony'. It is said in another way of a proportion of mixed ingredients, such as when something has been mixed in a proportion of 2:1 or 4:3. For it seems that something which has been mixed in this way – where, say, one ingredient in the mixture is double, the other half – has been mixed   15 harmoniously and that this particular kind of mixture is a harmony.

    With the first kind of harmony, the harmony is not the same as what is produced from the things brought into harmony. For when the wood in a bench is put together harmoniously it does not follow that the bench is therefore a harmony; and when stones are arranged harmoniously it does not follow that the temple that has been produced from their harmony is thereby a harmony as well. With this

20 kind of harmony, the harmony is one thing and what has been produced from things composed harmoniously is another. The same also holds for harmony when taken as a proportion. For supposing that certain things have been mixed in a certain proportion and harmoniously, it does not thereby follow that what has been produced from this sort of mixture is [itself] a harmony and a proportion.[234]

26,1 A cithara's being in harmony, moreover, is not the same as its making a certain sort of sound. For it is no less in harmony when it makes no sound, whereas the sound that is produced out of and from this sort of harmony is something other than the harmony from which it is produced.[235]

Someone might deny that a proportion is a harmony whenever

5 things are mixed in a certain proportion, since the proportion of 2:1 is not a harmony when it occurs in wine and honey. For there is harmony in a specific kind of composition of melodies and rhythms, not in just any random thing or in any random proportion.[236] For every harmony is constituted by a determinate proportion. But the mixture of hot, cold, dry, and moist things – that is, the mixture of elements that the soul is a form of – is not constituted by a determi-

10 nate proportion. For the same soul persists even when the powers in a mixture are strengthened or weakened to a certain extent. For if someone were to say that in general the mixture of just any thing in some proportion is a harmony, this would commit one to saying that everything composed is in harmony, since some proportion is to be found in every composed thing.[237]

In contrast, the soul would be a harmony, or a harmonious composition of certain bodies, rather for those who make the soul out of a

15 specific kind of mixture and composition of things.[238] This group includes the Stoics, who claim that the soul is breath composed in a certain way from fire and air.[239] It also includes the Epicureans, since on their view the soul is composed from many different bodies.[240] Even on Plato's view, the substance of the soul is constituted from a

20 composition of things and composed in a certain proportion, as he says in the *Timaeus*.[241] As I was just saying, the soul would be a harmony for someone who speaks like this rather than for someone who claims that the soul is a disposition, power, and form that supervenes on a certain kind of blend and mixture of simple bodies.[242] For on the view of those who think that the soul is in a way the very things that are composed, the composite gets what it is to be a soul

25 from a certain kind of composition; so if this composition is a harmony, then the composite would get what it is to be a soul from the

harmony. But for someone who thinks that the soul is not the things composed simply as such, but instead a power that emerges above a certain sort of blend and mixture of the primary bodies, the blend of matter will have a proportion, but the soul will have its being not in virtue of the harmony and blend (as they are committed to saying), but in virtue of the power that emerges above it.[243]   30

The parts of the soul: how many and which ones?

We have made clear what the essence of the soul is and what follows   27,1
from it, to the extent it was possible to offer a general overview of it in a short space. The next thing to speak about are its parts, how many there are and which ones, after we have shown that there are several parts, though a finite number [of them].[244]

To show that the soul has several powers and not just one power   5
which seems to be several – as Democritus and various others thought,[245] because of the changes and activities [it undergoes] at different times, in relation to different things, and by different means – it is sufficient to point to the conflict of powers with one another, which occurs both in people who control themselves and in those who do not.[246]

But it could be shown most clearly by the fact that (1) nature does not seem to do anything superfluous[247] and (2) there are things* that have a power of soul, but cannot engage in other activities beyond it,   10
even when there are objects present which the activities corresponding to these powers concern.[248] For if someone were to claim that these activities do not occur in them [solely] due to a lack of organs, he will undermine the claim that nature does nothing superfluous. For the soul's being capable of engaging in many activities will be superfluous in them, since it will be prevented by nature itself from   15
engaging in these activities due to a lack of organs.[249]

How could it not be absurd, moreover, to claim that a human does not differ from frogs or any other random animal with respect to the power of the soul, but with respect to some organic body? This view will not differ from the belief in metempsychosis that some maintain, if the difference between animals and between their activities does   20
not come from the powers of the soul, but rather from organs. For even though the same soul will be in all animate things, they will engage   28,1
in distinctive activities in virtue of the differences in their bodies, which is just what [the proponents of metempsychosis] maintain.[250]

That there are not infinitely many powers of the soul

It is evident from what has been said that there are several powers of the soul. But it is also evident that there are not infinitely many powers,[251] from the fact that   5

1. nature does nothing superfluous
2. an infinite number of powers would be* superfluous

since an animal cannot engage in activity corresponding to infinitely many powers.[252]

Furthermore, since the parts of the body that has a soul are limited, it makes sense that the parts of the soul in it are limited too.[253]

Furthermore,

1. nature does everything for something[254]
2. in cases where one thing is first and another second, the first is always directed towards the second.

10   But

3. the soul is a nature and by nature there is a certain order among the powers in it.

Therefore,

4. there is a power that is highest among them, and the ones that precede it are for its sake.

For if the sequence of the soul's powers went on infinitely, it would undermine the principle that nature does everything for something.[255]

* * *

Since the powers of the soul are finite in number, we must investigate how many there are and which ones. Consider the following argu-
15   ment. As has already been stated,[256]

1. in cases where one thing is first and another second, where one is less advanced and another more advanced, it is not possible to formulate the essence accurately and in detail with a general characterisation.

For while the nature of the object is most fully expressed in the more advanced cases, the general characterisation cannot make them
20   explicit, since such a characterisation would no longer fit the less advanced cases and so would no longer be general.[257] But

2. the soul is this sort of thing.

For among the powers of the soul, some are first and simpler, and so because of this are also less advanced, while others come after them, and still others yet again above them, so that all of them are related to each other in such a way that the earlier powers can be separated
25   from the subsequent ones, but the subsequent ones cannot occur

without the earlier ones.[258] (As I said earlier, our account concerns the soul of things that are subject to coming-to-be and perishing. For the definition stated above is in fact [a definition] of this [type of] soul. For the soul of the gods – if this even ought to be called a 'soul' – is said to be a soul homonymously with this.)[259] But then

3. it is necessary for anyone speaking about the soul to give an account of each of its powers individually.[260]   29,1

The first [power] of the soul, then, in animate things which are subject to coming-to-be and perishing is the [power] for nourishing [oneself], to which the [powers] for growing and for reproducing are both linked.[261] For the animate is separated from the inanimate by this first power. Thus we attribute being alive, which is due to soul's   5
presence, to things that have at least this power; and being alive belongs to all animate things, not only plants, on account of the power for nourishing [oneself], just as perceivers perceive on account of the power for perceiving. For of necessity when living things lose the former power, they die, whereas everything that has a share in it is alive. Even living things that possess additional powers are alive because of the first power's presence. It is for this reason that we   10
define being alive in terms of nourishing oneself and growing.[262]

The [power] for perceiving and striving, as well as the [power] for desiring and representing constitute the second [type of] soul. These [powers] cannot themselves occur in anything apart from the [power] for nourishing [oneself], despite the fact that the [power] for nourishing [oneself] also exists apart from them (since the [nutritive power] in plants is like that).[263] Things that have the [power] for perceiving – that is, animals, since an animal is defined by this power[264] –   15
necessarily have the [power] for nourishing [oneself] too. But the [power] for perceiving is linked to whatever the [power] for desiring and representing is linked to; conversely, the [power] for desiring and representing is also linked to the [power] for perceiving.[265] And both the [power] for representing and the [power] for perceiving are linked to whatever the [power] for striving and changing place is linked to, since anything moved spatially in place in virtue of the soul present   20
in it is, of necessity, capable of representing, perceiving, and nourishing [itself] as well. It is not the case, on the other hand, that everything capable of representing and perceiving is thereby capable of moving spatially as well.[266]

The last type of soul power is the one generally called 'rational', yet contains within it the powers for deliberating, believing, knowing, and understanding.[267] These are the soul's most advanced powers,   25
both because they possess something of superior value in themselves and because a soul that has these specific powers also has all the   30,1
other powers of soul (although not everything that has those powers also has a share of these*).[268] For this reason, even though there are

many soul powers in [living] things in which the rational power is present, the soul constituted from them all is one, because no subsequent power can occur without the power that comes before it.

5 Rather, they all belong to it as parts, where successive [powers] are joined to the preceding ones and the preceding ones are because of this expanded and developed.[269]

In virtue of the difference in souls and soul powers just mentioned, there is also a quite general division of animate things, in virtue of which we say that some things that have a soul are plants and others

10 animals, and some animals are rational and others non-rational. Those which have all of the powers just mentioned are called 'rational' and 'advanced' in reference to the highest power in them.[270] Humans are the only animal of this sort. All those, on the other hand, that do not have a share in reason, but have perception, are non-rational animals, both those which have the power of changing place in addition to perception and those that have perception apart from this. They are referred to in this way [viz., as non-ra-

15 tional] due to an absence and lack of the highest power. Plants are [animate things] governed solely by the power for nourishing [oneself] and reproducing.[271]

Since, then, the soul is like this and for this reason cannot be revealed through a general characterisation intelligibly, it is necessary for those who speak about the soul to develop their account of each of its

20 powers individually. For this is how the kind of essence and nature it has will be discerned.[272] Our account of them will continue only until the nature of each [soul] and the differences between [their] powers have been indicated, since the puzzles and queries that can be raised about each of them would be inappropriate to the present treatise, as they

25 would require much more leisure to pursue. For the endless review of claims and difficulties which arise for each power would get in the way of setting out the nature of the soul intelligibly.[273]

Though we speak of various parts of the soul, it does not follow that we thereby make the soul into something extended. For not everything which has parts is necessarily an extended thing. For number is not extended either, even though it is composed from parts. But in addition to not being divisible into parts in the way an extended thing

31,1 is, the soul is also not divisible into parts in the way a number is. For we do not divide the soul as though it were composed from the parts into which we divide it as separate things.[274] Rather, we divide the soul by ennumerating the powers it has and by ascertaining the differences between them, just as if one were to divide an apple into

5 its fragrance, lustre, shape, and flavour. For dividing an apple in this way is not like dividing a body, even though the apple is certainly a body, nor is it like dividing a number.[275]

* * *

Now, given that

    1. life belongs to each living thing through the presence of a soul[276]

and

    2. plants are alive

it should follow that

    3. plants have a soul

and

    4. their soul is the power in virtue of which they are alive.

But

    5. plants are alive in so far as they are nourished and grow.[277]

Therefore,

    6. their soul and form is the power in them for nourishing   10
    [themselves] and growing.[278]

For every compound is said both to be and to engage in activity in virtue of each [component] in the compound: it both is what it is and engages in its own activities, first, in virtue of its disposition and form, and second, in virtue of the matter in it that underlies it.[279] The second [component] in virtue of which it is a given thing is what has received [something] within itself;* while the first is what it has   15 received. For example, the healthy animal, which is composed from health and a body, is said to be healthy due to health and also due to the body, where health is the disposition and form the body has received, and the body, in so far as it is healthy in a secondary sense, is the underlying matter that has received health.[280] If,   20 then, in the case of being alive, living things are alive due to the soul first and the body second, since they are composed from a soul and a body and they are said to be alive due to both, that is, due both to the soul and to the body, then it can also be shown from this that the soul is a form of the body and what this particular kind of body has received, while the body is the soul's matter and what has received [it].[281]

    The soul for nourishing [oneself] is therefore a form of the body   25 that has it. It is clear that this form is the soul, and not simply a nature, from the fact that none of the other things are alive that are held to have a nature, but not a soul. For none of the simple bodies is said to be alive, since something is said to be alive in virtue of a soul's presence. Certainly everything that has a soul is alive, and nothing   32,1 is alive which does not have a soul.[282]

    Furthermore, if

1. the powers in virtue of which seeds are active are similar in kind to those which belong to the things the seeds are produced from,

then

2. the powers in virtue of which the seeds of animate things are active will themselves be soul powers.[283]

But

5   3. all the seeds produced from animate things are first active in virtue of the power for nourishing [oneself].[284]

Therefore,

4. the power for nourishing [oneself] is a soul power.

Given, then, that the power for nourishing [oneself] is both a soul and first among the soul's powers, we should speak about it first and show just what its essence and nature is.[285] The account of the soul for reproducing is linked to the account of the soul for nourishing [oneself].[286] For just as being nourished and growing are activities that
10   belong properly to the soul for nourishing [oneself], so too does reproducing something similar to what sows seed. For making another thing like oneself is a function that belongs to living things which are not maimed (as eunuchs are) or generated spontaneously, but fully developed, so that they all can share, in the way that they can, in existing forever and in a likeness to the divine. For everything
15   formed naturally longs for this and does everything natural for its sake.[287] But

1. the soul is what is responsible for something animate doing what is in accordance with its own nature

and

2. generating something like itself is one of the things an animate thing naturally brings about,

since plants and animals that have not been maimed are able to produce things like themselves in virtue of their own nature. Therefore,

20   3. the power for reproducing is also a soul power.

But

4. plants, which only have the soul for nourishing [oneself], are able to reproduce in addition to being nourished and growing.

Therefore,

5. the power to reproduce is part of the power and soul for nourishing [oneself] too.[288]

The account for both, then, will be a shared one.

Since in all subjects one comes to know what is less clear by means of things which are more clear,[289] one ought to approach the present case in this way as well. In particular, since the activities correspond-   25 ing to the soul's powers are clearer than the powers from which they arise into activity – perceiving, for example, is clearer than percep- tion and being nourished clearer than the power for nourishing [oneself][290] – we should begin with being nourished. For in addition to being more intelligible, being nourished is also prior with respect to the definition of the power from which it arises. For those things, which [other] things include in their own definition, are prior in definition to those which are not contained in their definition.[291]   30 Being nourished is related in this way to the power for nourishing   33,1 [oneself]. For being nourished takes place in what is nourished due to the power for nourishing [oneself], whereas the power for nourish- ing [oneself] does not require its activity in order to be. For it is impossible for activities arising from dispositions to be without the dispositions, whereas the dispositions can also be found without the   5 activities.[292]

But in fact anyone who speaks about being nourished ought to speak about nourishment first. For being nourished cannot be made intelligible if nourishment – that by which something nourished is nourished – remains unknown. The same order of inquiry will hold for the soul's other powers too. For in their case as well the activities are more intelligible than the dispositions. But the account of the objects that the activities are directed towards is linked to the discussion of the   10 activities.[293] Anyone, therefore, who intends to show what the soul for nourishing [oneself] is ought first to speak about nourishment.

There are two kinds of nourishment

Nourishment seems to be of two kinds, since (*i*) what we ingest from outside, though still uncooked, is called 'nourishment'* as well as (*ii*) what has already been digested and incorporated.[294] Because of this   15 duality in nourishment, it is sometimes said that contrary is nour- ished by contrary, while at other times that like is nourished by like.[295] For nourishment that is still uncooked and undigested (that is, the first kind of nourishment) is contrary to what is nourished,[296] since a transformation has to take place in it for it to be assimilated to what is nourished – for cooking is just this sort of thing – and a transformation is in every case [a transformation] into a contrary. For there is no transformation of something white, in so far as it is   20 white, into anything except black or one of the intermediate colours, which likewise comes about in virtue of a transformation into a contrary; nor is there a [transformation] of something hot into anything except cold or, conversely, of cold into [anything except] hot. What is sweet, in so far as it is sweet, is not transformed into white

25 or black, or cold or hot, but into a contrary flavour.[297] So, too, in the case of nourishment that is still uncooked: if it is transformed by cooking and comes to be like what is nourished, then prior to this cooking and transformation it must be contrary to it. For this reason, all nourishment of this kind must be capable of being cooked and of being transformed into what is nourished by it.[298]

34,1   In this way, then, a contrary is nourishment for a contrary. But not every [contrary]. For it is not the case that everything which is transformed into its contrary is thereby capable of nourishing it. What is high-pitched, for example, is transformed into something low-pitched and *vice versa*; what is shapeless into something shaped; and what is white into something black. But it is not the case that they are thereby nourished because of this and made to grow by* the

5 things which have undergone a transformation to become the same.* The contraries that serve as nourishment, rather, are those which, by transforming into their contraries, can cause the contraries into which their transformation has resulted to grow. But bodies are capable of causing growth. Nourishment, therefore, must be a body which is contrary to and distinct from what is nourished.[299] But even though nourishment must be the sort of thing which can enlarge [something], it does not follow from this that anything which enlarges something enlarges it in the way that nourishment does. For

10 in fact the simple bodies, which we call 'elements', are enlarged by those [bodies] which are transformed into them, but not in the way that [something is enlarged] by nourishment. For water is said to be nourishment for fire [only] in a broader sense, since the only things that are nourished in the fundamental sense are those which have a soul for nourishing [oneself], since that is what nourishing belongs to. Therefore, nothing inanimate is nourished, even if it grows.[300]

So nourishment is a contrary, since the first [kind of] nourishment

15 is so. But in so far as what has already been incorporated also counts as nourishment, and like is incorporated into like, what is alike is nourishing too. For nourishment, as they say, is 'the part of nourishment that nourishes',[301] and what has been incorporated is nourishing, and what has already become like what is nourished is of this kind.[302]

What is nourished is something that has a soul for nourishing [itself]; nothing else is nourished.[303] This is clear from the following.

20 Although it can be said that what nourishes and what is nourished each becomes larger from the compounding of likes – since one could not become larger instead of [the other]* in the compound, as each is alike – it cannot be said that what has been transformed from

nourishment has [itself] been nourished and grown by means of nourishment. Rather, that to which it has been added [has been nourished and has grown], because the latter possesses a soul that nourishes and remains untransformed, while the nourishment,   25 which has been transformed by its power, is incorporated into the animate thing that persists.[304]

On the activity of being nourished

This is the sort of thing nourishment is, then. The activity of being nourished, in contrast, comes about when the soul for nourishing [oneself] transforms nourishment ingested from outside by cooking   35,1 [it], thereby assimilating and incorporating it into the body whose form and power it is.[305]

Heat is the soul's tool for nourishing [oneself]

In activities and transformations of this sort, heat is [the soul's] tool.[306] Because of this, some even thought that this is what nour-ishes, transferring the power of the source and principle that is acting to that by means of which it acts, since they saw that nothing can be   5 nourished apart from it*.[307] Now while heat is also capable of produc-ing change, there is no determinate or orderly change that primarily has heat as its source and principle. When something is being nour-ished, on the other hand, it develops in a certain sequence and order and has a limit, which are characteristics of soul, not fire.[308]

* * *

Things that are nourished also grow by means of what they are nourished by, as has already been said.[309] To grow and to be nour-ished are not the same, however: they do not occur at the same times,   10 nor does each of them have the same function. For an animal is always being nourished for as long as it exists – it is for just this reason the most continuous of soul activities.[310] But things which are nourished are not always growing, since they are nourished as long as they exist, but some also shrink as they age. The function of what nourishes is to preserve what is nourished, but [the function] of what causes growth is to add to the magnitude of what is nourished. So   15 among powers there is accordingly one that is able to preserve the being and essence [of a living thing] – since the power for nourishing [oneself] is of this kind – while the [power] for growing is primarily able to produce an increase in size.[311]

After the activities just mentioned, of growing and being nour-ished, next comes reproducing and leaving something behind like oneself, since it is not the case that whatever has each of the other

20   [powers] has it too, but rather all those which are not maimed or
      undeveloped, as was stated earlier.³¹² Of the powers that belong to
      the soul for nourishing [oneself], this is the last to develop. For the
      activity corresponding to it, since it naturally belongs to [living
      things] that are already developed, is developed at that stage too.³¹³
      For to reproduce something like itself, as was already said before, is
      each natural thing's end.³¹⁴

          These, then, are the activities of the soul for vegetation* or first
25   soul:³¹⁵ nourishment, growth, and reproduction. But then the powers
      from which these activities arise should also be apparent.³¹⁶ The
      power for nourishing [oneself], which is soul's first power,³¹⁷ can
      preserve what possesses it through its own activity, which occurs in
36,1 response to the presence of nourishment.³¹⁸ The soul's power for
      causing growth can cause the body that possesses it to grow by means
      of nourishment through its own activity. Finally, the soul's power for
      reproducing can produce something similar to that which possesses
      it.³¹⁹ It uses nourishment itself in a way too, since the seed by means
      of which reproduction occurs is the end product of the final stage of
      nourishment, as has been shown elsewhere,³²⁰ since [the power for
5   reproducing] is a more developed [power] than those which precede
      it. For the activity of the power for reproducing does not contribute
      to [the living thing] itself, its* preservation, or its development.
      Rather, in [living] things which are already developed it is responsi-
      ble for the generation of another thing like [themselves],³²¹ through
      a longing for a kind of 'reinvigorated immortality'. Through this
      power, nature provides what is mortal with a share in immortality,
      in the way that is possible for it.³²²
10   There are three things involved in being nourished: that which
      nourishes, that which is nourished, and that with which it is nour-
      ished. The soul for nourishing [oneself], or first soul, is that which
      nourishes; that which is nourished is the body whose form is the
      power just mentioned; and that with which it is nourished is the
      nourishment.³²³ The same account holds for growing and reproducing
      as well.³²⁴

          Now, given that

          1. it is proper to name all things after the end [*telos*] and the
          most advanced [*teleiotatou*] part of their makeup,³²⁵

15   thus, for example, we say that a human is rational, even though [a
      human] is also able to perceive; and

          2. the first soul's end, as has been shown, is to produce some-
          thing similar to oneself³²⁶

      it would make sense, then, that

          3. the first soul is called [the soul] 'for reproducing',

since it produces something similar to what possesses it, even though in addition to this it is most of all [a soul] for nourishing [oneself] and for growing.

The soul and power for nourishing [oneself] is responsible for the initial formation of the animal's body as well as for its being, increase, and growth.[327] For its function is to enable whatever it happens to be in to nourish itself and to grow. Since this soul is [already] present in the seed when it is sown,[328] once it receives matter suitable for it,[329] it forms the [matter] in such a way that what is formed from it comes to be like what emitted it through nourishment and growth and so becomes responsible for nourishing itself and growing when nourishment is present.[330] What is inside the womb engages in activity on its own solely in virtue of this soul power, since even though it possesses the sources and principles for the other powers and suitable conditions for the dispositions that its parent likewise possessed, it does not yet have these in activity, since in a way it does not yet possess the parts through which the activities of those powers [are exercised].[331]

Why parts detached from plants live and develop, while those from animals no longer do

Although some parts detached from plants can live and develop, those detached from animals no longer can.[332] We should regard the following as responsible for this.

Plants only have the soul for nourishing [oneself], which is present throughout the entire body. Because of this, plants are simpler and do not need as many organs. Any of their parts that can keep the power for nourishing [oneself] in it after being detached by means of abundant nourishment is preserved and becomes like the whole [plant]. For these parts engage in activity in virtue of the same power that enables things generated from a seed to engage in activity, since this is also what their culmination consists in.[333]

In the case of animals, though, [the powers] are not distributed throughout the entire [body] in this way and so not in the detached part either. For the soul of animals is not homogeneous in the way that the soul of plants is, nor is there the power of some of these [souls] present in them as it is in seeds. This is because, first, these parts cannot receive some of these [souls] themselves,[334] and second, they cannot draw nourishment in just any way, but only through certain specific organs, which cannot be added to things that have not been formed from a seed principle, as roots can to plants.[335] For roots are formed easily in the presence of nourishment and grow without needing much management. But no animal can be nourished without the specific organs for nourishing [itself], and it cannot form them without the seed that possesses their powers.[336]

5   For this reason, even though animals are nourished in the womb,
it is still as parts of the mother bearing them.* For while they are
nourished in virtue of the power in them, they receive nourishment
in so far as they are parts [of the mother]. Hence, animals still inside
the womb are not yet said to be an animal or alive simply as such and
on their own.[337]

The parts of animals often do live for a little while, though, after
they have been divided, in so far as (with regard to soul powers) the
10   parts can retain traces of the activities and powers they possessed
when they were unified and connected to the whole [animal].[338]

On the soul for perceiving

This, then, is what the soul's first power is like. Next after the soul
for life and vegetation[339] – the soul which has been shown by our
arguments about it to be a form of the body that possesses soul and
whose powers were just said to be the powers for nourishing [oneself],
15   growth, and reproduction[340] – after the account of this soul, then, the
next to be discussed would be the soul for perception, since this soul
is second after the previous one. For anything that has a further soul
power necessarily also has the power for perceiving, just as it has the
power for nourishing [oneself].[341] And it is this power in virtue of
which living things, in addition to being alive, are also thereby
animals as well.[342]

20   Perception is a large topic and deserves a treatise of its own.[343] But
in a nutshell, one could say in general as regards the soul for
39,1   perceiving that it is a power of soul in virtue of which whatever
possesses it is able to have cognition of the perceptibles it receives
with an activity related to them, by becoming like them through a
kind of alteration.[344] For just as the power for nourishing [oneself]
requires nourishment to be active, since its activity concerns this, so
the power for perceiving likewise requires perceptibles, since its*
5   activity concerns them:[345] it is for being aware of them and having
cognition of them.[346] Because of this, when they are not present it is
not active, but is rather perception in power,[347] analogous to those
who have a kind of knowledge, but are not engaged in the activity
corresponding to it. For in a similar way they are knowers through
their power and inactive perception is perception through its
power.[348]

Perceptibles are external because perception is directed towards
10   something useful, since it is for obtaining or avoiding something, and
these things are external.[349] The perceptible and the sense are unlike
[each other] before the activity [of perception], but in activity they
come to be alike, since perceiving occurs in virtue of a sort of likening
that comes about through alteration. For perception in activity is the
perceptible's form coming to be in what can perceive apart from the

matter.[350] But if the likening occurs through alteration, clearly they   15
are different and unlike before the alteration, as was also shown to
be the case with nourishment. It makes sense, then, to say that the
sense is modified by what is like in one way, and in another way by
what is unlike, since it is alike [now] because it was modified.[351]

This modification comes about in the primary body that has the
soul for perceiving through certain organs, which are of a different
nature than the perceptibles which they serve, because they have a   20
power to be modified by [perceptibles]; and whenever one is modified
in these ways, it relays the modification to* [the primary body].[352]
[The primary body] is situated in the neighbourhood of the heart,
where the governing part of the soul is also entirely present, as our
discussion will show as it proceeds. For it makes sense that the
highest form is located where what it is to be an animal is present   40,1
most. But what it is to be an animal is present most in what is hot
and moist, and the region around the heart is like this. For it is an
origin and well-spring of the blood with which we are nourished and
also of breath, and these are moist and hot.[353]

Such, then, is the general characterisation of perception. Now
given that

1. there are five parts of perception;[354]   5
2. they are related to each other in a similar way to the parts of
the soul,* where one is first and another subsequent;[355]
3. standardly, when things are related in this way, a general
characterisation does not ever express the nature of the subject
matter in question intelligibly; rather, if one intends to speak
about these things appropriately and in detail, one must always
develop an account of each of them individually;[356]

it then follows that

4. anyone who speaks about perception ought to speak about   10
each part individually.[357]

The power for perceiving's parts are touch, taste, smell, hearing, and
seeing or rather sight. Of these, touch is separated from the rest
(though taste is in a way also a [form of] touch), as there are in fact
some animals who only have this sense. But it is impossible for any
of the other senses to be found without touch in any animal. For it is
not possible for there even to be an animal in the first place without
this sense.[358]   15

But those who intend to speak about the powers for perceiving and
the activities corresponding to them must, since the activities of each
sense concerns a perceptible of its own, analyse perceptibles first
briefly, if they are to make these [activities] clear, since perceiving
occurs by likening* to them.[359]

On what is intrinsically and extrinsically
perceptible

20   Now, to speak generally, some perceptibles are (A) intrinsically perceptible (*kath' hauta*), while others are (B) extrinsically perceptible (*kata sumbebêkos*).[360]

Of those which are intrinsically perceptible, some are (A1) perceptible to one sense exclusively (*idia*):* some, like colours, are perceptibles of sight exclusively; others, like sounds, are perceptibles of hearing exclusively; others of smell, as odours are; others of taste, as flavours are; and still others of touch, as the tangible contrarieties

25   are, including [degrees of] heat and cold, dryness and moisture, roughness and smoothness. For these are perceptible to the corre-

41,1   sponding sense, but no other sense can perceive them intrinsically.[361]

Other things, however, which are intrinsically perceptible are (A2) common (*koina*): these are the kind of thing that can be grasped by perception, but there are several senses which transmit them.[362] For the perceptible exclusive to each sense occurs together with features the perceptual organs include when they relay them to the sense of

5   these things.[363] Change, rest, number, shape, and extension are this sort of thing.[364]

(B) Those things are *extrinsically* (*kata sumbebêkos*) perceptible which,* because they happen to belong (*sumbebêkenai*) to some perceptible, are themselves called 'perceptible' too. For example, if someone were to say that foam is perceptible, it would be because foam happens to be white, which is perceptible.[365] So things said to be perceptible in this way are not perceptible at bottom, because the

10   sense is not modified in any way by them in so far as* they are such things.[366]

Of the things that are intrinsically perceptible, the senses make mistakes with regard to common perceptibles, since the senses are not modified [by them] in such a way as to be like the corresponding objects. For perceptual error consists in just this: due to certain circumstances, the modification that occurs in the sense is of a different sort than and unlike that from which it arose.[367] In contrast, [the senses] are most true with regard to exclusive perceptibles, as

15   long as they preserve the conditions in which they have the capacity to be aware of these perceptibles. These are, first, that the perceptual organs are healthy and in their natural state; second, the position of the perceptible (for sight cannot have awareness of what is located behind oneself); and third, the commensurateness of the distance, since an awareness of perceptibles does not occur at just any distance from the perceptual organs. Beyond these conditions, the medium through which there is awareness of perceptibles must also be in a

20   suitable condition for transmission to the perceptual organs. For it is

42,1   not possible to see if the transparent [material in the medium] is not illuminated. Finally, [the medium] must not be disturbed by anything. For one cannot hear what one wishes when loud sounds create a disturbance.[368]

* * *

Colours[369] and things which are not seen in the light, but are seen in   5
the dark, are both perceptibles exclusively of sight.[370] The latter
cannot be colours, though, since they do not fall under the definition
of colour. For colour is what is capable of producing change in that
which is actively transparent.[371] Air, water, and any solid which does
not have a colour of its own are transparent,[372] and when they are
changed in a certain way by colours, they are able to transmit to sight
so that there is awareness of [colours]. They become actively trans-   10
parent whenever they are illuminated, for colours can produce
change in them if they are in this condition.[373] For it is clear that light
and transparent [materials] that have been illuminated are changed
in a certain way by colours, from the fact that in many cases when
colours are seen through the light, one sees the [transparent mate-
rial] come to be the same colour and carry the colour along with it.
For it itself appears golden from the presence of gold, purplish from   15
murex dye, and greenish from foliage. Often one can see facing walls
or the ground to be this sort of colour, as though they were tinged with
the colour of these things, or even people, if they happen to be
standing nearby, because what is illuminated relays this particular
type of colour from one set of things to the other by being modified.[374]
For the colour comes to be present in what is illuminated and in light   20
in the same way that light comes to be present in what is transparent,
though what is transparent does not receive light or light colour in
virtue of an effluence or in the way matter [receives something].[375]
In fact, when the things that produce these [effects] have gone
away, the colour immediately leaves the light as well (in the case
where the things that tinge it go away) and light leaves the   43,1
transparent (in the case where what illuminates it is not present).
The sort of change that arises from both sources occurs in what
receives them in virtue of a presence (*parousia*) and a particular
sort of relation (*skhesis*), much as [the reflections] in mirrors come
to be present in them.[376]

Now illuminated things, as I said, are actively transparent.[377] For   5
when something can actively appear through (*diaphanesthai*) them,
they are actively transparent (*diaphanê*) in the fundamental sense,
receiving their culmination and their own form (in so far as they are
transparent) from light.[378] For light is the activity and culmination of
transparent [material] in so far as it is such.[379]

How there comes to be light in the transparent[380]

10   This light comes to be by the presence of fire or the divine body in the transparent. For light comes about in virtue of the illuminant's relation to things whose nature it is to be illuminated.[381] For light is not a body and so comes to be instantaneously.[382]

If colour is visible in light, then it is also able to change it. For, as has been shown in the inquiries into how we see, the perception and cognition of colours occurs because (*i*) what is actively transparent – that is, what is illuminated – is first modified by the colour, since colour is able to change it, and then (*ii*) the eye is modified by this [sc.
15   what is transparent], since the eye itself is also transparent.[383] (Things seen in the dark, therefore, cannot be colours. How these are seen and in what circumstances has also been addressed in the writings on how we see.)[384] For light, which has been tinged anew by
20   each visible thing along a straight line to the eyes aligned with it,
44,1   relays the exclusive modification, since it was itself modified due to them;[385] and [the eyes] in turn are also able to receive a reflected image themselves because they are both smooth and transparent.[386] So given that

> 1. seeing occurs because the perceptual organ received the colour and in some way becomes likened to it;[387]
> 2. what can receive colour is something that lacks a colour of its own or can be seen only with difficulty;[388]
> 3. what has this characteristic most is transparent [material]
5   that is moist and without a definite shape;[389]
> 4. both air and water are this sort of thing,[390]

[it follows that]

> 5. the perceptual organ through which there is awareness of colours is composed of these [materials].[391]

For the interior of the eye is composed of water,[392] for the following reason. Of the transparent [materials] that lack a definite shape, water straight off can retain the modification produced in it by colour,* because of its density and consistency; for air is not like
10   this.[393] Seeing, then, comes about through the activity concerning visible things, which in turn comes about through the eyes' power for seeing, in virtue of a likening to [visible things]. The power for seeing, in contrast, is that in virtue of which its possessor can, when altered by visible things, become aware of them and have cognition of them, through the activity concerning them.[394]

As regards light – something that is visible in the highest degree and responsible for other visible things' being seen[395] – it has already
15   been stated just what it is, namely, an activity of transparent [mate-

rial] that lacks a definite shape, in so far as it is transparent.[396] But
light is also said to be the transparent [material]'s colour, in so far as
it is transparent.[397] For in the same way that colour is in things that
have colour, light comes to be in transparent [materials] and is
responsible in the way just mentioned. Colour, which can change
what is transparent in this way, is itself in transparent [material]
too, but in something with a definite shape.[398] For every body, be-   20
cause of its ability to receive colour, has a larger or a smaller share
of the nature we call 'transparency',[399] since this is the proximate
matter of colours. For if there is a colour, there must also be the
nature that can receive it.[400]

Transparent [material] without a definite shape – something
which is and is said to be transparent (*diaphanes*) in the highest
degree because it receives daylight (*phaos*), that is, light (*phôs*), and
is responsible for other things' appearing (*phainesthai*) – is coloured   25
by something external [to it].[401] For light is in a way a colour of what   45,1
is transparent in the form stated above[402] and occurs in it due to the
presence of something whose nature it is to illuminate it. This is what
fire and the divine body are like.[403] For light comes about in virtue of
their having a certain relation to it [sc. the transparent material].*
Hence, it is illuminated when they are present, but when they leave,
the light departs together with them.[404]   5

The transparency in solids, in contrast, has the colour inside,
co-mingled and compresent.[405] Hence, it is not present in it at one
time and not another, as happens with light in transparent [materi-
als] without a definite shape.[406] Among [materials] which are
transparent in this way, some are more and others less transparent,
because of a certain amount of mixing in of a minimally transparent
body, such as earth. For it impedes the transparency of whatever it   10
has been mixed into.[407] It is also responsible for the difference between colours. For the colour in any transparent [material] is due to
the presence of something bright (*leukon*) – for fire is in fact just this
sort of thing – whether as something external to it or mixed in with
it. But the difference in degrees of transparency and the mixture of
various amounts of something whose nature it is to illuminate it
produces the differences between colours. For [the colour] is bright   15
and luminous in things in which the transparent is purer and in
which there is more colourant, but it is less so and dull, already
tending towards dark (*melan*), in things where the transparent is
present [only] to a certain extent. When there is something mixed in
with the transparent [materials], however, that makes them transparent in actuality, they have a colour of their own compresent with
them, which is called 'colour' in the fundamental sense (since light is
not like this).[408]

Colour is also the boundary of transparent [materials] with a   20
definite shape in so far as they are transparent.[409] For in so far as

they are a body, their boundary is a surface; but in so far as they are transparent, it is a colour. The colour is thus compresent with the surface.[410] For colours make their appearance (*phantasia*) on the surface, since only the boundary of bodies is apparent (*phaneron*),* and the colour is both apparent and something that appears (*phaino-*

25   *menon*).[411] For that in virtue of which bodies are coloured is also that in virtue of which they are visible;* but they are visible in virtue of

46,1 the boundary. So it makes sense that colour is said to be the boundary of the transparent in a [body] with a definite shape in so far as it is transparent.[412] The power present in fire and other things which are able to produce light makes them visible in the highest degree and is responsible for other colours being seen as well, since these things can produce light, by which things seen are seen. We should regard this nature as responsible, when mixed in larger or smaller quanti-

5   ties in transparent [materials] with a definite shape, for the production of colours and the differences between them.[413]

That colour is the boundary of the transparent, in so far as it is transparent, is indicated by the fact that transparent [materials] which do not have a boundary of their own – those without a definite shape are of this sort – do not have a colour of their own either, since

10   the boundary of a body is compresent with its boundary as something transparent. For [these materials] are tinged by something from outside in the same way as they are bounded and shaped by it.[414] For anything whose boundary is definite* as a body is also [definite] as something transparent; and anything transparent whose boundary is definite has a colour of its own, since the boundary and the colour coincide.[415] Yet although they coincide, they are not the same. For a

15   single body has a single surface; but it is not the case that if there is a single surface, there is also a single colour, since it is possible for the same surface to have even contrary colours in it.[416] Transparent [materials] with a definite shape have a boundary, whether they are illuminated or not, but they only have a colour when they are illuminated as well.[417]

Commentary

1. [1,2] By restricting his discussion to the souls of bodies that come to be and perish, Alex. effectively brackets any questions regarding divine souls from consideration and how his account might apply to them (cf. 28,25-29,2; *Mant.* 104,10; also *in Metaph.* 373,5-8). This group would include not only the First Cause, which is a non-bodily understanding or *nous* (89,9-15; cf. *Quaest.* 1.25, 40,8-9) – if it can even be said to have (or be) a soul – but also, importantly, the soul of the divine and eternal body which constitutes the celestial spheres (*Quaest.* 1.25, 40,9-30). This restriction fits with Arist.'s own view that we should not generalise from 'the perceptible region around us' (*ho peri hêmas tou aisthêtou topos*), where bodies come to be and perish, to the universe as a whole, since the bodies of the celestial spheres are eternal (*Metaph.* 4.5, 1010a29-30; cf. Alex. *in Metaph.* 310,23-33; 77,24-6). In Alex.'s view, bodies that come to be and perish – the subject of what he calls 'Third Philosophy' (*in Metaph.* 251,36-7) – are to be found exclusively in the region beneath the moon, which is the domain of contingency, fate, and providence (*Mant.* 181,21-7; 182,32; *Quaest.* 1.25, 41,10-11; cf. 2.19, 63,15-26; *in Meteor.* 6,5-6).

2. [1,3] 16,18. The Greek *ousia*, although often rendered as 'substance', is derived from the participle for the verb 'to be'. It can thus signify both (*a*) something that really is, i.e. a being or a substance, as it often does below – Alexander says that Aristotle always calls beings (*ta onta*) 'substances' (*ousias*, *in Metaph.* 117,25) – but also (*b*) *what* something really is, its essential nature, especially when it is used (as here) in locutions of the form 'the *ousia* of *X*'. Understood in this second way, it is not limited to the essence or form of composite individuals, but can be used for the essence of other things as well, including souls. On this broader sense, see Alex. *in Metaph.* 374,37-375,9 (cf. Arist. *Metaph.* 5.8, 1017b21-2). Alex. develops the question of the soul's *ousia* somewhat differently in the opening of the *Mant.* 101,3-18.

3. [1,2-4] Alex. follows this programme, but only in broad outline. He does claim explicitly at 16,18 to have stated the essence of the soul and he focuses directly on the number of powers at 27,3-28,13 and the powers themselves at 28,13-31,6. But his remark at 27,1-2 suggests that the whole treatise up to that point has been a discussion of the essence of the soul (2,10-26,30), just as the differences between the powers will in some sense be the subject for the remainder of the treatise (31,7-92,11), as is confirmed by his formal conclusion at 92,12-15 (before what are, in effect, two appendices, 92,15-94,6 and 94,7-100,17).

The questions Alex. sets here are modelled on those with which Arist. begins his *DA* (1.1, 402a7-8). But they are more specific: Arist. says that in addition to the 'nature and essence of the soul', we should investigate its attributes (*hosa sumbebêke*) and whether any belong to the soul alone. Alex. does not raise the latter question here, which is potentially much broader in scope, and focuses exclusively on the powers of the soul instead.

4. [1,6] That is, Apollo: cf. *Fat.* 31, 202,9; 203,1.8.16.20.24. The epithet refers to Apollo's slaying of the dragon Python, in establishing his own shrine at Delphi. For the different versions of the myth, see Fontenrose 1959. For a recent introduction to Apollo's role in prophesy, see Graf 2009, ch. 3, and for the Delphic oracle, Johnston 2008, 22-60.

Someone might question the sincerity of Alex.'s appeal to divine prophecy here in light of his own reservations about divine foreknowledge: at *Fat.* 30, he argues that not even the gods can know that contingent events will happen, only that they might or might not (see esp. 200,24-201,3 and 201,13-21). But Alex. still believes that prophecy and petitionary prayer have a useful function, since on his view, unlike the Stoics', we can avert fate, and through prophecy the gods advise us to resist the consequences of a baser nature (*enhistasthai têi tês phuseôs kheironos akolouthiai, Mant.* 185,33-186,4 at 185,36; cf. *Fat.* 6, 171,7-11; 17, 188,11-17; and 31 passim). In these passages, Alex. is concerned not only with the nature of the species, as here, but with the nature of an individual as well (17, 185,11-33; cf. 6, 170,9-171,7).

5. [1,6-8] In contrast with the tradition that ascribes this saying to the Seven Sages (see Wilkins 1917, 1-2, 6, 8), Alex. speaks of the command as divine in origin, as other later authors do (Cic. *Leg.* 1.58-9, cf. *Tusc.* 1.52; Juv. *Sat.* 11.27; Jul. *Or.* 6, 183A, 188B), though Alex. goes further by appealing to Apollo's special authority in virtue of his foreknowledge. Arist. may have been gesturing in this direction in his lost dialogue *On Philosophy*, when he claimed the command was older than the sages, originating instead from the Pythian oracle (Clem. *Strom.* 1.14.60.3 = Arist. fr. 3 Rose³).

6. [1,8] I have retained the gender of the masculine pronouns in the Greek here, as less disruptive and distorting than more neutral alternatives we prefer today. It is clear that Alex. has in mind every human (*anthrôpos*, 2,1), not just men.

7. [1,9] Elsewhere, Alex. maintains that one of the universally shared intuitions (*koinai ennoiai*) about fulfilment (*eudaimonia*) is that it consists in 'living in accordance with nature and the life in accordance with nature' (*to zên kata phusin kai ton kata phusin bion, Mant.* 162,32-163,1). He argues that virtue alone is not sufficient to secure it: if we are deprived of either the goods of the body or of the soul, we are not living in accordance with nature (163,1-18). The phrase 'in accordance with nature', he claims, should be 'understood to mean in accordance with *nature's intention*' (*kata to boulêma tês phuseôs akouetai*, 163,13-18, cf. 163,21-3. 28-31).

The most striking parallel for this conception of fulfilment, as well as for the whole opening argument (see next note), comes from an Academic, Antiochus of Ascalon (first century BCE), who similarly uses the phrase 'living in accordance with nature' (*secundum naturam vivere*) to define the end or aim of life (Cic. *Fin.* 5.26; 2.34 = Antiochus fr. 9a Mette; cf. 5.44, *Acad.* 1.19). Antiochus disavows any originality here: he repeatedly represents his views as shared by the Old Academy, the Peripatetics, and (with qualifications) the Stoics. The view seems a natural one for Peripatetics to hold; but the formula 'living in accordance with nature' is not attested for Peripatetics prior to Alexander. The evidence for the Old Academy, in contrast, is unequivocal. The definition is attributed several times to the fourth head of the Academy, Polemon (fourth to third century BCE), who wrote a treatise with that title (Cic. *Fin.* 2.34 = fr. 127 Gigante; 4.14 = fr. 129; for the title, Clem. *Strom.* 7.32.9 = frs. 97, 112); and the general view is also credited to the third head of the Academy, Xenocrates (fourth century BCE) at Cic. *Fin.* 4.15-18 (= fr. 79 Heinze), as well as to Aristotle (ibid.). It may conceivably be behind the definition attributed to the second head of the Academy, Speusippus, too (Clem. *Strom.* 2.133.4 = fr. 101 Isnardi Parente).

The Stoics also use this phrase. Zeno, who studied with Polemon (*SVF* 1.10-11,

13), wrote a treatise with that title as well (D.L. 7.4 = *SVF* 1.41) and is said to have 'followed Xenocrates and Polemon in their view that the elements of fulfilment are nature and what is in accordance with nature' (Plut. *Comm. Not.* 1069F = *SVF* 1.183; Cic. *Fin.* 4.61). It is also listed among the Stoics' various definitions of the end (Stob. *Ecl.* 2.77.16-19 Wachsmuth = *SVF* 3.16 = LS 63A 1; cf. 2.78.1-6; Mich. *in EN* 598,30-2 = *SVF* 3.17). But the Stoics' use of this notion differs in two key ways. (1) In characterising the end, the Stoics emphasise our being in agreement with the nature of the cosmos *as a whole* (D.L. 7.89 = *SVF* 1.555), and not just with the specific nature of human beings, as Alex. and Antiochus claim. (2) The Stoics seem to distinguish a life lived 'in agreement' with nature (*homologoumenôs têi phusei zên*), a more canonical definition of the end, from one which is lived merely in accordance with nature (*Fin.* 4.25-6, 4.43). The so-called 'natural goods' are not goods, strictly speaking, on their view: while things that contribute to the life in accordance with nature (*khreian sumballomenên pros ton kata phusin bion*) are 'preferred' (*proêgmena*) and so have 'value' (*axia*), they are morally 'indifferent' (*adiaphoron*, D.L. 7.105 = *SVF* 3.126; Stob. *Ecl.* 2.80.3-4 Wachsmuth = *SVF* 3.136). We are to choose them because, and only in so far as, they fit in with the plan and order of nature as a whole, that is, because they agree with nature as a whole, and not because they are good in themselves. On this difference, see N. White 1979, 148-9, 151-3, 157-8; 1985, 61, 66-8; Striker [1983] 1996, 289; [1991] 1996, 224. Alex. criticises the Stoics on precisely this point, arguing that they will have trouble assigning the life in accordance with nature to any of their categories of value (*Mant.* 167,17-168,1 = *SVF* 3.45).

    8. **[1,4-2,4]** The overall argument here is surprising if one associates the Delphic command with knowing one's own personal traits and limitations, a subject on which Aristotelian psychology has little to say. Alex. takes the command instead to concern our common nature as humans and more generally as beings who 'come to be and perish' (1,2), that is, as *mortals* (an interpretation which had some currency in antiquity: see Wilkins, 1917, ch. 7) and so is arguing, in effect, that the recognition of mortality is essential to a life lived in accordance with nature and thus to human fulfilment. Alex.'s controversial views on the mortality of the human soul at the end of the treatise are thus already foreshadowed here in its opening argument. Interestingly, he does *not* invoke the notion of reflexive self-understanding, so central to his own theory of the understanding (*nous*), which would figure prominently in interpretations of the Delphic command by later Platonists (Wilkins 1917, ch. 8 offers a preliminary survey). For a thorough history of the maxim, see Courcelle 1974-75, t. 1.

    The closest antecedents we have for Alex.'s argument are again Academic (see preceding note). An extended version of the argument is attributed to Antiochus of Ascalon by Cicero: see *Fin.* 5.44; cf. 5.26-7, 34. 41; 4.25-6; also Aug. *CD* 19.3. Earlier evidence for antecedents is thinner. Arist. mentions the Delphic command in his extant writings only in passing (*Rhet.* 2.21, 1395a20-6; though cf. *MM* 2.15, 1213a13-26); he appears to have discussed it in his lost dialogue *On Philosophy* (frr. 1-3 Rose[3]), but we do not know how extensively or to what end. The Stoic evidence is somewhat better: according to the emperor Julian, the Stoics made the Delphic command the 'core' of their philosophy (*kephalaion tithentai philosophias*) and wrote many treatises on it (*Or.* 6, 185D-186A). There is perhaps some basis for this assessment in Epictetus (1.18.17; 3.1.25; cf. 1.6.25; 2.6.14) and in Seneca (*Cons. ad Marc.* 11.1-5; *NQ* 3, praef. 15; cf. *Ep.* 94.28; 121.3), but there is little before them. The best parallel is an argument that it is impossible to fulfill the Delphic command without a knowledge *of the natural world generally* (Cic. *Fin.*

3.73 = *SVF* 3.282; cf. *Leg.* 1.61 = *SVF* 3.339; Epict. 1.1.10; I am grateful to Brad Inwood for discussions on the Stoic evidence). The closest parallels before Antiochus are in Plato: Socrates' describes his efforts to obey the Delphic command in the *Phaedrus* as an attempt to find out what sort of being he is, a monster like Typhon or one that has a share in the divine (229E-230A); and in the *Alcibiades I* it is argued that to know ourselves is to know our souls (130E), though it seems there to be more a matter of knowing the individual self rather than the nature of the species. (There are other contrasts as well, of course: Plato is concerned primarily with our immortal and rational self, rather than the mortal nature we share with animals. I am grateful to Richard Sorabji for emphasising this.)

9. [2,4-9] Notice that Alex. does not assign some kind of ultimate authority to Arist.'s views, dismissing any who disagree. His wording suggests rather that others do attain the truth in some measure, but that Arist. does to a much greater extent and so deserves our full efforts at understanding him. Accattino and Donini 1996 (= AD) aptly cite Arist. *Metaph.* 2.1, 993a30-b7, which argues that while everyone manages to get at some part of the truth, some do more than others.

10. [2,10 title] The section titles are found in the principal manuscript V (Venetus Marcianus gr. 258) and in the Aldine edition of 1534, but are printed by Bruns only in the apparatus. I have printed them here because, even though they might not stem from Alexander, they are nonetheless a part of the tradition and generally helpful.

11. [2,13] 'Art' here renders the Greek *tekhnê*, which should not be understood as restricted to fine arts, but applies to any kind of productive and practical knowledge, of knowing how to make or do things, including the art of housebuilding, the art of medicine, and even the art of governing. As such, it implies a grasp not only of the general regularities in nature, but also the causes responsible for producing various effects (see esp. Arist. *Metaph.* 1.1, 981a12-b9; cf. *An. Post.* 2.19, 100a6-9). The analogy between nature and art that Alex. exploits here is central for Arist. as well: see esp. *Phys.* 2.8, 199a9-b33; *PA* 1.1, 639b14-23; see also G.E.R. Lloyd 1966, 287-90.

12. [2,12-15] 3,2-21. The rhetorical comparison with the products of art, as well as the language of marvels and wonders (cf. 11,5-13), is reminiscent of the famous passage where Arist. exhorts his readers to the study of the parts and materials from which animals are composed (*PA* 1.5, 644b23-645a26, esp. 645a10-17).

Alex.'s confidence about his readers' being more easily 'convinced' (*pisteusomen*, 2,14) contrasts strikingly with Arist.'s more guarded remark at the opening of his *On the Soul*, that this is a subject about which it is 'the most difficult, in each and every way, to secure conviction.' (1.1, 402a10-11)

13. [2,17-18] 11,5-13. Alex. is alluding to Plato's *Phaedo* (91C-D), where Socrates addresses the 'doubts and fears' Simmias has because he regards the soul both as (*i*) something 'more divine and more noble than the body' (*kai theioteron kai kallion on tou sômatos*; cf. 94E) and (*ii*) a 'tuning' (*harmonia*) or disposition of the body, a theory that has relevance for Alexander's own treatment of the soul (note his use of *epharmozein* here at 2,17). The preceding section of the *Phaedo* (89C-91C) also stresses the difficulty of arriving at settled views in these matters and the consequent risk of 'misology'. It may also be the case, as both AD (105) and Bergeron and Dufour 2008 (= BD), 234 suggest, that Alex. is responding to contemporary Platonic views here, citing a fragment of Atticus that excoriates Arist. for rejecting the incorporeal nature of the soul (Euseb. *PE* 15.9.7-8 and 11, 2.370.4-9 and 371.1-6 Mras = fr. 7.34-43, 57-63 des Places).

14. [2,18-22] Arist. *DA* 1.3, 407b13-26; 2.2, 414a22-7. As AD point out (106),

Alex. does not carry out such a detailed examination here (see also Donini 1971, 68). At most he speaks in broad, schematic terms about the increasing complexity of bodies, from simple bodies to plants and then animals (see 8,13-11,13).

The English 'regulation' renders *oikonomia*; cf. 38,2. In an extended simile, Arist. describes nature, in using different material to form the parts of the body in the embryo, as a 'good house-manager' (*oikonomos*), who lets nothing go to waste (*GA* 2.6, 744b16-21). The Stoics also speak of the 'regulation' or management (*dioikêsis*) of the universe: Alex. *Fat.* 22, 192,12.28 = *SVF* 2.945 = LS 55N; Plut. *Stoic. Rep.* 34, 1050A = *SVF* 2.937.

15. [2,23] I have used the phrase 'origin and principle' throughout to render the important term *arkhê*, apart from a few cases where only one of these senses could be in play. In general an *arkhe* is a source, origin, or basis of a thing or process, that in some sense determines or characterises what issues from it or (in another of its senses) governs or rules it.

16. [2,25-3,13] *Mant.* 101,22-6. The distinction between matter and form, which Alex. introduces here simply as the opinion of the experts, is one of the most central and characteristic Aristotelian doctrines. For the view that all perceptible substances are composed of matter and form and more generally for the distinction betwen matter, form, and the composite formed from them, see esp. *Cael.* 1.9, 277b30-278a10; *DA* 2.1, 412a6-12; *Metaph.* 7.8, 1033b12-19; 8.1, 1042a24-31; 8.2, 1043a14-28; 12.3, esp. 1070a9-13.

17. [3,7-9] *Mant.* 102,1-7. Arist. uses statues frequently as an example to illustrate various points about the four causes, but the one closest to the present context is *GA* 1.18, 724a23-6, where Arist. speaks of the material being shaped (*skhêmatisthentos*), as Alex. does at 3,6 above. Cf. also *Metaph.* 5.2, 1013b6-9; *Phys.* 1.5, 188b19-20; 1.7, 190b5-6; 2.3, 195a32-5. Arist. also uses other artefacts to make key points about the soul: he uses the example of a house to show how psychological states should be defined (*DA* 1.1, 403b3-9) and an axe to explain the way in which the soul is a form of the body (2.1, 412b10-17).

18. [3,9-11] Alex. here relies on the analogy with nature he makes fully explicit just below (3,19-21, with note): the form or design produced by art is itself said to be 'art', just as the form of a natural object is its nature. Arist. says that art is the form of the product at *Metaph.* 7.9, 1034a24; *GA* 2.1, 734b36-735a3; 2.4, 740b25-9; cf. *PA* 1.1, 640a31-2.

19. [3,11-13] Elsewhere Alex. generalises this description to all matter, as an underlying subject suitable for receiving the form in question, at *Mant.* 148,25-7; *in Sens.* 44,25-7.

20. [3,15-16] *in Meteor.* 197,3; *Eth. Prob.* 25, 148,15; cf. *Mant.* 101,28-102,1. Both parts of this antithesis occur nearly verbatim in a passage believed to derive from Arist.'s lost dialogue, the *Protrepticus* (B13 Düring = Iambl. *Protr.* 49.28-50.1; cf. B14 = Iambl. *Protr.* 50.2-14). But the positive claim, that art imitates nature can be found in the extant works too: see *Meteor.* 4.3, 381b3-9 (cf. a9-12); *Phys.* 2.2, 194a21-2; 2.8, 199a15-17. See G.E.R. Lloyd 1966, 287-90. Ian Flora has pointed out to me that we also find versions of the positive claim in e.g. Philo (*Ebr.* 90, 2.176.13-14 Cohn-Wendland = *SVF* 3.301) and Galen (*UP* 1.408.5-13 Helmreich). On the theme more generally in antiquity, see Close 1969, 469-72.

21. [3,17-19] *in Meteor.* 177,20-178,10. Much of Arist.'s theory in the *Meteorology* is based on his distinction between two types of emission (or, as it is often rendered, 'exhalations'), one vaporous, the other fume-like or smoky (*Meteor.* 1.4, 341b6-12; 3.6, 378a19-20). Metals are the result of the vaporous emission's being compressed and solidifying (3.6, 378a26-31). For the specific claim that bronze, like other metals that can be melted, is made of water, see Arist. *Meteor.* 4.10, 389a7-9; cf. *Metaph.* 5.4, 1015a9-10; 5.24, 1023a28-9 (cf. Alex. *in Metaph.* 421,33-4; 430,8-9). On Arist.'s account of metals, see Eichholz 1949.

22. [3,19] *in Meteor.* 212,24-33. Alex. suggests at the very end of this commentary that the form of natural bodies can be understood quite generally as a certain kind of 'solidity or consistency' (227,11-14; cf. 226,5-6). On solidification in general, see Arist. *Meteor.* 4.6-7.

23. [3,19-21] Arist. *Phys.* 2.1, 193a31-b8. See n. 18 on 3,9-11 above.

24. [3,22] *Mant.* 103,32-3; Arist. *Cael.* 1.2, 268b26-7; 1.5, 271b17-18; *PA* 2.1, 646a12-24. AD are right to note (107) that 'compound' here cannot mean 'composed of matter and form', as it generally does (e.g. 2,27), since for Alex. all bodies, including simple bodies, are compounds of matter and form (see 3,27 below). What distinguishes compound bodies is that their *matter* is also a body and so itself a compound of matter and form. This analysis can be reiterated until we finally reach simple bodies, which, though compounds of matter and form themselves, have matter that is *not* a compound of matter and form and so not a body either.

25. [3,24-5] This last generalisation extends to celestial bodies: see Alex.'s discussion of their underlying matter in *Quaest.* 1.10 and 15.

26. [3,28-4,4] Alex. here articulates a traditional conception of 'prime matter' (*materia prima*), an ultimate material substrate underlying all bodies, which has no form as part of its own nature beyond its mere receptivity to forms (for the latter, see *Quaest.* 2.7, 52,28-30; cf. 1.15, 27,22-3). It is inseparable from the bodies it underlies and so from form, but in itself is nothing in actuality. For Alex. on matter 'in the fundamental sense' (*kuriôs*), see *in Metaph.* 159,11-17 (cf. 158,9-14; 159,3); 430,3-6; *Quaest.* 2.24, 75,5-10.16-19, which explicitly identify it with 'prime matter' (*prôtê hulê*). For Alex.'s views on prime matter more generally, see also *in Metaph.* 213,2-4; 357,13-18; 359,10-11; 421,34-6; *in Meteor.* 224,14-19; *Quaest.* 1.17, 30,2-6. For the description of it as 'formless', see *Mixt.* 11, 226,15; *Mant.* 104,19; 'shapeless', *Quaest.* 2.7, 52,20-53,30 (cf. 2.3, 49,30-1); and also 'unshaped' (*arrhuthmistos*), 1.10, 21,1-2.

Arist. uses all of these phrases himself to describe matter: 'formless and amorphous' (*Cael.* 3.8, 306b17), 'amorphous' (*Phys.* 1.7, 191a10), 'shapeless' (*Phys.* 1.7, 191a2; cf. 1.5, 188b20; 1.7, 190b15), and 'unshaped' (*Phys.* 2.1, 193a11). He also speaks of matter 'in the most fundamental sense' (*GC* 1.4, 320a2-5) and even of 'first' or 'prime matter' (*GC* 2.1, 329a23, a29; *Phys.* 2.1, 193a29; *Metaph.* 5.4, 1015a7-10; 9.7, 1049a24-7; *GA* 1.20, 729a32; cf. *Metaph.* 5.6, 1017a5; 8.4, 1044a23; *GA* 2.1, 733b26). Arist. explicitly notes, though, that this last phrase can be used for either end of the hierarchy, for the last or 'proximate' matter of a substance as well as for the first or ultimate one (*Metaph.* 5.4, 1015a7-10), and in a number of these cases he uses quite ordinary materials as examples, such as the element water. The best reasons for thinking Arist. is committed to prime matter are his views about the transformation of the elements into one another (e.g. *GC* 2.1, 329a24-35 (cf. a8-11); 2.7, 334a15-25; *Cael.* 3.8, 306b16-21), together with the requirement that some matter must persist through change that can equally possess or lack even these elemental qualities (see esp. *Phys.* 4.9, 217a21-33; *Cael.* 4.5, 312a30-3; *GC* 1.4, 319b2-4; 1.5, 320b12-14; 2.5, 332a17-20, a34-b1). The closest he comes to describing such a qualityless substratum is in a thought experiment in *Metaph.* 7.3, 1029a7-30, for the admittedly negative purpose of showing that it cannot be substance. But the interpretation of these passages remains controversial. For classic examinations of the evidence for prime matter, see: *contra*, Charlton [1970] 1983, 129-45 (also Rashed 2005, xcii-ciii); and *pro*, C.J.F. Williams

1982, 211-9. For more recent interpretations, with references to the literature: *contra*, M.L. Gill 1989, ch. 2 and Appendix; *pro*, F. Lewis 2008.

Many of the key features of prime matter, though, can be found uncontroversially in Plato's characterisation of space as the 'mother' and 'receptacle' of all perceptible qualities (*Tim.* 49A-52B): he says that it is 'amorphous' (*amorphon*, 50D7, 51A7, cf. 50C1), without any other nature (50E2, cf. B7-C2), invisible (51A7), and completely receptive (51A7; cf. 50B8, D4-E1). There can be little doubt of the profound influence this passage has exercised over the development of the notion (Charlton [1970] 1983, 141-5), since Arist. understood this conception of space to play the same role that he assigned to matter (*Phys.* 4.2, 209b11-16).

Alex.'s precise formulation, though, has two nearly verbatim parallels in the tradition, which suggest that by his time it was already something of a philosophical commonplace.

(1) A report deriving from the doxographer Aetius (*c.* 100 CE) attributes the view to both Aristotle and Plato (or just Plato, in Stobaeus' version) that matter is 'bodily, amorphous, formless, shapeless, and qualityless in its own nature (*sômatoeidê amorphon aneideon askêmatiston apoion*), but comes to be a receptacle of forms, like a nurse, wax tablet, and mother' (1.9.4-5, *Dox. Gr.* 308.4-9); a very similar version occurs again in Alcinous' summary of Plato's doctrines from perhaps the mid-second century CE (*Didask.* 8, 162.32-39, 163.4-10 Whittaker). The same themes, expressed somewhat differently, had been already attributed two centuries earlier by Antiochus of Ascalon to both Academics and Peripatetics (Cic. *Acad.* 1.27). For further parallels for the individual terms, see Whittaker 1990, 96 n. 139. It should be noted (against AD, 107) that the parallels for the Peripatetic Boethus (first century BCE) are merely verbal, since the pre-existing matter he describes as 'amorphous and formless' is expressly distinguished from the underlying substratum: ap. Them. *in Phys.* 26,20-4; Simpl. *in Phys.* 211,15-18 (passages which may stem from Alex.'s lost commentary on the *Physics* – see Moraux 1973, 170).

(2) One of our testimonies for the Stoics provides another verbatim parallel. Calcidius reports that Zeno of Citium (fourth to third century BCE), the founder of the Stoa, believed that just like wax and the many shapes it can take on – see Alex.'s use of this comparison below at 4,9-20 – 'in the same way there is no form or shape or any other quality that belongs intrinsically to the matter underlying all things [*sic neque formam neque figuram nec ullam omnino qualitatem propriam ... fundamenti rerum omnium silvae*], though it is always inseparably conjoined with some quality.' (Calc. 292, 295.3-6 Waszink = *SVF* 1.88 = LS 44D 3; cf. 311, 311.7-8 Waszink; Origen *Orat.* 27.8, 368.2-10 Koetschau = *SVF* 2.318). Elsewhere we find Zeno and Chrysippus, the third head of the school (third century BCE), defining substance (*ousia*) as the 'prime matter' of all things and the Middle Stoic, Posidonius (second to first century BCE), describing it as 'qualityless and amorphous' in itself, though it always has some given quality and shape: Stob. *Ecl.* 1.132.27-133.11, 18-23 Wachsmuth = Arius Didymus fr. 20, *Dox. Gr.* 457.25-458.11 = LS 28q and in parts, *SVF* 1.87, 2.317 and Posidonius fr. 92 Kidd; cf. Calc. 290, 294.8-9 Waszink = *SVF* 1.86, cf. 293, 295.17-18 Waszink; D.L. 7.150 = *SVF* 2.316; Ps.-Galen *Qual. incorp.* 19, 273-4 Giusta = *SVF* 2.323a; Simpl. *in Phys.* 227,23-6 = *SVF* 2.326. As one of the Stoics' two fundamental principles, matter is described as 'qualityless' and 'shapeless' substance (*apoios ousia*, D.L. 7.134 = *SVF* 2.300 = LS 44B 2; *askhêmatistos*, Sext. Emp. *Adv. Math.* 9.75 = *SVF* 2.311 = LS 44C 1, cf. 9.11 = *SVF* 2.301). See also 18,2-3 below.

These two parallels may not be independent. If the older Stoics actually used the word 'matter', it suggests an Aristotelian influence, as was long thought (see esp. Hahm 1977, ch. 2). But even those who are more sceptical of Aristotelian influence, like Sandbach (1985, 35-6), still link Stoic views with the Academic tradition, esp. Xenocrates. There is thus no reason to think that Alex. is simply appropriating Stoic views here. And there is in any case a critical difference between their views. For Alex., although prime matter is a constituent of every body, it is *not* itself a body, since it is not a compound of matter and form (3,26-7). For the Stoics, in contrast, prime matter *is* a body, since it is capable of being acted upon (D.L. 7.134 = *SVF* 2.299 = LS 44B 3, retaining the MSS reading – see LS 1.274, 2.266; this is confirmed by Alex. *Mixt.* 11, 225,3-5 = *SVF* 2.310).

27. **[4,5]** The phrase 'simply as such' here renders the Aristotelian technical term *haplôs*, which indicates that a term is to be understood without further qualification or restriction. See e.g. Arist. *Top.* 2.11, 115b29-35 (cf. *GC* 1.3, 317b5-7); Alex. *in Top.* 215,22-216,10; also Arist. *GC* 1.3, 317b5-7.

28. **[4,8]** *Mant.* 120,2; *Quaest.* 1.8, 17,10; 1.17, 30,3-6; *Mixt.* 13, 228,22; Arist. *GC* 1.5, 320b16-17; cf. 2.1, 329a24-7.

29. **[4,8-9]** In fact, Alex. does not explicitly say earlier that the matter of compound bodies can exist on its own: when he introduces the distinction at 3,23-4, he says only that their underlying matter is a natural body. He assumes that all natural bodies can exist on their own, apart from any further mixture or compound they may enter into or from any form they may take on. This is confirmed below at 4,23-5 and 17,11-12.

30. **[4,9-15]** cf. 6,20. The example of wax is used to make a similar point at *Quaest.* 1,8, 18,32-4, 19,3-6; 2.7, 53,25-30. The last passage notes that while qualityless 'in its own nature', matter is not qualityless 'in its very being', since it always has some quality or other; *Mant.* 121,32-4 adds that it is only separable in thought (*epinoiai*). Alex. may have in mind Arist. *Cael.* 3.7, 305b29-30 and *Metaph.* 5.26, 1024a4-5 which notes that the same wax can take on different shapes; cf. also *GC* 1.10, 327b14-15, which argues that shape is not something mixed with wax. Arist. also uses wax prominently as an example in *DA* 2.1, 412b6-8, but he is concerned there with the unity of matter and form and not Alex.'s point that although having a shape is essential to wax, no particular shape is.

Compare Descartes' use of a similar argument based on the variable qualities of wax in the Second Meditation (AT 7.30-2) to show that we can only perceive the essence of wax and bodies in general by the intellect alone.

31. **[4,18-20]** If having a particular form were part of the nature of prime matter, then it would be a body, compounded of matter and form itself. But then anything which had prime matter as its matter would be a compound body, contrary to the hypothesis that we were considering the matter of a simple body. In addition, if the form that was essential to prime matter were the form of one of the elements, such as fire, then prime matter could not serve as the matter of another simple body like earth, since on the present hypothesis it would cease to exist if it were to lose the form of fire.

32. **[4,20-2]** *Mixt.* 13, 228,20-1; *Quaest.* 1.17, 30,5-6. Alex.'s claim that forms in general – or at any rate those forms that come to be in something (he remains silent on eternal substances) – cannot exist apart from matter, even less than matter can exist apart from form, is essential to his overall position concerning the soul in this treatise. Despite the explanatory and metaphysical primacy of form (including the soul), it is nevertheless existentially dependent on body.

33. **[4,23]** cf. 10,24; 44,21. Alex. uses the term 'proximate matter' (*prosekhê hulê*) to refer to the matter that directly underlies a compound body, in contrast with the various matters beneath it that constitute the proximate matter (or

constitute the matter that constitutes the proximate matter, and so on). In contrast with prime matter, it is the 'last' or highest matter in the hierarchy rather than the first or ultimate one: see esp. *in Metaph.* 358,36-359,4 (cf. 359,10-11); also 212,35-213,4; cf. 357,16-18; 430,3-6. (In the case of the elements, first and last trivially coincide: *Quaest.* 2.24, 75,5-10.) Although the phrase 'proximate matter' does not occur in Arist., the notion does: see esp. *Metaph.* 5.4, 1015a7-10.

34. [4,24] The phrase *tode ti*, literally a 'this-something', is a technical expression Arist. uses to speak in the abstract of something that belongs to a specific kind, a particular instance or token of a certain type. This is usually an individual substance (*Metaph.* 7.3, 1029a27-30; cf. Alex. *Mant.* 101,18-21), but not always: see, e.g., 6,8; 7,12 below. For a discussion of the expression's semantic range in Arist., see M.L. Gill 1989, 31-4. For Alex.'s use of the phrase, see Sharples 1999.

35. [5,1] Following the Hebrew translation's construal of *ekeinôn* and *toutôn*.

36. [5,1-2] *Mant.* 103,29; Arist. *Metaph.* 8.3, 1043b21-3; cf. 7.17, 1041b29-30; 12.3, 1070a13-20. For a recent treatment of the Aristotelian texts, see Katayama 1999. Alex.'s claim here is limited: he denies that the *form* of an artefact is an *ousia*, something that is in the most fundamental sense of 'is' (see n. 1 above, on 1,2). As for the artefacts themselves, he believes they are substances only in virtue of the natural substances underlying them: *Mant.* 121,17-19; cf. Arist. *Phys.* 2.1, 192b16-23. See n. 51 on 6,2-3 below.

37. [5,2-3] 3,9-11.

38. [5,1-4] *Quaest.* 1.21, 35,6. The Aldine edition reverses the natural order of each of these inferences, using 'therefore' (*ara*) instead of 'because' (*hoti*).

39. [5,5] A substantial question of interpretation turns on how we read the second occurrence of the Greek *kai* in 5,5. If we take it (*A*) in its most common sense, as in my translation above, to mean 'and' or 'as well as', then heat and dryness *together with* the lightness that emerges above them (see n. 40 on 5,5-6 below) are the form of fire. Alternatively, we might take it (*B*) as epexegetic or even corrective, as AD seem to, to mean 'or rather' (*anzi*), with the result that it is *not* hot and dry, properly understood, which are the form of fire, but just lightness (AD xii, 110; cf. Accattino 1995, 187-8). In favour of (*A*), one might point to the fact that matter is said to underlie *them*, using the plural pronoun *toutois* (5,7), which suggests that lightness is either *part* of the form of fire or just *a* form of fire (as 5,11 might also be understood). On the other hand, one might find some evidence for (*B*) in the argument at 7,14-21 that 'the form and nature' of simple bodies must be *simple* and responsible for a single, simple change, such as upwards motion (Accattino 1995, 190).

A serious difficulty for (*B*) is that lightness, like the two elemental qualities, belongs to elements other than fire: just as heat also belongs to air and dryness also belongs to earth, so lightness belongs to air as well as fire (*Mant.* 126,25-8; *Mixt.* 4, 218,2-5; *in Metaph.* 259,17; cf. *DA* 8,22). But then lightness cannot by itself be the form of fire. It is only the *combination* of heat and dryness, and thereby lightness, which is distinctive of fire. (It may thus be significant that Alex. is non-committal about the precise identity of the form of fire at 20,25-6.) To adopt (*A*), though, we must take Alex.'s argument at 7,14-21 as claiming either (*i*) that the nature of fire is capable of a single *change* in the narrow sense that it is capable of only a single *motion* in space, or (*ii*) that *each* form or part of a form is simple and responsible for a single *change*, so that lightness would be responsible for motion upwards, heat for heating, and dryness for drying.

It should be noted that Arist. himself distinguishes lightness and heaviness from the two fundamental contrarieties of hot and cold and of moist and dry, which constitute the 'forms and principles' of bodies and thus their differentiae as bodies: *GC* 2.2, 329b6-17; 2.3, 330a30-b7; *DA* 2.11, 423b27-9; cf. *Meteor.* 1.2, 339a13-14; *PA* 2.2, 648b9-10. He regards lightness and heaviness, in contrast, as 'consequences' of the elemental qualities (*akolothousin, PA* 2.1, 646a16-20), from which they 'derive' or 'trace back to' (*anagontai, GC* 2.2, 330a24-6; cf. 329b32-4). On both of these points, Alex. agrees: for hot, cold, wet, and dry as elemental qualities, see *Mixt.* 13, 229,30-230,5; *Mant.* 127,3-5.12-17; *in Meteor.* 4,25-5,1; for lightness and heaviness as consequences of these, see *DA* 58,26-59,1 in addition to 5,5-6 with accompanying notes; also cf. *in Meteor.* 14.18-19.

Arist. himself does not, however, draw an analogy between the elements' form and the soul, as Alex. does here. Gottschalk (1986, 253-4; cf. 1987, 1113-14) argues that the Peripatetic Andronicus of Rhodes (first century BCE) set a precedent here, but Accattino (1995, 187 n. 13) is rightly more circumspect.

40. [5,5-6] Literally, 'is generated from and above' them (*ek ... kai epi ... gennômenê*); cf. 24,23-4.28; 26,27-9. This pregnant use of the preposition 'above' (*epi*) recurs at key points throughout the treatise: see the Greek-English index, under '*gennasthai epi*' and also '*epigignesthai*' (on which, see n. 229 on 25,2 below). I have chosen the language of emergence here, not only because it fits well with the spatial imagery, but because Alex. uses it, as nineteenth- and twentieth-century emergentists do, to advance a *non-reductivist* position (against Accattino 1995, 187, 199-200; AD 110). Although certain higher-level properties, such as lightness, depend upon and covary with lower-level properties present 'beneath' it, higher-level properties are nevertheless distinct, new causal powers. This is especially clear in the case of lightness, the power to move upwards, which is not identical to the power to heat or to dry or to a mere combination of the two, even though it is always found together with heat. This nuanced combination – of distinct new causal powers, which nonetheless depend on and covary with lower powers beneath them – is crucial to his characterisation of the soul as something which emerges from the specific blend and composition of the body, but is not identical to it, in virtue of having distinct powers. In general, the higher-level form does not belong to the underlying bodies from which the compound arises (*Quaest.* 2.24, 75,24-6). See n. 90 on 10,17-19, n. 92 on 10,24-6, and n. 229 on 25,2 below.

Several centuries later, John Philoponus will draw an even more fine-grained distinction between those characteristics that merely 'supervene' (*epiginesthai*) on other characteristics underlying them and those which 'follow' (*hepesthai*) or are the 'result' (*apotelesma*) of them. He takes these last two relations to be *stronger* than mere supervenience: what follows from something is explained by it or is even reducible to it. Philoponus accepts what he calls 'supervenience', while rejecting these stronger notions: see Sorabji 2003, 156-8, with updates in notes in 2004*a*, 1.193-5 and 199-204 and in the new introduction to his [1987] 2010, 33-4; see also Berryman 2002. For translations of the key texts from Philoponus, see Sorabji 2004*a*, 1.199-203. But Philoponus uses 'supervene' differently than Alexander, in so far as he does *not* require covariance: Philoponus' argument at *in DA* 51,13-29, for example, assumes that it is possible to have different psychological states, while holding the total bodily state fixed. As both Sorabji and Berryman acknowledge, the supervening qualities are *not* 'a direct function' of the changes in the underlying mixture for Philoponus but are underdetermined by it.

Alex., however, does *not* distinguish between 'supervenes' and 'follows' in the way Philoponus does (*pace* Sorabji), but frequently uses these terms as equivalents. In claiming that higher-level forms 'supervene' on the mixture of underlying materials, Alex. *accepts covariation* and so supervenience in the contemporary technical sense of the term, as I have been using it, unlike Philoponus. He is fully explicit on this point with regard to the soul: the different types of soul covary with different types of body (*summetaballousin*), the type of soul being a consequence (*epêkolouthêsan*) of the underlying constitution (*sustasei*) and blend (*krasei*), from which it follows (*hepetai, Mant.* 104,27-34; for further discussion of this text, incl. its authenticity and relation to Alex.'s *DA*, see n. 92 on 10,24-6 below). But Alex. also *rejects reduction*, maintaining the explanatory primacy of the supervenient form: see n. 90 on 10,17-19 below; cf. n. 92 on 10,24-6. He thus accepts a stronger relation between body and soul than Philoponus does, while also rejecting Galen's still stronger, reductionist view.

Alex.'s ultimate position about the soul and the body, though, is just an instance of a more general view about the relation between matter and form. As he states below, differences between forms follow (*hepesthai*) quite generally from differences in the underlying matter on which they supervene (*tôn ginomenôn ep' autais*, 10,24-6); and in his commentary on the *Topics*, he discusses a specific case at length. The white colour of snow, which supervenes (*epiginomenon, in Top.* 51,3) on underlying material conditions, which he elaborates in great detail (50,18-29), *follows necessarily* from them (*ex anankês parakolouthein*, 50,20; *ex anankês hepetai*, 50,23; *epakolouthoun*, 50,30; cf. *epakolouthounta*, 50,10). But while he regards the underlying material conditions as part of the essence of snow, its white colour is only an extrinsic feature (50,29-51,4; cf. 50,9-11). So in this case it is clear that while the snow's colour is a necessary consequence of underlying conditions and inseparable from them, it is nevertheless a distinct and irreducible feature.

One of Alex.'s main points in the passage above is that this non-reductive, layered metaphysical conception is not peculiar to life and consciousness, but something present throughout nature, right down to the chemical and physical properties of the elements, much as modern emergentists later claimed. See my 1997, esp. 309-19 and 347-54; cf. also Accattino 1995.

41. [5,8] Todd notes (1974, 212 esp. n. 20) that while the term rendered here as 'receptive' (*epidektikos*) is not itself found in Arist., it is plausibly based on *GC* 1.4, 320a2-5 (which does in fact use *dektikos*).

42. [5,8-9] Arist. holds that the four elementary bodies can all be transformed into one another, if not directly, then through a cycle of changes: see esp. *GC* 2.4-5; *Cael.* 3.6.

43. [5,11-15] Alex. here sets up a crucial analogy for his view of the soul: that although it is a power for change, it does not undergo change itself because it is inseparable from the body (21,22-24,17). He explicitly appeals to an analogy with heaviness at 22,7-10 and 18-20, though he takes this characteristic to belong to forms *in general* (22,14-15; cf. *Phys.* 5.1, 224b5 and 11-12).

44. [5,16] Although commonly rendered 'cause', the Greek *aitia* and its cognate *aition* are closer to the English 'because': an *aitia* is something cited in an explanation as responsible for a certain state of affairs, its ground or *explanans*. In many cases, this is a cause; but not all explanations are causal explanations. I have chosen to stay closer to the verb from which the Greek term is derived, *aitiasthai*, to hold responsible or accountable, even when causes are involved, to show that this broader explanatory notion is at issue.

45. [5,17] The Aldine edition again reverses the natural order of this inference, using 'therefore' (*ara*) instead of 'because' or 'for the following reason' (*hoti*).

46. [5,19] 3,26-7.

47. [5,20] Arist. *GC* 2.2, 329b6-10; *DA* 2.11, 423b27-9.

48. [5,20-1] 3,28-4,4.

49. [5,21-2] 4,7-9.23-5. Cf. 17,11-12.

50. [5,22-6,2] 4,20-5,1.

51. [6,2-3] See esp. Arist. *DA* 2.1, 412a6-12; 2.2, 414a14-16; *Metaph.* 7.10, 1035a1-4; 7.13, 1038b2-3; 8.1, 1042a26-31; 8.2, 1043a26-8; 12.3, 1070a9-13. By restricting this doctrine to natural substances here, Alex. goes somewhat beyond Arist. (though 412a11-12 might suggest it). Alex. unambiguously denies that either artefacts or the forms of artefacts are substances in their own right, but only in so far as natural substances underlie them: cf. 5,1-2 and *Mant.* 121,17-19.

52. [6,3-4] *Mant.* 121,23-5; 122,4-15. Note the strong explanatory priority Alex. assigns to matter and form. It is not simply that parts of a compound substance must be substances themselves; the latter fact is what explains the former. On the principle that the parts of substances are substances in Alex., see Rashed 2007a, ch. 2. Arist. has reservations about this principle, at least if stated without further qualification: *Metaph.* 7.13, 1039a3-8 (though compare a14-19); 7.16, 1040b5-16, 1041a4-5. There are nonetheless traces of it in the corpus: cf. *An. Pr.* 1.32, 47a24-8; *Phys.* 1.6, 189a32-3. On the last two passages and Alex.'s comments on them, see Rashed 2007a, 51-2.

53. [6,4-6] Elsewhere Alex. only claims that the *forms* of artefacts are qualities and not substances (5,2; *Quaest.* 1.21, 35,6); here artefacts themselves are said to be qualities. Having explicitly restricted substantial forms to natural objects, he cannot regard the artefacts as substances in their own right (5,2), but at most in an extended sense in virtue of their materials (*Mant.* 120,5-7, 121,17-19).

54. [6,6-7] The worry Alex. considers here is triggered by his conclusion at 5,18-19. He need not have the Stoics exclusively in mind here, though they certainly fall within the target zone, since they take the two principles of bodies, matter and divine reason, to be bodies themselves (D.L. 7.134 = *SVF* 2.299 = LS 44B 3, retaining the MSS reading – see LS 1.274, 2.266). See also Alex.'s criticism of the Stoic mereological principle that every part of a body is a body at 18,10-27 below.

55. [6,8] Here *tode ti* does not designate an individual, but just a determinate kind of thing in any category. See n. 34 above on 4,24.

56. [6,8-10] Arist. *Phys.* 1.5, 188b21-6; 1.8, 191b13-16; *GC* 2.4, 331a14-16.

57. [6,12-13] *Mant.* 121,29-30.

58. [6,13-14] Arist. *GC* 1.3, 317a32-b5; *Cael.* 3.2, 302a3-7.

59. [6,14-15] *Quaest.* 2.19, 63,8-28; cf. *in Metaph.* 103,8; 158,7-13; 159,10-26; 213,2-17; *in Meteor.* 6,15-16; 78,11-12. Also Arist. *Cael.* 1.10, passim; 2.1, 283b26-284a13; cf. 2.14, 296b33. The Stoics accept that there is always body, since god is eternal and a body (see n. 54 on 6,6-7), even though they believe the world-order (*diakosmêsis*) is perishable: Philo *Aet.* 9, 75.14-76.3 Cohn-Wendland = *SVF* 2.620; cf. 131, 113.5 = *SVF* 1.106.

60. [6,19] 4,9-15.

61. [6,6-20] See the closely parallel argument at *Mant.* 121,31-122,4. Alex.'s argument has the structure of a constructive dilemma: either there was a time when bodies first came about or there have always been bodies; but either way, he argues, bodies come from non-bodily items in some sense. But Alex. is not indifferent between the two. Alex. does not himself accept the first horn, but the second: there have always been bodies. But he introduces a key distinction: since each body comes from another body, it does not come from what is not a body *tout court*, but only from what is not the particular sort of body it is. In this way, he can accept the general principle, while avoiding the absurdity of the first horn, of non-bodily items existing separately on their own. Bare matter and form are only abstractions and never exist apart.

As 5,18-19 shows, however, Alex. is still committed to non-bodily items, even if they do not exist separately. His counterargument above relies on a *diachronic* model throughout: Alex. focuses exclusively on the pre-existing items bodies are *produced from* (*ek*). But the initial objection can equally be raised on a *synchronic* model: someone might worry whether bodies can be *composed from* (*ek*) non-bodily items like form and matter, and ultimately prime matter, at a single instant. Alex. believes that they can and are, but does not defend it here.

62. [6,21-2] *in Metaph.* 20.5-6. This claim about the central role of form is extended below to the form of compound bodies (7,4-5), and eventually to the souls of living things. BD nicely observe (238) that this general principle underlies the claim made in the opening argument that the soul is that in virtue of which each human is a human (2,1) and so provides the key to self-knowledge.

63. [6,28] *Mixt.* 13, 229,30-230,2.

64. [6,30] 'Culmination' (*teleotês*) is one of Alex.'s key technical terms in *On the Soul*. Arist. himself uses it only twice (*Phys.* 3.6, 207a21; 8.7, 261a36), though the idea is completely orthodox. It derives from *telos*, the Greek word for end or goal, and thus signifies the full realisation of some given kind of thing, closely related to *entelekheia*: see esp. 16,5-7. The alternative rendering *teleotês* as 'completion' captures its etymology, but understates the normative role of the end that is so crucial to Aristotelian teleology, while rendering it as 'perfection' overshoots the mark and introduces irrelevant theological overtones. On Alex.'s use of this term, see Todd 1974, 213-14.

65. [6,30-7,2] *in Metaph.* 349,14-16.

66. [7,2] Arist. *Metaph.* 9.8, 1050a15-16; cf. 5.4, 1015a10-11; 5.24, 1023a33, together with Alex.'s brief comments, *in Metaph.* 359,30-2 (cf. 21-2) and 422,16-17.

67. [7,6] *in An. Pr.* 46,2-16; 29,1-30,6.

68. [7,9-13] *Mant.* 116,18-31. Arius Didymus (first century BCE), in his summary of Aristotelian physics, speaks similarly of bodies making and being modified 'by non-bodily powers' (*tais asômatois dunamesi*, fr. 5, *Dox. Gr.* 449.12-14 = Stob. *Ecl.* 1.141.19-22), though Kupreeva 2003 has questioned the dates for this evidence (309 n. 40). And while Arist. himself does not contrast bodies and their non-bodily items or powers in just so many words, he does come reasonably close to it at *Sens.* 4, 441b12-15: 'nothing is naturally such as to act or be modified in so far as it is fire or earth, nor does anything else in fact; everything acts or is modified just in so far as there is a contrariety in it.' In his commentary, Alex. construes this as a claim about bodies in general (*in Sens.* 73,10) and portrays the Aristotelian view as positioned midway between the Stoics and the Platonists: 'For Arist. does not think that bodies act or are modifed, as the Stoics maintain, or on the other hand that non-bodily items do, as the Platonists thought, but rather [bodies do so] in virtue of the non-bodily contrarieties in them' (73,18-21). Bodies thus act in virtue of their features or powers, which are not themselves bodies, much as someone today might claim that bodies act in virtue of their properties. Both of the competing views are thus in a sense right and in a sense wrong. When Alex. speaks of 'Platonists', he might have in mind Plato himself, *Phaedo* 100A-105C (cf. 95E-96A), or still more likely Arist.'s critique of Plato at *Metaph.* 1.9, 991b3-9; *GC* 2.9, 335b7-24. The Stoic claim that only bodies can act or be acted on is central to their ontology: Cic. *Acad.* 1.39 = *SVF* 1.90 = LS 45A; Aet. 1.11.5, *Dox. Gr.* 310.6-7 = *SVF* 2.340 = LS 55G; Plut. *Comm. Not.* 30, 1073E = *SVF* 2.525 (cf. 40, 1080F); Sext. Emp. *Adv. Math.* 9.211 = *SVF* 2.341 = LS 55B; Stob. 1.138.14-139.4 = *SVF* 1.89 & 2.336 = LS 55A; Nemes. *Nat. Hom.* 2, 20.14-17, 21.6-9 Morani = *SVF* 1.518 = LS 45C; Euseb. *PE* 15.14.1, 378.19-379.2 = *SVF* 1.98 = LS 45G; cf. Sext. Emp. *Adv. Math.* 8.263 =

SVF 2.363. On the dispute between Alex. and the Stoics on this point, see Kupreeva 2003, 307-15.

69. [7,18-20] Arist. *Cael.* 1.2, 268b26-269a1, a25-7; 3.3, 302b6-8; 3.4, 303b4-5. On different possible construals of the argument at 7,14-20 see n. 39 on 5,5 above.

70. [7,22] 3,24-7.

71. [7,23] 8,9-10. The comparative *teleioteros*, here rendered by the phrase 'more advanced', can be used to indicate not merely whether something is fully developed, and so superior in comparison with members of its own kind, but also whether it is superior across kinds, as here. Similar remarks apply to the semantic range of the superlative and the various privative forms: see the Greek-English Index under '*teleios*' and '*ateles*'. For the normative force of teleological notions, see n. 64 on 'culmination '(*teleiotes*) at 6,30.

72. [7,24-8,1] Note that while the higher-level forms of compound bodies in some sense depend on matter, they do so *via* form: the lower-level forms of the underlying bodies, which serve as proximate matter, 'contribute' (*suntelei*, 7,24; 8,11) to the higher-level form and so help to explain its complexity and sophistication (8,13-15).

73. [8,3-5] A single simple body – that is, one of the four elements – can serve as the (pre-existing) matter for a different body, by being transformed into it. But such transformations only result in a different element and thus another simple body, because they only involve an exchange of elemental qualities (*GC* 2.4-5, passim; cf. 2.7, 334a16-26). To get a compound body, therefore, more than one type of body is needed. Arist. actually goes further, arguing that every compound body ultimately includes *all four* elements: *GC* 2.8, 334b31-335a9.

74. [8,10-12] Alex. begins to lay out the ways in which the nature of a higher-order form depends upon the underlying matter, in particular on the forms of the underlying bodies: see esp. 8,15-17; 10,17-19 and 24-6; 11,11-13; and 23,29-24,4, with their corresponding notes.

75. [8,12-13] Arist. uses this phrase, but to describe the understanding (*nous*), which is capable of receiving all forms, and so is a 'form of forms' (in the way that the hand is a 'tool of tools') at *DA* 3.8, 432a1-3. Alex.'s point is quite different: as the form of proximate matter, the higher-level form is in a sense the form of the lower-level forms so combined and organised.

76. [8,16] This is the first use of the notion of a distinctive mixture (*mixis*) or blend (*krasis*) that will become central to Alex.'s explanation in the pages that follow. See n. 90 on 10,17-19. Elsewhere, Alex. distinguishes between mixtures and blends, the latter being a species of the former: blends are those mixtures where the ingredients are not preserved separate from one another, but come to have a single underlying substratum (*Mixt.* 13, 228,27-36; cf. Arist. *Top.* 4.2, 122b30-1); see Joachim 1903, 73-4. In the *DA*, Alex. typically uses 'mixture' in conjunction with 'blend' to signifiy the species.

77. [8,15-17] The different character of higher-level forms depends upon differences in the underlying matter, specifically their forms. See 10,17-19 and 24-6; 11,11-13; and 23,29-24,4, with their corresponding notes.

78. [8,17-18] Alex. clearly has in mind the matter of a simple body or element here, that is, prime matter, since a compound body will have not one, but several bodies as its matter, which would contribute to its difference (8,5-13).

79. [8,17-25] Alex.'s argument is that in the base case of elemental bodies there is already a striking amount of diversity, which is due solely to the different pairings of elemental qualities, since the matter in this case is entirely without forms of its own and so makes no distinctive contribution. In the subsequent cases of compound bodies, the matter consists of several types of body, which will also contribute forms of their own and so will only add further to the diversity of the bodies that result. Arist. speaks of 'couplings' (*suzeuxeis*) of elemental qualities in elemental bodies at *GC* 2.3, 330a30-b7.

80. [9,1-4] *Mant.* 105,10-12 (cf. 103,36-8); Arist. *DA* 2.2, 413a25-31. The simplest living things, plants, differ from simple bodies in their causal powers. The three cited here – the power to eat and be nourished, to grow, and to reproduce – are the distinctive powers of the 'soul for nourishment' (*threptikê psukhê*). See below at 9,11-14 and then at greater length at 29,1-10 and 31,7-38,11.

81. [9,4-7] The different forms of plants are explained by the different blend of materials underlying them. This strong explanatory claim presupposes a covariation between plant forms and their matter: there is no difference in the type of plant without some corresponding difference in the type of material blend. The former types supervene on the latter.

It is surprising that throughout this discussion Alex. does not mention differences in structure and in 'anhomoeomerous' or non-homogenous parts, which are mentioned only at the end of the treatise (98,4-5), but are prominent elsewhere (e.g., *in Meteor.* 224,24-225,16 and 227,15-22, where he signals the subsequent discussion of this topic in *PA* 2). Taking structure into account would not, I think, fundamentally alter Alex.'s emergentist strategy (see n. 40 on 5,5-6), but it would complicate the detail considerably, and he may have left it out of his presentation for convenience's sake. (His remark about parts at 10,28-9 is non-specific.)

82. [9,12] For both Alex. and Arist. this claim represents the core of the common concept of soul or *psukhê*: it is the 'principle of life' (*arkhê tôn zôiôn*, Arist. *DA* 1.1, 402a6-7), that in virtue of which living things are alive and perform the activities distinctive of living things (2.2, 414a12-13), whatever that in fact turns out to be. Different theories differ over just what that is and its precise nature. As BD point out (240), this is the first mention of soul since the beginning of the treatise.

83. [9,12-14] 78,5-6; 92,18-20; Arist. *DA* 2.2, 414a12-14. AD rightly stress (117) how with these assumptions, Alex. moves from speaking merely about the forms of complex bodies like plants to souls proper.

84. [9,14-22] Here again Alex. argues that the principles Arist. applies to the soul are just instances of a broader pattern, which is already at work at the most basic level of elemental bodies. The study of the soul is to this extent continuous with the rest of natural science, a point he makes again later in his treatment of the soul using the example of the heaviness of the element earth (23,29-24,3; on heaviness as a form, cf. n. 39 on 5,5 above). He appears to have made a similar point in his lost commentary on the *de Caelo*: see Simpl. *in Cael.* 380,29-381,2.

In the present case, he is concerned with the distinction between 'potentiality' and 'actuality', that is, between a power (*dunamis*) and its exercise or activity (*energeia*). Alex.'s reading is notable for its unambiguous, emphatic identification of form with the power, something which is at best implicit in Arist.'s view. In this way, Alex. gives explanatory primacy to powers, esp. causal powers, even though powers are defined by reference to their exercise (contrast Arist. *Metaph.* 9.8, 1050b2-6). Alex. develops the point here as a consequence of Arist.'s view that while a power and its exercise can both be viewed as stages of completion or *entelekheia*, the soul is to be identified as the *first* completion (*DA* 2.1, 412a21-8; cf. Alex. *Mant.* 103,10-20). Alex. frames it here as a metaphysical principle which holds of forms and powers quite generally, substituting his own favored term, culmination (*teleiotês*), for completion. He links the two terms explicitly below at 16,4-10.

85. [10,3] 2,26-3,2; 3,23-5.

86. [10,7-8] 6,24-7,8.

87. [10,8-10] The claim that perception distinguishes animals from other living things and so is a part of their definition is fundamental in both Arist. and Alex. For Alex., see 29,14-15; 40,14-15; 78,6-7; 92,21-3; *Mant.* 105,12-13; *Quaest.* 2.27, 77,14-15; *in Sens.* 3,19-20; 9,1-2; *in Top.* 17,9-11; 160,20-1; 376,11-15; 381,17; 394,6-7; 407,23-4; as well as the formulaic definition of animal as 'perceptive animate substance' (*ousia empsukhos aisthêtikê*): *Quaest.* 1.11, 21,25-6 (= 23,27-9); 22,9-12 (= 24,11-14); *in Metaph.* 161,8-9; *in Top.* 93,1-3; 124,1-2; 355,21-4; 405,2-5 (commenting on Arist. *Top.* 135a16); 407,23-4; 432,1; 463,11-15; 493,3-4. Cf. also *DA* 30,13; 66,5; 67,2; 93,17-18; *in Sens.* 5,21-4; 8,2-3; 9,1; *in Top.* 16,23-4; 89,16-17; 391,6-7; *in Metaph.* 198,29-30; 315,33-4; 316,18-19.

For Arist., see *DA* 2.2, 413b1-4; 3.12, 434a27-31; *Sens.* 1, 436b10-12; *Somn.* 1, 454b25; *Iuv.* 1, 467b24-5; 3, 469a18-20; 4, 469b4; *PA* 2.5, 651b3-5; 2.8, 653b22-3; 3.4, 666a34; *GA* 1.23, 731a30-b4; 2.1, 732a12-13; 2.2, 736a29-30 (cf. b1); 2.5, 741a9-10; 5.1, 778b32-3; *Metaph.* 1.1, 980a27; *EN* 9.9, 1170a16; cf. *Top.* 5.2, 129b26; *DA* 3.2, 427a14-16; 3.13, 435b5-7, b16-17; *HA* 1.3, 489a17-18; 4.8, 533a17-18; *PA* 2.1, 647a21; 2.8, 653b22-3; 2.10, 656a3-4; 3.4, 666a34; 4.5, 678b2-4; *GA* 3.7, 757b15; 5.1, 778b32-3; *Metaph.* 7.10, 1035b14-18; *EN* 6.2, 1139a20; though compare the caveats at *HA* 8.1, 588b17-18 and *PA* 4.5, 681a19-20.

88. [10,12-14] Throughout *On the Soul*, Alex. frequently appeals to 'analogy' (see under *analogia* and *analogon* in the Greek-English Index). But in this passage, he also intends it to carry the quantitative sense of a proportion, where the central terms are identical: in a series of three terms, $A : B :: B : C$, as regards how advanced (*teleios*) each is. The golden ratio is an example of this kind of proportion.

Underlying this proportion is a deeper analogy, though, concerning the relation that holds between the higher-level forms at each stage and the lower-level ones directly beneath them: each new level emerges from and is in some sense determined by the previous one (see n. 90 on 10,17-19 below).

89. [10,14-17] Alex., much like Arist., thinks that the relation between the souls of different animals replicates the larger relation that holds between animals and plants: but where Arist. is only concerned with a kind of independence (whether one set of powers can be found instantiated without the others), Alex. makes a much stronger, quantitative claim about the proportionality that holds between them. It is not clear exactly which differences Alex. has in mind here, however, and so just how extensively this proportionalilty is supposed to hold: some animals have only the sense of touch, others have more than one sense, and some have all; some animals can move, while others cannot; some have memory, while others lack it.

90. [10,17-19] The nature of these differences is in some sense to be accounted for (*aitia*) by differences in the underlying bodies, specifically their number, mixture, blend, and formation (*kata te plêthos kai kata poian krasin te kai mixin kai sustasin*): see 8,15-17.22-5. This claim presupposes that the higher forms *covary* with these underlying factors: given a certain mixture or blend of bodies, a certain higher-level form follows or is a consequence, something stated explicitly below at 10,24-6. If so, these higher-level forms *supervene*, in the technical sense, on the mixture of underlying bodies: which higher-level forms occur is a function of the 'blend, mixture, and formation' of the underlying bodies. Cf. 8,10-12; 11,11-13; 23,29-24,4; 25,2; 26,22.

Someone might worry whether this dependence on matter conflicts with the explanatory primacy Alex. assigns to form and that the 'bottom-up' account he introduces here clashes with his 'top-down' approach elsewhere (e.g., 7,9-14). But there is in fact no contradiction. The matter which is responsible for higher-level forms is always a body of some sort and so has a form of its own. All bodies differ from one another in virtue of their forms, moreover, and Alex.'s claim is simply that such differences at lower levels have consequences at higher levels, since higher-level forms *covary* with certain kinds of underlying bodies and hence with their forms and thus supervene on them in the technical sense (*Mant.* 104,27-34 and also discussion in n. 92 on 10,24-6 below). In so far as these bodies underlie the higher-level compound, they are material factors of it. But it is still their forms that play the key role. Contrast this sort of case with prime matter, which is without any determination or form of its own. It is precisely because prime matter can equally occur with any given form or without it that *no* form covaries with prime matter and so none supervenes on it in the technical sense. Even the simplest case of supervenience presupposes lower-level forms that determine the matter, as when lightness emerges from the heat and dryness of fire (5,4-6); neither heat nor dryness, in contrast, emerges from or supervenes on prime matter. The only matter that can be responsible for higher-level differences is matter that *has a form of its own* and is therefore already a body.

91. [10,19-20] Though proverbial (*Corpus paroem. gr.* Diog. 2.97; cf. App. prov. 1.41 Leutsch-Schneidewin), this saying occurs prominently in the methodological remarks that conclude Arist.'s function argument at *EN* 1.7, 1098b7; cf. *Polit.* 5.4, 1303b29-31. But the closest parallel may be *SE* 34, 183b22-6, which develops the point most fully and uses the superlative *megiston*, rather than the comparative. Ian Flora points out to me that the superlative can also be found in Plato *Rep.* 2, 377A (cf. *Laws* 6, 753E6-754A2), which Arist. himself may have in mind.

92. [10,24-6] It is because matter is an *arkhê*, an origin and principle, of the difference in forms that it is responsible (*aitia*) for these differences, as Alex. claims above at 10,17 (see accompanying note). The difference in higher-level forms is here clearly said to be a *consequence* (*hepesthai*) of differences in the matter. These need not be causal consequences of the matter, but simply a question of *covariation*: necessarily, whenever there is matter of a certain kind, there is a higher-level form of a certain kind – there cannot be any difference in the forms without some difference in the underlying matter. In light of this, AD are wrong to claim (115) that there is 'absolutely no passage' in *On the Soul* where matter is said to be a sufficient condition for organic form (and likewise BD 33-4), against Moraux (1942, 41). Both sides wrongly assume that such sufficient conditions would entail a very strong form of reductionist materialism. But an emergentist strategy like Alex.'s can accept sufficient conditions while rejecting reductionism. See n. 40 on 5,5-6.

That Alex. does regard the underlying matter as a sufficient condition in the present passage is confirmed by a parallel passage, *Mant.* 104,27-34: the body's blend (*krasis*) is responsible (*aitia*) for the soul's coming into being in the first place (104,28); the difference between souls is a consequence (*epêkolouthêsan*) of the specific formation (*sustasei*) of the body and one covaries with the other (*summetaballousin allêlois*, 30-1); and the difference in souls is a consequence (*hepetai*) of the specific blend of the body (33). For further discussion, see my 1997, 348-9.

Some have worried (e.g., Sorabji 2003, 156 and 2004*a*, 193, 194-5, following Sharples) that *Mant.* 104,28-34 diverges from the view in Alex.'s *DA* and might not even be written by Alex. But the concern is unfounded, as the two texts do not differ on these key points at all. Alex. states equally in the *DA* that higher-level forms, including the soul, follow (*hepesthai*, 10,25; 26,29) from the underlying blend and mixture, which is therefore said to be in some sense responsible (*aitia*, 10,17) for the higher-level form and an origin of it (*arkhê*, 10,24).

93. [11,1] I have used 'organic' here for the Greek *organikos*. One might worry that this rendering is a false friend: the Greek *organon*, from which it derives, is used not only for physiological organs, but for implements, tools, instruments, and anything quite generally that serves as the means for some specific function or end. There is a dispute, moreover, about its use in Arist.'s definition of the soul in *DA* 2.1 as the form of a natural body (412a28-b6), where it has variously been taken to signify that the body either (*a*) has organs or (*b*) is itself organ-like or tool-like. (For discussion, see Menn 2002, 108-11.) Alex. clearly favours the first reading, (*a*). He characterises the *organikon* body as one 'that has many different parts able to subserve the soul powers' (16,11-12; *Quaest.* 2.8, 54,9-10) and explicitly rejects the view that the soul uses the body 'as an organ' or 'tool' (*hôs organôi*) at 23,24-8. He takes Arist.'s use of the word in the definition of soul as an elaboration of the earlier phrase 'capable of having life' (*Quaest.* 2.8, 54,6-9.11), thus bringing it even closer to ordinary connotations of the English 'organic'. I have accordingly translated *organon* as 'organ', which Alex. uses almost exclusively for physiological organs in *On the Soul*. (For the rare exceptions, cf. 35,2 and 96,8.)

94. [11,2] Alex. is gesturing broadly at elements of Arist.'s definition of the soul at *DA* 2.1, 412a19-b6.

95. [11,5-6] Alex. returns to the strategy he advanced at 2,10-25: that once we understand how marvellous nature is, we will no longer be puzzled as to how bodies can be endowed with the powers characteristic of living things. See n. 97 below on 11,11-13.

96. [11,7] 5,11-15.

97. [11,11-13] Alex. extends the proportion between different kinds of forms to the matter underlying each of them, because of their dependence on this matter: if the difference between forms is a function of the difference in the underlying matter's composition and make-up (7,21-8,25; 9,4-7; 10,17-19.24-6), then the matter of more advanced forms, such as the souls of animals, will itself be more complex and advanced than the matter of less advanced forms, such as the souls of plants. Instead of positing a non-bodily soul separate from all matter, whose powers are 'more divine and greater' than those of any body (cf. 2,17-18), Alex.'s solution to the earlier aporia is to appeal to a layered conception of nature, where increasingly complex forms depend in some way on the increasingly complex bodies that serve as their matter. What is important about these underlying bodies are their forms and powers, which depend, in turn, on the simpler bodies underlying them, whose forms and powers depend on the bodies underlying them, and so on again until we ultimately reach the elemental forms and prime matter. At each level, new forms emerge as a result of the complexity and organisation of the forms of the bodies underlying them.

98. [11,14] AD suggest (122-3) that the reason Alex. does not make this claim about living things (*ta zônta*) generally, but restricts himself here to animals (*ta zôia*), is that he is arguing dialectically from what has been agreed upon (*homologeitai*), since the Stoics deny that plants have a soul: *Mant.* 105,6-12; 118,12-14 = *SVF* 2.711 (cf. 118,19-21); cf. *DA* 31,25-32,1 below. See also Galen *Intr.* 14.726.7-11 Kühn = *SVF* 2.716 = LS 47N; Philo *Leg. Alleg.* 2.22-3, 1.95.7-20 Cohn-Wendland = *SVF* 2.458 = LS 47P.

99. [11,15] Throughout this treatise, I have rendered the Greek construction *esti ek tinos* – literally, 'is from something' or 'is out of something' – as 'is composed out of'. Arist. distinguishes different senses of 'from' or 'out of something' in a number of passages (*Metaph.* 5.24, passim; cf. also 2.2, 994a22-b3; 8.4, 1044a23-5). But for the most part his discussion does not line up with Alex.'s here, which exclusively concerns different kinds of composition. (Arist. *Metaph.* 14.5, 1092a21-35 is closer in this regard, but not much.) Alex.'s discussion has more to do with the distinction between different types of mixture or combination that Arist. discusses in *GC* 1.10, esp. his distinction between 'composition' (*sunthesis*) and mixture (*mixis*) at 328a5-15, corresponding to (*a*) and (*b*) above. Alex. refers to the first case as 'juxtaposition' below (*parathesis*, 12.2). He explicitly links 'juxtaposition' and 'composition' at *Mixt.* 13, 228,28-34.

But Alex. is not canvassing different types of composition here just for the sake of completeness. His strategy is more pointed. The three kinds of composition directly correspond to three theories of the soul's relation to the body: atomists like the Epicureans think that soul atoms are juxtaposed with other atoms in the body (*a*); the Stoics hold that there is a 'total blending' of the two (*b*); and the Aristotelians make the soul the form of the body (*c*). Afterwards, Alex. will make an additional argument (12,7-13,8), directed against substance dualism and so effectively against the Platonists, to round out his critical survey.

100. [11,15-17] This sort of mixture, where the ingredients are preserved intact in their original form (like rice and beans), is what Alex. himself calls 'juxtaposition' (*parathesis*) below at 12,2; see also his use of this term to characterise one of the Stoic forms of mixture at *Mixt.* 3, 216,17-22. For Epicureans and atomists generally, all mixture is of this type, including the body and soul: Epic. *Ep. ad Hdt.* 63-6 = LS 14A 1-5; Lucr. 3.425-58 = LS 14F 2-3.

101. [11,17-18] 15,5-8; *Mant.* 116,7; *in Metaph.* 334,31-4; cf. also *DA* 13,22 and *Mant.* 116,12, which use the example of honeyed wine; also cf. Arist. *Metaph.* 8.2, 1042b15-17. Alex.'s use of these examples and the terminology suggest the Stoics' view, esp. in the *Mant.* passage: 'the whole soul pervades the whole body and is blended with it' (*hôs holon di' holou diêkein kai kekrasthai tôi sômati*, 116,5-6); for the attribution to Chrysippus, see *Mixt.* 4, 217,32-218,1 (= *SVF* 2.473, p. 155, ll. 24-30 = LS 48C 10) together with 3, 216,4-14. But the view Alex. goes on to elaborate in the present passage differs in key respects: see n. 102 on 11,18-20. Both of these views, it should be noted, hold that the *animal* is a blend of soul and body, which is quite distinct from the view that the *soul* itself is a blend of the bodies underlying it, as Galen claims in *Quod animi mores*. Regarding the latter view, see n. 226 on 24,18-20 below and Alex.'s discussion of *harmonia* theories of the soul more generally at 24,18-26,30.

102. [11,18-20] Alex.'s characterisation here differs from that of the Stoics. According to Chrysippus, the ingredients are *preserved* in total blending and *can* be extracted from it again – in fact, the possibility of extraction is a 'distinctive characteristic' of blending (*Mixt.* 3, 216,25-217,2 = *SVF* 2.473, p. 154, ll. 19-28 = LS 48C 4; cf. *Mant.* 6, 220,20-2). The case Alex. describes above, in contrast, is what the Stoics call 'fusion throughout' (*sunkhusei di' holôn*), in which the ingredients perish and some third thing is created (*Mixt.* 3, 216,22-5 = *SVF* 2.473, p. 154, ll. 15-19 = LS 48C 3; cf. Philo *Conf. Ling.* 184-7, 2.264.23-265.15 Cohn-Wendland = *SVF* 2.472). For a quick overview of the Stoic theory of blending, see LS 1.292-4 and M. J. White 2003, 146-9. For more detailed studies, see Todd 1976, 21-88; Sorabji 1988, ch. 6; E. Lewis 1988.

Alex., however, is not trying to report Stoic doctrine faithfully here. As at *Mant.* 116,5-13, he blends his presentation of their view with his own criticism, drawing out what he thinks are the real options and consequences, since he finds the whole notion of total blending absurd: he argues that it collapses either into juxtaposition or, if there is mixture throughout as here, fusion (*Mixt.* 7, 220,23-221,25; cf. 1, 213,2-13). In the latter case, the ingredients will not be preserved, as the Stoics claim, but perish (7, 221,11-15.20-5). This accords with his own view, according to which the ingredients in a blend are not preserved in actuality – that would be juxtaposition – and so could in a sense be said to 'perish' when the blend comes into being: see 12,5-6 below, but also *Mixt.* 13, 228,34-6; 15, 231,15-19.25-6. (Alex. would embrace this designation even more strikingly if we were to accept, with Todd, Montanari's emendation *phthora* at 230,15 and 19, in place of the MSS's *mixis*; on which, see Todd 1976, 178.) But it is critical to note that even for Alex. this is *not* complete annihilation (*out' ... pantapasin phthareiê*), since the ingredients are in a way preserved (*sôzomenôn*): see *Mixt.* 14, 230,17-19 especially, but also 231,10-12; 15, 232,13-18.28-31. Alex. adopts the orthodox Aristotelian position that the ingredients still exist in one sense (namely, potentially) though not in another (actually): *GC* 1.10, 327b23-31, 328b17-19.

103. [11,20-1] This is, of course, the Aristotelian alternative Alex. favours. See above, 2,25-3,13 (incl. the example of the statue at 3,7-9).

104. [12,2-3] 15,15-17; 20,6-7; 21,10-11; *Mant.* 104,21-2; cf. 115,30-4. Alex. assumes here that the body of a living thing is animate throughout, a point on which certain Stoics agree (*Mixt.* 4, 217,36 = *SVF* 2.473, p. 155, ll. 25-8 = LS 48C 10; Hierocles *Elem. Eth.* 4.6-8 Long). Alex.'s position might be thought to be a straightforward consequence of Arist.'s hylomorphism: since the soul is the form of the 'whole living body' (*holou zôntos sômatos*, *DA* 2.1, 412b17-23), one might think that no part of the body could be without at least the most basic vital powers of the soul. (The soul for perception is a different matter, since not all parts of the body are sensitive: see 74,29-75,2 and 97,4-6 below, with notes.) Arist.'s views about homonymy also suggest this, as when he claims that 'there will be no part [of the body] without a share of soul, except in name' (*GA* 2.1, 735a6-8, cf. 734b23-7; also 1.19, 726b22-4). But Arist. does not always regard this as a consequence of his views. At the end of *MA* 10, he says that 'there need not be soul in each part [of the body]' (703a36-7); rather the other parts 'live by being naturally attached' to the body's central principle, in which the soul, like a ruler, resides (703a29-b2). Nussbaum suggests (1978, 153) that Arist. is merely denying that each part is a 'separable *animal*' with a soul of its own. But on the most straightforward reading of the Greek, Arist. is making the stronger claim that there need not be any *soul* present in certain parts of the body at all. Tracy more plausibly suggests (1983, 336-7) that the claim is meant to apply to the soul only in so far as it is *an efficient cause* of change, which is the main concern of the argument in that context, and so is compatible with his view elsewhere that the soul is the form of the entire body while the heart is the principle or origin of the activities that distinguish living beings as such; on this reading, Arist. is simply rejecting multiple principles (cf. *PA* 3.4, 665b27-9).

105. [12,3-4] Alex. appears to be drawing a categorial distinction between the character (*poion*) of an animal and its size (*poson*). But presumably he has in mind the broader sense of character here, in which one can speak of the genus and differentia of a substance as a kind of characteristic, rather than just those which more strictly fall into the category of quality (*poiotês*): Arist. *Categ.* 5, 3b13-21; *Metaph.* 5.14, 1020a33-b2, b14-15; 5.28, 1024b4-6; *Top.* 4.2, 122b16-17 (though compare *Metaph.* 7.12, 1038a19-20); Alex. *in Metaph.* 399,1-6; 400,28-31; 429,12-14.17-19; *in Top.* 314,22-4. If so, then the argument is not merely dialectical, as AD 123 suggest, in order to win Stoic concessions, but something Alex. can and should accept on his own terms (as one would expect if the present argument is to count as a demonstration): the soul contributes not merely to the size or quality of a living thing, but to its essence and substance as well.

106. **[12,5-6]** The argument here is clearly meant to run as follows: (1) if the animal is a blend of soul and body, then the soul and body perish when the animal comes to be; but (2) when the soul and the body perish the animal does not come to be, but rather dies; therefore, (3) the animal is not a blend of body and soul. The Stoics would deny (1), since on their view the ingredients are *preserved* in a true blend. But Alex. rejects this account of blending and so does not concede it here even for the sake of argument. On the differing views of blending and the dialectic, see n. 102 on 11,18-20 above.

107. **[12,8]** Alex. uses the phrase 'itself just on its own' (*autê kath' hautên*) to indicate that the soul, though an *ousia* in the way a form is (6,2-4), is not an independent substance that can exist itself just on its own. This way of putting it gives added emphasis to his rejection of substance dualism, since the phrase is used first by Plato to distinguish the Form of *F* from the many things which are *F*: the Form is just *F* itself on its own, taken by itself without anything else to which it attaches. Alex. uses it here as elsewhere in the treatise to speak more generally of whether a given thing as such can exist independently: see the Greek-English Index, under *auto kath' hauto*. Platonists are clearly a target here, as AD rightly suggest (124), though Alex. need not have any specific ones in mind: they cite Atticus fr. 7 Des Places and Alcinous *Didask.* 25, but neither uses the phrase *autê kath' hautên*. Like Arist., Alex. clearly intends the argument that follows to be a broadside attack against substance dualism in general.

108. **[12,9-13,8]** Alex. expands and develops the programmatic argument from Arist. *DA* 1.1, 403a3-25. The differences are instructive. Arist. starts from a puzzle about whether there are any states or 'modifications' (*pathê*) that belong to the soul exclusively or whether they are all shared by the body and the soul (a2-5), and suggests guardedly that 'most seem' to fall into the latter category: he lists several emotions as well as perception in general. Understanding (*noein*) is the one he says is most likely to belong to the soul alone, but even that will not be separable if it requires representation (a8-10). He then lays down the condition that the soul will be 'separable' if, and only if, some modification is exclusive to soul (a10-12), but then argues that the body undergoes something concurrent with all modifications of the soul (a16-19), concluding that these modifications are all 'enmattered *logoi*' (a24-5), using examples again drawn from the emotions.

Alex. is more forthright, comprehensive, and systematic. He begins by unambiguously endorsing the general thesis that *all* activities of the soul involve the body necessarily and without exception, and immediately sets this within the context of his broader naturalistic strategy, by putting it on all fours with the motions of the inanimate elements (12,9-11; cf. 23,26-24,3). He then runs through the gamut of activities, starting with the vital functions shared by plants (12,12-13); the cognitive, emotional, and appetitive activity of animals, (12,13-19); and finally thought (12,20-1). Regarding the latter, he shows no signs of hesitation: it falls under the general thesis equally with the rest. In all of these cases, the activities are described as occuring either *through* the body (*dia tou sômatos*, 12,14.17-18.21; compare *Sens.* 1, 436b6-7) or *when* the body undergoes the corresponding change (12,13.15.16.17.19). It is not clear if the difference between these phrases amounts to anything more than elegant variation, but it is worth noting that Arist. is willing to use the former phrase, which if anything is the stronger of the two, with the cognitive functions of perception, representation, and thought.

Alex. also introduces an important nuance at 12,9-10 (cf. 21-2) when he pairs activities (*energeiai*) of the soul with the changes (*kinêseis*) in the body, instead of Arist'.s vaguer and more neutral talk of 'modifications' (*pathê*) common to the soul and the body. Arist. does draw a distinction between activities and changes in *Metaph.* 9.6, 1048b18-35, and it is plausibly behind his treatment of perception in *DA* 2.5 as being a kind of completion and so either not an alteration or an alteration of a different sort (417a21-b16). Although this is compatible with there being a change in the body corresponding to the activity in the soul, the text does not explicitly state it. Alex., in contrast, insists on *both* an activity in the soul *and* a corresponding change in the body, and he applies this across the board to all modifications of the soul, not just those involved in cognition, as an instance of a general pattern that holds throughout the whole of nature down to the four elements. This distinction is critical for Alex., who wants to uphold Arist.'s view that the soul does not *itself* undergo change (21,22-24,17; 78,24-79,21), while still maintaining, as he does here, that all psychological activity involves change *in the body*.

109. [12,10-11] Although Alex. could conceivably have in mind natural objects here quite generally, since their natures are internal principles of change and rest (Arist. *Phys.* 2.1), he is more likely alluding to the tendency of the four elements to move towards their natural places: Arist. *Cael.* 4.3-5, passim; *Phys.* 8.4, 255b13-20. Alex. identifies the 'natural tendencies' (*kata phusin ... rhopai*) of natural bodies as lightness and heaviness at *in Metaph.* 72,34-6; cf. *in Sens.* 73,26-9. At one point, he draws a general analogy between the form of living things and of the four elements at *in Metaph.* 357,25-9, as the origin and principle of changes they naturally undergo, and specifically identifies the former as souls and the latter as 'tendencies'; he explicitly contrasts these two principles of change at *Quaest.* 2.3, 49,1-4 and in the Arabic translation of a treatise attributed to Alexander, against Galen's theory of motion: see 67a14-22 (Rescher and Marmura 1965, 17).

110. [12,14-15] 76,15-78,2; Arist. *DA* 3.10, 433b16-21; *MA* 10, passim. On desire generally, see Alex.'s discussion of striving (*hormê*), *DA* 73,14-80,15, since he regards desire as a type of striving (74,1).

111. [12,17] Although commonly translated as 'imagination', *phantasia* is something that has a wider and more central role in psychology, for Alex. as well as for Arist. It designates a form of representation that is generated initially from perceptions and possesses content that is perceptual in character, but also serves as a basis for the content of memories, dreams, desires, passions, and even thought (although in the latter case, further conceptual operations are required). It thus plays a key role in Arist.'s and Alex.'s explanations of most higher mental states. For more on the term and its use, see Alex.'s main discussion of it at 66,9-73,13, as well as Arist.'s in *DA* 3.3. passim, along with my 2006, 331-5; for more detail, see my 1996 and 1998.

112. [12,17-18] 68,4-10; 69,14-70,5; *in Metaph.* 312,2-5; Arist. *DA* 1.1, 403a8-10; *Mem.* 1, 450a27-b11; 2, 453a14-30; cf. *DA* 3.3, 428b11-14.

113. [12,19] Although Arist. uses the term *hormê* (see Bonitz 525b47-526a10) Alex.'s use is endebted to the Stoics, for whom it is a key technical term in their moral psychology: *hormê* is an intentional state directed at the pursuit or avoidance of something and initiates the corresponding motion. The common rendering of the term as 'impulse' wrongly suggests a primitive and instinctual drive or even a blind force. For more on the term and its use, see Alex.'s main discussion of it at 73,14-80,15 below.

114. [12,20-1] The conditional here is not merely hypothetical: on three different occasions, Arist. insists that we cannot think without a representation, thus affirming the antecedent: *DA* 3.7, 431a16-17 (cf. b2); 3.8, 432a8-10; *Mem.* 1, 449b31. Alex. uses *phronein* here in its broad sense, for thinking in general, instead of understanding (*noein*), which Arist. uses in the parallel passage at 403a8-10, in order to make clear that the point about dependence on *phantasia* and the body is not limited to some specific form of thinking, but holds for all thinking quite generally. It would weaken Alex.'s argument if he were appealing mainly or exclusively to practical thinking, as AD suggest (125).

115. [12,21-4] Alex. develops this pivotal claim of Arist.'s (*DA* 1.1, 403a10-12) in several interesting ways. As before, he frames it in terms of the pairing of activities in the soul with changes in the body (see n. 108 on 12,9-13,8 above). But he also states it in terms of conceivability: the soul is inseparable from the body provided that the activity of the soul cannot even be *conceived* (*labein*) apart from a body. Given how strong the antecedent is, the claim is somewhat weaker than it might otherwise appear, since it would not address cases where the correlations to the body are merely nomically necessary, not conceptually. Finally, Alex. offers an explanation for the claim, not found in Aristotle: without a body, such a power could not be exercised and so would be otiose or superfluous (*matên*). But as both Arist. and Alex. often say, nature does nothing superfluous: see n. 247 on 27,9; also 27,13; 28,4; 98,9 below.

116. [12,24-5] In the first half of this statement, Alex. ties the inseparability of the soul to its being the form of the body. But the second half is stronger still, in so far as it emphasises the explanatory role of the body's capabilities. On the meaning of *epitêdeiotês*, see Todd 1972.

117. [13,1-8] Of the three cases Arist. presents as evidence for his thesis that the states of the soul are 'enmattered *logoi*' at *DA* 1.1, 403a19-24, Alex. only presents the first two, which involve variations in strength, in a slightly generalised form. Note that Alex. takes Arist.'s use of *pathêmata* at 403a20, as many modern commentators do, to be referring to external provocations (13,1; cf. 13,4), rather than conditions in the body. He also takes the condition of the body in the second case merely to be one of being primed and predisposed towards anger (13,5), rather than 'the same state one is in when one is angry' as Arist. says (*hotan orgai to sôma kai houtôs ekhêi hôsper hotan orgizêtai*, 403a22). The phrasing of Alex.'s last remark here, about the body being in a certain state (*pôs ekhein*, 13,8), could be an allusion to Stoic terminology for their third category, but it is hard to see what point that would serve.

118. [13,10-14,3] Arist. *Phys.* 4.3, 210a14-24; cf. *Metaph.* 5.23, 1023a23-5. Since Alex. is going to use this division of senses as the basis for an extended argument by elimination (cf. 15,26-8), he has to assume that it exhausts all the relevant alternatives. So it is worth noting that while his list substantially overlaps Arist.'s, it does not do so entirely: Arist. includes several causal senses (efficient and final) which Alex. omits, while Alex. includes the presence of ingredients in a mixture. (The list from Arist.'s *Phys.* does not include the inherence of extrinsic characteristics either, though an example of it is given at *Metaph.* 5.23 1023a13 and it of course underlies the central distinction of the *Categ.* at 2, 1a23-b3.) Given the range of senses here, Alex. cannot plausibly dismiss these others as being too far afield, esp. since Arist. argues the soul is also an efficient and final cause (*DA* 2.3, 415a8-12). Alex. might think that these senses are to be understood in terms of the sense in which form is in matter, but it would still require argument.

Alex. offers additional arguments against (*c*), (*e*), and (*g*) at *Mant.* 115,28-116,1, on the assumption that the body which has a soul is animate throughout. See n. 104 on 12,2-3.

119. [13,22] 15,7; see n. 101 on 11,17-18 above (on honeyed water).

120. [14,2-3] 9,14-18; 23,29-24,3.

121. [14,4-5] Alex. alludes here to Arist.'s cryptic remark at the end of *DA* 2.1 that it is unclear whether the soul is a completion or *entelekheia* of the body 'as a sailor is of a ship' (*hôsper plôtêr ploiou*, 413a8-10). Alex.'s remark suggests that, far from being unclear, it is straightforwardly covered by the senses of 'in something' he has already enumerated, although he will still discuss it on its own below at 15,9-26 for good measure; see also 20,28-21,10; 79,19-20. The analogy itself suggests a form of substance dualism, in so far as the pilot, who governs and controls the ship, is a distinct, independent entity that can be separated from it (although Descartes himself explicitly rejected this analogy in the Sixth Meditation, AT 7.81). On the analogy see Tracy 1982.

122. [14,5-7] 12,3-4. Alex. assumes here that every part of a body is a body. But he cannot accept this without further qualification, since he rejects the unqualified version as confused at 18,10-27 (cf. 6,6-12). If the principle holds at all, it holds only for those parts which 'contribute to the body's size and continue to exist after they are carved' (18,15-17).

123. [14,8-9] The phrase 'body passing through body' (*sôma dia sômatos khôrein*) refers to the interpenetration of bodies, which Alex. associates above all (though not exclusively) with the Stoic theory of total blending and consequently with their view that the soul pervades the entire body (see n. 101 on 11,17-18 above). Alex., like Arist., regards the idea that two bodies can be in the same place as absurd and argues against it at length: see n. 189 on 20,8-19 below.

124. [14,10-11] Alex. offers no argument for this claim: he may just take it to be patently absurd that the soul is composed from parts of the body; or, alternatively, he may be assuming that the compositional principle mentioned earlier at 14,6 goes hand in hand with the converse principle, that anything composed of bodies is itself a body. Neither hypothesis quite explains his silence, though, since elsewhere he does not hesitate to offer an argument against a position he thinks absurd or to work over again a point he has recently covered.

125. [14,12-14] The first objection (12-14) is to the point so long as individual souls and bodies are our sole concern. But it is silent about the possibility that soul *in general* is a species of body *in general*, which would have the consequence that any given soul is an *individual* body. The second objection (*eti te*, 14) moves to close this gap, by implicitly denying that soul is a body, as it surely is not a body on the view Alex. has been developing, since forms in general are not bodies (5,22-6,2; *Mant.* 113,26-8). But in the present context, Alex. cannot help himself to the view that the soul is a form without begging the question, since the purpose of the entire argument is just to establish that the soul *is* the form of the body (13,9; 15,26-9); and given that he makes a point of starting from agreed upon common ground (13,10), he ought not to simply take it for granted that the soul is not a body, since others (like the Stoics and Epicureans) insist that it is. Nevertheless, Alex. relies on this premiss repeatedly in the *reductio* arguments that follow: 14,18; 15,5-9.14-15. He does, however, offer a battery of arguments for the claim elsewhere, though, independent of his view that the soul is a form: see *Mant.* 113,25-118,4.

126. [14,14-16] Presumably Alex. is referring to the claim at 14,12-14 that species and genera are universals, whereas the soul and the body are particulars.

127. [14,16-17] Whatever is predicated truly of the genus is predicated truly of the species: *Categ.* 5, 2b17-22; cf. 3, 1b10-15. But in the present case, the consequence is manifestly unacceptable, since if no soul is a body on Alex.'s view, then it follows that no body is a soul either, by conversion. Even on his opponents' views, not all bodies are souls; and that is all that is needed for this objection to strike home.

128. [14,18] Arist. *Phys.* 4.5, 212b7, b28-9; 4.1, 209a26-7; cf. 4.4, 211a17-23. Alex. again needs the premiss that the soul is not a body to be established independently: see n. 125 on 14,12-14 above. Plotinus 4.3.20 develops and builds on the arguments here.

129. [14,19-20] Alex.'s objection seems to be that everything has absurdly swapped roles: if (*e*) were right, the soul would be a body and the body would be a place, that is, something that contains bodies. The simple disjunction of alternative views on place he mentions does not appear in Arist. The first alternative, empty extension (*diastêma kenon*), seems to be an imprecise way of referring to space (*khôra*), which Arist. describes as the extension between the boundaries of the containing body, considered as something over and above any bodies that might occupy it (4.4, *Phys.* 211b14-29, 212a3-5). Alex. may possibly be conflating this notion with the common conception of emptiness or 'void' (*to kenon*) as 'extension with nothing in it', according to Arist. (4.6, 213a27-9; 4.7, 213b31, 214a5-6, a20). Alex. might also have Platonic and even Stoic conceptions of space in mind here: *Tim.* 52A-B; Sext. Emp. *Adv. Math.* 10.3-4 (= *SVF* 2.505 = LS 49B); cf. Ps.-Galen *Qual. incorp.* 2, 19-23 Giusta (= *SVF* 2.502 = LS 49E). The second alternative, the boundary of what contains the occupant, is of course Arist.'s own favoured definition of place: *Phys.* 4.4, 212a20; *Cael.* 4.3, 310b7-12. For recent treatments of Arist.'s concept of place, see Algra 1995, chs 4-5; Morison 2002.

130. [14,20-2] The claim that the animate body's differences are due to the soul is just an instance of Alex.'s more general position that the differences between bodies are due to their forms (7,9-11); even the contribution of matter is through the forms of the underlying bodies which consititute it (7,24-8,13).

131. [14,23-4] Arist. *Phys.* 4.2, 209b28-9; 4.4, 212a14-18, which both describe a vessel as a 'transportable place' (*topos metaphorêtos*).

132. [14,24-15,1] In a number of passages, Alex. discusses the suggestion that the soul might be in the body as an extrinsic characteristic or 'accident' (*sumbebêkos*) inheres in a subject and emphatically rejects it, devoting many arguments against it: *Mant.* 119,21-122,15 (esp. 120,9-17); *Quaest.* 1.8 passim, esp. 17,34-18,4 and 19,9-15; 1.17 passim, but esp. 30,14-22; 1.26 passim; also ap. Simpl. *in Cael.* 279,5-14; *in Phys.* 270,26-31.

Despite these repeated denials, Moraux nonetheless takes Alexander to be committed to the view that the soul is just an accident of the body and so posterior to it, in contradiction with both himself and with Aristotle (1942, xix, 42-4; cf. 9-10, 33, 45, 170, 177, 178). But this is obviously an uncharitable and willful distortion of what Alexander actually says and should be resisted. Moraux confuses being supervenient with being causally or metaphysically posterior (see 49 n. 2 and 43-4, respectively). But neither in fact follows: on the contrary, Alex. himself consistently argues against such inferences, as in the present passage. See also nn. 90 and 92 on 10,17-19 and 10,24-6.

Alex.'s first argument here connects Arist.'s classification of the soul as a substance or *ousia*, in so far as it is a form (DA 2.1, 412a19-20, cf. a6-9), with the claim in *Categ.* 5 that individual substances alone can receive contraries (4a10-b19). By taking this characteristic of concrete substances to apply to substantial forms, Alex. accepts the consequence that the soul can itself be the subject of extrinsic characteristics (*Mant.* 121,25-7). One might worry whether this has the further consequence that the soul can itself undergo change, and not just extrinsically, against his express position (21,22-24,17).

133. [15,2-5] *Mant.* 119,31-120,17; cf. *Quaest.* 1.17, 29,31-30,22. For something to inhere in a subject, the subject must already be some specific thing (*tode ti*) on its own. But without its form, the matter of a substance is not the specific thing it becomes in the substance, except potentially. Hence, substantial forms must be in matter in some way other than inhering in a subject in the way an extrinsic characteristic does. For translations of Alex.'s other texts and reactions to them by later commentators, see Sorabji 2004a, 3.122-5; on Alex.'s view, see Ellis 1994; Sharples 1999. Alex. may be reacting here to earlier Peripatetics, such as Boethus, who held that form does not belong in the category of substance, but in non-substantial ones, such as quality or quantity (ap. Simpl. *in Categ.* 78,17-20), and so would inhere in matter.

Alex.'s denial that the soul inheres in the body in the way an extrinsic characteristic does has a further consequence relevant to current debates regarding Arist.'s psychology. If the soul were an extrinsic characteristic of the body, which the body could equally have or lack, then the same body could exist as such either before or after its serving as the matter of the living thing. In denying that the soul is extrinsic to the body, Alex. insists that the organic body gets its nature as an organic body from the soul (15,3-5; *Mant.* 120,13-17; *Quaest.* 1.17, 30,14-22): it is a living body *essentially* and so only comes to be such together with the soul when the living thing first comes into being. When the body ceases to function and to be alive, it remains a body only in name or 'homonymously' (Arist. *DA* 2.1, 412b20-3; *Meteor.* 4.12, 389b31-390b2; *PA* 1.1, 640b34-641a5, a17-21; *GA* 1.19, 726b22-4; 2.1, 734b23-7, 735a7-8; *Pol.* 1.2, 1253a20-5; Alex. *in Meteor.* 223,25-224,11 and 225,3-33). It is precisely this feature of the body/soul relation on Arist.'s theory that J. L. Ackrill finds problematic in his landmark article (1972/73), since it is in tension with the conception of matter as something that underlies all change, including substantial change, and so pre-exists the substance's coming to be and survives its passing away.

134. [15,7] 13,22; see n. 101 on 11,17-18 above (on honeyed water).

135. [15,5-9] Alex. is operating from within his own framework here rather than a rival one, like the Stoics'. According to the Stoics, the soul is blended with the body (see n. 101 on 11,17-18); but on their conception of blending, the ingredients and their natures are preserved, not destroyed, and they are indeed all bodies. What Alex. describes here the Stoics would call 'fusion' (*sunkhusis*; see n. 102 on 11,18-20). So Alex.'s first objection is not effective against the Stoic view of blending when taken on its own terms. The second objection would be effective, on the other hand, provided Alex. can establish independently that the soul is not a body (see n. 125 on 14,12-14).

136. [15,9-10] Alex. takes up again the ship's pilot, something he mentioned briefly before at 14,4-5 and will return to below at 20,26-21,21. In his view, this suggestion is ambiguous between two cases: (1) where the pilot is understood as a form of the body and so falls under (*h*); and (2) where the pilot is taken to be in a place or vessel, and so falls under (*e*). He can thus divide the question: if the suggestion is just a variant of (*h*), the conclusion he is arguing for in the present section, it does not require rebuttal (though he still rejects the analogy: see 20,26-21,21); but if not, it encounters objections. As AD note (128-9), Alex. puts the possibility of the first construal in the optative (15,11), whereas he puts the second in the indicative (15,14), to indicate he regards it as the real target.

In discussing whether the soul is in the body in this way, Plotinus (4.3.21.5-21; cf. 4.3.17.21-31; also 1.1.3.21-3) seems to be responding directly to details in the present passage (see n. 128 on 14,18 above). Against Alex., some commentators even take Arist. to endorse a version of the pilot view: Simplicius *in DA* 96,3-10 and Philoponus *in DA* 224,28-37. (Themistius leaves it unresolved: *in DA* 43,30-5.)

Porphyry embraces the metaphor and develops it at length, even allowing for a succession of pilots at *ad Gaurum* 10.4-6, 47.5-48.8 Kalbfleisch (on which James Wilberding has valuable notes, with further references, in his translation in this series, 2011).

137. [15,10-13] On construal (1), what is important about the pilot is simply that he guides and regulates the behavior of the ship as a ship, and not that there is some actual *homunculus* deliberating and operating the ship – in effect, construal (2). Although it may sound odd to modern ears, a very Aristotelian way of framing this option is in terms of art, just as Arist. sometimes speaks of the art itself as the efficient cause, rather than the artisan (e.g., *Phys.* 2.3, 195a3-8; *GA* 1.22, 730b19-23; 2.1, 734b36-735a4). For a full elaboration and defence of the comparison with art, see Menn 2002, esp. 95-6, 99, 114-17, 136-9.

For the inseparability of dispositions, see *Mixt.* 9, 222,31-2. For the inseparability of forms, see *DA* 17,9-15; cf. *Mixt.* 13, 228,17-20. Alex. may use both terms here for dialectical reasons: the same objection will serve regardless of the specific version this view assumes, since his point will hold more generally for anything which is not a substance in its own right, but belongs to a substance: cf. Arist. *Categ.* 5, 2b5-6; *Phys.* 1.4, 188a6, a12-13; *GC* 1.10, 327b22 (cf. 1.3, 317b10-11, b31-3; 1.5, 320b24-5).

138. [15,14-15] If the point of the comparison is that the soul is like a person, then it too will be embodied. Note the stronger use of *meta* + genitive here: if it merely meant 'conjoined with', as it often does (e.g., 4,12-17; 5,20), Alex. could not validly infer that the soul *is* a body. If an opponent accepts this consequence, Alex. again needs independent grounds to argue that the soul is not a body (see n. 125 on 14,12-14). But his purpose here may be more tactical and *ad hominem*: such a result would be an embarrassment to substance dualists and shows that they cannot afford to take the comparison too literally.

139. [15,15-17] 21,10-11; for the general assumption, see n. 104 on 12,2-3. This second objection is the more important one: even if one does not take the pilot to be literally embodied, the comparison still implies that the soul has a specific location in the body, like the pilot at the helm; otherwise, it becomes difficult to distinguish this option from (1).

On the responsiveness (*sumpatheia*) of the whole body, see 100,1-8; for the claim that different parts of the body have an accompanying awareness (*sunaisthêsis*) of each other, see *in Metaph.* 363,21-4 (cf. 321,24-30). Contrast this with the absence of such awareness between different persons or even unconnected senses (*in Sens.* 163,11-14; cf. 36,12-17). A difficulty for the present argument is that Alex. elsewhere accepts Arist.'s view that parts of the body like hair, bones, and nails are not sensitive at all: 74,29-75,2 and 97,4-6.

Both notions have Stoic antecedents, though. According to the Stoics, the responsiveness of one part of the body is a feature of unified bodies generally, and so of the universe as a whole, which is itself a unified animate body (Sext. Emp. *Adv. Math.* 9.78-80 = *SVF* 2.1013; cf. Alex. *Mixt.* 3, 216,14-17 = *SVF* 2.473; 10, 223,7-9.30-3 = *SVF* 2.441; 12, 227,8-9 = *SVF* 2.475; Cleom. *Motu circ.* 2.164.4 Ziegler (cf. 1.8.16-21) = *SVF* 2.534). Cleanthes even appeals to the responsiveness of body and soul to each other as an obvious datum, from which he can argue that the soul must be corporeal (Nemes. *Nat. hom.* 2, 21.6-9 Morani = *SVF* 1.518 = LS 45C). The awareness of the entire body plays an important role in their theory of *oikeiôsis* as well: the Stoic Hierocles (first century CE) explains that the initial awareness an animal has of its own body is due to the blending of the soul with the entire body (Hierocles *Elem. eth.* 4.39-53 Long = LS 53B 5-9). Superficially, this might seem to conflict with Chrysippus' assertion that although a pain occurs in the foot, the awareness that accompanies it is in the chest (that is, the heart), where the governing part is located, and in no other part (Galen *PHP* 3.7.4, 212.14-18 De Lacy = *SVF* 2.900; cf. 3.1.25, 172.20-6 De Lacy, = *SVF* 2.886). But Hierocles also describes the awareness as reaching the governing part (4.49-53). These positions can be reconciled by distinguishing between act and object: although the animal has awareness *of* all the parts of the body, the *act* of awareness itself occurs solely *in* the governing part. Galen also employs the notion of the responsiveness of different parts of the body extensively. For the general notion, see Siegel 1968, 360-72; and specifically with regard to vision and referred pain, Siegel 1970, 121-2 and 187-9, respectively.

140. [15,17-22] 21,11-13; the suggestion that the soul on this view does not move the animal naturally, but by force, is more fully elaborated at 21,13-16. Arist. uses a similar *reductio* at *DA* 1.3, 406b2-5 (cf. a22-7), regarding the possibility of the soul's displacement, and draws the further conclusion that dead animals might be reanimated. On such a view, the body would not be essentially animated, but would be the sort of thing it is independently of the presence of soul.

141. [15,22-6] The precise nature of this objection is unclear, since an infinite regress hardly seems inevitable. In fact, it seems perfectly coherent to go back just one step: if, e.g., one took the soul to be like the 'governing part' (*hêgêmonikon*) of the soul in Stoicism, which is a body and could be regarded as like a pilot. Alex.'s objection cannot rule such a case out, but at most urges a polemical correction, namely, that such an explanation is inadequate unless it appeals to the form of this body (in which case the theory has changed its stripes in favour of Aristotelianism).

142. [15,28-9] *Mant.* 116,15-18; cf. 6,21-9; 10,7-10.

143. [16,1-2] 9,11-14; 10,4-14; 10,28-11,7; 12,6-8.

144. [16,2] *Quaest.* 2.10, 55,9. In this treatise, when Alex. speaks of 'enmattered' forms, he typically has in mind the forms of natural objects that serve as the object of thought (83,19; 87,5; 88,4.11; 89,13; 90,2; cf. *Mant.* 108,3.21; *Quaest.* 1.25, 39,28). In the present passage, though, he is likely to be alluding to Arist.'s characterisation of states of the soul as 'enmattered accounts' (*enhuloi logoi*) in the programmatic argument in *DA* 1.1 (403a3-25 at a25), which Alex. has just reprised at 12,7-13,8.

145. [16,2-4] 10,26-11,5.

146. [16,5] 6,29-7,3.

147. [16,5-6] Although Arist. occasionally uses the term 'culmination' (*teleiotês*) – see n. 64 on 6,30 above – he does not use it in this context. What Alex. is saying here is rather that where he himself uses 'culmination', Arist. typically uses the term 'completion' or *entelekheia*. 'Completion' occurs prominently in Arist.'s general definition of the soul in *DA* 2.1, and again in 2.5, to distinguish two levels of realisation: the first, where something actually has the power to perform certain activities, and the second, where it is actually performing them: 2.1, 412a22-7 (cf. 412b27-413a1); 2.5, 417a21-b16. On Alex.'s use of these terms, see Todd 1974, 213-14.

148. [16,7] Arist. *DA* 2.1, 412a27-8.

149. [16,8-10] 9,15-26; *Mant.* 103,11-20; Arist. *DA* 2.1, 412a22-7 (cf. 412b27-413a1). As AD rightly note (130), Arist. does not use either of the terms 'disposition' (*hexis*) or 'power' (*dunamis*) for the first completion in *DA* 2.1. But he explicitly uses 'power' in this way at *DA* 2.5, 417a21-b16 and *Phys.* 8.4, 255a30-b3. AD also suggest that 'disposition' can be derived from 417a32, but the parallel is not exact. For further discussion of the Aristotelian antecedents, see BD 246-7.

150. [16,10] Arist. *DA* 2.1, 412b5-6.

151. [16,11-12] *Quaest.* 2.8, 54,9-10; also see n. 93 on 11,1 above.

152. [16,12-13] The traditional rendering of the *dunamei* as 'potentially' wrongly suggests that Arist. is concerned with the form of bodies which are not yet alive, but could become so. But Arist. is quite clear that he is describing the body that *actually* has the soul (412b25-6) and so has life by or in virtue of its power.

153. [16,12-18] *Mant.* 104,11-17; *Quaest.* 2.8, passim. Life, according to Arist., is 'said in many ways', and amounts to performing the various activities Alex. lists here, which distinguish the animate from the inanimate (*DA* 2.2, 413a21-5). But something that possesses these abilities is alive even when it is not exercising them: being inactive or asleep is different from being dead or inanimate, since in the former case one actually has the power to function in these ways and not in the latter (cf. 2.1, 412a23-6, 412b28-413a1). Hence, the soul is defined in terms of the powers to perform these various activities, rather than the activities themselves (2.2, 413b11-13).

154. [16,18] This answers the first question on the agenda Alex. sets out at the very beginning of the treatise. See n. 3 on 1, 2-4.

155. [16,18-17,1] For the order of three main types of souls, see Arist. *DA* 2.3, esp. 414b20-415a12.

156. [17,1-8] 28,14-29,1; 30,17-20; cf. 40,4-10; *Quaest.* 1.11a and b, passim. As Arist. himself emphasises, the definition given in *DA* 2.1 is only 'an account of the most general sort' (*koinotatos logos*, 412a5-6; cf. b4-5) and merely a 'sketch in outline' (413a9-10). The underlying problem, according to Arist., is that different types of souls form an ordered sequence (2.3, 414b20-415a1) and such sequences lack a genus prior to the individual species: *Metaph.* 3.3, 999a6-11; *EN* 1.6, 1096a17-23; *EE* 1.8, 1218a1-15; *Polit.* 3.1, 1275a35-b2; cf. *DA* 1.1, 402b5-9. For a detailed examination of the Aristotelian view, see Lloyd 1962.

Moraux attacks Alex.'s interpretation in the present treatise as tendentious and erroneous (1942, 50-62). He misrepresents Alex., though, as *denying* the possibility of a general definition and of an essence common to all souls. But Alex. begins the present passage by *affirming* that there is an essence of the soul (16,18) and goes on to discuss its general characterisation. What he denies is that such a general definition can be fully perspicuous (*saphê*, 17,1) or reveal the nature of each type of soul intelligbly (*gnôrimôs*, 30,18). For a detailed critique of Moraux, see AD 131-2.

157. [17,9] Alex. devotes the arguments of the two previous sections (11,14-13,8 and 13,9-17,8) to demonstrating that the soul is a form. But the view has been explicitly in play since at least 9,11-12 and in preparation since 2,25. Cf. also 31,20-5.

158. [17,9-10] Showing that each of these three characteristics belongs to form sets the agenda for what immediately follows: after a brief argument to show that the soul is inseparable (17,11-15), Alex. argues at greater length that the soul is non-bodily (17,15-20,26; see also *Mant.* 113,25-118,4), before turning to the claim that the soul cannot undergo change on its own (21,22-24,17).

159. [17,11-12] 4,8-9; 5,21; *Mant.* 117,20-1; Arist. *Metaph.* 8.1, 1042a29-31. The key to Alex.'s argument here is his general view that bodies are composites and so already have the matter and form needed to exist on their own (4,22-5; 5,21). Since the soul is a form, it cannot exist on its own (5,22-6,2), but needs the body of a living thing as its matter. Alex. passes over in silence here the awkward fact that on his own view the *body* of a living thing, in so far as it is organic, also cannot exist on its own as such apart from the soul or the living thing (15,3-5 and n. 133 on 15,2-5; *Mant.* 120,13-17; *Quaest.* 1.17, 30,14-22), despite the fact that it is a body and so something that, according to 17,11-12, should be able to exist on its own.

160. **[17,12-15]** Although the form in question is a substance, it cannot exist on its own as the composite body can. Instead it is always the form of something and so cannot exist apart from the matter of the composite. This requirement, in Alex.'s view, is common to both Arist. and the Stoic doctrine of principles or *arkhai*, and is to be contrasted with the Platonic view of form (*in Metaph.* 178,15-19 = *SVF* 2.306; I am grateful to Ian Flora for this reference). But it is also to be contrasted with the Stoics' view of the relation between the soul and the body. As BD rightly point out (249), the soul *can* be separated from the body on their view, precisely because it *is* a body: see esp. Nemes. *Nat. Hom.* 2, 22.3-6 Morani (= *SVF* 2.790 = LS 45D). This is what allows them to endorse some form of *post mortem* existence: Arius Didymus fr. 39, *Dox. Gr.* 471.18-24 = Euseb. *PE* 15.20.6, 2.385.9-12 = *SVF* 2.809 = LS 53W; Aetius 4.7.3, *Dox. Gr.* 393.1-7= *SVF* 2.810.

Regarding the inseparability of limits, Arist. recounts a Platonic argument in *Metaph.* 3.5, which claims that limits are prior to bodies because they can exist without bodies, and not *vice versa* (1002a4-8), contrary to what Alex. claims here. But in commenting on the passage, Alex. reaffirms that limits cannot exist without bodies in reality, but only in thought (*in Metaph.* 229,31-230,1).

161. **[17,15]** If every body is something that can exist on its own (17,10-11), and the soul cannot (17,14-15), then the soul cannot be a body.

162. **[17,15-17]** Repunctuating with von Arnim (= *SVF* 2.394), as AD rightly urge (133), although I would offer a different justification. With Bruns' punctuation, the sentence reads: 'The form cannot be a body along the lines of those who claim, like the Stoics, that *everything*, whether it is matter or from matter, is a body.' This not only misrepresents the Stoic view, which includes non-bodily items, but also makes no sense of the argument that follows in the text. What Alex. offers is an *ad hominem* argument against a Stoicising view: if every *body* is either matter or composed from matter (as the Stoics claim), and a form is neither, then no form is a body. The minor premise of this argument presupposes von Arnim's construal and so confirms his punctuation, against Bruns.

The premise that every body is either matter or composed from matter is very likely an inference on Alex.'s part from the fact that one of the two Stoic principles from which the entire cosmos is composed is matter, and is itself a body, unlike Aristotelian prime matter (D.L. 7.134 = *SVF* 2.299 = LS 44B 3, retaining the MSS reading – see LS 1.274, 2.266; cf. Alex. *Mixt.* 225,3-5 = *SVF* 2.310). The Stoics, moreover, explicitly maintain that qualities (*poiotētes*) are bodies (Plut. *Comm. Not.* 50, 1085E-1086A = *SVF* 2.380; Galen *Nat. Fac.* 2.4, 168.12-14 Helmreich = *SVF* 2.410; Simpl. *in Categ.* 217,32-3 = *SVF* 2.389 = LS 28L 1; 271,20-2 = *SVF* 2.383 = LS 28K; cf. Alex. *Mant.* 124,9-10 = *SVF* 2.432). This is surely due to their view that qualities like prudence, temperance, and even life are causes and only bodies can be causes: see esp. Stob. 1.138.14-22 Wachsmuth (= *SVF* 1.89 = LS 55A 1-3). If Stoic qualities are to be analysed as 'breath in a certain state' (*pneuma pôs ekhon*), as Alex. takes them to be (*in Top.* 360,10 = *SVF* 2.379), then they will in general be composed of matter.

Alex. offers a battery of arguments against the view that qualities are bodies at *Mant.* 122,16-125,4; similar arguments can be found earlier in Plut. *Comm. Not.* 50, 1085E-1086B; Alcinous *Didask.* 11, passim; Ps.-Galen *Qual. incorp.*, passim. On this tradition, see Kupreeva 2003, esp. 304-15.

163. **[17,17-18]** The dialectic is complex. Alex.'s overall aim is to examine different ways of construing his own theoretical terms. But the option he is considering and arguing against here is one that incorporates distinctively Stoic views (n. b. *Stoikôn paides*, Ps.-Galen *Qual. incorp.* 1, 10-11 Giusta = *SVF* 2.377).

Matter, for example, has to be understood in the Stoic sense, since on Alex.'s own view only prime matter is qualityless (on prime matter as qualityless, see references in n. 26 on 3,28-4,4). Forms, on the other hand, can be viewed as a kind of qualification, even on an Aristotelian view, at least in a broad sense (see n. 105 on 12,3-4); in fact, Boethus had claimed that forms belong in non-substantial categories, such as quality or quantity (ap. Simpl. *in Categ.* 78,17-20); see n. 133 on 15,2-5 above.

164. [17,18] Notice Alex.'s reinsertion of form here. One might worry that this undercuts the effectiveness of Alex.'s argument, since an opponent might well reject a further analysis into matter and form. But Alex.'s objection has a more general force. His rationale is presumably that if the second half of the original disjunction, 'being composed of matter', is to differ from the first, then it cannot mean being composed solely of matter, but must involve some other element, whether we regard this as an Aristotelian form or a Stoic quality or something else. The question is then whether this additional element can also be a body.

165. [17,18-19] It is difficult to make good sense of this objection. It is cavilling if Alex. is claiming that the second form, as a proper part of a whole, is both the same and not the same as the whole (as Kupreeva 2003, 317 appears to take it), since then it would merely equivocate on 'same'. For there is nothing absurd in (*a*) the second form's being a proper part of the composite (namely, the first form) and so *not identical* with it, while also (*b*) being the *same kind* of thing, namely, a form. Alex. might instead be making a more general complaint about the view's overall strategy: if parts of composites such as forms are themselves composites, then there is no longer a clear difference in their respective theoretical roles. But so construed, the objection is obviously not fatal and, worse, it can be raised against Alex.'s own conception of matter: apart from prime matter, all other matter on his view is a body (3,23-5) and so a compound of form and matter; but he does not think that this prevents such a compound from serving as matter in some even more complex body.

166. [18,1] The MSS read *to eidos* here, which would have the form somehow possessing a form not different from itself. Bruns reasonably emends it to *to einai* (as followed here), referring to 88,12-13. But the relevant parallel is surely 18,6.

167. [18,2-7] Alex. has presented his opponents with a series of dilemmas: either forms are bodies or they are not; if they are bodies, then either they are matter or they are composed of matter and form; if they are composed of matter and form, then either the component form is also composed in this way, leading to an infinite regress, or at some point such composition comes to a stop. But if composition comes to a stop, the last form will neither be matter nor composed of matter. Why, then, should it still be considered a *body*? Alex. now completes his *reductio* with a final dilemma. If the last form is a body because it 'has its being with matter' and so cannot exist apart from it, something analogous would have to be said of the last matter, namely, that it 'has its being with form'; but this would conflict with the Stoic definition of matter as 'qualityless' (18,2-3; see the penultimate paragraph of n. 26 on 3,28-4,4). But if, on the other hand, matter is qualityless because form is not part of its nature, though inseparable from it, then something analogous will have to be said of the last form too: even though the last form is inseparable from the corresponding matter, it is definitionally independent of it and *so not a body*, against the initial hypothesis. Alex.'s opponents have thus been forced to accept Alex.'s own position (5,18-6,2 and 6,6-20; though compare *Mant.* 115,12-14). For related criticisms, see Plut. *Comm. Not.* 50, 1085E-1086B. For a somewhat different analysis of the argument, see Kupreeva 2003, 317-20.

168. [18,7-10] The objection appears to be that any change in quality, on this view, would entail a change in mass or quantity, since if the new form is itself embodied, it will add some matter of its own to the composite: cf. *Mant.* 116,1-2.13-15. But this does not follow, since the former quality or form which is lost in the change would be embodied too and might well depart with its own matter in tow; so no general conclusions can be drawn about a net gain or loss.

169. **[18,10-14]** Von Arnim includes the present passage as a fragment of Chrysippus (*SVF* 2.793), but we have no other testimony for the argument as a whole, much less an explicit attribution to Chrysippus. The mereological principle offered as the first premise (18,10-13; cf. 14,6) is attributed almost verbatim to the Stoic Apollodorus (second-century BCE), down to the examples (fr. 7, *SVF* vol. 3, p. 260.12-14 = Stob. 1.19.5, 167.9-12 Wachsmuth = Arius Didymus fr. 24, *Dox. Gr.* 460.14-16). But the second premise of Alexander's argument can hardly be attributed to the Stoics; it again seems to be part of the Stoicising interpretation of form which Alex. has been critiquing. See nn. 162 and 163 on 17,15-17 and 17,17-18 respectively.

Since the argument is valid – if, at any rate, one adds the reasonable assumption that an animal is a body – and Alex. accepts both this tacit premise and the second premise above (cf. 6,2-4), he should reject the first premise, that the parts of a body are necessarily a body. But while he clearly rejects any unqualified, general version of this principle as involving a fallacy of division (6,6-12), he does in fact employ a version of it himself earlier on (see n. 122 on 14,5-7 above). For a different account of this argument, see Kupreeva 2003, 321-4.

170. **[18,17]** As AD point out (136), this claim does not hold for *organic* parts of living bodies, at least not without further qualification, since a dead or detached hand is no longer a hand except in name or 'homonymously' (*DA* 2.1, 412b20-5; *Meteor.* 4.12, 389b31-390b2; *PA* 1.1, 640b34-641a5, a17-21; *GA* 1.19, 726b22-4; 2.1, 734b23-7, 735a7-8; *Pol.* 1.2, 1253a20-5). Alex.'s main point will still hold, though, for the compositional matter that makes up the organs and the body. What matters most to the kind of division here is its being something quantifiable, as Alex. makes clear in his discussion of the different meanings of 'part' in commenting on *Metaph.* 5.25: when animal is divided 'as something with size' (*hôs poson*), it is divided into head, trunk, and so on (*in Metaph.* 424,17-19).

171. **[18,17-21]** Arist. *Metaph.* 5.25, 1023b19-22.

172. **[18,21-3]** For the contrast, cf. 12,3-4; 14,6-7.

173. **[18,24]** 18,15-17.

174. **[18,25-7]** 6,24-7,8, together with 5,19-6,6.

175. **[18,25-19,1]** Von Arnim also includes this passage as a fragment of Chrysippus (*SVF* 2.793), but again we do not have any other testimony or attribution for the argument as such. The first premise is obviously related to the first premise of the previous argument above, which is Stoic in origin (n. 169 on 18,10-14). But they are nonetheless distinct: the earlier principle concerns mereological division, whereas this one concerns composition, and neither entails the other. It is reasonable to think that Stoics like Apollodorus would have endorsed both, but we have no independent evidence. We have no direct evidence that the Stoics endorsed the second premise of the present argument either, although again it is reasonable, in so far as they speak of the sense organs (*aisthêtêria*) as 'parts of the soul': Aet. 4.21.2-3, *Dox. Gr.* 410.30-411.13 = *SVF* 2.836 = LS 53H 3; D.L. 7.110 (cf. 157) = *SVF* 2.828. For discussion of this argument, see Kupreeva 2003, 324.

176. **[19,1-3]** Alex. does not challenge the validity of the argument, but its soundness. In his view, the second premise is never true, no matter how we understand the word 'sense' (*aisthêsis*): taken in one way, a sense is a part of the soul, but so understood, it is not a body; taken in the other way, it is a body, but not a part of the soul. Alex. relies here on the Aristotelian view that the sense (*aisthêsis*), taken as a part of the soul, is distinct from the perceptual organ (*aisthêtêrion*), which is a body – in fact, a sense is the form of a perceptual organ: *DA* 2.12, 424a24-8; cf. 2.1, 412b17-25. If 'sense' is used more loosely to speak of the organs, it no longer designates a power of the soul.

177. [19,3-5] Alex. seems to be relying on the position he attributes to the Stoics above (17,15-17), that every body is either matter or composed from matter, with the added assumption that the second alternative, if it is to go beyond the first, must include the addition of some quality or form. See n. 164 on 17,18.

178. [19,6-9] See 26,15-17 (= *SVF* 2.786), with accompanying note; also *Mant.* 115,6-12 (= *SVF* 2.785). According to the Stoics, not all breath or *pneuma* is animate, since it pervades the entire cosmos and underlies all things (*Mixt.* 3, 216,14-17). It constitutes soul only with the addition of a certain quality: Galen *Hipp. Epid.* 17b.251.1-6 Kühn = *SVF* 2.715; *QAM* 4, 45.5-8 Müller = *SVF* 2.787; D.L. 7.157 = *SVF* 1.135; Sext. Emp. *Pyrr. Hyp.* 2.70 = *SVF* 1.484. More specifically, the breath turns into soul at parturition, when it is chilled by the outside air: Plut. *Stoic. Rep.* 41, 1052F, 1053C-D = *SVF* 2.806; Hierocles *Elem. eth.* 1.5-27 Long; Plot. $4.7.8^3$.1-3 = *SVF* 2.804. For a comparison of Stoic embryology with Alex.'s own views, preserved at Simpl. *in Phys.* 311.1-19, see Kupreeva 2003, 327-30.

179. [19,9-16] On Alex.'s view, the soul is a substance and therefore has a distinct essence of its own, which breath as such does not share, since on the Stoic account it is not always alive. It cannot become a soul, therefore, unless there is a change in its essence, in which case it would no longer be breath, but would have transformed into soul. Compare this, as Alex. suggests, with other natural bodies: when air becomes fire, it is no longer air. The alternative is to view soul merely as an extrinsic characteristic of the underlying breath, which it can equally have or lack (19,14-16). Alex. is in effect pressing the Stoics on their holism here. To the extent that there is a single substance, underlying all things, which is merely differentiated in different places and times by different qualities, the soul and all the phenomena associated with it would simply be phases or states of breath and living things simply parts of the whole cosmos. These are consequences the Stoics might well embrace, but which Alex. takes to be highly counterintuitive and to undermine the soul's status as a substance. On this argument, see also Kupreeva 2003, 325-30.

180. [19,18-20] Another dialectical possibility, which Alex. countenances only briefly, is that there are two types of breath, one inanimate and the other animate, so that there is a sense in which soul is breath, namely, it is a kind or species of breath. But a genus, Alex. points out, cannot exist as such on its own. The Stoics' own corporealism in any case precludes this option: for them breath is not an abstract kind or type, under which they fall, but a concrete body which pervades the cosmos and exists on its own. They cannot abandon such a core claim without completely changing their theory.

181. [19,21] Alex. again seems to be critically examining a hybrid Aristotelian view, as in the previous section (see nn. 162 and 163 on 17,15-17 and 17,17-18), which accepts the letter of the doctrine that the soul is the form of the body, but construes form in a corporealist way. This might seem otiose, in so far as the target here is only a special case of the one in the previous section: any of the general objections there against taking form to be a body should apply *a fortiori* to any specific kind of body, such as fire or air. But the discussion here is not redundant, as Alex. limits himself for the most part to objections which are peculiar to this variant. The different theories may also have different provenances. The view discussed in the immediately preceding section concerns Stoic influences, and while the mention of fire and air here might also suggest the Stoic notion of breath or *pneuma* – or even Presocratic views, as Ian Flora has suggested to me, such as Democritus (Arist. *DA* 1.2, 405a8-13 = DK 68 A 101) or Heraclitus (Arist. *DA* 1.2, 405a25-6 = DK 22 A 15) or still earlier Anaximenes (Aet. 1.3.4, *Dox. Gr.* 278.12-15 = DK 13 B 2) – the appeal to *form* specifically suggests a hybrid view which may be Peripatetic in origin. We do not have evidence of anyone advancing precisely this claim. But given the way Alex. reports the view (*hoi legontes*, 19,21), the commitment to form (19,21; 20,23) and the details Alex. later adds (19,26-8), it seems unlikely that it is a purely dialectical construction. AD tentatively suggest (137-8) that there are resemblances to the view reported at *Mant.* 112,11-16, which they (following Moraux 1967, on the basis of *Mant.* 110,4) take to derive from Aristotle of Mytilene (second century CE), who may have been one of Alex.'s own teachers: according to this view, fire or something fire-like supervenes on the blend of ingredients in each body and serves as an instrument of the divine understanding; but as AD note, this passage does not explicitly say that this fire is the *soul* or *form* of the body. Opsomer and Sharples 2000, moreover, have argued that the *Mant.* passage refers not to this later Aristotle from Mytilene, but to the original one, from Stagira. For a discussion of corporealist views held by later Peripatetics, see Kupreeva 2003, 331-5.

182. **[19,24]** 2,25-7,8, esp. 2,25-3,15.

183. **[19,24-8]** Alex.'s inference does not turn on the notion of a culmination by itself, since he considers the form of even a simple body, such as the heaviness of earth, to be a culmination (9,17-19), and it does not result from some mixture. The consequence Alex. draws in the text above follows instead from the fact that the soul is the form and culmination of a particular kind of complex body. Therefore, if the soul is fire or air or the like, as claimed, then an apparently elemental body would instead be the form and culmination of this complex body and would come into being, as the soul does, when the complex body is created from a mixture of ingredients.

184. **[19,31-6]** On Alex.'s view, although the ingredients in a blend are not present in it in actuality, they do not perish entirely, but persist in potentiality (*Mixt.* 14, 230,17-19). In particular, their qualities and matter are unified into those of the blend and are present in actuality: 230,26-34; 231,1-4.10-12. Consequently, fire would have to exhibit the qualities of its ingredients on this view, which it manifestly does not. For more on Alex's view, esp. as compared with the Stoic view, see n. 102 on 11,18-20. On Alex.'s use of *mixis* and *krasis* in the *DA*, see n. 76 on 8,16.

185. **[19,36-20,1]** Alex.'s criticism suggests that the proponents of this view did not offer any explanation for why fire or air held a privileged position. Instead, he takes the view simply as a claim about one of the elements and in effect sets up an indifference argument as a challenge: unless there is a relevant difference between elements, either they each should be forms of the remaining elements or, if they cannot all be, then none should be a form of the others. Alex. presupposes that they are all elements or principles and so on a par with one another.

186. **[20,4]** For this use of *mêden mallon*, where we would use 'no less', see also *Fat.* 175,17 and 176,10 (Sharples 1975, 251 n.8; 1983, 134 and 242 ad loc.).

187. **[20,1-6]** Alex. continues to examine how, on the present proposal, the body that is supposed to be the soul is related to the other bodies as their form. Just above he questioned whether it could be a mixture of them, since it would then have to exhibit their powers as well, which it does not (19,31-6). Here he considers

the body in question simply as a body produced out of the others: if a new body is produced, then only its powers should remain in the animal (20,1-4). But the powers of the other bodies are in evidence no less than fire's, so it cannot be a new body produced from them (20,4-5). Alex. concludes that it cannot be a form and so not a soul either (20,6), but it is not clear whether this is *ad hominem* – viz. *on this proposal*, it would not be a form or a soul – or whether it conflicts with the nature of forms on anyone's view, including Alex.'s. The *ad hominem* reading seems more plausible, since Alex. does not elsewhere seem committed to the view that the form's powers are the *sole* powers in the animal (20,1.5).

188. [20,6-7] Alex. sets up a dilemma here, each of whose horns he regards as leading to a *reductio*: either (*a*) the body which constitutes the soul on this view does not completely pervade the body of the living thing or (*b*) it does and so requires that one body passes through another body. The first option is one he has already objected to before (see n. 104 on 12,2-3; also *Mant.* 104,21-2) and he offers no further argument here. The second is the target of the remainder of this paragraph (20,7-19).

189. [20,8-19] 14,8-9; *Mant.* 139,29-141,28; *Quaest.* 2.12, passim; ap. Simpl. *in Phys.* 530,9-30. Alex. regards the view that one body can extend or pass through another body to be one of the most distinctive and unacceptable consequences of the Stoic theory of blending, which applies not only to the relation of the soul to the body, but of divine reason to the matter of the entire cosmos. Although Alex. often characterises their view simply by reference to this consequence, he recognises elsewhere that they did not themselves fully appreciate the importance of this commitment to their overall theory (*Mixt.* 12, 227,1-10). See Todd 1976, 73-88, who argues even more strongly that this phrase is not used by the Stoics at all (74), despite von Arnim's use of it as a subtitle for a section on their theory of blending (*SVF* vol. 2, p. 151, l. 7); in Todd's view, it is 'an independent notion imposed on them rather than an actual doctrine of theirs' (228). But it may not be an unjust inference for all that: see the apparently direct reports of Stoic views at *Mixt.* 3, 216,14-17; 4, 217,27-9.33-6; 218,1-2; 6, 219,9-10. For a quick overview of the Stoic theory of blending, see LS 1.292-4 and M.J. White 2003, 146-9. For more detailed studies, see Todd 1976, 21-88; Sorabji 1988, ch. 6; E. Lewis 1988.

Alex.'s reference at the end of this paragraph (20,18-19) to a more lengthy treatment is almost certainly to his *de Mixtione*, which is largely devoted to opposing the Stoic theory of blending and above all the notion that body passes through body. Some of the criticisms he makes here can also be found there: it is counterintuitive that what is full can receive something further (5, 218,17-19.21-4); and if two bodies can pass through each other, nothing prevents indefinitely many from doing so or even the largest body (6, 220,13-16; cf. *Mant.* 140,22-5; 141,9-22). The second criticism appears to be Academic in origin, tracing back perhaps even to Arcesilaus himself (third century BCE): see Plut. *Comm. Not.* 37, 1077E-1078E, with the reference to Arcesilaus at 1078C. Alex. is no doubt also influenced by Arist.'s frequent references to the absurdity of two bodies being in the same place, which he takes an opposing position he is criticising to be committed to: e.g., *DA* 1.5, 409b2-4; 2.7, 418b13-18; *Phys.* 4.1, 209a4-7; (cf. 4.5, 412b25); 4.6, 213b5-12; 4.7, 214b6; *Cael.* 3.6, 305a19-20; *GC* 1.5, 321a5-10. Todd even goes so far as to suggest (1976, 85) that Alex. *DA* 20,6-19 says little more than what Alex. would have said in commenting on Arist.'s argument at *DA* 1.5, 409b2-4.

190. [20,19-22] Although Alex. had earlier spoken of an *analogia* or proportion between the forms of living things, namely, souls and the forms of the simpler bodies that make up the bodies of living things (10,15 and 11,12), here he seems to have in mind just the analogy or parallel between souls and other forms in general, including the simplest ones, those of the elements, such as the lightness of air or the heaviness of earth (5,11-15; 9,14-26; 22,7-12.18-21), and even the forms of artefacts (3,2-15), against AD 140. Alex.'s objection appears to be that in none of these other cases is the form plausibly a body like fire or air, or itself a mixture of other bodies. If so, then Alex. is arguing that an advantage of his naturalistic approach is its *uniformity* in the treatment of form: souls are just one kind of form among many, differing only in the specific powers and activities they concern; their general characteristics, in contrast, are shared by all forms, from those of the simplest natural bodies to the products of art.

191. [20,22-6] Alex. aims to drive a wedge between his opponents' corporealism and their commitment to the notion of form: it would be *more* consistent for them to hold that the soul was the form of fire, rather than the elemental body itself. Alex. of course would not accept this modification either, because of the immense complexity which on his view distinguishes the form and matter of living things from that of simple bodies (8,25-11,13).

AD (140) take Alex.'s use of the optative here to indicate that his opponents did not explicitly identify the soul as form with a simple body. But 19,21-3 leaves little doubt that they spoke of soul both as a form and as a body like fire or air; so the only thing left open to question is whether they regarded fire and air as *simple* bodies, which they might not have, if they regarded them as mixtures (19,26-9).

192. [20,26-30] 14,4-5; 15,9-26; 79,19-20. Although Alex. has already discussed and rejected the notion that the soul might be like the pilot of a ship, he mentions it here as another way of developing the corporealist suggestion that the soul, though a form of the body, is itself a body; it is possible that this was part of his opponents' actual view. Of the two options he considered earlier, this corresponds to the second (15,13-26), which regards the pilot as a concrete individual, which can exist separately from the ship, rather than a completion or *entelekheia* (15,10-13). Alex.'s first objection is simply that the pilot, so construed, is not necessary for the ship's being a ship and so cannot be its culmination and form.

193. [21,4-5] 16,7; Arist. *DA* 2.1, 412a27-8.

194. [21,1-10] The second argument considers a more nuanced conception of the pilot: on this view, he *is* part of the completion of the ship, in so far as he is necessary to its activity as a ship. But Alex.'s objection turns on the same point as before: since the pilot is separable, the ship remains a ship without the pilot; hence the pilot contributes at most to the *second* completion of the ship, not the first. But there cannot similarly be an animal without a soul; and it would be an animal only in name or homonymously: see n. 133 on 15,2-5. The soul is thus a first, and not a second, completion and so is like the shape of the ship rather than its pilot.

195. [21,10-11] Alex.'s line of reasoning here and in what immediately follows is very similar to his earlier treatment: see 15,15-17. The duplication of arguments suggests a certain amount of editorial indecision. But it is difficult to decide where the arguments are better suited. Systematically, they fit quite naturally in his earlier discussion of how the soul is in a body and whether it constitutes a distinct sense of 'being in'; but the arguments also look as though they were inserted there as an afterthought. In the present passage, in contrast, there seems to be little systematic reason to raise the pilot analogy again. But this suggests that the reason it was included here is that the actual proponents the theory now under discussion invoked it.

For the general assumption that the soul pervades the entire body, see n. 104 on 12,2-3; also 20,6-7; *Mant.* 104,21-2.

196. [21,11-13] 15,17-21. AD detect in the use of the aorist participle *khôristhe-isan* here a suggestion of a possible resurrection after death (142), similar to the parallel passage in Arist. (*DA* 1.3, 406b4-5). But nothing in the present passage requires that the separation in question occur at death.

197. [21,13-16] This objection is only hinted at in the earlier version, when Alex. states that the soul, so construed, would move the body 'by force' (*biai*, 15,17). The final remark, that on this conception the soul would be a body (21,16), marks Alex.'s disagreement, but it hardly constitutes an independent objection, since his opponents here are openly corporealist. AD 143 suggest that it is meant instead to be an embarrassment to Platonic or, more likely, Platonising opponents, possibly even the Peripatetic Xenarchus (first century BCE; cf. Aet. 4.3.10, *Dox. Gr.* 388.16-20), whom they conjecture are the source of the comparison with the pilot (140-2). But this is just speculation; there is nothing in the text that requires the hypothesis. Moreover, if Platonists were the target, Alex.'s objection at 21,11-13 and 15,17-21 would completely misfire, since from their perspective the possibility of the soul's exiting and entering the body, which Alex. rejects out of hand as absurd, would be regarded as a positive *advantage* of the theory, not a flaw.

On forced motion and bodily resistance, cf. 79,10-11 below. BD also cite a highly relevant fragment of Alex. quoted by Simplicius (*in Cael.* 379,18-23), which similarly argues, regarding the soul of the heavens, that 'if a soul is moved by force, it must be endowed with a body, since it is impossible for a body to be moved by something else without contact and resistance, which are bodily features' (20-1). For further discussion, see the rest of their comment at 254.

198. [21,16-21] Depending on how we construe the phrase 'in this way' (*houtôs*, 21,17) in the first clause, Alex. might be challenging either the view that (*a*) the soul is like a pilot, or (*b*) the soul is one of the simple elements, or more broadly still the view that (*c*) the soul is a body. Since this last claim is the one most recently mentioned in context (21,16), and none of Alex.'s criticisms here turn on any specific form this view might take, (*c*) is the most reasonable option: Alex. is raising a general worry about how the soul and the body can constitute a single, unified living thing on corporealist theories, especially given how unlike each other they are in nature (*tas phuseis diapheronta*, 20,19). Although Arist. himself does not press this issue against his predecessors in this exact form, he does complain that they give little thought to what enables soul and body to interact together (*DA* 1.3, 407b13-26), in contrast with his own theory, where there is no more question of why they are one than there is with wax and its shape (2.1, 412b6-9). This question about the soul-body relation is quite distinct from his worry about what makes the soul one or the body one, and whether either gives the other its unity (1.5, 411b6-19). Still less does it make an explicit statement about the mortality of the soul (*pace* AD 141, 143).

199. [21,22] Alex. has been arguing at some length that the soul is the form of the living body (see n. 157 on 17,9 above) and so as a consequence has three characteristics (17,9-10): it is (*i*) inseparable from the body (17,11-15), though (*ii*) non-bodily (17,15-20,26), and (*iii*) incapable of undergoing change on its own. In the present section, he argues for the last of these three characteristics.

AD, we should note, reject the section break in MS V (preserved above and by Bruns), taking 21,22-4 instead as the end of the previous section, where it is supposed to make a merely apparent concession, intended ironically, to Platonic opponents (143). But 21,22-4 can be much more straightforwardly understood as exploring the consequences of Alex.'s own position, since he himself holds that the soul is inseparable. The sentence that immediately follows at 21,24-5, moreover, draws out the consequences of 21,22-4 and links them directly to the subject of the present section, and hence should not be separated from it.

200. [21,24] Alex. addresses the question of individual survival much more directly than Arist., who generally speaks only about whether the soul or its parts are 'separable' (*khôristos*) from the body (*DA* 2.1, 413a4-7; 2.2, 413b27-8). Alex. refrains from denying personal immortality here outright, because on his view the human understanding (*nous*) lacks a dedicated organ (84,10-24) and so is *not* a form of part of the body; whether this enables it to survive death is left unsettled here. In this respect, Alex. follows Arist., who frequently hedges his claims with the suggestion that the understanding *might* prove an exception: *DA* 1.1, 403a8-12; 1.4, 408b18-25; 2.2, 413b24-7; *GA* 2.3, 736b21-9; cf. *DA* 2.3, 414b18-19, 415a11-12. In the end, Arist. distinguishes two understandings, one of which he declares to be immortal and eternal, while the other is perishable (*DA* 3.5, 430a22-5); but he does not make fully explicit what this implies for individual humans. In contrast, when Alex. draws a similar distinction at *DA* 90,11-91,6, he states explicitly that the immortal intellect only comes to be in us 'from outside' and is not itself a part or disposition of our soul (90,23-91,4); what he calls the material understanding perishes along with the rest of the human soul (90,13-16). The question of human mortality is arguably present in the background throughout Alex.'s treatise, hinted at already at the very beginning: see n. 8 on 1,4-2,4.

201. [21,25-6] cf. 78.24-5. Alex. is now beginning to pick up the sequence of Arist. *DA* again with 1.3, 405b31-406a4. (His last extensive comment on Arist.'s *DA* was at 12,9-13,8, concerning Arist. *DA* 1.1, 403a3-25.) For the argument that not everything responsible for a change need undergo change itself, and that some of them in fact must not be changed, see Arist. *Phys.* 8.5, 256b13-24, 258b4-9 (cf. 258a1-4); *GC* 1.6, 323a13-14; 1.7, 324a30-4; cf. *Metaph.* 12.7, 1072a25.

202. [21,29-22,2] For the claim that what produces change by contact must itself undergo change, see Arist. *Phys.* 3.2, 202a5-9; *GC* 1.6, 322b32-323a12; cf. Alex. *Quaest.* 2.23, 74,5-6. The four types of change Alex. mentions correspond exactly to Arist.'s list of the four basic types of motion produced by something else (*hup'allou phora*), in terms of which all other spatial motions can be accounted for: *Phys.* 7.2, 243a16-244a4; for the details of the reduction, see Wardy 1990, 127-9. Alex. gives a slightly enlarged list of bodily motion through contact, as BD note (255), at *Mant.* 122,22-123,3. AD question (144) whether Alex. might be diverging from Arist., who considers all types of change and not just spatial change at *DA* 1.3, 406a13-14. But there is little divergence, if any: Arist. himself immediately goes on to argue that all of these changes occur in space and so therefore would imply that the soul is in place itself (406a16-22).

203. [22,5-6] That is, they are all inseparable on their own from the things that have them. The soul was argued to be a form at length above: see n. 157 on 17,9.

204. [22,5-12] Arist. argues prominently and at length that the soul does not move the body or produce change of any sort by undergoing it itself in *DA* 1.3 and portions of 1.4 (408a4-b18, cf. 408b30-409a30) – in fact, he regards it as 'an impossibility' (406a2), a position that sets him apart from materialists like Democritus and dualists like Plato (see Menn 2002). But Arist. nowhere offers the general reason that Alex. does here, that this is a characteristic of powers and dispositions generally, and hence of forms like the soul. The closest Arist. comes is to say that arts or *tekhnai* produce their effects without being modified themselves (*GC* 1.7, 324a34-b6), and they are powers and principles of change (*Metaph.* 9.2, 1046b2-4) and dispositions (*EN* 6.4, 1140a6-10, a20-1). Similarly, he regards the endpoint of every change, 'whether a form, a modification, or a place', not to be subject to change itself, since it is what the change is a change *to* (*Phys.* 5.1, 224b11-13, cf. 4-7). Ian Flora has also suggested to me that the point about separability is implicit in the contrast between natural and mathematical sciences at *Metaph.* 6.1, 1026a13-16; 11.7, 1064a31-3. (Arist.'s point in *DA* 2.5, that certain activities of the soul like perception are not modifications is quite different, since it does not turn on the proper subject of change, as here, but on the type of change undergone.)

Alex.'s point in the present passage is fundamentally metaphysical. To claim that the soul undergoes change is in effect to make a category mistake: it is the wrong sort of thing to undergo change. For something to undergo change, it must be a subject in its own right and hence separable; anything which is inseparable cannot undergo change even if it is responsible for that change. Alex.'s point is thus much more general: it applies not just to the soul, but to all forms, powers, and dispositions, animate or inanimate, all the way down to the elemental level. Here as elsewhere, Alex. underscores the continuity of psychology with the rest of natural philosophy by invoking the example of earth's heaviness or fire's lightness: see nn. 40 and 190 on 5,5-6 (cf. n. 43 on 5,11-15) and 20,19-22 respectively, as well as 22,18-20 and 23,29-24,1 below.

Alex. is reported elsewhere (Simpl. *in Phys.* 964,9-23 and *Parisinus suppl. gr.* 643, 101r, as reported in Rashed [1997] 2007, 146-7) to have argued that the soul cannot undergo change because it is without parts and according to Arist., nothing without parts can undergo change (*Phys.* 6.4, 234b10-20; 8.6, 258b24-6). *Prima facie*, this appears to conflict with the present treatise, which assumes that the soul *has* parts: see 18,26-19,3 above and more generally under *meros tês psukhês* and *morion tês psukhês* under *psukhê* in the Greek-English Index. But these are not parts in the sense at issue in the argument. Arist. himself, it should be noted, does not apply the argument from *Phys.* 6.4 to the soul, although he does employ a version of it against Xenocrates' theory of the soul at *DA* 1.4, 409a1-3.

205. [22,13-15] Arist. distinguishes between something's undergoing change on its own or intrinsically (*kath' hauto*) and undergoing it in virtue of something else (*kath' heteron*) or extrinsically (*kata sumbebêkos*) and argues that the soul is changed only extrinsically: *DA* 1.3, 406a4-22; 1.4, 408a30-4; for the general distinction, cf. *Phys.* 8.4, 254b7-12. Although he rarely uses the expression, he does speak of 'joint change' in the relevant sense at *Top.* 2.7, 113a29-30.

Alex. continues to be more general and metaphysical in his reasoning than Arist. (see n. 204 on 22,5-12 above): not just the soul, but *every* form undergoes change jointly (*sunkineisthai*) with its body, precisely because the form is inseparable from it; it is necessarily a part of the changing thing. But talk of joint change amounts to little more than saying that the *composite* of matter and form undergoes change, since Alex. clearly does not take it to imply that the form itself undergoes change intrinsically.

206. [22,15-23] Alex. again stresses that what holds for the soul holds equally for inanimate things too, right down to the elemental level (22,18-20; see n. 204 on 22,5-12 above). In fact, he is careful to point out that this is so not merely with regard to changes that animate and inanimate objects share, such as forced motion due to external causes, but also with respect to changes that belong to living things precisely in virtue of being alive. The distinction between different types of motion unsurprisingly has Aristotelian antecedents: see *Phys.* 8.4, 254b15-20 (although note the still finer distinctions at 8.6, 259b1-14).

207. [22,24-23,6] Alex. need not have a specific opponent in mind here, since Arist. represents his predecessors as generally committed to this view, from

Democritus to Plato, though in so far as it specifically targets the claim that change is part of the *essence* of the soul (22,27), he may have Plato especially in mind, who uses this to argue for the soul's immortality (*Phdr.* 245C-E). AD 144-5 rightly note that Alex. uses the first Stoic inference schema (*modus ponens*) as part of a *reductio ad absurdum*, since he will reject both alternatives at 23,6ff.

208. [22,23-7] Arist. takes the natures of things to be principles that govern *both* the initiation of a type of change *and* its cessation (*Phys.* 2.1, 192b8-23), and so generally takes change and rest to be correlative and on a par with one another (5.6, 229b23-8). But if the soul can equally be at rest or changing, then change does not belong to the essence of the soul: cf. Alex. *in Top.* 321,12-16. On the meaning of *apoklêrôsis*, see Sharples 2004, 75 n. 236.

It is worth noting how much simpler and more direct Alex.'s criticism of Plato's position is, using familiar Aristotelian doctrines, than Arist.'s own fairly baroque argument about change and the essence of the soul at *DA* 1.3, 406b11-15 (discussed by Alex. in *Quaest.* 2.2, 46,22-47,27 and most recently in Shields 2007, esp. 152-4).

209. [23,2-3] On several occasions, Arist. characterises coming to know and understand as coming to rest, in so far as arriving at a conclusion involves the dissolution of uncertainty or disturbance: *DA* 1.3, 407a32-4, but also esp. *Phys.* 7.3, 247b10-248a6 (cf. 5.1, 224b13).

210. [23,4-5] All of the conditions Alex. describes here are bodily ones (see also n. 114 on 12,20-1 above), even though acc. to Arist. understanding is the activity that seems to belong 'most properly' to the soul (*DA* 1.1, 403a8). But Alex.'s description here of bodily disturbance in the young and old, the drunk and the sober, as an impediment to knowledge itself draws on Arist. *Phys.* 7.3, 247b13-248b6; cf. *DA* 1.4, 408b22-5.

211. [23,6-24] This passage is an exposition and development of Arist. *DA* 1.4, 408a34-b18, which J. Barnes memorably described as the 'celebrated Rylean passage' ([1971/72] 1979, 33-4) because it seems to share Ryle's basic insight (1949, 16-24) that to treat the mind as a subject of mental states in its own right, rather than the person, is a category mistake. Even if Shields' reservations (2007, 156-60) about attributing Rylean concerns to Arist. were justified, it is plain that Alex. understands Arist. in this way: the soul cannot be the subject of such activities precisely because it is a power of the body and inseparable from it (22,2-6; cf. 23,24-8); to think it can be a subject, rather than the composite to which it belongs, is just a category mistake. Thus the 'Rylean' reading of Arist. goes back at least to Alex.

212. [23,9-11] Notice that Alex.'s claim here is completely general and un-hedged: *every* activity that is characteristic of living things as such belongs to the living thing and not the soul. The soul is *a fortiori* not the subject of *cognitive* activities either, such as perception or even understanding, which on Alex.'s view lacks a dedicated bodily organ. The soul, as a form, is the power in virtue of which living things engage in those activities, not what engages in them itself. Cf. 23,26-8 below.

213. [23,11-13] Because of the absence of manifest, external changes in the body, we are misled in certain cases into thinking that a psychological activity could only belong to the soul – cases, presumably, like those listed at 23,15-17. Alex. seems to suggest that if we had better knowledge of the inner workings of living bodies, we would be less tempted to make this mistake. Arist. is actually more explicit here, saying that the heart undergoes a specific change in anger and fear and that thinking (*dianoeisthai*) 'either involves something of this sort or perhaps something else', whether it involves movement or alteration or some other kind of change (408b8-12). But Arist. likewise complains, in a quite different context, of the faulty conclusions others draw from ignorance of the internal workings of the body: *Respir.* 3, 471b23-9.

214. [23,15-21] Alex. expands Arist.'s list of activities, by bringing together other examples mentioned in the larger context of Arist.'s remarks (408b5-30).

215. [23,20] The *aulos* is a double reed instrument much like a shawm or oboe (West 1992, 81-5), especially classical and baroque oboes, which lack the elaborate mechanical system of keys we are familiar with today.

216. [23,18-22] Alex. modifies Arist.'s point slightly here. Arist. appeals to artistic activities simply as clear, parallel cases where we take the human being to be the agent, and so concludes we should treat psychological activities similarly. Alex., in contrast, draws an analogy directly between art and the soul: both are powers and dispositions, but neither is itself the agent. (Arist. regards art as responsible for change, but not subject to change itself: for references, see n. 204 above on 22,5-12.)

Alex. also modifies Arist.'s examples: he keeps weaving, but replaces house-building with oboe-playing and wrestling. It may be to avoid making the point turn on incidental features of these arts, by offering a broader range of examples: unlike weaving, neither oboe-playing nor wrestling results in a concrete product, and wrestling further does not use any other instrument than a person's own body.

217. [23,26-8] This sort of instrumentalism is emblematic of Platonic views (*Alc. I* 129C-130A), and can be found in first- and second-century CE authors such as Plutarch (*de Pyth. Or.* 21, 404B; *Sept. Sap.* 21, 163D) or Galen (*UP* 1.2, 1.13-2.2 Helmreich; see Moraux 1984, 778). But even Arist.'s own characterisation of the soul as the form of a body that is *organikon* (*DA* 2.1, 412a28-b6) could be taken as implying that the living body is itself a tool or organ which the soul *uses*, and in fact Arist. does occasionally say that the soul uses the body as an art or an artisan uses tools: *DA* 1.3, 407b25-7; *EE* 7.9, 1241b17-19, b22; *Protr.* B59 Düring = Iambl. *Protr.* 41.15-20 Pistelli. For a reading of Arist. along these lines, see Menn 2002; also Plut. *Quaest. Plat.* 8.2, 1006D. (Thanks to Jan Opsomer for the Plutarch references.)

Alex. rejects this understanding of *organikon*, however (see n. 93 on 11,1 above) and here he explicitly argues against an instrumentalist characterisation of the soul's relation to the body. The soul is comparable to an art on his view, but neither art nor the soul can be said to *use* any instrument or organ. To think that they can is a category mistake: only a separable substance, like an artisan, can use tools, and the soul is *not* like an artisan in this regard (against *EE* 7.9, 1241b17-19, b22).

218. [23,29-24,4] Alex.'s characterisation of the soul as a power, form, and completion, which comes from a mixture and blend has not been stated this succinctly before, but it was developed at length at 7,21-11,13; see esp. 8,10-13.15-17; 9,11-12; 10,17-19.24-6; and 11,11-13, with their corresponding notes. The example here of an elemental form, heaviness, again underscores the quite general nature of this claim: see n. 204 on 22,5-12 above.

219. [24,5] Alex. maintains the Aristotelian view that the governing part is located in the heart and its immediately surrounding region (39,21-2), a thesis he defends at length in the final section of this treatise (94,7-100,17), as a kind of appendix (see n. 3 on 1,2-4). In speaking of a 'leading' or 'governing' part (*to hêgêmonikon*) of the soul Alex. is adopting the popular terminology of the Stoics, who prominently use it for the central faculty of the soul, which they also locate in the heart: see 98,24-5 below (= *SVF* 2.839); also Aet. 4.21, *Dox. Gr.* 410.25-9 = *SVF* 2.836; D.L. 7.159 = *SVF* 2.837. Mansfeld (1990, 3109 n. 222) takes the adoption of Stoic terminology to be significant and an indication that the question has already become a scholastic *topos*. On the Stoic conception generally, see Annas 1992, 61-70. This consensus appears to have held until Diogenes of Babylon; on later, heterodox Stoics, see Mansfeld 1990, 3095 n. 145.

The Peripatetic Strato (d. 269 BCE), who succeeded Theophrastus as third head of the Lyceum, is reported to have had views about the *hêgemonikon*: fr. 111 Wehrli = Plut. *de Lib. et Aegr.* 4, 53.13-54.9 Ziegler-Pohlenz at 53.22-3. But the terminology in our sources is more likely due to the influence of Stoic terminology, than evidence of independent Peripatetic terminology.

The core notion of a central, governing part of the soul, though, is undeniably in Arist. himself. He says that in deliberation, we reason until we can trace back the beginning of action 'to the governing part of oneself' (*hautou eis to hêgoumenon*), and it is this that makes decisions (*prohairoumenon, EN* 3.3, 1113a5-7). He locates this principle, moreover, in the heart (or in bloodless animals in what is analogous to the heart), which he speaks of as the 'chief' or 'controlling' part of the animal (*kurion, kuriôtatê, Iuv.* 3, 469a4-10 (cf. 4, 469b11-13); cf. *Metaph.* 7.10, 1035b25-7) which operates from a 'governing location' (*arkhontos khôra, Iuv.* 4, 469a33-4). He identifies it more specifically as the source of each of the animal's principal activities. It is, as we have seen, the source of the animal's movements: *PA* 2.1, 647a24-6; 3.3, 665a10-15; 3.4, 666b14-15; *MA* 7, 701b24-32; 9, 702b12-28. But it also serves as the source of perception and life more broadly: *Somn.* 2, 455b34-456a6; *Iuv.* 1, 467b18-27; 2, 468a20-3; 3, 469a5-20; 4, 469a23-34, b1-6; *PA* 2.1, 647a24-31; 2.10, 656a27-9; 3.3, 665a10-15; 3.4, 666a11-18, a34-5; 4.5, 678b1-4; *MA* 11, 703b23-4; cf. *Metaph.* 5.1, 1013a4-6; 7.10, 1035b25-7. Even thinking (*dianoeisthai*) depends crucially on internal parts such as the heart: cf. *DA* 1.4, 408b7-12, cf. b25-7. For a discussion of the heart's central role and its compatibility with Arist.'s mature hylomorphism, see Tracy 1983; in fact, BD 257 explicitly compare Tracy's compatibilist position with Alexander's.

220. [24,5-6] In describing the part of the body where the governing part is located as animate '*prôtôs* and in its own right', Alex. may be claiming (*a*) that it is the *first* part of the animal's embryo to be formed and so to be animate on its own, in contrast with a parent's seed, which is animate only in so far as it is part of another living thing; or (*b*) that the source and principle of the activities of animate things as such is itself *pre-eminently* animate; or (*c*) both of these to some extent; and depending on which is in play, Alex.'s explanation (*gar*) of where the governing part is located will differ accordingly. In favor of (*a*) is Arist.'s frequent claim that the heart is the first part of the animal to be formed and so neither prior nor posterior to the new living being: *Iuv.* 3, 468b28-31; *PA* 3.4, 666a10-11, 20-2; *GA* 2.5, 741b15-16; 2.6, 742b1-2; *Metaph.* 7.10, 1035b25-7. Alex. appeals to this temporal priority below as evidence that the source and principle of nutritive activities is located in the heart (95,6-8). But (*b*) cannot be ruled out either or hence (*c*). Alex. uses *prôtôs* in the sense of 'pre-eminently' at 89,2 in explicating one of his central tenets about explanation and the sorts of things that can serve as grounds or principles (88,26-89,8). Arist. himself remarks that 'the essence and defining character' of a living being in some sense resides *in* 'the first, governing [part]', such as the heart or brain (*Metaph.* 7.10, 1035b25-7).

221. [24,6-7] It is not the governing part of the soul, but a part of the living body, the heart, in which the governing part resides, that uses the 'organic' or instrumental parts (*tois organikois meresin*). As Alex. goes on to make clear, this includes sense organs as well (24,9-11). For Arist., this phrase primarily designates the limbs, which are constituted out of bones, muscle, and flesh (*PA* 2.2, 647b22-5) and are contrasted with the senses as heterogeneous structures that subserve motion and other activities (*PA* 2.1, 647a2-5, a24-30; cf. *HA* 1.6, 491a26). See also *DA* 3.9, 432b25-6; *IA*, 3, 705a20; 4, 705b22; *EN* 3.1, 1110a15-18; cf. *GA* 2.6, 742a28-b6. Alex.'s use of this phrase elsewhere (*Eth. Prob.* 9, 129,22; 12, 133,12) is in keeping with Arist.'s usage.

222. [24,7-9] Alexander's comparison with art relies on the original sense of *organon* as a tool. Like art, nature uses tools as well, except that in this case the tools or organs are an intrinsic and congenital part of the natural substance: see Arist. *GA* 2.1, 735a2-4; cf. 1.22, 730b11-24.

223. [24,13] Alex. has argued at length in this treatise that the soul is a form (see n. 157 on 17,9). But he may have in mind the specific point here that forms are responsible for the differences between things with regard to causal powers (7,9-11.13).

224. [24,11-15] The passage closely follows Arist. *DA* 2.4, 415b8-28, which likewise characterises the soul as what is responsible for the living body as its origin and prinicple (b8) in three of the ways that something can be responsible (b8-12): as the essence of the living thing (b12-15); as that for the sake of which the body functions (b15-21); and as the source from which change originates (b21-8).

225. [24,16-17] 28,8, with corresponding note; see also *in Metaph.* 121,16-18; 160,17-18; 349,14-16; *Quaest.* 3.12, 102,31-103,1; cf. *in Top.* 171,21-172,3. Although this statement might sound like an affirmation of universal teleology, it contains an important restriction. For an Aristotelian, not everything in the natural world is 'produced by nature': this subset contrasts not only with things produced by art (and so by reason), but also with those which arise by chance or spontaneously (Arist. *Phys.* 2.5, 196b17-33). Arist. even denies that eclipses have a final cause (*Metaph.* 8.4, 1044b8-12). For Alex.'s discussion of these distinctions, see esp. *Fat.* 4, 167,16-168,24.

226. [24,18-20] Alex., of course, is one of the people who subscribe to (1): on supervenience, see n. 229 on 25,2.

The claim that the soul is a *harmonia*, (2), first appears in Plato's *Phaedo*, when the Pythagorean Simmias suggests that the soul is a blending or tempering of elemental forces in the body, similar to the *harmonia* or tuning of a lyre, in opposition to one of Socrates' arguments for immortality (85E-86C). The English cognate 'harmony' is to a certain extent a false friend, since a *harmonia* is not in the first instance something heard – in fact, Alex. explicitly denies that it is below at 25,24-26,2 – but rather the harmonious fitting together of the parts of the instrument that can produce such sounds, its being tuned in a certain way. The Greek term originally applied even more broadly still, to any artefact that has been well joined or fitted together, as when Alex. speaks of the *harmonia* of a bench or a temple below at 25,16-19; and it was common to think of *harmonia* in natural cases too, such as health of the body (see 25,4-7 below). Given the range of cases, it would be awkward to use the English 'tuning', even though more correct, especially since we speak of non-musical items as being 'in harmony' or 'harmoniously constructed'. For more on the meaning and etymology of the term, see my 1997, 219-22, esp. nn. 21, 23, and 27 for references.

Both Plato and Arist. reject the view that the soul is a *harmonia*, although not for entirely the same reasons (Plato *Phaedo* 91E-95A; Arist. frr. 37-47 Rose[3]; *DA* 1.4, 407b27-408a28). One of their shared concerns is mental causation. In Arist.'s view, a *harmonia* cannot be responsible for change, whereas he regards this as one of the most characteristic features of the soul (*DA* 1.4, 407b34-408a5). The concern with causation is obviously important for Alex. too, who identifies the soul as a power and disposition (see, e.g., 22,5-6 above). The blend of the underlying body

determines which powers supervene on it (see 10,17-19 and 24-6, with corresponding notes), but these powers are not thereby identical with or reducible to the
blend. They are genuinely new causal powers that emerge (see n. 40 on 5,5-6). On
the *harmonia* theory and the subsequent debate over it, including Alex. and Galen,
see my 1997.

227. **[24,22-3]** On emergence, see n. 40 on 5,5-6 above; also 25,7-9; 26,27-9; cf.
24,28.

228. **[24,23-25,2]** Alex.'s observation about drugs is meant to be simple and
direct: in their case, he thinks, it is just evident that the power of the mixture is
one thing and the proportion of ingredients quite another; if the soul is a power,
then it too will differ from any underlying proportion or harmony. BD offer an
alternative reading (258), based on differences in the power of different dosages,
which nonetheless maintain the same proportion of ingredients, but this is unnecessary and much more complex than what the text actually says.

Medical drugs are used as a star example by the Stoics and above all by Galen,
who often speaks of the powers of the 'four-fold drug' (*tetrapharmakos*), which is
not the same as any of its ingredients. For the Stoics: Alex. *Mixt.* 3, 216,4; 4, 218,6
(= *SVF* 2.473); Philo *Confus. Ling.* 187, 2.265.11 Cohn-Wendland (= *SVF* 2.472).
For Galen, see *Hipp. Elem.* 1.455 K; *MM* 10.281, 352, 353, 882, 883 K; *MMG* 11.84,
138 K; *SMT* 12.328 K; *Comp. Med. Loc.* 12.602, 604, 610 K; *Comp. Med. Gen.* 13,
593 K; *HNH* 15.18 K; *adv. Lyc.* 18a.240, 241 K; *Hipp. Fract.* 18b.598 K, in addition
to those cited by Moraux (1984, 740, n. 214), namely, *Hipp. Elem.* 1.452 K; *HNH*
15.32 K; *CAM* 1.242 K; *CC*, CMG Suppl., 2.3.2. For discussion, see my 1997, 350.

229. **[25,2]** The verb rendered here as 'supervenes', *epigignesthai*, is not an
innovation on Alex.'s part: Arist. himself speaks of form 'supervening' on matter at
Metaph. 7.10, 1035a5, a12; 7.11, 1036a31-2, b6. For Alex.'s conception of supervenience, see n. 40 on 5,5-6, n. 92 on 10,24-6, and n. 90 on 10,17-19; cf. 24,18-20 above
and 25,7-9 and 26,22 below.

230. **[25,2-4]** In articulating his position, Alex. may be distinguishing himself
carefully from his predecessors. Galen reports (*QAM* 4, 44.12-20 Müller, translation available in Sorabji 2004a, 1.187, §6a, text 13) that Andronicus of Rhodes, the
first century BCE Aristotelian and editor of Aristotle's works, 'says that the soul
is either a blend or a power that follows on the blend' (*êtoi krasin einai phasin ê
dunamin hepomenên têi krasei*, 18-19) and criticises Andronicus for adding 'power'
rather than just identifying the soul with the blend, as Galen does himself
(44.20-45.3; cf. 37.5-23). Alex.'s position can be seen as directly opposing Galen's
criticism, by defending the second of Andronicus' two alternatives (against the
harmonising interpretation of Michael of Ephesus, *in Parva nat.* 135,22-30). For
discussion on these differences, with further references, see my 1997, 351-2; on
Andronicus' views about the soul, see Moraux 1973, 132-4.

231. **[25,4-7]** Arist. *DA* 1.4, 408a1-5 (though, as Ian Flora points out, Alex.
thankfully sidesteps Arist.'s pun here). Arist. takes health to be constituted by a
blend and balance (*en krasei kai summetriai*) of hot and cold: see esp. *Phys.* 7.3,
246b3-10; cf. also *Top.* 6.2, 139b21; 6.6, 145b7-11; *PA* 3.12, 673b26. At *Metaph.* 7.7,
1032b7 and 18-20 he suggests that it consists in an equable state (*homalotês*). On
Arist.'s view within the context of the Greek medical and philosophical tradition,
see Tracy 1969, esp. 157-63.

232. **[25,2-9]** Alex.'s strategy here is that of a non-reductive materialist: although the soul *supervenes on* materials composed in a certain way, it is not
identical with these materials, their composition, or the materials composed in this
way (in the way that health might be); rather, the soul is a distinctive new power

that emerges from this combination. The ontological distinction between what supervenes on certain base conditions and the base conditions themselves is what allows him to block the inference at 24,18-20: the soul depends on matter, but it is not identical with matter. The firmness of this distinction allows Alex. a more eirenic and nuanced view. In his overall account, the *harmonia* of the body – its being composed, mixed, and blended in appropriate ways – has a legitimate and important role, as part of the base conditions on which the soul supervenes. It is just not what the soul itself is.

Arist.'s response to the *harmonia* theory, in contrast, is more aggressive and less forthright. He issues a broadside attack on the theory, disambiguating *harmonia* into two senses and then categorically rejecting each possibility with a barrage of rhetorical questions, suggesting the hopelessness of any such identification (*DA* 1.4, 408a10-13 and a13-26, respectively). But he is silent on whether there is anything like a *harmonia* in his theory, leaving him open to the suspicion that he protests too much.

In what follows, Alex. accepts Arist.'s disambiguation, but as part of a positive exploration of what a *harmonia* is (25,9-23), not as a criticism. He reserves his objections solely for the view that the soul is *identical* with a *harmonia* (26,3-13), something he thinks other theorists come closer to than Arist. does himself (26,13-30).

233. [25,9-15] Arist. *DA* 1.4, 408a5-9. Alex. follows Arist.'s characterisation of the two senses of *harmonia* almost verbatim, adding only (*i*) that the elements of a harmony in the first sense cannot have anything of the same sort in between them (which, as BD 259 note, is how Arist. characterises things *in succession* at *Phys.* 5.3, 226b34-227a6 and 6.1, 231a23); and (*ii*) the examples of specific ratios. But unlike Arist., who proceeds directly to criticisms of the *harmonia* theory (see n. 232 on 25,2-9 above), Alex. just incorporates these two senses of the term into his explanation of what *harmonia* might mean, without using them as a key part of his objection.

234. [25,15-23] Regardless of whether we take a *harmonia* to be the concrete compounding or composition (*sunthesis*) of elements or instead the abstract proportion (*logos*) by which they are composed, the *harmonia* will be distinct from the compound that arises from (*to ginomenon ek*) this mixture. This ontological distinction does not directly challenge the *harmonia* theory, which never claimed that the *harmonia* is the living being as a whole. It is simply part of Alex.'s exploration of what precisely a *harmonia* is.

235. [25,23-26,3] The *harmonia* of a musical instrument, like a cithera or lyre, is not any melody or sound it produces, but the underlying tuning which is responsible for those sounds. In this respect, the English 'harmony' is a false friend: see n. 226 above on 24,18-20.

236. [26,3-7] The initial objection is that having a certain proportion is not sufficient for being in harmony, since a given proportion is a harmony in some cases and not others. Musical cases of harmony are clearly regarded as paradigmatic here. What is unclear is whether the objection contests the earlier, non-musical cases of *harmonia* given at 25,4-7 and 16-19, or only certain cases like honeyed wine (on which, cf. 13,22 and 15,7). Rejecting all non-musical cases would involve a narrowing of the original semantic range of *harmonia*: see n. 226 on 24,18-20 above. But the objection does not require such a narrowing: the argument would work just as well so long as there are certain cases, like honeyed wine, where there is a proportion, but a native Greek speaker would not use the word *harmonia*. Alex. does not seem to share this linguistic intuition in any case: in what preceded, he does not mark off wider uses of *harmonia* as infelicitous.

237. [26,7-13] Despite Alex.'s use here of the explanatory particle 'for' (*gar*), this objection is logically independent of the preceding one. For even if a given proportion always constituted a harmony, wherever it occurred, it would not follow that *all* proportions are harmonies, the point contested here. The suggestion that only determinate proportions are harmonies would be familiar from Greek music theory, where all the tones of musical scales are taken to be ratios of whole numbers, and so determinate and 'commensurable': Arist. extends this requirement to colours at *Sens.* 3, 439b25-440a3, suggesting that the generally recognised ones might all be due to determinate ratios of white and black, analogous to musical tones, while indeterminate ones are infinite in number; see also Alex. *in Sens.* 54,4-55,8. If this is right, then the soul could not be identified with a proportion *tout court*, but only with certain commensurable proportions.

Alex. immediately goes on to develop two further objections, which effectively constitute a dilemma, depending on whether or not one accepts the claim that every harmony is a determinate proportion:

If (1) harmonies are restricted to determinate proportions, there is a further disanalogy with musical harmonies (26,9-11): the mixture of elemental powers in living things is not limited to a single, fully determinate proportion, but can *vary within a certain range*; hence the soul cannot be identified with any one of the proportions in this range rather than another.

This variation has greater significance than Alex. acknowledges here, since it should pose an analogous difficulty for his own theory: though not identical with the harmony and proportion of elemental powers mixed in the body, the soul nevertheless supervenes on them (see n. 229 on 25,2 above); therefore, if living things can tolerate a certain amount of variation in these proportions, the soul must supervene *on a range of* proportions, rather than just one. This is not so much an inconsistency for Alex. as a complication, since supervenience allows for the possibility of multiple realisation: a higher-order power can supervene on a number of different underlying bases, each of which is sufficient individually for the presence of the higher-order power. By acknowledging that the underlying powers in the living beings can vary in strength – as any Aristotelian surely must, given the ordinary changes in heat and cold that occur in digestion and the movement of limbs (a point well made by AD, 149) – Alex. is committed to *multiple realisation*: if the soul is to supervene on the underlying mixture, it must be the case that *any* proportion within certain limits (*heôs tinos*, 26,10) will suffice for the soul and its powers. But only within these limits: if the underlying conditions range beyond them, they will no longer support the existence of a soul.

If, on the other hand, (2) harmonies are *not* restricted to determinate proportions, the *harmonia* theory will face a different problem (26,11-13): there will be too many harmonies, since every composite will be a mixture of elements or powers in some proportion, whether commensurable or not. But then, the worry seems to be, there would be nothing distinctive about the soul's being a proportion, beyond perhaps being some specific one. On Alex.'s view, in contrast, there is an important difference: even if all composite things exhibit proportions, different powers will supervene on different mixtures; and the soul will be identified by specific powers and not the proportions as such on which it supervenes.

238. [26,13-15] If the opposing view is to be distinct from Alex.'s own, as AD rightly point out (150), it must be understood in such a way that the soul is constituted from the mixture and so in some sense *the same* as it, rather than (as on Alex.'s view), a distinct power which emerges from it.

239. [26,15-17] On the place of 26,13-20 generally in the doxographic tradition, see Mansfeld 1990, 3108-9.

On the Stoic view that the soul is a type of breath or *pneuma*, already attributed to Zeno (D.L. 7.157 = *SVF* 1.135) and Cleanthes (Sext. Emp. *Pyrr. Hyp.* 2.70 = *SVF* 1.484), see n. 178 on 19,6-9 above. The claim that this *pneuma* is specifically a blend of fire and air, however, appears to trace back to Chrysippus: see Galen *QAM* 4, 45.5-25 Müller (= *SVF* 2.787), which, as Ian Flora points out to me, is an especially close parallel to Alex.'s report, and immediately follows the passage about Andronicus which Alex. may have been responding to, discussed above in n. 230 on 25,2-4. For the more general view that *pneuma* is a mixture of air and fire, see Alex. *Mixt.* 10, 224,14-15 (= *SVF* 2.442); 11, 225,5-8 (= *SVF* 2.310); Galen *PHP* 5.3.8, 306,23-7 De Lacy (= *SVF* 2.841); D.L. 7.156 (= *SVF* 2.774); cf. Simpl. *in Categ.* 218,1 (= *SVF* 2.389). For a discussion of the evidence, and in particular the value of Alex.'s reports, see Sorabji 1988, 85-9.

240. [26,17-18] Epicurus is reported to have said that the soul was a 'blend' (*krama*) of four things, one of which is like fire, another like air, another like breath or wind and a fourth without any name, which is responsible for awareness: Aet. 4.3.11, 388.21-389.8 = Usener 315 = Arrighetti[2] 159 = LS 14C; cf. Plut. *Adv. Colot.* 20, 1118D-E = Usener 314= Arrighetti[2] 158. See Kerferd 1971, 90. For Epicurus' conception of blending, see Alex. *Mixt.* 2, 214,28-215,8 = Usener 290.

241. [26,18-20] Alex. may have in mind here Plato's description of the creation of the world soul at *Tim.* 34C-35B, which is constituted from a complex mixture of being, the same, and the different. But more likely he is simply relying on Arist.'s report that in the *Timaeus* Plato made the soul 'from the elements' (*ek tôn stoikheiôn, DA* 1.2, 404b16-17). As Mansfeld points out (1990, 3109), Calcidius reports that anti-Platonists had claimed that the *Timaeus* and the *Phaedrus* were in conflict on just this point, of whether the soul was composite (*in Tim.* 228, 243.13-18 Waszink).

242. [26,21-2] See n. 230 on 25,2-4; also 24,19-23; 25,7-9.

243. [26,26-30] See n. 40 on 5,5-6 above; see also 24,22-3 (cf. 24,28); 25,7-9. Here Alex. makes an even finer distinction than he had before, regarding the soul and the bodies that underlie it. The underlying mixture of bodies on his view is in some sense responsible for the new power that emerges from it and supervenes on it, which he identifies with the soul: see 10,17-19 and 24-6. But neither the underlying mixture nor its proportion constitutes the essence or being of the soul, that is, what it is to be a soul. The soul gets its essence solely from the power itself, not the mixture from which the power emerges.

244. [27,1-4] This sentence signals the end of the first part of the programme laid out at the beginning of the treatise (1,1-3): Alex. indicates at 16,18 that he has stated the essence of the soul, and then discusses various consequences of this characterisation, including the fact that it is (*i*) inseparable from the body (17,11-15), while nevertheless being (*ii*) non-bodily (17,15-20,26), (*iii*) incapable of undergoing change in itself (21,22-24,17), and (*iv*) not a harmony (24,18-26,30). Alex. now proceeds to the second part of his programme, concerning the parts or powers of the soul, starting with the claim that there is more than one part (27,4-28,3), though not infinitely many (28,4-13), and then characterising the differences between them (28,13-30,17).

Alex. takes it for granted that the 'parts' of the soul (*merôn autês*, 27,3) are 'powers' (*dunameis*, 27,5). Nevertheless, more is at issue than simply differentiating powers: he is concerned more with how powers are grouped together as parts within the whole soul and how they are distributed across different kinds of living thing: see nn. 246 and 249 on 27,4-8 and 27,8-16 respectively. This distribution shows that there are many parts or powers of the soul, even though there is only one soul in each living thing: 30,2-3; cf. 28,3; *Mant.* 118,6-7. An independent set of arguments for the plurality of powers is offered at *Mant.* 118,6-119,20.

   245. [27,6-7] The reference to Democritus (= Luria fr. 459) may be little more than an inference, as AD suggest (152), from Arist.'s assertion that Democritus 'says' that the soul (*psukhê*) and the understanding (*nous*) are 'the same' (*DA* 1.2, 404a27-8, 405a8-9 = DK 68 A 101) and that he 'makes' all the objects of senses into objects of touch (*Sens.* 4, 442a29-b1 = DK 68 A 119); the evidence from Philoponus, as AD point out, is itself based on Alex. and so not independent (*in DA* 35,10-16 = DK 68 A 105; *in DA* 71,19-34 = DK 68 A 113). But we should note that in context Arist.'s claims are dubious conjectures themselves, made for polemical purposes. Democritus in fact speaks in a number of fragments about psychological conflict and even *akrasia* (DK 68 B 214, 236, 234). By Alex.'s standards (27,7-8), this should commit Democritus to distinct parts of the soul in conflict with each other, although his words only speak of a conflict between the individual and a part of himself. On this point, see Kahn 1985, 16-17.

   Democritus, however, is probably just a beard for the Stoics, who are more likely Alex.'s main target here. The Stoics attribute a strong form of unity to the soul. Thus, while they recognise many 'parts' of the soul, these are physical extensions of the breath in the governing part to the various bodily organs (Aet. 4.21.1-4, *Dox. Gr.* 410.25-411.24 = *SVF* 2.836 = LS 53H; Iambl. ap. Stob. 1.368.12-20 = *SVF* 2.826 = LS 53K); and for Chrysippus, at least, the characteristic activities of living things are in an important sense activities *of the governing part itself* (Sen. *Ep.* 113.23; cf. Aet. 4.21.1, *Dox. Gr.* 410.25-9) and so of a single thing being exercised in different ways (Sext. Emp. *Adv. Math.* 7.307, 359 = *SVF* 2.849; Plut. *de Virt. Mor.* 3, 441C = *SVF* 3.459). This is true, significantly, even in cases of psychological conflict: struggles between reason and the passions are to be understood as the governing part vacillating between different objects, being drawn one way and then the other sequentially over time: Plut. *de Virt. Mor.* 7, 446F-447A = *SVF* 3.459 = LS 65G. Alex. explicitly attributes this sort of vacillation to the Stoics, interestingly, with regard to perceiving objects in different sense modalities at *in Sens.* 167,6-8.

   246. [27,4-8] *Mant.* 118,6-9 (= *SVF* 2.823). Alex. here refers to the experience of psychological conflict, of being 'torn in different directions', something which occurs in the *enkratês*, someone who overcomes this conflict and maintains control, as much as in the *akratês*, the person who loses control and does something he believes he should not. The latter term is often translated as 'having a weak will', but the Greek does not mention the will and is not limited to cases where a specifically moral weakness is involved: any failure to do what one thinks should be done, for whatever reason, is relevant.

   Arist. does not make this first argument about parts. In general, his approach is taxonomical: he emphasises that different types of living things along the *scala naturae* are capable of different activities; and he takes this to imply that there are distinct powers of the soul, some of which can exist apart from the rest (*DA* 2.2, 413a20-414a3; 2.3, 414a29-b1, 414b32-415a12). But such arguments would be inadequate against the Stoics, who also differentiate living things along the *scala naturae*, but regard each level as having a distinct and unified form of *pneuma* of its own, which includes the powers of those beneath it (see Inwood 1985, 25-6): thus plants have a nature, while animals have soul, and humans and gods possess reason (Philo *Quod Deus sit Immut.* 35-46, 64.1-66.15 Cohn-Wendland = *SVF* 2.458 = LS 47Q; *Leg. Alleg.* 2.22-3, 1.95.7-20 Cohn-Wendland = *SVF* 2.458 = LS

47P). Arist.'s arguments would likewise be ineffective against the sort of opponents Alex. targets below (27,12-28,2), who take all souls to be endowed with the same powers, even if some are unable to exercise them on account of the body they currently inhabit. The fact that living things exhibit different activities is thus not decisive for either group of philosophers.

Perhaps with this shortcoming in mind, Alex. chooses a quicker and more decisive argument, drawn from Plato. In *Republic* IV, Socrates argues that the soul has three parts: the appetitive, the competitive, and the rational (434D-441C). He makes the crucial point that such conflict is not merely diachronic, but synchronic: it is possible to want *contrary* things *at a single time*, something that would be impossible, he claims, if the soul were undivided (436B-437A; see also Alcinous *Didask.* 24, 176.41-177.3 Whittaker). Alex. plainly does not accept Plato's tripartition of the soul, but he does little more than allude to Plato's argument here. He does not explain which parts of the soul on his own account would be in conflict or make further use of psychological conflict in the present treatise. It is striking that he does not even name Plato: perhaps it is to distance himself from the specifics of Plato's account or otherwise diminish it. Alex. does, however, endorse the critical point elsewhere that a single power cannot act in different ways at a single time (*Mant.* 118,31-5). This claim is in fact stronger than Plato's, which only denies that a power can act in *contrary* ways at once, and as Richard Sorabji rightly points out, even more controversial.

247. [27,9] Alex., like Arist., uses this principle about the natural order to argue primarily for the *absence* of certain features or powers, which would be to no purpose or 'superfluous' (*matên*) in a particular species, were they present. For Alex., see *DA* 28,4-6; 98,8-9; *Mant.* 157,15-18; 164,25-7; 183,25-6; *Fat.* 11, 178,11-12; 179,25-6, but esp. *Mant.* 163,24-30, where Alex. bases this principle on an analogy with art, characterising nature as 'a kind of divine art' (*tekhnê tis theia*). The sage and virtue are also said to choose nothing superfluous: *Mant.* 165,29-30; 166,11. For Arist.'s use of this principle, see *Cael.* 1.4, 271a33; 2.11, 291b13-14; *DA* 3.9, 432b21-6; 3.12, 434a31-2; *Resp.* 10, 476a11-15; *PA* 2.13, 658a8-9; 3.1, 661b23-4; 4.11, 691b4; 4.13, 695b19; *IA* 2, 704b12-18; 8, 708a9-12; *GA* 2.5, 741b4-5; 2.6, 744a36-7; 5.8, 788b20-4; *Polit.* 1.8, 1256b20-2. For discussion of Arist.'s use of this principle and its variants, see Lennox [1997] 2001.

In a somewhat different usage, a process can be said to be to no purpose or 'in vain' when in a particular case it does not issue in its natural outcome. Arist. appeals to this usage to provide an etymology for a 'fortuitous outcome' (*to automaton*) at *Phys.* 2.6, 197b22-30, which Alex. adopts at *Mant.* 178,26-9. But that clearly is not the sense at issue here.

248. [27,9-11] Bruns inserts *zôia* after *tina* at 27,9, following the Hebrew translation, which restricts the point to variations between different kinds of animals, presumably with regard to their different abilities to perceive objects in different sense modalities. But Alex.'s point is intelligible as it stands, and even more poignant, as it would apply to plants as well as animals: the idea that plants, as well as worms and anemones, might have the power of sight and hearing, but just lack the organs, is quite obviously absurd. AD 153 add extra arguments for this reading based on the exact form of the Greek expression.

249. [27,8-15] This second argument is also not present in Arist., but the target here seems somewhat different than in the first. The issue is no longer simply whether a theory distinguishes between different powers, but whether they are distributed differently across living things, as Alex. and Arist. and even the Stoics think (see n. 246 on 27,4-8). The opponent Alex. has in mind here thinks that all living things have the same powers, in virtue of having a soul, and differ only as to which they can exercise, a difference which is to be explained by the body, whereas Alex. and Arist. think that there are different types of soul, which only overlap partially in their parts or powers. There is no reason to think that the Stoics are still in view here, much less the primary target.

Alex.'s objection to this view is *not* simply that we would be ascribing powers to living things that could not exercise them: Arist. himself allows that a living thing could continue to have a power, even though the organ had failed (*DA* 1.4, 408b19-25). The problem rather is that on this theory certain things could not exercise these powers *by nature*, because of their proper bodily constitution, and not by becoming deformed, injured, or decrepit. To have a power by nature that cannot be exercised by nature is superfluous and violates a teleological conception of the soul and its powers. On Arist.'s view, a difference in powers implies a difference in organs (*GA* 4.1, 766a22-3) and which organs something has is to be explained by reference to its powers and activities, not *vice versa*: see esp. *PA* 4.10, 687a10-14; *GA* 1.2, 716b23-5; cf. also *PA* 1.5, 645b14-20; 4.12, 694b13-14.

250. [27,15-28,2] This argument is an extension of the preceding one, heightened by the comparison with metempsychosis or the transmigration of souls, which Arist. also rejects out of hand: *DA* 1.3, 407b13-27; cf. 2.2, 414a22-5. The objection does not turn so much on the religious elements, or its commitment to the disembodiment of the soul and its successive reincarnations, but rather on the fact that it severs any correlation between what powers a soul has and its bodily organs.

Arist. associates this view with the Pythagoreans in the first passage cited above, as it commonly is: Xenophanes' quip about beating a puppy presupposes that it is a view for which Pythagoras was already known at the time (D.L. 8.36 = DK 21 B 7); the attribution is explicitly confirmed later by Aristotle's student, Dicaearchus (Porphyry, *Vita Pyth.* 19 des Places = fr. 40 Mirhady): for a review of the evidence, see Huffman [2005] 2009, sec. 4.1, and more generally Huffman 2009. Herodotus (2.123) suggests that the doctrine is Egyptian in origin. But the view is certainly found later in Empedocles and Plato. For Empedocles: DK 31 B 115, 117, 126, 137, B 147, along with testimony from Diogenes of Oenoanda (fr. 42 Smith); for a general discussion of Empedocles' view, see Inwood [1992] 2001, 55-68; for discussion of the Diogenes of Oenoanda fragment, see Inwood 2009. For Plato: *Phaedo* 81B-82C, 107D-E, 113A; *Phaedrus* 248C-249C; *Rep.* 10, 614B-621B, esp. 617E-618A and 620A-C; *Tim.* 41D-42D, 76D-E, 90E-91A and 91D-92C; *Laws* 10, 903D; cf. *Meno* 81A-B; *Phaedo* 70C-D, 72A-D; *Laws* 9, 870D-E; 10, 904A-C; for a general discussion, see Ehnmark 1957. The view can also be found in later Platonists like Alcinous (*Didask.* 25, 178.33-9 Whittaker).

251. [28,3-13] Alex. takes up the second preliminary question mentioned at 27,3-4, before a discussion of the specific parts of the soul. The trichotomy of one power *vs* finitely many powers *vs* infinitely many powers is purely systematic in motivation: no known philosopher maintained that there were infinitely many. The latter position might be suggested, as AD (154) and BD (261) note, by Arist. *DA* 3.9, 432a23-b7. But Arist. just raises it there as an obvious absurdity, solely for purposes of a *reductio*. By offering arguments against it, Alex. takes it more seriously as a theoretical possibility.

252. [28,4-6] If a living thing cannot exercise an infinite number of powers, then the powers it does not and cannot exercise will be superfluous, which violates Arist.'s teleological principle that nature does nothing superfluous (on which, see n. 247 on 27,9). More interesting, perhaps, is the supporting argument Alex. offers for premiss (2), namely, that an animal cannot exercise an infinite number of powers. The exercise of different powers does not itself seem to present a logical difficulty, as the exercise of a single power in contrary ways might (see 27,4-8 above, together with *Mant.* 118,31-5). So the problem is presumably that there might be an infinite number of them: perhaps no finite creature can engage in an infinite number of activities, either simultaneously or over time. Alex. does not elaborate further.

253. [28,6-8] This argument relies on a general correspondence between the functional parts of the body and the parts or powers of the soul. But it need not be one-to-one. For while Arist. thinks that nature in general follows the better course of assigning one organ for one function, this is not always possible, in which case a single organ can subserve two or more functions and powers: see esp. *PA* 4.6, 683a20-6 and *Pol.* 1.2, 1252b1-5; also *PA* 2.16, 659b34-660a2; 3.1, 662a16-24; *DA* 2.8, 420b16-22; *Sens.* 5, 444a25-7; *GA* 5.8, 789b9-12. But so long as no part of the body can serve an *infinite* number of functions, and there are only a finite number of such parts, as Alex. claims, there will not be an infinite number of functions and hence powers corresponding to them.

A more pertinent objection would be that the correspondence does not hold in the opposite direction, from functions to parts: Alex. allows that in some cases there is *no* bodily part corresponding to a given function, since on his view, like Arist.'s, the understanding lacks a dedicated organ (84,10-24; for further references, see n. 200 on 21,24). But this need not open the floodgates: so long as the understanding is unique in this regard, or even one of a limited number of cases, Alex. can uphold his conclusion that there will not be an infinite number of powers of the soul.

254. [28,8] See 24,16-17 above, with corresponding note. Arist. *DA* 2.4, 415b16-17; *Somn.* 2, 455b17-18; cf. *Metaph.* 1.9, 992a29-31; 11.8, 1065a26-7.

255. [28,8-13] The central notion on which this argument rests – namely, that the parts of the soul constitute an order or sequence – derives from Arist.'s extended comparison of the different types of soul with the series of geometrical figures in *DA* 2.3, 414b20-31, an argument which Alex. goes on to develop immediately below at 28,14-29,1. But his treatment of it here is very different in a number of ways. First, Alex. claims quite generally that the earlier members in series of this sort bear a reference to *subsequent* members, and not (as one might expect) *vice versa*. In this respect, such series differ from cases of 'focal meaning', where many things are characterised by reference back to a single, primary member (*pros hen*), as Alex. elaborates at *in Metaph.* 263,25-33: in series of the sort at issue here, earlier members 'contribute' to later ones (*suntelein*, 263,30.32), which are 'higher' or 'more advanced' (*teleiotera*, 263,33). Second, the order Alex. appeals to here is specifically a teleological one, where earlier parts of the soul are *for the sake of* the subsequent ones: cf. 75,31-76,6 below. Arist. never makes such claims. Third, Alex. claims that this specific type of series cannot go on infinitely, in order to show that the parts of the soul must be finite in number. But this is certainly not true of this type of series in general: Arist.'s examples, of polygons and counting numbers, both continue indefinitely. But one thing cannot be for the sake of another, and that thing for another, and so on indefinitely: a series of teleological explanations must ultimately reach a final good, in terms of which all the earlier ones must be understood; otherwise, it is unintelligible what they are all for. This assumption, which underlies Arist.'s reasoning about our practical aims and aspirations and the highest good in *EN* 1, is explicit at *EN* 1.2, 1094a18-22 and defended at *Metaph.* 2.2, 994a8-10 and esp. b9-16, and Alex.'s discussion of the latter at *in Metaph.* 159,27-160,27.

256. [28,15] 16,18-17,1. See further n. 155 on 16,18-17,1; also 30,17-20; 40,4-10; *Quaest.* 1.11a and b, passim.

257. [28,17-20] 17,2-5.

258. [28,23-5] 92,15-94,6; cf. 40,10-15. The kind of separation (*khôrizesthai*) at issue is a special one Arist. elaborates in this context: see esp. *DA* 2.2, 413a31-b7; cf. 1.5, 411b27-30. It concerns the separation of parts or powers of the soul, not within an individual – these cannot be separated from one another (1.5, 411b19-27) – but across different kinds of living thing: some powers occur in certain species without others. Plants, for example, have nutritive powers, but no perceptual or rational ones. This sort of 'taxonomic' separability is non-symmetrical, moreover: even though nutritive powers can be found without perceptual powers, the latter never occur without the former. Alex.'s point in the passage above is that this sort of separability runs in one direction only, from lowest to highest: the nutritive powers are separable from the perceptual, and the perceptual from the rational, but not *vice versa* in either case: see 30,3-4. For more on this notion of separability, see my 1999, 208-10.

259. [28,25-9] Alex. refers to the opening line of the treatise, where he restricts the scope of his inquiry to the souls of things that come to be and perish: see 1,2 with accompanying note. The reason he insists on the qualification here is that if the gods have souls in the same sense as other living things, they would pose a counterexample to the claim he has just made at 28,23-5 about the separability of powers, since in their case, a higher power does occur without a lower one. The clearest case is the Prime Mover or First Cause, which for Alex., like Arist., is a non-bodily understanding (89,9-15; *Quaest.* 1.25, 40,8-9; cf. 2.19, 63,20-1; Arist. *Metaph.* 12.7, 1073a3-7) and so has a rational power, but cannot have the nutritive or perceptual powers, which require organs. For the possibility that Arist. himself might have been concerned about this case, see my 1999, 210 (for reservations, see Accattino 1992, 42). Arist. certainly draws the relevant contrasts at *DA* 2.2, 413a31-2 and 2.3, 415a8-12, which AD 155 offer as a possible source of Alex.'s remarks here.

But Alex.'s use here of the plural 'gods' may indicate, as AD 155 suggest, that he is thinking of the celestial spheres as well, which he, like Arist., regards as animate: Arist. *Cael.* 2.2, 285a29-30; 2.12, 292a18-21; Alex. *Quaest.* 1.1, 3,10-14; 1.10, 20,30; 1.25, 40,9-11; 2.19, 63,18-20; see Accattino 1992, 40-51. Unlike the Prime Mover, the celestial spheres are embodied. But being eternal, they will not have any of the nutritive powers or, according to Alex., perceptual powers either: this, at any rate, is how he interpreted Arist. *DA* 3.12, 434b4-7 in his lost commentary on the *DA*, according to Ps.-Philop., *in DA* 595,37-596,14, although Alex.'s original wording was no doubt closer to Them. *in DA*, 123,24-9, which is clearly drawn from the same passage (cf. also 44,22-4; 125,21-30). Alex. does, however, attribute desire and striving to the celestial spheres: *Quaest.* 1.1, 3,15-19; 1.25, 40,10-23.)

To exclude both kinds of counterexamples, then, it is necessary to restrict the characterisation of the soul here to things which are *not* eternal, but 'subject to coming-to-be and perishing' and thereby exclude all divine beings, whether embodied or not. In support of this restriction, Alex. suggests that when one speaks of the gods as having a soul, it will be a soul in a different sense than the general characterisation of its essence given above (16,10.18-20). It will thus be a soul 'only in name' or homonymously, since although it will share the same name, it will not share the same definition (Arist. *Categ.* 1, 1a1-6). The general characterisation above claims that the soul is the first completion 'of a natural organic body' and so straightforwardly fails to apply to the Prime Mover, who has no body. The case is less obvious for the celestial spheres, since they have a body which moves and is animate, and so ought to be a natural body (*Quaest.* 1.10, 20,23-30). But presumably Alex. would deny that their body is organic. According to Simplicius, Alex. claimed that while divine beings were animate, they could not be said to be animals (*zôia*) except homonymously, since they lack the power to perceive and to nourish themselves (*in Cael.* 463,3-6).

Arist. is less forgiving. He does not speak of the general characterisation given in *DA* 2.1 as a definition (*horismos*), as Alex. does (28,26), but maintains instead that life is 'said in many ways' (*DA* 2.2, 413a22; cf. 1.1, 402b5-9) and so is homonymous even when applied to *plants and animals* (*Top.* 6.10, 148a27-31, a passage on which Alex. fails to say anything in his commentary). Homonymy is much less pervasive for Alex., who assumes that his general conclusions apply univocally to all souls in the sublunary realm. The crucial divide for him is between the mortal and the eternal. (BD 263 explain the homonymy in a way that, if correct, would make the argument at 28,26-9 circular.)

260. [28,28-29,1] Arist. *DA* 2.3, 415a12-13.

261. [29,1-3] This power of the soul is first because it can exist without the others, while the others cannot exist without it, at least not in the sublunary realm, where things are born, grow, and decay – note Alex.'s repetition of this crucial restriction (see n. 259 on 28,25-9). Thanks to Ian Flora for the point about 'first'.

Alex. speaks of the various abilities to be nourished, grow, and reproduce as powers that are 'linked' (*sunezeuktai*). This appears to have an almost technical sense here (which it lacks in Arist.), such that one thing cannot be separated (*khôrizesthai*) from another if they are 'linked'. If so, it is a non-symmetrical relation: although all three powers named here are mutually inseparable from each other, the inferences at 29,16-22 suggest that some can be linked to another, without the other being linked to it.

Arist. likewise claims that the power for growing and decaying is inseparable from the power for nourishing oneself: *DA* 3.12, 434a22-6. But he occasionally makes an even stronger claim: he says that the power for nourishing oneself and the power for reproducing are 'the *same* power' at *DA* 2.4, 416a19; cf. *GA* 2.5, 740b36-7. It is possible to read Alex. this way as well: AD seem to think that there are not three 'really distinct' powers here, but only three expressions for the same power. Much depends, though, on what is required for being 'really distinct'. Alex. does claim these powers are inseparably linked and speaks of them conjointly as 'the first power'. But he nowhere asserts that they are *same* and he could not in any case claim that they are same in being; at most they would be the same in number. Arist. himself, it is worth noting, distinguishes the being of these three powers, at *DA* 2.4, 416b11-17.

It is also worth noting the terminology Alex. begins to use here. He constructs adjectives for different powers and souls from the verbs for particular activities together with the suffix *-ikos*, denoting ability. I have chosen to emphasise the verbal notion in my translations, rather than use the corresponding abstract construction in English: thus, I have used 'the power for growing', for example, rather than 'the augmentative power' (*auxêtikê dunamis*) and 'the soul for desiring' rather than 'the desiderative soul' (*orektikê psukhê*). Both forms of expression are equally awkward in English. But emphasising the verbal notion makes the straightforward nature of many of Alex.'s inferences more evident.

262. [29,3-10] Arist. *DA* 2.1, 412a13-15; cf. 2.2, 413a20-b4. It is not clear that Arist. would *define* life as Alex. does at 29,10, though, since Arist. holds that 'being alive' is 'said in many ways' (*pleonakhôs*, 413a22), which suggests he thinks it is homonymous between the different forms of life and so does not permit the sort of univocal account Alex. gives here (see the end of n. 259 on 28,25-9). In fact, elsewhere Arist. seems comfortable accepting his predecessors' view that the animate is distinguished from the inanimate by (self-) movement and perception: *DA* 1.2, 403b25-7; cf. 3.3, 427a17-19; 3.9, 432a15-16.

263. [29,12-14] Arist. *DA* 2.2, 413a31-b4. On the notion of separation, see n. 258 on 28,23-5 above. For Alex.'s use of 'representation' (*phantasia*), see n. 111 on 12,17 above; for his use of 'striving' (*hormê*), n. 113 on 12,19.

264. [29,14-15] Alex. clearly is developing Arist.'s claim at *DA* 413b2, but the stronger form that Alex. gives it here, involving definition, is frequently made in Arist.'s corpus: for references, see n. 87 on 10,8-10 above.

265. [29,16-18] Arist. *DA* 2.2, 413b22-4; 2.3, 414b1-15; 3.7, 431a13-14; 3.11, 433b31-434a5; *Insomn.* 1, 459a15-17; *MA* 8, 702a17-19; cf. *DA* 3.10, 433b28-9, though compare *DA* 3.3, 428a9-11. Alex. explicitly makes the point here that these powers mutually entail each other, which would be otiose if 'linking' (*sunezeuktai*, 29,17) were symmetrical (see n. 261 on 29,1-3 above). The powers named here, then, cannot occur without the others, but come as a package for anything capable of perception and so are shared by all animals.

For Alex.'s discussion of the power for representing, see 66,9-73,13 below.

266. [29,18-22] 30,13-15; Arist. *DA* 2.2, 413b2-4. In contrast with the preceding lines, the powers named here do not mutually imply each other. Anything capable of (self-) motion must have the power for perceiving and representing, but not *vice versa*. Some animals are stationary, even though they are capable of perception and some crude form of representation (on this last point, see n. 265 on 29,16-18). The basic powers of perception are thus separable from the power of locomotion, but not *vice versa*. For the claim that some animals have perception, but are stationary: Arist. *DA* 1.5, 410b18-20; 2.2, 413b2-4; 2.3, 415a6-7; 3.9, 432b19-21 (cf. b13-14); *HA* 1.1, 487b6-11; *PA* 4.7, 683b4-11; cf. *DA* 2.3, 414b17; 3.12, 434b7-8; *HA* 8.1, 588b12-17.

If the power for striving (*hormetikê dunamis*) is always connected with the power of locomotion, as 29,18 suggests, then there will be a similar asymmetry between the power for striving and the power for desiring: the power for striving will be inseparably linked to the power for desiring, but not *vice versa*. The fact that Alex. treats them very much in tandem in his extended discussion of the power for striving below (73,14-80,15) only shows that he thinks the power for striving is linked to the power for desiring (73,26-8) and that striving is even a kind of desire (74,1); it does *not* show that anything capable of desire is capable of striving, as the converse would require. On the term 'striving' (or 'impulse', as *hormê* is often misleadingly translated), AD 156 rightly note a possible Stoic influence, but Arist. himself also uses the term (see Bonitz 525b47-526a10). On the origin of the expression, see also BD 264. Alex.'s notion of striving is in any case different from the Stoic one. See n. 113 on 12,19 above and more generally 73,14-80,15 below.

267. [29,22-4] Arist. *EN* 6.1, 1139a6-17; cf. *DA* 3.3, 427b24-6 and 428a3-5.

268. [29,22-30,2] The 'rational' powers, all of which involve the use of concepts in some way, are inseparable from the lower powers, at least in mortal beings, even though the lower powers are separable from them: for the non-symmetric notion of separation, see n. 258 on 28,23-5; and for the restriction of the claim to mortal beings, see n. 259 on 28,25-9. For the use of *teleioteros* to mean 'more advanced' in cross-species comparisons, see n. 71 on 7,23.

It is noteworthy that Alex. includes the powers of practical and theoretical reason together under one head, as AD 156-7 point out. For antecedents they cite *EN* 6.1, 1139a6-17 and 6.5, 1140b25-30, even though Arist. speaks of these two kinds of reason as distinct 'parts' of the soul (1140b25; cf. 1139a3-6).

269. [30,2-6] Alex. emphasises the unity of the rational soul here, as it comprises all of the psychological powers and not just rational ones. Because the rational powers are inseparable from the others, they cannot be found apart from them in sublunary beings and so must in some way together constitute a whole, of which they are 'parts' (30,5). AD 157 worry unnecessarily whether Alex. intends his remarks about unity to be *restricted* to rational souls. But nothing in the text precludes the perceptual soul, for example, from exhibiting a similar sort of unity. If anything, Alex.'s remark that the lower powers are 'expanded and developed' (*auxêsin te kai epidosin ... lambanousôn*, 30,6) by the addition of higher powers suggests that organic unity is to be found in more complex souls quite generally, where the higher powers are not merely added on as distinct modules or components, but instead enrich and augment the lower powers through more complex interactions. Feeding and reproduction in animals, unlike plants, can manifest itself in quite varied and complex hunting and mating behavior, for example, precisely because perception is involved.

BD 264-5 take Alex. to be making a further point here, namely, that in each living thing there is a single soul, composed of multiple powers, rather than a plurality of souls. Although this is no doubt Alex.'s view, he does not explicitly reject a plurality of souls here.

270. [30,10-12] 36,13-15.

271. [30,6-17] Alex. is not simply making the claim that there is a *scala naturae* among living things in the sublunary realm, from plants to animals to humans, but that this is grounded in the corresponding hierarchy of souls and powers. In this case, it is clear that the order of explanation is the reverse of the order of discovery: we posit various powers of the soul in response to the range of activities we observe in living beings and then establish the hierarchy of powers based on how they are distributed conjointly or independently among plants, animals, and humans. But we make these theoretical posits precisely in order to account for the patterns we observe among living things, and so accord the souls and soul powers explanatory priority.

272. [30,17-20] 17,1-8; 28,14-29,1.

273. [30,20-6] Alex. makes clear that the present treatise is intended only as a systematic overview of the subject, unlike (presumably) his lost commentary on Arist.'s *DA* or the more detailed treatments of particular topics or puzzles that we find in the *Quaest.* and *Mant.*

274. [30,26-31,2] The two senses of 'part' Alex. rules out here are both quantitative, in line with the first sense of 'part' given in Arist. *Metaph.* 5.25 at 1023b12-15; see Alex. *in Metaph.* 423,33-9. But Alex. is more specific. By ruling out (*i*) continuous extensions, Alex. effectively rules out the soul's being a body, as on the Stoic view, where the parts of the soul are parts of the breath or *pneuma* extending from the governing part of the soul (Aet. 4.21.1-4, *Dox. Gr.* 410.25-411.24 = *SVF* 2.836 = LS 53H; Iambl. ap. Stob. 1.368.12-20 = *SVF* 2.826 = LS 53K). For Alex. the parts of the soul are not arrayed spatially themselves, except extrinsically in virtue of the organs (*in Metaph.* 417,14-19). And by ruling out (*ii*) numbers, he also rules out any conception of the soul as an aggegrate of discrete parts ('composed from parts into which it is divided'). For Alex., the powers of the soul must exhibit a stronger unity or integrity.

Arist. discusses critically the view that the soul is a magnitude and a number at, respectively *DA* 1.3, 407a2-19 and 1.2, 404b27-405a7, but neither passage provides a close parallel.

275. [31,2-6] A very similar argument, at least in outline, is attributed to the first century BCE Aristotelian, Nicolaus Damascenus (Porph. ap. Stob. 1.353.12-354.6 Wachsmuth): he argues that the parts of the soul are not quantitative, but qualitative parts, like the parts of art or of philosophy (see Moraux 1973, 481-5). Alex.'s use of a body as an example instead may have a polemical purpose, since the apple example also appears in a report of the Stoic view, which similarly treats the parts of the soul as qualities (Iambl. ap. Stob. 1.368.12-20 Wachsmuth = *SVF* 2.826 = LS 53K). Stoic qualities are bodies, however (see n. 162 on 17,15-17), and Alex.'s point here is precisely that the qualities of the apple, though parts of a body, are not bodies themselves. (In point of fact, the parts of the soul are not even qualities for Alex., strictly speaking, but parts *of the form*: in *Metaph.* 424,29-31.) It is impossible to determine whether the apple example, which also occurs at *in Sens.* 165,26-166,2, comes from the Stoics originally or from an earlier Peripatetic, or whether Iamblichus is actually borrowing it from Alex. in reporting on the Stoics. For discussion, see Inwood 1985, 30-2, esp. n. 55.

276. [31,7] 29,1-10, esp. 4-5; 31,28; 92,17; *Mant.* 105,12; 118,19; cf. 103,9-10.

277. [31,8-9] 30,15-17.

278. [31,7-10] 9,11-14.23-6; *Mant.* 118,19-21. BD 266 suggest that this argument derives from the more general argument Arist. offers at *DA* 2.2, 414a4-14. Ian Flora has suggested to me that 413a25-b2 provides an even closer parallel.

279. [31,10-14] This statement is striking for the way in which it acknowledges the role of matter, even if secondary to form. Generally, Alex. simply says that it is in virtue of the form that bodies are the kinds of things they are and do the kinds of things they do (6,21-3; 7,9-14). But the difference may just be one of emphasis, since it is also Alex.'s view that matter contributes to what a body is and can do indirectly, in so far as differences in the underlying matter are responsible for which forms supervene (10,14-26).

280. [31,16-20] N.B. Bruns' edition misnumbers the lines here, with only three lines between those marked 31,15 and 31,20. I will treat 31,19 as missing and otherwise respect the numbering printed. Bruns suggests a lengthy insertion at 31,18 to bring the use of 'primary' and 'secondary' in line with those above. But this is unnecessary, since *deuterôs* here is not a precise parallel to *deuteron* at 31,13 above: it marks the derivative sense in which the *body* can itself be said to be healthy, in contrast with the animal, which is healthy in a primary or fundamental sense (*kuriôs*). For the use of *deuterôs* to mark a derivative application of a predicate, see above 8,22.

At 25,4-7, as AD 160 point out, Alex. contrasts the soul and health, suggesting that the latter is more like a harmony and a balance, which the soul is not, much as Arist. does, we might add: see n. 231 on 25,4-7. But Arist. also treats health as an example of a form received by a body, as AD rightly observe: see next note.

281. [31,20-5] The claim that the soul is the form of the body has been one of Alex.'s central points in the treatise so far: see n. 157 on 17,9. For the comparison between health and the soul, as forms of the body, see Arist. *DA* 2.2, 414a4-14: though one is an accidental form and the other a substantial form, each is that by which (*hôi*) something lives and is healthy, respectively, in contrast with the underlying subject and matter.

282. [31,25-32,1] *Mant.* 105,4-12; 118,12-16.19-25. It is sometimes thought that Alex. is objecting here to a Stoic view, since they think that the breath or *pneuma* in plants constitutes a nature (*phusis*) but not a soul (*psukhê*): see esp. Philo *Leg.*

Alleg. 2.22-3, 1.95.7-20 Cohn-Wendland = *SVF* 2.458 = LS 47P; *Quod Deus sit Immut.* 35-46, 2.64.1-66.15 Cohn-Wendland = *SVF* 2.458 = LS 47Q; Galen *PHP* 6.3.7, 374.18-19 De Lacey = *SVF* 2.710; *Foet. Form.* 3, 68.9-17 Nickel = *SVF* 2.712; 6, 104.16-19 Nickel; *Hipp. Epid.* 17b.251.1-6 Kühn = *SVF* 2.715; cf. Origen *Orat.* 6.1, 311.16-312.10 Koetschau = *SVF* 2.989 = LS 53A. For discussion of the Stoic *scala naturae*, see Inwood 1985, 21-7. But if the Stoics were Alex.'s target, his objection would actually misfire: on the Stoic view, simple bodies and stones belong to a lower echelon: they do not have a nature, as plants do, but only 'cohesion' (*hexis*). So the Stoics would be indifferent to Alex.'s objection that simple bodies are not alive at 31,27-8, as an *ignoratio elenchi.* Galen is more likely to be Alex.'s target here. Galen not only begins his *Nat. fac.* by defending the distinction between nature and soul (without mentioning cohesion), but claims that the Aristotelian view amounts to the same thing in different and unusual language, while his distinction conforms more closely to ordinary usage: 1,1, 101.1-15 Helmreich; cf. *adv. Iul.* 5, 18a.266.9-13 Kühn; *Caus. Sympt.* 7.129.9-10 Kühn; *Subst. Nat. Fac.* 4.759.9-15 Kühn; *HNH* 15.123.14-124.7 Kühn. Alex. is concerned to show that the difference is not merely verbal and to give these terms their proper extensions: things which are not alive still have a nature, but nothing without a soul is alive.

283. [32,1-4] The powers by which seeds operate will be powers of the progenitor that produced them, presumably because seeds are originally proper parts of the progenitor. (2) is then offered as an instance of (1), with 'seed' now used in its proper, biological sense. The connection between 'animate' and 'soul power' in (2) is more plausible in the Greek, since both key terms are based on the word 'soul' or *psukhê*: the powers of animate things (*tôn empsukhôn*) are themselves soul powers (*psukhikai*).

AD 160-1 give *Mant.* 118,25-6 as a parallel and argue that this argument is directed at the Stoics, accusing them effectively of inconsistency, since they hold that the power for reproducing is a part of the soul in contrast with the power for nourishing oneself and growing, which merely belong to nature (see n. 282 on 31,25-32,1 above): Aet. 4.21.2-3, *Dox. Gr.* 410.30-411.13 = *SVF* 2.836 = LS 53H 3; Aet. 4.4.4, *Dox. Gr.* 390.5-13 = *SVF* 2.827; D.L. 7.110 (cf. 157) = *SVF* 2.828, although Panaetius appears to have assigned all of these powers to nature (fr. 86 van Straaten; for discussion, see also Sharples 2004, 58 n. 168). AD's remarks apply straightforwardly to the argument in the *Mant.*, which explicitly concerns the part for reproducing (*to gennêtikon morion*) and reports the view of unnamed philosophers who might be the Stoics ('they say'). But the argument here does not mention the power for reproducing at all, only the power active in seeds (32,2) and the power for nourishing oneself (32,4-5), and so does not object to inconsistent treatment of different powers. Seeds figure in the argument here primarily to establish certain powers of the progenitor, by (1); and then Alex. crucially claims in (2) that the seeds of living things are active in virtue of *soul* powers. It is not clear that the Stoics would have agreed with (2): they can easily argue that the first activities of the developing embryo are expressions of nature, not soul.

284. [32,4-6] Arist. *GA* 2.1, 735a15-21 (cf. a2-4).

285. [32,6-7] Although Alex. is usually scrupulous about distinguishing powers from the souls that are constituted from them, here he explicitly states that the power for nourishing oneself is a soul. But the soul for nourishing oneself is a special case, since it is constituted by just one kind of power, the power for nourishing oneself, and so the distinction between the power and the soul is a very fine one (much like the difference between a singleton set {*a*} and its sole member, *a*). Whether the power for nourishing oneself can itself be subdivided is a further question: see nn. 261 and 288 on 29,1-3 and 32,15-22, respectively.

286. [32,8] For Alex.'s use of 'linked' (*sunezeuktai*), see n. 261 on 29,1-3.

287. [32,11-15] cf. 36,6-9. The lines above (apart from the example of the eunuchs) are a very close verbal echo of Arist. *DA* 2.4, 415a26-b2; see also *GA* 2.1, 731b31-732a1, 735a17-19; cf. *Oecon.* 1.3, 1343b23-5. Arist. makes a similar claim about the endless cycle of elemental transformation at *GC* 2.10, 336b26-33 (cf 2.11, 338b6-19); *Metaph.* 9.8, 1050b28-9. But the point is made most generally by Plato, beginning with the reproduction of living things at *Symp.* 206E-207A, 207D-208B; cf. also *Laws* 4, 721B-C. Alex. may also have in mind the middle Platonist theme of 'likening oneself to God' (*homoiôsis theôi*), as AD 161 suggest: cf. *Quaest.* 1.25, 40,17-19. But there are also parallels in Arist. himself: *EN* 10.7, 1177b33-1178a3.

The example of eunuchs may derive from Arist. *Metaph.* 5.12, 1019b15-19, on which Alex. comments at *in Metaph.* 393,2-17.

AD 161 point out that the Greek in 32,15 is ambiguous, perhaps intentionally: *panta* here can either be the subject (as they take it in their translation) or the object of *prattei* (as translated above). The first reading is weaker by making its meaning nearly the same as the previous clause: '... and everything naturally acts for its sake.'

But however we construe it, the statement at 32,14-15 goes well beyond Alex.'s earlier claims about natural teleology at 24,16-17 and 28,8. The natural activity of natural objects is not merely directed at an end intrinsic to itself – namely, its complete realisation as a member of its kind – but at participation, in some limited degree, in God's perfection and eternity.

288. [32,15-22] Arist. *GA* 2.1, 735a16-19; 2.4, 740b29-37; *DA* 2.4, 416a19. Alex.'s argument here leans heavily on (3), the claim that the soul which plants have is only a soul for nourishing oneself. But he is entitled to this premiss, given the notion of separability on which his taxonomy of souls rests (see n. 258 on 28,23-5): unless there are living things that have one of these powers, but not the other, they belong to the same type of soul. Alex. here speaks of the soul for nourishing oneself as a power again (see n. 285 on 32,6-7), but it is even more noteworthy that he speaks of the power for reproducing *as a part* (*morion*, 32,22) of the power for nourishing oneself: compare 29,1-3, with corresponding note on the relation between these powers.

289. [32,23-4] Alex.'s methodological remark here seems to be a simplification of the familiar Aristotelian principle that we proceed from things which are more evident and intelligible *to us* (*gnôrimôteron hêmin*) to things which are less so, but more intelligible in themselves and without qualification (*gnôrimôteron haplôs*), and so can be used to illuminate the 'obvious' facts from which we started: this is the principle briefly alluded to at *DA* 2.2, 413a11-12, but more fully developed at *Phys.* 1.1, 184a16-b14; *An. Post.* 1.2, 71b33-72a5; *EN* 1.4, 1095b2-4; *Metaph.* 7.3, 1029b3-12; and as applied to definition, *Top.* 6.4, 141a26-142a16. But Alex. does not draw the distinction between a relative and an absolute use here, and more importantly he speaks about the starting points simply as 'clearer' (*dia tôn saphesterôn*), in keeping with non-Aristotelian usage rather than Aristotle's more nuanced phrasing, that we start from what is *less* clear, but more obvious (*ek tôn asaphôn men phanerôteron de*, *DA* 2.2, 413a11-12).

290. [32,25-7] Arist. *DA* 2.4, 415a16-20; cf. 1.1, 402b10-14. In claiming that activities are 'clearer' (*saphesterai*) – to observation, presumably – than the powers from which they arise, Alex. goes beyond Arist., who only claims that we should study them first because they are prior in account (*kata ton logon*, 415a19-20).

Arist. does say elsewhere that in cases where one thing is prior to another in this way, knowledge (*gnôsis*) of the first precedes knowledge of the second (*Metaph.* 9.8, 1049b16-17), but he has definitional knowledge in mind there, which is unlikely to be at issue in these lines; in fact, Arist. claims that what is prior in knowledge (*to têi gnôsei proteron*) can come apart from what is prior in account at *Metaph.* 5.11, 1018b29-34.

291. [32,29-30] This sentence is difficult. On the most natural way of construing the Greek pronouns in 32,29-30, the sentence would read 'those things are first in definition which include in their own definition [other] things in whose definition they do not enter.' That is, it would claim that *A* is prior in definition to *B* just in case *B* is part of the definition of *A*, but *A* is not part of the definition of *B*. (In a note, Bruns makes clear this is how he takes it.) But this gets things the wrong way around, since it makes the definition of *A* dependent on *B*. As priority in definition is standardly formulated, *A* is prior because *A* is *not* dependent on *B*, but *B* is dependent on *A*: *A* is part of the definition of *B*, but *B* is not part of the definition of *A*. See Arist. *Metaph.* 7.10, 1035b4-6; 13.2, 1077b3-4; also 10.8, 1049b12-17; cf. Alex. *in Metaph.* 386,33-5. To get around this difficulty, AD propose translating *kata ton logon* as 'in essence', while construing the pronouns in the same way (162-6). But this is no improvement, even if we grant the rendering of *logos*, since it still has the dependence relations running in the wrong direction: *A* cannot be prior in essence to *B* if it includes *B* in its essence, while *B* does not include *A*. They are forced to look for a non-standard reading of priority in essence, which is essentially teleological in nature, based on Philoponus' report of Alex.'s comment on *DA* 2.4, 415a20 at *in DA* 264,15-22. (For another possible reading of Alex.'s comment, see n. 292 on 32,30-33,5.)

The sentence at 32,29-30 is in line with the standard doctrine, however, if we construe the pronouns as BD do (267-8), taking *tina* to be the subject of *periekhei* and the genitive *hôn* to depend on *prôta*, as rendered in my translation above. There is a very similar difficulty in the construal of the same point at Arist. *Metaph.* 13.2, 1077b3-4, where Ross in his notes similarly takes the genitive *hosôn* at b3 as dependent on *protera*. This is not the most obvious reading of the Greek, but it is a possible construal and the best way to make sense of the text as it stands.

292. [32,30-33,5] At first glance, Alex.'s explanation (*gar*, 33,1) seems quite odd. In order to support his claim that being nourished is prior in definition to the nutritive power (32,27-9), he seems to change the subject twice, by arguing that *powers* have a kind of *existential* priority to their corresponding activities. But another way to take Alex.'s line of thought would be as follows: the way in which activities are prior has to be in definition, since they are *not* prior in being, but rather powers are.

293. [33,7-10] Arist. *DA* 2.4, 415a20-2; cf. 1.1, 402b14-16. Like Arist., Alex. holds that the activity of each of the soul's powers involves an object, and therefore cannot be understood or defined without reference to that object and without some understanding of what makes it a suitable object for that activity.

294. [33,13-15] *in Meteor.* 186,21-6; cf. *in Sens.* 108,10-14. Arist. draws the same distinction at *DA* 2.4, 416b3-7, in connection with the issue of whether like is nourished by like or contraries by contraries (see n. 295 on 33,15-16 just below); *GC* 1.5, 321b35-322a3. (The distinction between two types of nourishment at *GA* 2.6, 744b32-6 is quite different.)

The notion of cooking (*pepsis*), sometimes rendered 'concoction', is central in Arist.'s natural works (see Lloyd 1996) and applies to many processes we would not ordinarily describe as 'cooking': in fact, Arist. explicitly states that it is an extended use of the term, for lack of any better (*Meteor.* 4.2, 379b14-17). As he defines it, cooking is the process of completing (*teleiôsis*) a thing by heat's acting on its matter (379b18-20). In many cases, this results from the object's own natural heat, as when fruit ripens, or food is broken down and digested (*PA* 3.14, 674b9-13, cf. b26-34), or in the formation of the homogenous materials that make up the body, such as bone, hair, or sperm (*PA* 2.3, 650a2-32). For the formal account of cooking, see Arist. *Meteor.* 4.2-3; Alex. *in Meteor.* 185,24-198,3; on the different uses of the term, see esp. the references in Lloyd 1987, 205 nn. 119-24.

I have accepted Bruns' deletion of *trophê legetai*, instead of retaining it with AD and inserting a *te*. It does not, in any case, affect the overall meaning.

295. [33,15-16] Arist. *DA* 2.4, 416a29-34 (cf. a21-2); *Phys.* 8.7, 260a30-2; Alex. also mentions the point briefly at *in Meteor.* 186,24-6.

Both Anaxagoras and Empedocles seem to be committed to the view that like is nourished by like. For Anaxagoras, see Simpl. *in Phys.* 460,15-20 = DK 59 A 45; cf. Aetius 1.3.5, *Dox. Gr.* 279.12-17 = DK 59 A 46. In fact, nourishment appears to have been one of the most striking cases for his general thesis that there is a portion of everything in everything (DK 59 B 6 & 11): the accretion of like by like in growth is possible because the similar homogeneous substances are *already* present in food. The evidence for Empedocles is somewhat more tenuous, but see esp. Plut. *Quaest. Conviv.* 4.1, 663A = DK 31 B 90; Aet. 5.27.1, *Dox. Gr.* 440.4-10 = DK 31 A 77; also cf. Simpl. *in Phys.* 381,31-382,3 = DK 31 B 62.

It is not clear who held the view that contraries are nourished by contraries. This may just be an application of Arist.'s claim regarding agent-patient interactions in general that 'most of his predecessors agreed' (*hoi pleistoi ... homonoêtikôs legousin*) that only dissimilar things could have an effect on one another (*GC* 1.7, 323b3-7).

296. [33,17-18] Repunctuating the text in line with the Hebrew translation (followed also by AD and BD).

297. [33,18-24] Arist. *DA* 2.4, 416a33-4. See also *GC* 2.5, 332a7-8; *Phys.* 8.7, 261a32-b1; *Metaph.* 4.7, 1011b34-5; 10.7, 1057a31; 11.11, 1068a1-4; 12.1, 1069b3; Alex. *DA* 59,11-12; *Quaest.* 1.7, 15,26, 16,6; *Eth. Probl.* 30, 162,7-9; *in Metaph.* 329,18-21; 423,28.

298. [33,25-9] Alex. here applies the general argument Arist. makes in *GC* 1.7, with regard to all agent-patient interaction: in order to interact, they must be initially contrary to each other, but potentially alike, since they will come to be actually like each other as a result of the interaction. The case is particularly strong with nutrition, since nourishment produces growth in what is nourished by adding to its mass; and it can do this only if it comes to be like the body that absorbs it as a result of digestion.

299. [33,28-34,8] Arist. *DA* 2.4, 416a21-5. Alex. elaborates Arist.'s argument further, though not fully. A distinction is needed between growth and alteration, which also involves a transformation from one contrary to another. In alteration, however, there is a single underlying subject, which changes in quality; in growth, a separate body is transformed and added to another, which does not change its nature or quality, but only increases in size as a result.

300. [34,8-14] Alex. is reconciling two Aristotelian passages here: *DA* 2.4, 416a25-9, which allows that water *is* nourishment for fire, and *GC* 1.5, 321a9-29, which seems to argue that the transformation of the elements is not growth, but generation and destruction. Alex. reads the first passage as being true only in a broader sense of 'growth', while the second is true in the fundamental sense. This is reasonable, since 416a25-9 only makes claims hedged by 'it seems' and 'it appears', and Arist. corrects this half a column later at 416b9-11, by denying that anything which is not alive can nourish itself, as Alex. emphasises at 34,13-14. Arist. elsewhere denies that fire can genuinely be nourished by moisture because it does not retain its identity from one moment to the next, but is in constant flux: *Meteor.* 2.2, 355a3-11; cf. Alex. *Mixt.* 16, 233,30-234,11. On water as nourishment for fire, see *Mant.* 149,11-13, where Alex. notes that it is the moisture in logs that burns; see also *in Sens.* 46,9-12.

301. [34,16-17] The aphorism points to a duality similar to the one Alex. has been emphasising: in a broad sense, food is nourishment, but more strictly it is only the part of it that nourishes and is incorporated into the body which is nourishment, the rest being waste. Accattino 1993 points out that Philoponus also quotes this phrase in this context (*in DA* 284,11-12) and explicitly attributes it to medical writers (*hoi iatroi*); and that it can be found in MS M (Marcianus gr. 269) of pseudo-Hippocrates *de Alim.* 8. The closest parallels from Galen, in contrast, all reflect the quite different reading in MS A of *de Alim.* (*trophê de to trephon, trophê de to hoion*). We can add that the phrasing Alex. quotes is also attributed to Hippocrates by Meletius *de Nat. Hom.* 101.13 Cramer.

302. [34,14-18] These remarks are Alex.'s gloss on Arist.'s solution at *DA* 2.4, 416b4-9. For a similar solution applied to perception, see 39,12-18 below (parallel to *DA* 2.5, 417a18-20).

303. [34,18-19] 34,14. *Mixt.* 16, 233,26-7.

304. [34,18-26] Arist. *GC* 1.5, 321a29-b10. Cf. Alex. *DA* 36,9-13; *Mixt.* 16, 234,11-15; 236,19-30; cf. 238,10-20. Alex. argues that there is a crucial asymmetry here between these two 'like' things, in spite of their symmetry in other respects. With respect to growth, what nourishes (in the second sense) and what is nourished are on a par, since the two are similar in kind, and so both are equally increased through the accretion of like by like. But with regard to being nourished, they are not symmetrical, since one is transformed into the other and not *vice versa*, and so only one is nourished by the other. The ground of this asymmetry is the presence of a soul (34,18-19), which Alex. had argued just above distinguishes nourishment specifically from the more general category of growth (34,8-14).

305. [34,27-35,2] Alex. is following the order of explanation set out at 32,23-33,12 (based on Arist. *DA* 2.4, 415a16-22): having finished his discussion of nourishment (33,13-34,26), he turns briefly to the activity of being nourished (34,27-35,8), along with the activities of growing (35,8-17) and reproducing (35,17-25), before finally discussing the powers underlying these (35,25-36,9).

On the need to transform the external nourishment before it can be assimilated and incorporated, see 33,18-19 (cf. 25-6) above.

306. [35,2-3] 96,5-8; *in Top.* 376,27-30; *in Sens.* 78,6-12; *in Meteor.* 186,35-187,3. In this passage, Alex. is surely continuing his elaboration of Arist. *DA* 2.4, by developing the claim at 416b28-9 that being nourished requires heat, which must therefore belong to all living beings (cf. also *Iuv.* 4, 469b11-12; *Resp.* 8, 474a25-8). For the specific claim that heat is a 'tool' or 'instrument' (*organon*) of the soul, see *GA* 2.4, 740b29-36, where Arist. says that the soul uses heat and cold as its tools in nourishment, growth, and reproduction; cf. also *PA* 2.7, 652b9-15.

According to Philoponus (*in DA* 288,5-19), Alex. discussed an interpretation of *DA* 416b25-9 – presumably in his lost commentary on the *DA* – whereby *both* heat *and* the soul for nourishing oneself are 'that by which' (*to hôi trephetai*) an animate thing is nourished, the soul as an unchanged changer and heat as a changed changer. But it is offered as an interpretation of an alternative manuscript reading, which Alex. may not himself endorse. See n. 323 on 36,9-13 below.

307. [35,3-5] Arist. *DA* 2.4, 416a9-15, which also cites certain unnamed philosophers as holding that the 'nature of fire' (*hê tou puros phusis*) is what is productive (*to ergazomenon*) in animals and plants and responsible for nourishing oneself and growing. Simplicius ascribes this view to Hippasus of Metapontum and Heraclitus at *in Phys.* 23,33-24,12, esp. 24,6-8. Arist. himself holds that heat simply as such is not responsible for these processes, but is only a kind of contributing factor (*sunaition pôs*, 416a14).

308. [35,5-8] These lines are a close reformulation of Arist. *DA* 2.4, 416a13-18, with some differences in emphasis. Alex. claims that all natural compounds (in contrast with the elements) observe a definite order in their activities and natural limits, which he attributes to their form: see esp. *in Metaph.* 103,31-104,18; also *Fat.* 4, 168,3-7.14-15; 6, 170,9-11; *in Metaph.* 32,1-5. Cf. *Mant.* 185,14-15; *in Metaph.* 101,28-30.

309. [35,8-9] 34,5-9.

310. [35,10-11] 74,23-5; cf. *in Top.* 167,8-11; Arist. *GC* 322a24-5; *Top.* 2.4, 111b24-6; cf. Arist. *Somn.* 1, 454b32-455a3; *EN* 1.13, 1102b4-5. AD 168 note that Alex. has 'animal' (*zôion*) at 35,11, where Arist. has the broader 'animate being' (*empsukhon*) at 416b13, and conjecture that Alex. might have written 'living thing' (*zôn*). Though possible, this is unnecessary: Alex. can use animals as an example without thinking that his claim applies only to them; or he may be using *zôion* as he sometimes does for living things in general.

311. [35,9-17] Arist. *DA* 2.4, 416b11-15; *GC* 1.5, 322a20-8; cf. Alex. *Mixt.* 16, 236,24-6. Since the power for nourishing oneself and growing are always coinstantiated (see n. 261 on 29,1-3) and both utilise nourishment (as he states here), Alex. needs to show that they are different in other ways: they can operate independently at different times (35,10-13), have different functions (35,13-15), and consequently involve different powers (35,15-17). For a more extended discussion of Alex.'s views on growth, see *Mixt.* 16, 233,23-238,23.

312. [35,19-20] 32,11-13.18-19; cf. Arist. *DA* 2.4, 415a26-8; 3.9, 432b23-5. On the face of it, this claim might seem to conflict with Alex.'s earlier assertions that the power for reproducing is inseparable from the other powers of the soul for nourishing oneself (29,1-3, with corresponding note; cf. 32,15-22). But they are compatible if we distinguish between types and tokens. The present claim concerns *individuals within* a species: even if the species as a whole has all three powers of the soul for nourishing oneself, a given individual may not, if it is immature or deformed. Claims about the separability of powers, in contrast, are based on whether there are any *species* where one power is found without the others. If there is no species that has the powers for nourishing oneself and growing, but lacks the power for reproducing, the power for reproducing will be inseparable. In the *DA*, Alex. simply treats them as inseparable, though it would be interesting to know whether he regards mules, which are infertile, as a species. Alex. does not appear to discuss the problem mules pose in his extant works, unlike Arist. (*GA* 2.8).

313. [35,20-2] On the reproductive changes during puberty (in humans), see *HA* 7.1 passim, which puts the first appearance of sperm at the age of 14 (581a12-14) though it is infertile until the age of 21 (582a16-17); cf. also *HA* 7.5, 585a34-b2; *GA* 1.19, 727a5-8; 1.20, 728b21-7. The appearance of the sexual organs is earlier, of course. He observes that a penis in a male embryo can already be detected by the fortieth day of gestation: *HA* 7.3, 583b14-20; cf. *GA* 4.1, 766b4-7 (though compare 2.4, 737b8-12).

314. [35,22-3] 32,11-16. Note that Alex.' claim here, as in the earlier passage, is not limited to living things (as BD seem to assume), but in some sense is meant to apply to all natural things.

315. [35,24] For the distinction between first and subsequent souls, see 16,18-17,1; 29,1-6; and esp. 38,12-13, where the first soul is also described as 'for vegetation' (*phutikê*), confirming Victorius' emendation of the MSS here, which read 'natural' (*phusikês*), to *phutikês*. AD 169 rightly cite Arist.'s pertinent use of the term for one side of the non-rational part of the soul at *EN* 1.13, 1102a32 and b29; BD adds *EE* 2.1, 1219b37.

316. [35,24-5] In line with the methodology given above (32,23-33,12), Alex. now turns from the activities of this type of soul to discuss the powers underlying it briefly (35,24-36,9): see n. 305 on 34,27-35,2. Since powers are defined by reference to the activities they give rise to, there is little Alex. has to add here beyond what he has already said.

317. [35,26] 29,2.

318. [35,26-7] Arist. *DA* 2.4, 416b14-19.

319. [36,2-3] Notice the omission of the phrase 'through its own activity' (*dia tês oikeias energeias*) which Alex. has used in the previous two cases (35,27; 36,2), as sexual reproduction requires the activity of another progenitor as well.

320. [36,3-4] Arist. *Somn.* 3, 456a34-b6; *PA* 2.3, 650b2-13; 2.4, 651a14-15; *GA* 1.18, 725a11-13, 726a26-7; 4.1, 766b7-9 (also b12-14); cf. 1.19, 726b1-5, b9-11; 2.3, 737a18-20. Alex.'s view, following Arist., is that the useful, nourishing part of food is extracted and refined through a process of cooking (*pettesthai*, see nn. 301 on 34,16-17 and 294 on 33,13-15 respectively), and then transformed into blood and distributed to the different parts of the body, which it nourishes and causes to grow. Through further cooking, the blood – the last or final nourishment – is turned into seed for producing another animal of the same sort: see 40,2-3 and 94,26-95,8 on blood (which is described as the 'last stage of nourishment' at 94,28) and 92,19-21 on seed.

Although Alex. states that this view 'has been shown elsewhere', there appears to be nothing in the extant works that corresponds to it. AD 169 reasonably suggest he is not referring to his own writings, but to Arist.'s *GA* (much as 97,26-7 refers to the *MA*).

321. [36,7] cf. 32,17; Arist. *GA* 2.1, 735a17-19.

322. [36,6-9] 32,11-15, together with accompanying note for references to Plato and Aristotle. The phrase 'reinvigorated immortality' (*athanasias episkeuastês*) at 36,8 comes from Plato *Polit.* 270A, which states that the heavens receive a 'reinvigorated immortality' when in the eternal cycle the craftsman god causes the heavens to move forward again, after having moved backwards under their own power, thus restoring forward moving life-processes to them. The details of this 'great myth' seem unimportant here, apart from the idea that something which is mortal in its own right might nonetheless adventitiously receive an extension of its life through something else, as part of a cycle. In particular, there is no suggestion in Alex. of divine intervention.

323. [36,9-13] Alex. here virtually reproduces Arist. *DA* 2.4, 416b20-3, with only minor changes. BD 271 suggest that Alex. interpreted this passage differently in his lost commentary on the *DA*, based on Philoponus *in DA* 288,5-19 (discussed above in n. 306 on 35,2-3). But Philoponus is concerned with a passage several lines later at 416b25-9, where there is a textual crux. Alex. may only be reporting there, as he often does, alternative readings and the consequent differences in interpretation, rather than endorsing it outright, and Philoponus' wording does not impute any stronger commitment on Alex.'s part than that. Themistius, in contrast, clearly does endorse the alternative reading: see his *in DA* 53,26-33. On the commentators' differing readings of this passage, see Moraux 2001, 333-4.

324. [36,13] Alexander is oversimplifying here: the threefold schema does not extend straightforwardly in the case of reproduction, since the soul that makes reproduction possible is only the same in species as the form of the body that is generated; they are not the same in number, as two distinct individuals are involved. Alexander does regard the seed, though, as 'that by which' (*di' hou*) something is reproduced and as a refinement of nourishment: see 36,3-4 above.

325. [36,14-18] Alex.'s argument is an expansion of Arist. *DA* 2.4, 416b23-5, with very close verbal echoes in (1), (2), and (3). A principle similar to (1) is attributed by Cicero (in a different context, concerning excellence and fulfillment) to Antiochus of Ascalon at *Tusc. Disp.* 5.22; *Fin.* 5.92. But it concerns the *largest* or *greatest* part, rather than the most advanced or complete one.

326. [36,16] 32,11-16.

327. [36,19-21] Arist. *GA* 2.1, 735a12-14; cf. 2.3, 736a35-b1. It is important to emphasise, here and in the lines that follow, both that (1) Alex.'s view is entirely faithful to Arist.'s account of reproduction in *GA* and (2) it is not in any way incompatible with his own account of the emergence of the soul from the body, as Moraux 1942 alleges (31-4, 38-43; cf. also Donini 1971, 81). On (1), see esp. Accattino 1988; on (2), see Sharples 1994*b*, Accattino 1995 and BD, 26-34, esp. 32-4.

The 'emergence' of the soul and other complex forms from the various forms in the matter underlying them need not be a diachronic process, as Moraux seems to assume, despite the language of 'emerging' or 'begetting'. It may instead refer to the *supervenience* that holds synchronically at any given time: in order for there to be a soul or other higher-level form at a given time, there must also be at the same time certain kinds of underlying material conditions that are *sufficient* nomologically for the higher-level forms to exist. The language of emergence and generation just underscores the novelty and irreducibility of the higher-level forms, which cannot be found apart from conditions like these. See, along with their corresponding notes, 5,5-6; 9,4-7; 10,17-19; 10,24-6; 23,29-24,4; 24,18-23; and 26,26-30.

What is crucial to observe is that none of these passages says anything about how *the underlying material conditions* are brought about: a supervenience thesis of this sort is, in the abstract, compatible with any number of causal stories. Nothing in Alex.'s emergentism, therefore, need contradict Alex.'s or Arist.'s view that 'man begets man', that is, that each living thing is always produced by another living thing of the same type, by means of its seeds. Reproduction is not the transmission of a soul that pre-exists in actuality, much less the magical generation of a new form by purely formal means. On the contrary, the seed of a living thing has the power to produce another living thing with a soul of its own *by effecting changes in matter*, which eventually lead to the appropriate combination of homogeneous materials and the constitution of organs from them. Clearly none of this precludes there being underlying material conditions which are a sufficient condition for the type of soul involved. On the contrary, one might even argue that such conditions are *required* if there is to be an explanation of why these material changes result in a new substance with a form of its own.

Finally, one should note that the agent which produces this underlying mixture is not the soul for nourishing oneself in the seed, as BD 33 suggests, since initially this soul is present only as a power: it does not attain the level of first completion until the heart is formed in the embryo and begins to draw nourishment. The agent is instead the seed itself, which produces the changes in the material furnished by the mother, which in turn leads to the production of the relevant homoeomerous materials and eventually the anhomoeomerous organs.

328. [36,22-3] Arist. *GA* 2.3, 736a31-6. Arist. makes clear that neither the seed nor the embryo has this soul in actuality before it has the organs necessary to perform the corresponding functions – it has soul only potentially, that is, through its power (*dunamei*): *GA* 2.3, 736b8-15, 737a16-18; cf. 2.1, 735a9-11; *Metaph.* 7.9, 1034a33-b1. Alex. also hedges on the status of an animal embryo: see 38,7-8 below.

329. [36,23] Repunctuating the text *epitêdeiou labêtai pros touto, sunhistêsin* with AD; see Accattino 1988, 81 n. 10 on Alex.'s use of *epitêdeios* with *pros* + acc.

330. [36,23-6] Arist. *GA* 2.3, 737a18-22; cf. 2.1, 735a12-14.

331. [37,1-3] A living thing cannot possess a power in actuality – that is, at the level of a first actuality or completion (*prôtê entelekheia*) – unless it is in a position to exercise that power (absent something extrinsic hindering or preventing it). But the powers of the soul require bodily organs for their exercise and so cannot be exercised before the relevant organs have developed. Prior to that time, then, a living thing can have such powers only potentially: Arist. *GA* 2.3, 736b22-4. The powers for nourishing oneself are present in actuality as soon as the heart or its analogue is formed, the first of the bodily organs: *GA* 2.1, 735a14-26; 2.5, 741b15-17. Other powers appear later, as the formation of the corresponding organs is staggered over the embryo's development: no power for perceiving can attain first completion before the relevant perceptual organs have been formed (736b1-5). For Alex. on the gradual emergence of powers, see below, 74,17-23; for the requirement that the organs must be present in order to possess the corresponding power, see 27,8-15 with note.

What is noteworthy here is Alex.'s vague reference to 'the other powers' (37,1). If this includes the rational powers, as it seems to suggest, then Alex. holds that the rational powers do not differ from others powers in this regard: they have not yet appeared because there are parts of the body on which their functioning depends. Contrast this with the central Aristotelian text on which Alex. depends here, *GA* 2.3, which takes the rational powers to pose a puzzle that needs to be solved (736b5-8). Unlike other parts of the soul, the understanding lacks a dedicated organ and so is not the form of any part of the body (*DA* 3.4, 429a18-27; cf. 2.1, 413a4-7): Arist. even claims that its activity is not a bodily one (*GA* 2.3, 736b29). Consequently, he regards it alone, of all the powers of the soul, as not involving a material contribution from the mother and so 'alone comes from without' (*monon thurathen epeisienai*, 736b27-8), that is, from the father. (For a more extended defense of this reading of Arist., see my 1999, 215-16.) Alex. agrees that the understanding is not the form of any part of the body; but he insists that it cannot function without bodily activity either (see n. 44 on 12,20-1 and n. 200 on 21,24 above). This might explain why the rational powers are the last to develop: they cannot be exercised until other powers, especially perception and representation, have themselves reached first completion; but these in turn depend on the development of organs that only emerge over time. (Alex. develops an entirely different reading of the understanding 'from without' below, however: see 90,19-21 and 91,2.)

332. [37,4-5] Arist. appeals to this fact repeatedly, but draws a more nuanced distinction than Alex. states here. In Arist.'s view, not just plants, but also certain insects like the centipede can survive dismemberment, at least for a little while; some animals like the tortoise can even survive the loss of an essential organ, like the heart: *DA* 1.4, 409a9-10; 1.5, 411b19-27; 2.2, 413b16-21; *Long.* 6, 467a18-23; *Iuv.* 2, 468a23-b15; *Resp.* 3, 471b203; *de Vita et Morte* 1 (= *Resp.* 18), 479b1-7; *IA*

7, 707a27-b5; *PA* 4.6, 682b30-2. On Aristotle's discussions of dismembered insects, see Sprague 1989.

Alex. oversimplifies Arist.'s view throughout most of this section, maintaining a strict dichotomy between plants and animals. At the end (38,8-11), he does mention that animals often survive dismemberment briefly, but it seems little more than an afterthought to bring himself in line with Arist.'s stated views. Alex. does not specify here whether all animals are capable of this or only some; nor does he explore how or in what circumstances animals manage to do this. At the end of the present treatise, he mentions that the tortoise and also the chameleon can survive the loss of their heart and adds, for dialectical purposes, that other animals can survive the loss of their head (100,9-13). But again he does not integrate this observation with his views here.

333. [37,5-11] Alex.'s argument here is elaborated more fully below at 37,18-38,4 (see accompanying note). But the key point is that nourishment is accomplished in plants without highly differentiated organs in disparate locations; and such differentiation as there is can be regenerated from most of the plant's parts, as they were originally generated from the seed.

334. [37,11-15] The Greek in this passage has been found difficult to construe. Bruns takes there to be a lacuna, inserts two clauses, and repunctuates the subsequent lines, altering the argument structure. But the text is grammatical as it stands and only requires a minor emendation of *oute* to *oude* at 37,14 (following Bruns' suggestion). The real difficulty is to identify the unexpressed antecedents for various terms. (*i*) It is not clear what *paresparmenai* at 37,12 modifies. AD take it to refer to 'souls' and accordingly insert *<hai psukhai eisin>* before *oukh homoiôs* at 37,12; but this would make the singular *hê tônde psukhê* in the next line awkward. Like BD, I prefer to take 'powers' (*dunameis*) as understood, since it is prominent in the immediately preceding lines and so would not need to be repeated. (*ii*) The antecedent for *ekeinôn* at 37,14 and 15 must be the same (against BD), but then it cannot refer to animals (against Bruns and BD), since the antecedent is said to be what is *received* at 37,15 (*dektika*). Like AD, I take these pronouns instead to refer to souls, explicitly mentioned at 37,13.

335. [37,11-18] Alex. is making two distinct points in these lines, which he interweaves throughout: (1) that in animals the soul is not 'homogeneous' (*homoiomerês*) in each part of the body in the way that it is in plants, and (2) that a separated part of an animal's body cannot regenerate the missing parts or acquire functions that were not originally developed in it from the seed.

(1) The lack of homogeneity is due to the close relationship between the actual possession of a power and the organs that subserve it: see esp. n. 331 on 37,1-3 above; cf. also n. 249 on 27,8-15. This is true not only of different types of powers, but even just the power for nourishing oneself by itself. Although this power is common to both plants and animals, it is realised in different ways in each: as one ascends the *scala naturae*, there is an increasing complexity in the way living things carry out even simpler functions and correspondingly a greater articulation in their bodily organs, which reflects a more highly specified division of labor: *Mant.* 103,38-104,5. As these organs are inevitably located in different parts of the body, physically separating them from each other destroys their ability to function together as a system. An animal can lose its eyes or limbs and still live (cf. *PA* 3.4, 665b24-6). But the permanent loss of parts of vital organs, as are required for digestion, eventually spells death: *Mant.* 104,5-8.

Alex. departs somewhat from Arist. here, who insists that the soul present in the divided parts is 'one in form' (*homoeideis*) both with each other and the soul of the original animal, despite the loss of organs, which can even remain sensitive for a time (*DA* 1.5, 411b19-27; *Iuv.* 2, 468b1-9, b12-14). In his view, the loss of organs explains why the divided parts fail to survive, but does not tell against the type of soul present in them.

(2) The dismemberment of animals generally implies a permanent loss: unlike plants, they cannot regenerate the missing organs. Arist. holds that this is the case with most animals and even insects (*Long.* 6, 467a20-2; cf. *PA* 4.6, 682b30-2), although he sometimes allows that simple insects like centipedes can survive because, like plants, the principle (*arkhê*) of their vital activities is present in each part (*PA* 4.5, 682a2-9).

336. [37,18-38,4] Plants can regenerate roots and stalk from any portion, since the principle (*arkhê*) is present in all parts potentially: *Long.* 6, 467a18-30; *Iuv.* 2, 468b5-9; *PA* 4.6, 682b30-2.

337. [38,4-8] 74,17-23. The question of whether the embryo is an 'animal' is a set topic in the doxographical tradition already by the first century CE (see Aet. 5.15, *Dox. Gr.* 425.14-426.14; cf. also Clement *Strom.* 8.10.3-4; Ps.-Galen *Def. Med.* 445, 19.451-2 Kühn), which typically represents Aristotelians as midway between Platonists and Stoics. The Platonists think the embryo is an animal, whereas the Stoics think that it is not, but like a plant (Plut. *Stoic. Rep.* 41, 1052F = *SVF* 2.806.1; Aet. 5.15.2, *Dox. Gr.* 425.18-22 = *SVF* 2.756; Ps.-Galen *Def. Med.* 445, 19.452.5-10 Kühn = *SVF* 2.757) – in fact, the Stoics regard nourishment and growth as due to nature, not soul (see n. 282 on 31,25-32,1 above). The Aristotelians, in constrast, think the embryo has a soul, but is only an animal in potentiality. See Moraux 2001, 363-3 n. 201, as well as Mansfeld's invaluable and meticulous discussion in 1990, 3186-90.

According to Arist., embryos actually possess the power of nourishment once they begin to 'draw nourishment' (*helkei tên trophên*, *GA* 2.3, 736b8-13). But prior to the development of perceptual organs, it only lives the 'life of a plant' (*phutou bion*, *GA* 2.3, 736b12-13; 3.2, 753b27-9; 5.1, 778b32-779a2; cf. *EE* 1.5, 1216a3-9); it is an animal only in its power and is still incomplete (*GA* 2.4, 740a24-7). Alex.'s view is somewhat stronger. It is not simply that the embryo at this stage is an animal only in its power; it is also not even receiving nourishment as an independent being in its own right, but is just *a part of another being*, its mother. Arist. himself only says more vaguely that it receives its nourishment from something else because it is 'an outgrowth' (*tôi pephukenai*, *GA* 3.2, 753b27-9). It is the Stoics, in fact, who seem to speak of the embryo as a 'part' of the womb (Aet. 5.15.2, *Dox. Gr.* 425.18-22 = *SVF* 2.756). It is perhaps worth noting in this context that Arist. thinks abortion is permissible before 'perception and life' (*aisthêsin ... kai zôên*) – life, presumably, *as an animal or a human* – have been realised (*Pol.* 7.16, 1335b19-26). Arist. believes this is 40 days for a male child and 90 for a female one (*HA* 7.3, 583b9-25).

Galen's position is broadly similar. He also compares the embryo to plants, like Arist. and the Stoics: see esp. *Foet. Form.* 3, 68.10-70.21 Nickel. But Galen is closer to Arist., since he does not hesitate to speak of the embryo as having a soul and regards it as becoming 'animal-like' prior to birth, as soon as a pulse is present: 3, 74.11-16 Nickel.

338. [38,8-11] Arist. *DA* 1.5, 411b19-27; *Iuv.* 2, 468b1-9, b12-14. Alex. here qualifies the oversimplified position he takes throughout most of this section, though without further exploring its theoretical ramifications (see n. 332 on 37,4-5 above). On 'traces' (*enkataleimmata*), see the note on. 62,22-63,4 in the second volume of this translation.

339. [38,12-13] For the first soul as the soul for life, see 29,1-10; as the soul 'for vegetation', see n. 315 on 35,24, where Alex. identifies its activities as nourishment, growth, and reproduction.

340. [38,13-15] The argument for the first soul as the form of the body occurs at 31,7-25. For the three types of powers involved, see 35,26-36,9 (cf. 32,6-23); the activities themselves are specified at 34,27-35,25.

341. [38,16-18] 29,12-22; 29,26-30,6. For Alex., this claim is true only if restricted to *mortal* beings: see the discussion of Alex.'s reading of Arist. *DA* 3.12, 434b3-8 in his lost commentary, ap. Ps.-Philop. *in DA* 595,37-596,14 (cf. n. 259 on 28,25-9 above).

342. [38,18-19] See 10,8-10 with corresponding note.

343. [38,19-20] In addition to *DA* 2.5-3.2, Arist. devotes an entire essay to perception (*Sens.*), on which Alex. has an extant commentary (*in Sens.*) and to which he may be referring here.

344. [38,21-39,2] cf. Mich. *in EN* 556,37-557,8, which contains a doublet of the entire passage (38,21-39,8). Alex. synthesises elements from several different discussions of perception in Arist. in this compact opening formulation:

(1) Perception is a form of cognition (*krinein*), in which one discerns or discriminates objects. For the meaning of this term, see n. 346 below on 39,4-5.

(2) Perception is understood as something relative to (*pros*) its objects and *vice versa*. This is explicit in *Cat.* 7 (6b2-8, b33-6, 7b33-8a12) and clearly implicit in *DA* 3.2, 425b25-426a27. Recognising the relational nature of perception does *not* imply, however, that the change involved is a *merely* relational one, a 'mere Cambridge change', where an object is said to undergo a change solely in virtue of changes in its relation to other objects rather than due to any modification intrinsic to itself (Geach 1969, 71-2): see Alex. *in Sens.* 127,5-128,6, esp. 127,5-12 and 128,2-6; more generally, *in Sens.* 16,15-16; 17,13; *in Metaph.* 324,33-325,1; 402,8-13; 406,25-407,15; 409,26-36; cf. *in Metaph.* 323,26; *in Top.* 71,4-7; 104,2-6; 218,21-2; 407,4-5.

(3) Perception comes about 'through a kind of alteration' (*dia tinos alloiôseôs*), as a result of which the perceptual organ that has the power is 'assimilated' or likened (*homoioumenon*) to the object; Alex. expands on this below at 39,10-18. Arist. classifies perception as this kind of modification or alteration in his first extended discussion of perception in general in *DA* 2.5. Like other agent-patient interactions, he regards perception as a case where the agent (the perceptible object) modifies or alters the patient (the perceiving subject), making it like itself, having been unlike before (417a14-21, 418a3-6). The kind of modification it undergoes does not destroy its nature, though, as other alterations might, but instead preserves the power to perceive by exercising it. Arist. concludes that perceiving is either not altering or an alteration 'of a different type' (*heteron genos*, 417b2-16; see also 3.7, 431a4-6). This explains Alex.'s qualification above, that perception is 'a *kind* of alteration' (*tinos alloiôseôs*, 39,2) or a kind of modification (*paskhein ti*), a qualification Arist. consistently makes himself: *DA* 2.4, 415b24; 2.5, 416b34; 2.11, 424a1; *Insomn.* 2, 459b4-5; *MA* 7, 701b16-18; *Phys.* 7.2, 244b10-12 (though n. b. 7.3, 248a6-9); it is also said to be a 'kind of change' (*kinêsis tis*) at *Somn.* 1, 454a9-11.

Alex. discusses whether perception is an alteration in more depth in *Quaest.* 3.2 & 3 (the former also refers explicitly at 81,17-18 to a discussion in his commentary, most likely his lost commentary on the *DA*, though see Sharples 1994a, 128 n. 197). Alex.'s considered position seems to be that (*a*) perception is not itself an alteration in the primary sense, but (*b*) it nevertheless occurs 'through' (*dia*) an alteration in the perceiver. For the contrast between (*a*) and (*b*), see *Quaest.* 3.3, 84,4-6.12-13;

3.9, 98,2-8; cf. also the analogy to the exercise of practical know-how (*tekhnê*) at *Quaest.* 3.2, 81,27-9. At *in Sens.* 9,5-6 Alex. suggests that Arist. says that perception is a modification *because* it comes about through a modification (*dia pathous*). He frequently makes the second point, (*b*), by itself in the *DA:* see 39,12; 50,11; 53,28; 54,21; 55,14; cf. 44,12; 59,8; also *Quaest.* 3.3, 83,3; 86,29-31; 3.9, 96,35. For (*a*) specifically, see *Quaest.* 3.3, 83,18; 84,18; 85,34-86,2; 86,23-5; cf. 84,8-12.

(4) It is interesting that Alex. does *not* mention the famous doctrine of 'receiving form without the matter' in his general characterisation here, but only a little later at 39,13 below. If the formulation above is a kind of formal *definition*, as AD suggest (175), its omission could be significant. But there is nothing that requires us to treat this formulation as anything more than a general summary, which can be filled in more as we go on.

345. [39,2-4] 33,7-10, with corresponding note; also Arist. *DA* 2.4, 415a20-2; cf. 1.1, 402b14-16.

346. [39,4-5] Alex. uses this pair of descriptions in defining most of the senses: each is a power for being aware of its objects and having cognition of them (*antilêptikê kai kritikê*). See 46,20-1; 50,9-11; 53,26-9; 53,30-54,2; 55,12-14; cf. 61,24-7; also *Mant.* 107,6-7; *in Sens.* 166,3. Both terms are central to Alex.'s treatment.

The verb for the first activity, *antilambanesthai*, and its corresponding noun, *antilêpsis*, are often rendered with cognates of 'apprehend'. But this is too abstract: in the *DA* Alex. never uses the term for understanding or thought, but only for perception. (Part A of the *de Intellectu* uses both terms for understanding at *Mant.* 107,7 but as part of a strong parallel with perception.) Alex.'s use of *antilêpsis* thus suggests the kind of direct, perceptual awareness we have of an object facing us. It is not used in these contexts to emphasise a connection with knowledge specifically, as the more abstract 'apprehension' might suggest, but something phenomenal and qualitative.

The verb for the second activity, *krinein*, and its corresponding noun, *krisis*, have been rendered by other scholars in various ways. Often cognates of 'judge' have been used, which would imply that it signifies a propositional attitude with a conceptual content as well as the subject's endorsement or commitment, much like belief. But it has been persuasively argued that, at least in Arist., this family of terms is used for a much more basic activity, of *discriminating* or *discerning* between different qualities, especially those on the spectrum of qualities that a given sense is sensitive to: see esp. Ebert 1983. Most of Alex.'s uses of this term are not decisive: he often speaks of engaging or being able to engage in *krinein* without further specification, beyond the mention of an object. Of the remaining cases, many can be understood in terms of perceptual discrimination, even when they involve content that seems more judgment-like, as when we perceive *that* contraries are contrary to one another (64,12-20). But not all of them can be understood in terms of discrimination and discerning. At 78,13-21 Alex. notes that there are many kinds of *krisis* other than perception: representing, endorsing, being aware, assuming, believing, knowing, reasoning, thinking, and understanding; cf. also 66,9-19; 72,3-5; 76,8-12; cf. Arist. *DA* 3.3, 427a20-1, 428a3-5. Discrimination may be what *perceptual* cognition consists in; but there is no reason to think all of these other sorts of cognition consist in discrimination for Alex. Because of this broad semantic field, I have rendered these terms with 'cognitive' and its cognates to express the general notion of a mental activity that has content and is involved in some way with knowing, in contrast with desiderative or practical attitudes. Alex. explicitly draws this contrast himself, splitting the capacities of the soul into two broad types, 'the cognitive' (*to kritikon*) and 'the practical' (*to praktikon*), at 73,20-6; 75,13-15; 76,1-3; 99,17-24. Emilsson also notes this contrast (1988, 122), but claims that the traditional rendering 'judgement' will still serve as well as 'cognition' for Alex.'s use of *krinein*. But this is not so. Judgement presupposes the subject's endorsement or rejection (cf. Salles 2001, 6 on the Stoic notion), whereas it is clear that some of the attitudes Alex. mentions, such as representation, do not. The content of judgements, moreover, is both propositional and conceptual, and so presupposes *logos*, whereas Alex. clearly believes that non-rational animals, who lack *logos*, nevertheless have *kritikai* powers too. What is essential is that all these activities are involved in the acquisition of knowledge, broadly understood, in contrast with desires or inclinations. If this is right, then Alex.'s identification of perception and cognition at *Quaest*. 3.9, 94,32-95,1 sounds less odd: for there is no independent reason to think that Alex. regards perception in general as a kind of *judgement*.

The term *gnôstikos*, which some translators render as 'cognitive', has a more limited semantic field, in contrast: *gnôstikos* and its cognates are used for higher epistemic achievements and in connection with knowledge in a narrower sense (see esp. 82,18 and its cognates at 1,6-9; 2,1; 66,17; 80,8; 82,13; 84,12). I have therefore used the more epistemic word 'apprehend' to render *gnôstikos* and its cognates.

347. [39,5-6] The term 'perception' (*aisthêsis*) is ambiguous: it can designate either the activity of perceiving or the power for it (cf. Arist. *DA* 2.5, 417a9-14; 3.2, 426a23-4). Before a perceptible object acts on it, it is perception only 'in power' (*dunamei*), at the level of first completion or actuality (cf. 425b29-31). Perception is always of objects which are present (*parontôn*) to the perceiver, unlike anticipation and memory, which are of future and past objects respectively: Arist. *Mem.* 1, 449b13-15, b27; cf. *Rhet.* 1.11, 1370a32-5; Alex. *DA* 69,11-14; *Quaest.* 3.3, 86,8-10; *in Top.* 116,28-9; cf. *DA* 66,24-8; *in Metaph.* 312,1-2.8-9; *Quaest.* 3.3, 85,15.

348. [39,6-8] Arist. uses the example of someone who possesses knowledge, but is not actively using it at the moment, to explain the difference between having the power to perceive and actually exercising it (*DA* 2.5, 417a21-b19), much as he had earlier to explain the idea that the soul is a 'first completion' or actuality (*entelekheia prôtê*, Arist. *DA* 2.1, 412a22-8; see above, Alex. *DA* 16,7-18). But if (*a*) actually exercising a power stands above (*b*) merely possessing it, actually possessing a power still stands above (*c*) merely having the power to acquire the power (on the latter, Arist. *DA* 2.5, 417a22-8, b29-32). (*b*) is thus Janus-faced: in comparison with (*a*), a perceptual power such as sight is a 'first completion', like the soul (412b27-413a3); but in comparison with (*c*), it can also be viewed as something higher than something else, a 'second power' (*deutera dunamis*), as Alex. calls it at *Quaest.* 3.2, 81,9; 3.3, 84,33-6.

On the neuter pronoun *ekeina* at 39,8, see Bruns' note in the critical apparatus and his entry in the index for Alexander's occasional practice of using neuter pronouns for nearby masculine and feminine antecedents.

349. [39,9-10] 71,26-72,5; 92,23-93,24; *in Sens.* 10,15-26; cf. *in Meteor.* 148,9-11. Alex.'s explanation for why perception is directed at external objects has no precise parallel in Arist. The chapter Alex. is summarising, *DA* 2.5, does mention that perceptibles are external and uses this to explain why perception is not up to us (417b19-25). But it does not refer to the final cause of perception or its role in action at all. Arist. does address the issue elsewhere, though, in *Sens.* 1. He. argues that the distance senses are for 'the sake of preservation' (*sôtêrias heneken*) because they can detect beneficial and harmful situations in advance, and so allow an animal to pursue or avoid what it ought (436b18-437a3; cf. *DA* 3.12, 434b24-7, though compare 3.13, 435b19-21). Pursuit and avoidance rely on our ability to discriminate between what is pleasant and painful, esp. in food, a sensitivity already present in the contact senses (*Sens.* 1, 436b12-18). Without the distance senses, mobile animals would not be able to find their food from a distance or evade predators and other dangers (*DA* 3.12, 434a32-b1); without the contact senses, which perceive food (2.3, 414b6-9; cf. 3.12, 434b18-22; 3.13, 435b22-3), the animal would not be able to seize or avoid what it ought (3.12, 434b13-17). Alex. adds to this observations on how the different distance senses contribute to preservation: smell allows animals to detect food, sight to detect predators, and sound both (*in Sens.* 10,16-25).

Arist. also argues that the distance senses are for the sake of the animal's well-being (*tou eu einai heneka*, 3.12, 434b24-7; 3.13, 435b19-21), esp. sight and hearing in animals with intelligence (*Sens.* 1, 437a1-17). Alex. greatly expands on Arist.'s brief remarks about the different contributions of sight and hearing to thought and differences in what they can discriminate: see *in Sens.* 10,26-14,6.

350. [39,13-14] Alex. briefly alludes here to a doctrine from a later chapter, *DA* 2.12, in which Arist. compares the senses to sealing wax: both receive the form of the object impinging on them 'without the matter' (*aneu tês hulês*, 424a17-24 at a18-19). Exactly what this phrase means and whether (and how) it qualifies the kind of likening involved is a matter of considerable dispute. Alex. will take this up later in the treatise, esp. in his comparisons of perception and understanding: see esp. 83,13-84,10; also 60,3-6; 66,13-14; 78,7-8; 92,21-3; *Quaest.* 3.7, 92,27-31 (cf. 92,35 and 93,9-11); 3.9, 95,20-1. In the present passage, Alex. does not seem to think that such qualifications affect his point about likening.

351. [39,10-18] Alex. elaborates the claim above (39,1-2) further. Even if perception should turn out not to be an alteration in the primary sense itself – see (3) of n. 344 on 38,21-39,2 above – it nevertheless occurs *in virtue of* a kind of 'assimilation' or likening (*kat' homoiôsin*) to the perceptible object, which comes about *through* an alteration (*di' alloiôseôs*, 39,12). Alex. is clear that what undergoes alteration and is likened is what possesses the soul (*to ekhon autên*, 39,1), that is, 'the *body* that primarily possesses the perceptual soul' (*ginetai to pathos touto en tôi prôtôi tên aisthêtikên psukhên ekhonti* sômati, 39, 18-19).

In the passage above, Alex. develops one of the main conclusions of the argument in *DA* 2.5, namely, that this change is understood along the same lines as alteration in general (cf. 417a1-2). The agent, in acting on the patient, makes the patient like itself, with respect to the active quality, so that in one way they must be unlike (namely, before the change), and in another alike (after the change): see *DA* 2.5, 417a18-20 and, for the general principle, *GC* 1.7, passim. In this respect, perception does not differ from nourishing oneself, as Alex. notes (39,16), glossing Arist.'s own back-reference at 417a19-20: at any rate, Arist.'s discussion of nourishment in *DA* 2.4 employs the same causal framework to reach an analogous result (416a29-b9). See Alex.'s remarks above, 33,15-34,18.

352. [39,18-21] Alex. begins to develop here the notion of a perceptual system, with the contrast between a central or 'primary' perceptual organ, where perception actually occurs, and the various peripheral organs which relay the modifications they undergo from perceptible objects to it. Alex. later famously compares the perceptual system to a circle, with the five peripheral sense organs at points on the circumference, relaying their modifications along radii that terminate in the common sense at the circle's centre: 63,8-64,11; cf. 64,17-65,2; 78,10-13; see Henry 1960. Alex. mentions the internal 'relaying' (*diadosis, diadidonai*) of perceptual stimulations from the peripheral organs to the central organ on a number of occasions: 39,21; 41,5; 63,16; 64,8; *Quaest.* 3.9, 97,5.12; *in Sens.*

59,12-15; cf. also *parapempôn* at *DA* 50,15-18 below and *diapempomena* at *Quaest.* 3.9, 96,33.36. In light of this, AD are surely right to correct the MSS *eit'* at 39,21 to *ep'*, a simple majuscule error. They point out that the construction *diadidonai ti epi ti* occurs several times in the treatise: 41,4; 42,19; 63,16; 64,8. Ironically, Alex. uses the verb *diakoneisthai* here (39,20) in its more common sense of 'serve', although elsewhere in this treatise he uses it most frequently to designate the transmission of a message from perceptible objects to the peripheral organs: see n. 362 on 41,1-3.

Alex. is systematising Arist.'s views here, based on scattered remarks across the corpus, but especially from the *Parva naturalia*. Several passages confirm that there is a single, common perceptual organ (*koinon aisthêtêrion*), to which all the other perceptual organs lead (*pros ho sunteinei talla*) and which is 'in charge' of them (*tou kuriou tôn allôn pantôn aisthêtêriou*), receiving all perceptibles (*dektikon pantôn tôn aisthêtôn*): *Somn.* 2, 455a12-b2; *Iuv.* 3, 469a10-16; *PA* 2.1, 647a24-30; cf. 2.10, 656a26-33; *GA* 5.2, 781a20-3. Arist. describes at some length the transmission of changes due to perceptual stimulations (*hai kinêseis hai apo tôn aisthêmatôn ginomenai*), which travel to the principle and origin of perception (*epi tên arkhên tês aisthêseôs katapherontai*) at *Insomn.* 3, 460b28-461a8 (cf. a8-b20).

The Stoics also claim that perception arises when an external impulse has been 'relayed' to the governing faculty (Galen *PHP* 2.5.35, 134.23-6 De Lacy = *SVF* 1.151, 2.882, cf. also 7.7.17, 472.29-33; Plot. 4.7.7.7-11 = *SVF* 2.858), as does Ptolemy (*de Judic.* 8, 13.6 Lammert). But we can find this usage in Plato already as well (*toutôn tas kinêseis diadidon eis hapan to sôma mekhri tês psukhês, Tim.* 45D; cf. *Tht.* 184D).

Alex.'s initial reference at 39,18 to a 'primary body' *may* derive from Arist.'s definition of a perceptual organ (*aisthêtêrion*) as the 'primary thing in which this sort of power' resides (*prôton en hôi hê toiautê dunamis, DA* 2.12, 424a24-5). But if so, then Alex. does not take this to refer to the peripheral organ that external stimuli *first* impinge upon, but rather the *ultimate* (*eskhaton*) perceptual organ, inside (*entos*) the animal, much as the organ of touch is described in Arist. as located not on the body's surface, but in something 'primary' beneath the flesh: *DA* 2.11, 423b29-31 (cf. b22-3); also 422b21-3; 3.2, 426b15-17; *PA* 2.10, 656b34-6 (2.8, 653b23-30, though compare 2.1, 647a19-21); and in the *Parva naturalia* Arist. describes the common sense as the 'primary thing that can perceive' (*prôton aisthêtikon*): 450a12, 451a17, 458a28. In any case, Alex. also uses both adjectives for the central organ (or sense), sometimes in close proximity: it is 'first' at 60,6; 65,8; 68,6; 69,22; 97,6; cf. *Mant.* 142,32; and 'ultimate' at 63,15.18; 64,8.18; *Quaest.* 3.9, 96,31; 97,5.10; *in Sens.* 168,3. For discussion, see Sharples 2005*b*, 349-50 nn. 17-18.

353. [39,21-40,3] On the soul for perceiving 'being situated in the area around the heart' (*hidrumenon peri tên kardian*, 39,21-2), see esp. 96,25-97,14; 98,1-7; 99,19-30). The location of the governing part and the soul's other powers is the subject of a lengthy appendix at the end of the present treatise (94,7-100,17). On the heat and moisture of the heart, see 94,17-20; *in Sens.* 40,22-3.

These details about the heart are entirely orthodox. Arist. locates the 'principle and origin of perception' (*arkhê tês aisthêseôs*) in the heart: see esp. *Iuv.* 3, 469a5-20; 4, 469a23-7, b3-6; *Somn.* 2, 455b34-456a6; also *PA* 2.1, 647a24-33; 2.7, 653b5-8; 2.10, 656a27-31 (cf. b24); 3.4, 665a10-13; 3.4, 666a11-18, a34-b1; 3.5, 667b21-31; 3.10, 672b14-19; 4.5, 678b1-4; *GA* 2.6, 743b25-7; *MA* 11, 703b23-4 (cf. 9, 702b20-1). The heart is described as a 'well-spring' (*pêgê*) at *PA* 3.4, 666a7-8 (cf. 666a11-18, a34-b1). On the heart as responsible for both the moisture and heat of blood, in connection with perception, see *PA* 3.5, 667b19-34; cf. 2.4, 650b22-3; *Somn.* 2, 456a6-10; heat and moisture are said to belong to animals naturally at *Long.* 5, 466a18-19. On heat and the heart more generally, *Iuv.* 4, 469b6-20; *Sens.* 2, 439a1-4; cf. *Resp.* 15, 478a24; *PA* 3.7, 670a23-6. On the heart as the origin of breath or *pneuma*, *Somn.* 2, 456a3-10; *MA* 10, 703a14-16.

The commitment to a central organ need not imply that perception *only* occurs there, however; still less does it reduce the peripheral organs to a purely interme-diary role like the external medium. But there are passages where Alex. seems to take extra steps in this direction. At *in Sens.* 34,3, for example, he says that neither the eye nor the vitreous humour *sees* and at 36,9 that the *power of sight* is not in the eye, but rather in the central organ; in fact, none of the senses can be in the peripheral organs, he argues, or we would not be able to compare their reports (*in Sens.* 36,11-19). But he does not make these denials expressly in the *DA*, which may therefore allow a more accommodating position, where, for example, the peripheral organs are first affected differently than the medium, but then transmit or even 'report' (64,2.20) their modification to the heart: see *DA* 60,14-17; 62,16-20; 63,28-65,2; also 44,6 where the eyes are said to be that 'through which' (*di' hou*) the awareness of colour arises. For a sensitive and thorough discussion of the evidence for both Arist.'s and Alex.'s position on this question, see Sharples 2005*b*, esp. 352-9.

354. [40,4-5] Alex. evidently has in mind the five senses here: sight, hearing, smell, taste, and touch. But in speaking of them as 'parts' (*merê*) of perception, he is thinking of them as different powers, much as perception is 'part' of the soul: see n. 244 on 27,1-4 above; cf. 19,2-3. The Stoics also speak of the five senses as 'parts', though as parts of the soul: Aet. 4.21.2-3, *Dox. Gr.* 410.30-411.13 = *SVF* 2.836 = LS 53H 3; D.L. 7.110 (cf. 157) = *SVF* 2.828.

355. [40,5-6] On the serial order of souls, see 16,18-17,1; 28,20-5; on the serial order of senses, see Alex.'s remarks just below at 40,11-15. Bruns inserts *phutikês* before *tês psukhês* at 40,5, in line with the Hebrew translation, thus making the comparison to a serial order specifically in the soul *for vegetation*, rather than the soul in general (as I have taken it). But the difficulties Alex. immediately goes on to discuss at 40,6-9 (see n. 357 below) are peculiar to the soul in general: since only the most rudimentary powers are possessed by living things universally, while the subsequent powers are not, a general characterisation could only mention the more rudimentary powers. The different senses present the same difficulty be-cause touch is the only sense possessed by animals universally. The three powers of the soul for vegetation (35,23-36,9), in contrast, are shared universally by all living things (or at any rate, those which have not been maimed) and so in fact *permits* a common account: 32,9-23.

356. [40,6-9] See esp. 17,1-8, with corresponding note; also 28,14-20; 30,17-20; *Quaest.* 1.11a and b, passim. I take the imperfect *ên* here to be a 'philosophical imperfect' expressing a general truth, rather than a back-reference (as AD 177 do).

357. [40,9-10] Just as Alex.'s discussion in this section is patterned after Arist.'s in *DA* 2.5, his procedure for the next 26 pages largely follows Arist.'s sequence in *DA* 2.6-12, including a preliminary discussion of the different kinds of perceptible, digressions on light and echoes, and a final discussion of perception in general: kinds of perceptible (40,20-42,3); sight (42,4-43,8) and light (43,8-46,19); hearing (46,20-47,24) and echoes (47,25-51,4); smell (51,5-53,29); taste (53,30-55,14); touch (55,15-59,24); and perception in general (60,1-66,8). Arist. offers no reason for proceeding in this way, though: the justification at 40,4-10 is wholly Alex.'s own.

358. [40,11-15] Alex. again brings together several different, but related doctrines here:

(1) The notion of separation involved is a taxonomical one: for details, see n. 258 on 28,23-5 above; 92,15-94,6; cf. *in Sens.* 10,12-15. Arist. draws the exact same parallel between the separability of the different senses and of different kinds of soul himself at *DA* 2.2, 413b4-7. He frequently states that touch can be found apart from the other senses, but not *vice versa: DA* 2.2, 413b4-7; 2.3, 415a3-5; 3.13, 435a12-13, b2; cf. *Sens.* 1, 436b13-14. Alex. frequently makes the following, somewhat weaker claim instead.

(2) Touch is necessary for there to be an animal at all and so belongs to all animals: Alex. *DA* 59,20; 92,23-93,19; 96,22-3; *in Sens.* 9,7-11; *in Top.* 116,25; 455,17; Arist. *DA* 2.2, 413b4-5, b8-9, 414a3-4; 2.3, 414b3; 3.12, 434a28-9, b9-14, b22-4; 3.13, 435b4-7, b16-19; *Sens.* 1, 436b13-14; *Somn.* 2, 455a27; *HA* 1.3, 489a17-19; 4.8, 535a4-5; *PA* 2.8, 653b22-4; cf. *EN* 3.10, 1118b1.

(3) For the claim that taste is 'a kind of touch' (*haphê tis*), see 51,26 (cf. 54,1); 93,4; *in Sens.* 39,23; 78,2; 105,4-5; also Arist. *DA* 2.9, 421a19; 3.12, 434b18, 21; *Sens.* 2, 438b30-439a1; 4, 441a3; *PA* 2.17, 660a21. But it is important to note that Arist. also denies that taste just *is* touch (*DA* 2.10, 422a10; 2.11, 423a20-1). His view seems to be that taste is of nourishment and so must be of a kind of tangible quality (*DA* 2.3, 414b6-9; 3.12, 434b18-19; cf. *Sens.* 4, 441b24-442a12). But if so, then we can only perceive it by being in contact with it – literally, by touching – and not through the medium of a foreign body (*DA* 2.10, 422a8-9; cf. Alex. *DA* 54,1-5; *in Sens.* 168,20-2).

On a philological note, AD 177 persuasively argue that *ê opsis* at 40,11 should be taken as corrective ('or rather sight'), since the frequent occurrence of *horasis* in the doxographical tradition is out of line with the strict distinction Alex. draws between the activity of seeing (*horasis*) and a capacity like sight (*opsis*), which is more appropriate here.

359. [40,15-19] Alex. relies here on Arist.'s methodological principle (*DA* 2.4, 415a14-23) that in order to understand a given capacity, we must look first to the activity or exercise of that capacity, and to understand that activity, we must look still before that at the kinds of objects on which it is exercised: see 32,25-7 and 33,7-10 above, with corresponding notes. But this order makes even more sense in the case of perception, where the animal's senses are in some way likened *to the objects* of perception, unlike nourishment, where the object is assimilated *to the animal's body*. By learning about the nature of perceptible objects in themselves, we therefore learn something about the nature of the effect they have on us.

360. [40,20-1] Alex adopts Arist.'s two-stage division of perceptibles at *DA* 2.6, 418a8-11, first broadly into those which are 'intrinsically' perceptible (40,21-41,5) and those which are 'extrinsically' perceptible (41,5-10), but then subdividing the first into those which are intrinsically perceptible to one sense 'exclusively' (40,21-41,1) and those which are intrinsically perceptible to several senses 'in common' (41,1-5). Arist. also discusses different kinds of perceptible at *DA* 3.1, 425a14-b10; 3.3, 428b18-30; *Sens.* 1, 437a3-17; cf. *Insomn.* 1, 458b4-6.

Arist. offers no independent characterisation of things which are perceptible 'intrinsically' (*kath' hauto*), literally, 'in virtue of themselves' or 'on their own'. But presumably any kind of thing will be intrinsically perceptible just in case it is perceptible *as such*, that is, it is perceptible in so far as it is an *F* or in virtue of being *F* (for some value of *F*), something that is *not* true of things which are perceptible only extrinsically (*DA* 3.1, 425a25-7). It is tempting, furthermore, to construe this distinction causally: *F*s are intrinsically perceptible because they can *bring about* perception (*poiêtikon tês aisthêseôs*) in virtue of being *F* (*Sens.* 6, 445b4-8; cf. 3, 439a17). The senses are *not* affected, in contrast, by extrinsic perceptibles in so far as they are such (*DA* 2.6, 418a23-4). But a causal reading is not unproblematic. While it applies straightforwardly to things which are intrinsically perceptible to one sense exclusively (cf. *DA* 2.6, 418a24-5), it is not clear whether or how this would apply to common perceptibles. Arist. never explains the causal mechanism by which we perceive common perceptibles and there are points where he speaks of them as if they might even be *extrinsic* to perceptibles exclusive to one sense: *DA* 3.1, 425a13-20, b4-10; 3.3, 428b22-4 (though contrast 3.1, 425a21-30). There is little discussion, or even awareness, in the literature on Arist. of this apparent conflict. But the expression 'in virtue of' can be understood in many ways, including definitionally (see, e.g., Sorabji [1971] 1979), and so its precise meaning in this context, for either Arist. or Alex., is very much open to debate.

The most Alex. says about what is intrinsically perceptible is negative. Time is not intrinsically perceptible because it is not 'some underlying nature which we perceive' (*hupokeimenê tis phusis hês aisthanometha*), but rather that in which the things we perceive are and occur (*in Sens.* 147,5-8). Similarly, small undetached parts of bodies, like the ten thousandth part of a millet seed, are not intrinsically perceptible, except potentially, because they do not as parts intrinsically exist, that is, on their own as such (and once they do, they are too small to be seen by themselves): see esp. *in Sens.* 116,21-3 and 116,7-122,23 passim. But these uses of 'intrinsically perceptible' seem to be different from Arist.'s sense or in the passage above, since both time and the colour of a ten thousandth part of a millet seed *are* both intrinsically perceptible in the sense given here (colour being perceptible on its own exclusively to sight and time common to several senses).

361. **[40,21-41,5]** Although usually translated as 'special', 'peculiar', or even 'proper' perceptibles, the meaning of the phrase *idia aisthêta* is best understood through its contrast with *koina aisthêta* (see n. 362 on 41,1-3), that is, as simply a question of whether something can be intrinsically perceived by just one sense *exclusively* or is *shared* by several; expressing the contrast in this ways avoids some of the epistemological connotations of the more traditional renderings. When Arist. first introduces exclusive perceptibles, he characterises them in two ways: as things (*a*) that cannot be perceived by another sense and (*b*) about which we cannot be mistaken (418a11-12). Alex. mentions only (*a*) in the present passage, deferring discussion of (*b*) until 41,13-15, which suggests that (*a*) is what defines exclusive perceptibles, while (*b*) may simply be a distinctive property they all possess. Alex.'s wording at 40,26 includes an important qualfication, which is absent from Arist.'s formulation, but is nonetheless required. Arist.'s considered position is not that exclusive perceptibles can be perceived by only one sense *tout court*, as his words at 418a11-12 might suggest, since each of these perceptibles can also be perceived by the other senses extrinsically (*kata sumbebêkos, DA* 3.1, 425a30-b3; see Alex. *Quaest.* 3.8 passim). What distinguishes them is that they are *intrinsically* perceptible (*kath' hauta*) to only one sense.

The examples Alex. gives here are the customary ones, with the exception of touch. Arist. holds that touch is sensitive to a number of tangible contrarieties, and the list differs on different occasions: see Arist. *DA* 2.11, 422b25-7; *GC* 2.2, 329b18-20. One might wonder whether the list of exclusive perceptibles is exhaustive for the other senses as well: Alex., at any rate, is willing to consider the possibility at 55,26-56,3 (commenting on Arist. *DA* 2.11, 422b27-33).

Arist. says that exclusive perceptibles are perceptible in the primary or fundamental sense (*kuriôs*) and that the essence of each sense is determined by its relation to them: *DA* 2.6, 418a24-5. This explains why the discussion of the different senses in *DA* 2.7-11 and *Sens.* 2-5 is so focused on these qualities, since they serve to differentiate the activities of the various senses and so help to define them, in line with his general methodology (*DA* 2.4, 415a16-23): see Alex. *in Sens.* 41,15-21. The tight connection between exclusive perceptibles and the individual senses is also meant to explain the authority that each sense has regarding the presence of such qualities in the perceiver's environment: *Metaph.* 4.5, 1010b14-17.

362. [41,1-3] Alex.'s division of things which are intrinsically perceptible is dichotomous: they are either intrinsically perceptible to exactly one sense (*idia*) or to more than one sense (*koina*). This cleans up Arist.'s presentation, which usually characterises the common perceptibles more narrowly, as things which are intrinsically perceptible to *all* the senses (*DA* 2.6, 418a10-11, a18-19). This leaves open a gap: anything that is intrinsically perceptible to more than one sense, but not to all, would be neither an exclusive nor a common perceptible by this characterisation. And it seems likely that several of the perceptibles Arist. calls 'common' would in fact belong to this middle group: it is hard to see how size or shape can be perceived by hearing, smell, or taste, as several commentators have pointed out (Simpl. *in DA* 126,27-37; Hicks 1907, 362, *ad* 418a19; cf. Alex. *in Sens.* 85,25-86,1; Them. *in DA* 57,36-58,5); and Alex. even denies that touch can be aware of number or distance (*in Sens.* 85,16, although this is somewhat surprising, since Arist. speaks about the relative authority of sight and touch regarding the number of objects perceived at *Insomn.* 2, 460b20-3). Arist. himself seems to recognise the issue elsewhere, though: at *Sens.* 4, 442b4-7, he says that perceptibles such as size, shape, roughness, and sharpness are 'common to all the senses' (b4) and then goes on to correct this, saying 'common to the senses, if not to all of them, then at least to sight and touch' (b6-7). Alex. adopts this more permissive construal as Arist.'s considered view. Such a distinction is already implicit in Aet. 4.8.6, *Dox. Gr.* 395.12-15. Galen goes even further, denying that size and shape can be perceived by any sense other than sight, 'except sometimes touch extrinsically', and that none of the others can perceive position and distance (*PHP* 7.5.35-8, 460.11-16; cf. 7.6.24, 466.26-7 De Lacy).

Later Alex. will deny that it is the five senses which actually have cognition (*krinei, krisis*) of common perceptibles – this belongs instead to the common sense alone (65,10-21). It is significant, then, that he speaks of the five senses here as 'transmitters' (*diakonoi*, 41,3), which is how they are also described in the pre-Galenic *Def. Med.* 116, atttributed to Galen (19.379.7 Kühn). As Alex. immediately goes on to say, the perceptual organs *relay* (*poietai diadosin*) the common perceptibles to 'the sense for them' (*epi tên aisthêsin autôn*, 41,4-5), that is, to the common sense. The Greek *diakonos* and its cognates are often used elsewhere simply to indicate a servant or the functions a servant performs taken quite broadly, and this can be the case even when Alex. is talking about the senses (see esp. 39,20 above, also *Mant.* 104,8). But *diakonos* can also refer to a specific kind of servant, a *messenger* (LSJ cite Aesch. *PV* 942 and Soph. *Phil.* 497). This sense predominates in Alex.'s works, esp. where the transmission of perceptible forms is concerned, often through an external medium: 41,3.20; 42,9; 52,20; 59,14; 62,5.12; 94,28; 95,1; 100,16; *Mant.* 145,27; *in Sens.* 25,21; *Quaest.* 1.2, 5,14-16; 6,9.13.20; 7,12; also cf. a report from his lost commentary ap. Philop. *in DA* 519,29 (= fr. IIIa Moraux). This sense is confirmed by Alex.'s repeated description of the medium as something that 'can receive and transmit' (*dektikon te kai diakonon*) perceptible forms: *Mant.* 145,26-7; *Quaest.* 1.2, 5,14-15; 6,9; 7,12. The last citation is the most telling. Alex.

uses elegant variation in a parallel between sight and smell: just as an odourless medium 'can receive and can *communicate*' (*mênutikon*, 7,10) odours, so the transparent medium 'can receive and *transmit*' (*diakonon*, 7,12; cf. 5,18-19) colours; we find the two terms used together again at *DA* 59,14 below. Thus, by undergoing a kind of alteration due to the object, the transparent medium '*reports* the form from the object that can be seen to sight' (*to eidos to apo tou horatou têi opsei* diangellontos, *Mant.* 141,35-6; cf. 142,31-143,1).

The Stoics refer to the senses as messengers that report back to the governing faculty, which acts like a monarch: Calc. 220, 233.5-6 Waszink = SVF 2.879 = LS 53G 7. But other philosophers make use of the comparison as well: Epicurus regards the senses as 'messengers of the truth' (*veri nuntios*, Cic. *de Nat. Deor.* 1.70); Ptolemy has the senses relaying their reports to the understanding, but 'like a messenger not interfering further' (*outhen epipolupragmonei kathaper angelos tis, de Judic.* 8, 13.5-8 Lammert); and Galen compares breath or *pneuma* to a messenger (*hôsper angelou tinos*), although it goes in the *reverse* direction, from the central organ to the peripheral senses (*PHP* 7.4.1, 448.7-9 De Lacy).

363. [41,3-5] As mentioned in n. 362 on 41,1-3 above, Alex. later identifies 'the sense' to which the common perceptibles are relayed as the common sense, which alone has cognition of them (65,10-21). What is striking here is Alex.'s insistence that common perceptibles accompany exclusive perceptibles at each stage of the process, not only in the distal object, where for example colour and shape always occur with each other (Arist. *DA* 3.1, 425b8-9), but also in the transmission from the peripheral organs to the central sense. Our awareness of common perceptibles is not the result of reorganising perceptual data at the final stage (as seems to be the case in Aet. 4.8.6, *Dox. Gr.* 395.1-12). Rather, common perceptibles are 'interwoven' (*sumpeplegmena*) from the start (*DA* 83,17-22), affecting the peripheral sense *along with* exclusive perceptibles like colour (65,11-16; cf. *in Sens.* 11,14-19).

Alex. offers detailed explanations of how we discern shape, size, distance, number, movement, rest, and number in vision, by means of the angle of the visual 'cone' extending to the object, variations in colour and other visible qualities, at *Mant.* 146,1-147,16 (quite possibly in response to Galen's complaints, *PHP* 7.7.4-8, 470.17-472.2 De Lacy).

364. [41,5] *in Sens.* 11,12-17; 84,11-16. Alex.'s list of common perceptibles here is exactly the same as Arist.'s at *DA* 2.6, 418a17-18; *Sens.* 1, 437a8-9; cf. *Insomn.* 1, 458b4-6. Arist. adds one (*hen*) to the list at *DA* 3.1, 425a14-16 and roughness, smoothness, sharpness, and bluntness at *Sens.* 4, 442b4-7. Alex. argues that these last four qualities cannot be subsumed under shape, because they do not fit its definition (*in Sens.* 84,13-16), but are common to very different perceptibles (*in Sens.* 84,16-18; *DA* 56,1-3). Alex. himself adds distance to the list at *DA* 65,13-14; *in Sens.* 84,11-13. One might have thought that distance could have been subsumed under extension (*megethos*). But Alex.'s explanation below of how we are aware of the distance of an object through hearing, sight, and smell suggests otherwise: *DA* 50,18-51,6 (with accompanying notes).

These lists are often compared to Plato *Tht.* 185A-D, where Socrates focuses on our awareness of certain 'common' features of perceptible objects, such as their being and not-being, or their being like and unlike, same and different, one and many, and somewhat further on admirable and shameful, and good and bad (186A). But Socrates' point in context is precisely that these features are *not* perceived by the senses, but rather by the soul, which alone compares and calculates (185D-186C; cf. 185B-C); Galen similarly claims that size, shape, motion, and number cannot be perceived by perception alone, but by reasoning and memory

(*PHP* 7.6.24, 466.25-8 De Lacy). Arist. and Alex.'s point is thus quite different. While they agree that there must be some single thing which has access to the reports of the various senses, they insist that we are nonetheless aware of these features *by perception* (hence the importance of a central or common *sense*). Moreover, they include quite mundane physical characteristics like size, shape, and change, while omitting the more transcendental characteristics that concern Plato, like being, sameness, and goodness. In fact, the only intersection between their respective lists concerns oneness and number.

    365. [41,6-8] Alex. returns to the primary division here, between those things which are intrinsically perceptible (*kath' hauta*) and those which are 'extrinsically' (*kata sumbebêkos*) perceptible (or, as commonly rendered, 'accidentally', 'concomitantly', or 'incidentally' perceptible). These are characteristics which are extrinsic to something perceptible – more literally, they 'happen to belong to it' (*sumbebêkenai*), perhaps even necessarily, as opposed to being part of its essence – and just because of this can be counted as perceptible themselves. So *A* is extrinsically perceptible just in case (*i*) *A* is an extrinsic characteristic of *B* and (*ii*) *B* is perceptible (intrinsically, one assumes). Arist. only offers examples of extrinsic perceptibles, rather than a fully general characterisation. But each time he does, he offers an explanation along the lines just sketched: with seeing Diares' son (*DA* 2.6, 418a20-3); seeing Cleon's son (3.1, 425a24-7); and even seeing a universal, colour (*Metaph.* 13.10, 1087a19-20' cf. *An. Post.* 2.19, 100a17). Alex.'s explanation conforms closely to Arist.'s first example, even down to the phrasing, especially if Bruns' clever suggestion is right: that the Greek for 'foam' (*aphron*) is a corruption of the name 'Euphronius' (*Euphron*), which the Hebrew translation appears to have taken to be a form of the word 'thoughtful' (*euphrôn*); Euphronius is perceptible because he happens to be white or pale (similar to Diares' and Cleon's sons), and this colour is perceptible. The suggestion that a substance like Euphronius can be an extrinsic characteristic of a perceptible like white might be surprising, as it seems like a reversal of the ontological priority developed in the *Categories*. But Arist. allows such locutions, so long as we do not take them to imply that the perceptible in these cases is the underlying subject: see *An. Pr.* 1.27, 43a33-6; *An. Post.* 1.22, 83a1-14.

    Nothing prevents something from being intrinsically perceptible *and* extrinsically perceptible, so long as it is so to different senses: sweetness is intrinsically perceptible to taste, but extrinsically perceptible to sight. In fact, every exclusive perceptible will be extrinsically perceptible to the other senses: *DA* 3.1, 425a30-1. But according to Alex. it need not be the case that every extrinsic perceptible be perceptible to each sense. In *Quaest.* 3.8 (passim), he argues that an extrinsic perceptible can be perceived by every sense only if the object has some qualities that are perceptible exclusively to each sense. He thus assumes we cannot perceive something extrinsically *with a particular sense* unless it has some perceptible quality exclusive to that same sense. I may be able to perceive a toxic gas extrinsically by smell and, if it has a colour, by sight too; but if it lacks a colour, I cannot perceive it by sight, either intrinsically or extrinsically according to Alex.

    366. [41,8-10] Taken at face value, Alex.'s denial that extrinsic perceptibles are perceptibles *au fond* or 'at bottom' (*tên arkhên*) is quite strong. It suggests a view we find expressed in other authors from time to time, that extrinsic perceptibles are *only indirectly* perceived (e.g. Hicks 1907, 360-1, cf. 363) or even that they are *not really* or *strictly* perceived at all (Ross 1961, 271). This reading is supported by Alex.'s hedged expressions in the previous line: things '*called* "perceptible" as well' and 'if someone were to *say* that foam is perceptible' (41,7).

    Arist. never quite says such things himself, though. He does say at *DA* 2.6,

418a23-4 that 'no sense is *affected* by this sort of perceptible in so far as it is such'. This implies that extrinsic perceptibles are both *ontologically extrinsic* and *causally extrinsic*: they are both extrinsic characteristics of some perceptible quality and extrinsic to the quality that is causally efficacious. But it does not follow that we do not perceive things *as* having these characteristics, or still less that they are not genuinely perceived at all (although that seems to be Alex.'s inference: *hoti*, 41,9). When Arist. says at 418a24-5 that exclusive perceptibles (*idia*) are *kuriôs* perceptible, he is *not* claiming that the other types are not 'strictly' perceptible (as e.g. Everson 1997, 18 renders it), but only that they are not what is *fundamentally* perceptible, as the exclusives are. In general, to say that something is extrinsically *F* is not for Arist. a way of denying that it is really *F* or is *F* only homonymously. On the contrary, it is a way of affirming that something is genuinely *F*, while noting that it is not so in virtue of itself (*kath' hauto*) – it is *F* in virtue of some extrinsic characteristic (*kata sumbebêkos*) and so not due to its own nature. It is thus open to Arist. to say not only that I genuinely perceive a human being, Callias, but that my perception is *of* a human being (*An. Post.* 2.19, 100a16-b1), that I see him *as* a human being. This is a genuine kind of perception, as much as seeing red or feeling something's roundness is.

Alex. may take a more moderate position elsewhere. In *Quaest.* 3.8 he insists that it is *not* the case that something which is only perceptible extrinsically by all of the senses is not perceptible *at all* (*oud' holôs aisthêton*, 94,4-5); if it were not perceptible by any sense, he continues, it would be imperceptible (94,5-6), against our hypothesis. In this text, then, something that is merely perceptible extrinsically is nonetheless perceptible. It is unclear, though, whether this represents a change of mind or only a change of emphasis. Moraux, for example, thinks the positions do not deviate much from each other (2001, 340).

367. [41,10-13] 70,10-12 (cf. 20-3). Alex. is reordering and reworking Arist.'s material here into a more systematic presentation. He has deferred speaking about error until this point, even though it is something Arist. raises towards the beginning of *DA* 2.6, when he speaks about the infallibility of perceiving exclusive perceptibles (see n. 361 on 40,21-41,5 above). But Alex. also emphasises the *fallibility* of perception here, unlike Arist., with both common and exclusive perceptibles, and thus things that can be perceived 'intrinsically'. Arist. does not even raise the issue of error with common perceptibles or place a limit on the infallibility of exclusive perceptibles in *DA* 2.6, but only later in *DA* 3.3 (cf. also *Sens.* 4, 442b8-10; Alex. *in Sens.* 84,9-10.22-3). Alex. is thus consolidating Arist.'s various claims and synthesising them to offer what he regards as the best Aristotelian position, or perhaps even Arist.'s considered position on error in perception.

Most of *DA* 3.3, 428b17-25 is concerned with how truth and falsehood in representations corresponds with different types of perception (which Alex. discusses below at 70,5-71,5). But at 428b22-5 Arist. claims that the greatest errors occur over common perceptibles (and therefore more, he seems to be claiming, than extrinsic perceptibles, which one might have expected were the most subject to error). But Arist. does not explain why. Alex. offers an explanation at *in Metaph.* 313,20-32: each sense only has authority over its exclusive objects, about which it reports truly, but not over 'extraneous' objects (*allotria*); and common perceptibles are 'in a way extraneous to each sense' (313,30). But the latter claim surely runs counter to Arist.'s division in *DA* 2.6, which makes common perceptibles *intrinsically* perceptible to all of the senses.

In the present passage, Alex. does not attempt to explain the difference in error, but only offers a remark about perceptual error in general: it occurs when the modification of the sense is 'not like' (*mê ... hôs ekhei, mê homoion*) the object perceived. It is unclear, though, what the phrase 'modification (*pathos*) of the sense' refers to. (1) If Alex. has in mind the modification *of the perceptual organ* that underlies perception, then he takes veridical perception to require a significant degree of likeness between the qualities of the organ and the qualities of the object (though he need not assume exact similarity, as so-called literalist interpretations demand; similarity in certain respects, such as the underlying proportions of the qualities perceived, might conceivably suffice as well). Alternatively, (2) Alex. might not have in mind a modification of the organ, but rather a state *of the sense* itself, that is, the power of perception. But this state could be 'like' the object only in so far as its *content* corresponds to it: the only way for a power to be 'red' is for it to be in an intentional state *about* something red. If so, then Alex.'s explanation above expresses a rudimentary correspondence principle: a perception is in error just in case it takes objects in the world to be a certain way when in fact they are not. (Compare Alex.'s characterisation of a false statement at *in Metaph.* 433,10-11.14-15.)

Arist. himself gives a closer characterisation of how this correspondence goes awry in *Insomn.* 1: when we mis-see or mis-hear, we see or hear something real, but not what we take it to be (*ou mentoi touto ho oietai*, 458b31-3). This comes about, he notes in the next chapter (while discussing a mistake about the number of objects perceived and hence a common perceptible), whenever a sense is *affected in the same way* as it would be due to perceptible objects – in such cases, what appears to us is the same as when we are perceiving veridically (*Insomn.* 2, 460b23-5). For more detailed discussion of the second passage, see my 1998, 272-9, esp. 276-7. For Arist.'s characterisations of truth as correspondence, see *Metaph.* 5.29, 1024b21-4; 9.10, 1051b4-5, b33-5; cf. *Int.* 9, 19a33. A very fine-grained discussion of Arist.'s commitment to a correspondence theory of truth can be found in Crivelli 2004, 129-38.

For the use of *hupokeimenon* to indicate the object of perception, as 'underlying' or corresponding to it, see 56,5-9; 60,14-16; 61,26; 69,6; 81,5; and in Arist., see esp. *DA* 3.2, 426b8-11; also 2.11, 422b32-4; 3.2, 425b14; *GC* 2.2, 329b13; *GA* 5.1, 781a15-17; *Metaph.* 10.1, 1053b1-3. This use is just a special case of the term's more general use for the object of a cognitive attitude or subject-matter of a field of study: see Bonitz, *Ind. Arist.* 798b60-799a27.

368. [41,13-42,3] Alex.'s qualifications here are significant. In general, Arist.'s position is that a sense is *never* wrong about those perceptibles exclusive to it, and in fact when he first introduces exclusive perceptibles in *DA* 2.6, he says it is *impossible* for a sense to be mistaken about them (*peri ho mê endekhetai apatêthênai*, 418a12), but only about *what has* the quality in question or *where* it is found: 2.6, 418a14-16; 3.3, 428b21-2; 3.6, 430b29-30; *Metaph.* 4.5, 1010b19-21. On the truth of such perception more generally, see 3.3, 427b12 (cf. 428a11); *Sens.* 4, 442b8-10; *Metaph.* 4.5, 1010b2-3. In one passage, however, Arist. qualifies this claim: the perception of exclusive perceptibles is 'true *or has the least possible falsehood*' (*alêthês estin* ê hoti oligiston ekhousa to pseudos, *DA* 3.3, 428b18-19). It is not clear whether Arist. only has in mind the related errors he mentions earlier, about the bearer of the quality or its location; or whether he is instead allowing that there can be errors about the qualities themselves, and if so, in which circumstances. He might have after-images in mind (*Insomn.* 2, 459b7-13); but it is not clear if these errors occur without representations (*phantasiai*) being involved. For discussion, see my 1998, 272 esp. n. 56.

Alex. sometimes repeats Arist.'s unqualified claim of infallibility about exclusive perceptibles: *in Sens.* 84,9-10.22-3; *in Metaph.* 311,31-2 (cf. 28-9); 313,20-1. But in the present passage, Alex. instead makes a comparative claim that perception of these perceptibles is the *most* true (*alêtheuousi malista*, 41,14) and later on that they are true only '*for the most part*' (hôs epi to pleiston, 66,15). He argues at *in Metaph.* 313,32-314,1 that differing conditions matter to the accuracy of perception: sight is correct about colour only when it is located 'at a commensurate distance and not far away' (*apo summetrou diastêmatos kai mê porrô*, 313,34-5; cf. *in Sens.* 50,22-4), and similarly for hearing and smell. Although Alex. mentions the iridescence of the pigeon's neck in different lighting and angles, he does not mention error in this context (*in Sens.* 51,1-3; cf. Sext. Emp. *Pyrr. Hyp.* 1.120). But he does discuss the mistakes weavers make in the choice of threads due to illumination and surrounding colours (*in Meteor.* 158,27-159,3). In general, Alex. concludes, the senses are *not* capable of cognising exclusive perceptibles accurately 'in just any condition or situated in any location whatsoever' (*hopôsoun ekhontôn ê hopoudêpote keimenôn*, *in Metaph.* 313,36; cf. *in Sens.* 127,20-1). Even Arist. acknowledges some of these facts himself at various points: that colours appear differently at different distances (*Metaph.* 4.5, 1010b5-6; cf. *Sens.* 3, 439b5-6); that dyed textiles appear to be of different colours when juxtaposed differently and in different illumination (*Meteor.* 3.4, 375a22-8); that wine tastes different depending on one's own condition (1010b21-3; cf. *DA* 2.10, 422b7-10); that the same things do not seem sweet to a healthy person and a sick one, or to a strong person and a weak one (*EN* 10.5, 1176a13-16); and in one passage, he even argues that there is not any variation in how things taste, *unless* a person's organs are 'damaged or maimed' (*diephtharmenôn kai lelôbêmenôn*, *Metaph.* 11.6, 1062b36-1063a3). But nowhere does he try to account for these facts in a systematic way.

This is precisely what Alex. sets out to do. He states the general position at *in Metaph.* 312, 24-31: things appear as they actually are most of all to 'the person who is in a *natural* state' (*tôi kata phusin ekhonti*, 312,29): to the perceiver who is at a commensurate distance, in good health and vigour, and awake. Natural conditions are not so much those which are normal or standard statistically, but those which are suited to the optimal, natural functioning of the perceptual apparatus. In the present passage, Alex. identifies five such conditions: (*i*) the health and condition of the organ, (*ii*) the direction in which the object lies, (*iii*) a suitably commensurate distance, (*iv*) the condition of the medium, and (*v*) the absence of interference. It is not clear where these details first originated. An almost identical list, though adumbrated with only five keywords, is sometimes attributed to the Stoics based on attributions in neighbouring contexts (Sext. Emp. *Adv. Math.* 7.424 = LS 40L). But it involves a modification of the old Stoa's criterion of truth: in addition to having a 'secure representation' (*katalêptikê phantasia*), it must also not be undermined by any 'obstacle' (*enstêma*), such as the failure of any of these conditions would present. The later Stoics credited with this strategy (Sext. Emp. *Adv. Math.* 7.253-8) are thus likely to be making a *concession* to objections raised by Academic sceptics: at any rate, we find the point elaborated very fully by Carneades, with a list of *nine* conditions, at Sext. Emp. *Adv. Math.* 7.183 (= LS 69E 4 in part) and more briefly in a presentation of Antiochus of Ascalon's position at Cic. *Luc.* 19. We have no way of knowing whether Carneades is the first to explore these ideas or whether he is adapting and developing the views of others.

369. [42,4] Although there is no subtitle in our MSS 'On Sight', the discussion of sight clearly starts here, beginning with the objects of sight (42,4-43,4). Alex. then focuses primarily on the medium of sight (43,4-45,5), with brief digressions along the way on how sight comes about (43,18-44,1), the eye (44,1-9), and the power of sight (44,9-13). At 45,5 he returns to the objects of sight and the nature of colour in particular (44,5-46,19).

370. [42,4-5] Arist. *DA* 2.7, 418a26-8. In the passage above, Alex. is paraphrasing the opening of *DA* 2.7, which identifies both colour and something 'which can be described, but lacks a name' – what we now call 'phosphorescent' objects – as visible. Arist. discusses them further at 419a1-7 as 'fiery and shining' objects that can bring about perception in the dark (*en tôi skotôi poiei aisthêsin*), though what they exhibit is not 'their own colour' (*to oikeion khrôma*, a2), that is, the colour they would show in the light. He identifies fungi, horn (Ross reads 'meat' instead, following Themistius), and the heads, scales, and eyes of certain fishes as having this ability (419a5), as well as the ink of the cuttle-fish (*Sens.* 2, 437b4-7; cf. a31-2). Alex. adds the eyes of lions and rabbits and the glow-worm (*pugolampis*) at *in Sens.* 18,12-13, fish bones and glow-worms at *Mant.* 128,5-7, stones and glow-worms (*lampuris*) at 138,15-16.22-3. On glow-worms and fireflies, see Arist. *HA* 5.19, 551b23-6 (cf. 4.1, 523b21); *PA* 1.3, 642b33-4; for the Greek terms and further ancient references, see Davies and Kathirithamby 1986, 158-9.

Alex. points out at *in Sens.* 17,5-7 that these objects do not in fact illuminate the medium and so do not make *other objects* visible, but merely shine themselves (though contrast *Mant.* 144,19-23 which says certain animals and stones 'illuminate the transparent'). We know that an earlier 2nd c. CE Peripatetic, Sosigenes, whom Alex. refers to as 'our teacher' (*ho didaskalos hêmôn, in Meteor.* 143,13-14; cf. Them. *in DA* 61,23; Ammon. *in An. Pr.* 39,24-5), discussed just these points in the third book of his *On Sight* (Them. *in DA* 61,22-32).

371. [42,5-7] 43,16-17. What Alex. refers to as the 'definition' of colour (*horismos*, 42,6) is not the definition of colour found in Arist. *Sens.* 3 (439b11-12, cf. a28-9), which Alex. discusses more fully below at 45,5-46,19, but rather a verbatim quotation of the beginning of *DA* 2.7, which states 'the very nature of colour' (*tout' estin autou hê phusis*, 418a31-b2) and is repeated later in the chapter as the essence of colour, what it is to be a colour (*to khrômati einai*, 419a9-10). Since phosphorescent objects are luminescent in darkness, when the medium is *not* illuminated and actively transparent, their apparent hue will not strictly be colours by this definition, or at any rate the objects' own colour (*oikeion khrôma, DA* 2.7, 419a1-6).

Although this may appear to be a merely verbal difference, the claim that colour can only be seen in the light has an important consequence. For 'what can be seen' (*to horaton*) cannot then be *defined* as colour, since other things can be seen as well, but only as the correlative of what can see (*to horatikon*). So when Arist. says that colour is an exclusive perceptible of sight, he should not be understood to be making a definitional claim, but a *causal* one: colour is what is *responsible* for certain objects' *being visible* (*to aition tou einai horaton, DA* 2.7, 418a31)

That which is actively (*kat' energeian*) transparent is that which has fully realised its nature as something transparent and so allows colours to be seen through it. Transparent materials achieve this state when they are illuminated and have light: n. 373 on 42,8-11 below. On the meaning and etymology of 'transparent' itself, see n. 378 on 43,5-8 below.

372. [42,7-8] Alex. continues with his summary of the opening of *DA* 2.7. At 418b4-9 (cf. *Sens.* 2, 438a12-15), Arist. mentions 'air, water, and many solids' as examples of what is transparent, which he characterises generally as that which cannot be seen intrinsically or on its own (*ou kath' hauto horaton*), but only through an *extraneous* colour (*allotrion khrôma*). Alex. takes this to show that it lacks a colour *of its own* (*oikeion khrôma*): see also *DA* 44,3-4; 46,7-9; *in Sens.* 43,20-2; 45,17-18; 50,4-7; cf. *DA* 59,14-15; *Mant.* 106,30-107,1; *in Meteor.* 200,25-6.

Alex. offers somewhat different explanations for why transparent bodies lack a proper colour, depending on whether they are (in effect) liquids and gases with only indefinite boundaries or solids with definite boundaries. Air and water, which serve as the medium of sight, have only indefinite boundaries that are determined by whichever bodies happen to be in contact with it. Alex. argues that it is precisely because air and water lack a definite boundary that they lack a colour of their own, since colour is the boundary of a definite body (*in Sens.* 48,22-49,4; *Quaest.* 1.2, 5,11-15; cf. *DA* 46,7-9); because of their 'looseness' (*dia manotêta*), they are unable to possess or retain any colour (*Quaest.* 1.2, 6,7-8.24-5). Such colour as they have comes, just like their boundaries, from other bodies (*in Sens.* 45,18-20; cf. 50,4-5).

But this account obviously will not apply to the solids mentioned in the passage above (*tôn stereôn*, 42,8), which do have definite boundaries: elsewhere Alex. mentions glass, horn, certain transparent stones (mica, stelenite), and tortoise shell as examples (*Mant.* 133,18-19; 149,26-9; *in Sens.* 26,27-27,1; 29,5-7; 44,1; 46,19; several of these are already mentioned in Arius Didymus fr. 17, *Dox. Gr.* 456,15). What explains transparency in their case, as well as for bodies with indeterminate boundaries, is the absence of earth (*in Sens.* 45,23-6), which obstructs and prevents bodies from admitting light (46,12-16; cf. *DA* 45,9-10). Transparent solids are solid because they have more earth in them than bodies with indeterminate boundaries (*in Sens.* 45,25); but they are still transparent because they nevertheless have more water than earth (46,6-9.19-21). Solids that contain larger amounts of earth have the ability to retain colours previously acquired, and this accounts for their having some colour of their own (47,8-15; contrast 46,21-47,8). So Alex. should not endorse the claim, without qualification, that colour is the surface *of a determinate body*: by his own admission, some of these bodies are transparent.

Later, Alex. will state that *all* bodies have transparent material in them on Arist.'s theory, some more, some less (see n. 399 on 44,20-1). But those with sufficient amounts of earth mixed in will be opaque (see n. 407 on 45,7-10). The only ones we can see through (*diopta*), as the above references make clear, are those which have much more water than earth in them.

373. [42,8-11] Colours affect the eye by affecting the transparent medium in between them, in such a way as to cause us to become aware of them: Arist. *DA* 2.7, 419a13-15; cf. *Sens.* 2, 438b2-5; 3, 440a18-19. On this 'transmission' (*diakoneisthai*), see n. 362 on 41,1-3 above. Colours can affect the medium, though, only when it is actively (*kat' energeian*) transparent, which occurs only when it is illuminated through the presence of light: see esp. Arist. *DA* 2.7, 419a11; Alex. *DA* 43,11-16 (cf. 4-5); *Mant.* 141,36-142,16; 143,35-144,6; 145,2-7; *in Sens.* 35,6-9; 59,4-12; 135,7-8; cf. also *Mant.* 146,21-5; *in Sens.* 105,9.

374. [42,11-19] *Mant.* 145,25-30; *in Sens.* 50,9-11; ap. Averroem *Comm. Magn. in DA*, 2.67.39-45, 231-2 Crawford. Alex. takes the phenomenon of tingeing to show that the transparent medium is 'changed in a way' (*kineitai pôs*, 42,12) by colour *in general*, even though in most cases the effect on the medium will not itself be visible to us. But it is precisely because the medium is affected (*tôi paskhein*) that it can relay colours to other things (*diadidontos*, 42,18-19; cf. *sunanapheron*, 42,14). On this qualification, see further n. 375 on 42,19-22. The example is potentially significant, because tingeing might seem to involve the medium's *literally* taking on a colour, at least in the sense that it visibly comes to be of that colour, even if this is not a change in its own proper (*oikeion*) colour. But Alex. will later deny that in ordinary cases the medium undergoes literal alteration when it relays colour or that the eye does either (62,3-7).

Both the phenomenon of tingeing and the specific examples Alex. uses to illustrate it can be found in other authors, most notably in Galen, who mentions the effect of a tree's foliage colouring the air for those beneath it and of a coloured wall on the air and other bodies, 'especially if it is blue or yellow or any other brilliant colour' (*PHP* 7.7.1-2, 470.5-11 De Lacy). The similarity naturally suggests that Alex. is depending in some way on Galen or possibly a common source (as Moraux claims, though without argument or positive evidence, at 1984, 758).There are some earlier parallels extant, although none as close. Lucretius, for example, describes the effect of awnings in early Roman theatre tents in *DRN* 4.72-89 as evidence of effluences, and the Peripatetic Strato is reported to have discussed the phenomenon before that, although we do not have further details (Aet. 4.13.7, *Dox. Gr.* 403.26-8). In Arist., the closest antecedent is *Sens.* 3, 439b1-2, which suggests that the occurrence of glare (*augê*) in air and water shows that they become temporarily coloured (*khromatizomena*). Differences in illumination (*en augêi toiaidi ê toiaidi*) further have an effect on how the colour of weavers' thread appears (*Meteor.* 3.4, 375a22-8).

375. [42,19-22] The comparison is, in the first instance, between the production of light in the medium and the medium's being tinged by the colour of surrounding objects: see *Mant.* 142,10-16, where the actively transparent medium is said to 'take on' colour 'as a kind of second light ... and a kind of second activity' (*hôs deuteron ti phôs ... lambanei deuteran tina tautên energeian dekhomenon*). But in both passages the medium's becoming tinged seems to be taken as evidence (*gar*, 42,11) for how colour affects the medium in ordinary cases, even when the medium does not itself become tinged, in bringing about sight of coloured objects. If so, then the reception of colour by light or the illuminated medium is an essential part of the transmission of colour through the medium for seeing in general. Alex. seems to have the transmission of colours specifically in mind when he draws the parallel again at *in Sens.* 59,7-15; 135,17-20 (expanding on Arist. *Sens.* 6, 447a10-11); *Mant.* 142,2-4; 144,31-145,7. His most explicit statement comes below at 43,18-44,1.

In passing, Alex. rejects two alternative accounts of these phenomena. (1) The first holds that light and sight are brought about by 'effluences' (*aporrhoai*), that is, by streams of matter flowing from objects. This basic idea is found in various authors, either alone or in combination with other mechanisms: it is attributed, for example, to Democritus (Theophrastus *Sens.* 50, *Dox. Gr.* 513.20 = DK 68 A 135; cf. Arist. *Div. Somn.* 2, 464a5-6, a9-11 and Alex. *in Sens.* 124,6-7) and invoked by Plato to account for colour in the *Timaeus* (67C; cf. 58C). It is standardly associated, though, with Empedocles, who might have been the first to coin the term: it occurs, at any rate, in his claim that effluences are emitted 'from all things' (Plut. *Quaest. Nat.* 19, 916D = DK 31 B 89). For Empedocles' claim that light specifically is an effluence, see Philop. *in DA* 344,34-345,2 = DK 31 A 57; cf. Arist. *DA* 2.7, 418b13-16, b20-3; *Sens.* 6, 446a25-8. For his claim that colour vision is due at least in part to effluences, see Plato *Meno* 76C-D = DK 31 A 92; cf. Arist. *Sens.* 2, 438a4-5; 3, 440a15-16; *GC* 1.8, 324b26-35; Theophr. *Sens.* 7, *Dox. Gr.* 500.28-9; Aet. 1.15.3, *Dox. Gr.* 313.8-20 = DK 31 A 92); Alex. *in Sens.* 24,7-9.

Arist. rejects any such account. He denies that light is an effluence and travels through the medium at *DA* 2.7, 418b14-15 and b20-6, arguing against the latter claim at length in *Sens.* 6 (446a20-b2, b9-13, 446b27-447a3, a8-10). He likewise denies that sight comes about by effluences at *DA* 2.10, 422a14-15; *Sens.* 3,

440a15-20. It is not surprising, then, to find Alex. defending a similar position: on light, see *Mant.* 128,14-15; 138,14-23; on sight, see esp. *in Sens.* 31,20-9; 56,10-58,22; 61,17-21; *Mant.* 130,10-12; 136,29-138,2; 141,33; cf. *in Sens.* 83,3-7; *Mant.* 134,28-136,28 (esp. 134,27). In these passages, Alex. is sometimes attacking specific, hybrid versions of an effluence theory, for example, one that involves simulacra or *eidôla* (*in Sens.* 56,10-58,22) or one which involves some extromission from the eye in addition to the effluence from the object (*Mant.* 136,29-138,2).

(2) More interesting is Alex.'s dismissal of the second alternative, that the transparent takes on light or light takes on colour in the way that *matter* takes on a form. One possibility, suggested by Accattino (1992, 52 n. 45) is that (*a*) Alex. is rejecting a rival view according to which light or colour, respectively, *is a body*, a view he explicitly rejects in the case of light: see 43,11 just below and the corresponding note for further references. These views are generally associated with the Stoics, but the only testimonia for this precise claim in von Arnim (*SVF* 2.432) are among the passages just cited and none identifies the Stoics by name. According to other sources, the Stoics maintain that light is not an effluence, but a change of the entire medium at once due to contact with and stimulation by the sun: Plut. *Fac. in Orb. Lun.* 18, 930F (= *SVF* 2.433b); cf. 5, 922E (= *SVF* 2.570); Galen *Hipp. Epidem.* 4.11, 214.24-215.3 Wenkebach-Pfaff (= *SVF* 2.433a). These claims could be reconciled if the Stoics think of light as a quality that pervades the illuminated medium, and so, given their materialist view of qualities, is also a body (*Mant.* 124,9-10). The qualified object that results, day, would also be a body, as they notoriously claim: see Plutarch *Comm. Not.* 45, 1084CD (= *SVF* 2.665).

Another possibility is (*b*) that Alex. is concerned here not with what kind of *object* light or colour is, but with the type of *change* involved. By rejecting effluences in the previous clause, he denies that light and colour are due to something travelling through space. To add that the medium does not receive them 'in the way matter' does (*oute hôs hulês*, 42,21) is to reject a different type of change, namely, alteration (*alloiôsis*). In this respect, these changes would be like perceiving, which on Alex.'s view is not itself an alteration, even though it involves alterations (see n. 344 on 38,21-39,2 above). This seems to be the clear sense of the phrase at 62,3-7, where Alex. denies that the eye receives colours 'as matter' and draws an explicit parallel with the illumination of the transparent medium; see also his explanation of why perception does not involve receiving a form as matter at 83,23-84,6. Alex. explicitly denies that illumination is an alteration elsewhere (*in Sens.* 133,13-14.19; 134,11) and insists that the medium does not undergo or receive a modification (*ou paskhei, ou pathêtikôs kineisthai/andekhetai/ekhei*) when it receives light or colour (*DA* 62,11-13; *Mant.* 144,34-145,2 (cf. 144,31-2); 145,6-7; *in Sens.* 42,26-7; 47,3-7; 50,16-18 (cf. 20-2); 52,2; *Quaest.* 1.2, 6,8-10.24-5; cf. *Mant.* 147,16-17) – this is one respect in which the transmission of colours differs from the transmission of odours or flavours (*in Sens.* 135,9-13). Alex. may have this point in mind earlier in the present passage when he twice hedges the claim that the medium 'undergoes change' with the qualification 'in a way' (*kinoumena pôs, DA* 42,8; *kineitai pôs*, 42,12; cf. *tis kinêsis* below at 43,1-2). Similar qualifications can be found elsewhere: when the transparent medium undergoes such changes, it is said to 'alter in a way' (*alloioumenou pôs, in Sens.* 141,34-5) or to 'vary and be modified in a way' (*trepetai pôs kai paskhei, Mant.* 142,2), a point Alex. immediately explains by distinguishing this variation (*tropê*) from what happens to things that are genuinely altered (*Mant.* 143,4-10). What the transparent medium undergoes is only a 'seeming alteration' (*tês dokousês alloiôseôs,*

143,17-18). (He does not always add such qualifications, though: see n. 383 on 43,11-16 below.)

Alex. characterises this change more positively in two ways. First of all, the illumination of the medium should be understood as a *completion* of its nature, the activity of a transparent material capable of being illuminated (see below, 43,7-8), and so not an alteration in which its nature and capacities are destroyed. The same could be said of the medium's becoming tinged by surrounding colours and even of the effect colours normally have on the medium when transmitted to the eye, if this change is to be understood on the same model (see the beginning of current note). But he also understands it as a kind of relational change, which he sharply contrasts with alteration: see n. 376 on 42,22-43,4 below.

376. [42,22-43,4] 43,8-9; 45,1-4. Arist. maintains that light is not brought about through the local motion of a body, but rather by the mere 'presence' (*parousia*) in the transparent medium of fire or something 'like it' (*DA* 2.7, 418b13-20; *Sens.* 3, 439a19-21; cf. 6, 446a20-447a11). Alex. develops this view further in a number of passages throughout his corpus and extends it here by applying the same claims to the tingeing of the medium by colour (and so presumably to the action of colour on the medium in general; see the beginning of n. 375 on 42,19-22 and also n. 385 on 43,18-44,1 below. In saying that these phenomena arise 'from both sources' (*ap' amphoterôn*, 43,2), Alex. has in mind the illuminant and the colour respectively, rather than the illuminant *together with* the medium and the colour *together with* the light, as Schroeder claims (1981, 217-18). Alex. has been treating the two cases in tandem from 42,19 on and is using 'both' here to refer back directly to the 'things that produce these effects' (*tôn tauta empoiountôn*, 42,22) a few lines before, which are explicitly identified as the colour (42,23) and the light (43,1). For a full defense of this reading, see Accattino 1992, 51-9, esp. 57.

Of Alex.'s claims about light (and on occasion colour), the following are especially relevant to the present passage:

(1) The presence of an illuminant in a transparent medium is logically speaking a sufficient condition for the illuminatation of the medium and is responsible for it (*hê aitia autou*, Mant. 144,19). But according to Alex. the medium is not altered or changed in the primary sense of the word when it is illuminated or tinged. Both phenomena come about *solely* in virtue of the relation (*kata skhesin*) of the medium to the illuminant or colour and so are at best 'mere Cambridge changes', much like something's coming to be to the right of something as a result of the other thing's being moved (see n. 344 on 38,21-39,2 above): see esp. *Mant.* 143,4-21; but also *DA* 43,9-10; 45,1-3; *Mant.* 142,3-8; 144,31-145,7; *in Sens.* 31,11-18; 42,25-43,1; 43,5-7; 52,8-12; 132,2-16; 133,23-6; 134,11-19; 135,12-13; *Quaest.* 1.2, 6,10-11.25-6; 1.21, 35,12-14. Alex. does speak in one passage of the medium 'being changed' by the presence of an illuminant (*kinoumenon hupo tês tou phôtizein pephukotos parousias, in Sens.* 59,8-10). But he immediately goes on to say it is only changed and disposed 'in a way' (*pôs*, 59,10-12), a qualification he uses elsewhere to indicate that it is *not* an alteration or change in the primary sense (see n. 375 on 42,19-22), much as he speaks here of the sort of change involved in both phenomena (*tis hê ... kinêsis*, 43,1-2).

These claims go beyond what Arist. explicitly says at *Sens.* 6, 446b27-447a11. In that passage, he only denies that illumination is the *motion* of a body passing through space (here *kinêsis*, 446b28, but cf. 446a25-b2 and the contrast between *alloiôsis* and *phora* at 446b28 ff.). In fact, Arist. appeals to the example of alterations like freezing as a comparison to show how illumination occurs and even speaks there of the medium's being 'modified' by light (*paskhei*, 447a9-10), without making the crucial qualifications which Alex. in contrast insists on at *in Sens.* 133,12-134,19. But Arist.'s position elsewhere is that something does not undergo change at all, except extrinsically (*kata sumbebêkos*), merely because its relations to other things shift: *Phys.* 5.2, 225b11-13 = *Metaph.* 11.12, 1068a11-13; *Phys.* 7.3, 246b11-12; *Metaph.* 14.1, 1088a29-35; cf. *Phys.* 3.1, 200b33-201a9. In his lost commentary on the *Physics*, Alex. appears to have developed this view further, by allowing that in these circumstances something could be said to change in a *broader* sense of the word, in so far as there is a realisation of one of its powers, in line with Arist.'s initial definition of change (*Phys.* 3.1, 201b4-5, cf. a10-11). But he then praises Arist.'s subsequent refinement and narrowing of the definition at 3.2, 202a7-9 (cf. 3.1, 201a27-9), so that not every realisation is a change in the primary sense of the word, but only changes in quality, quantity, place, and being. See esp. Alex. *apud* Simpl. *in Phys.* 437,18-28, together with 436,24-35 and 437,1-6 (= 409,27-32). Mere Cambridge changes, then, are not changes in the primary sense of the word, and Alex. elaborates Arist.'s views on light and colour with this systematic consideration in mind. For more on mere Cambridge changes in Aristotle and post-Aristotelian philosophy, see Sorabji 2004*a*, 2.64-8; 3.79-88.

(2) Alex. takes the twin facts that light and colour are present immediately (*euthus*) whenever their sources come to be present and disappear immediately together with them to be evidence (*sêmeion*) that the presence of light is due to relational facts: see esp. *Mant.* 143,11-29 and *in Sens.* 134,11-19; 135,9-17; also *in Sens.* 31,15-18; 47,4-6; cf. *Mant.* 145,2-5; *Quaest.* 1.2, 6,17-19; *in Sens.* 52,10-12. Such transitions are instantaneous (*akhronôs*), occuring simultaneously (*hama*) throughout the medium as a whole (*athroon*), both far away from the source and nearby: *in Sens.* 31,13-15; 132,11-16; 133,18-27; 135,21-2. This is not true of spatial motion or even alteration, at least not when the latter takes place over a sufficiently large area: *Mant.* 138,16-18 (cf. 139,17-19); *in Sens.* 123,6-11; 132,17-133,6. For more on instantaneous transitions, see n. 382 on 43,11 below.

This is a point, interestingly, on which Galen would have agreed. He contrasts the effect of heat in the air with light: the former lingers after the source has been removed, while the latter does not, but disappears along with it (*PHP* 7.5.11, 454.27-9 De Lacy).

(3) The presence of an illuminant or colour is a specific kind of relation (*poian skhêsin*, 43,3), of one thing's being spatially located in another. Alex. standardly uses the example of something's being to the left or to the right of something to illustrate the notion of a relation. But not all relations are spatial: at one point, Alex. uses the relation between a father and a son alongside what is to the left or right as examples of a *skhêsis* (*in Sens.* 134,17-19; see Accattino 1992, 56 n. 50). At 56,8-10 below, Alex. characterises the terms for perceptible qualities – 'what can be touched' (*hapton*), 'seen' (*horaton*), or 'heard' (*akouston*) – as the names of a relation, rather than the underlying object.

377. [43, 4-5] 42,9-10.

378. [43,5-8] Alex. offers a similar etymology at *Mant.* 148,7-9 and *in Sens.* 45,20-1: although all bodies have a share in transparency (*diaphaneia*) on Arist.'s view, Alex. notes that the only ones we call 'transparent' are those which are 'see-through' (*diopta, Mant.* 148,7); we specifically (*idiôs*) call 'transparent' those through which (*di' hou*) colours appear (*phainetai*); cf. *DA* 44,23-5 below. See also the further etymological elaboration of 'appearing' (*phainomenon*) in terms of 'light' (*phaos*) at *in Sens.* 45,11-14 (accepting Diels' emendation of the lacuna).

Alex. describes light as the form (*eidos*) of the transparent at *in Sens.* 35,13-15. But he also questions this at *Quaest.* 1.21, 35,9-16, on the grounds that the transparent can exist without it, and suggests that it is instead a kind of modification (*pathos ti*), which occurs in virtue of relational facts, involving the presence of something like fire. On light as the culmination (*teleiotês*) of the transparent, see n. 379 on 43,7-8.

379. [43,7-8] *DA* 2.7, 418b9-10; 419a11. On light as the activity (*energeia*) of the transparent, *DA* 44,13-15; *Mant.* 142,1-2 (cf. 148,14-16); *in Sens.* 35,8-9; 39,20-1; see also n. 373 on 42,8-11 above; as the culmination (*teleiotês*) of the transparent, see *Mant.* 142,8-10; cf. *Quaest.* 1.2, 7,1-4; and as the completion (*entelekheia*) of the transparent, *in Sens.* 35,13-15; 42,25; *Quaest.* 1.2, 7,3-4; 1.21, 35,9-10; cf. *Mant.* 144,29.

380. [43,8 title] The section title in manuscript V seems out of place, coming almost at the end of the discussion of light (42,19-43,11). Alex. does return below to the nature of light briefly at 44,13-15 and 44,23-45,5. But the principal topic in this section is the nature of colour in bodies (44,16-46,19), after a brief recapitulation of how colour affects the eye via the medium (43,11-44,1), the nature of the eye itself (44,1-9), and the power of sight (44,9-13). Light is discussed only in so far as its treatment has points of contact with that of colour. For an overview of the entire section on sight, see n. 369 on 42,4.

381. [43,8-11] 43,2; 45,1-3. On the relational nature of light, see n. 376 on 42,22-43,4 above. On light as the presence of fire or something like it, see 45,1-3; *Mant.* 144,18-19.23-4; 145,2-3; *in Sens.* 43,5-7; 132,7-8 (quoting *DA* 2.7, 418b16-17). Fire is not the only kind of thing naturally suited to illuminate the medium. Alex. also takes the 'divine body' (*theion sôma*) – that is, the celestial sphere which carries the fixed stars – to be a source of illumination: *DA* 45,3; *Mant.* 142,5. He refers to it at *Mant.* 144,19-22 as the 'aetherial body' (*to aitherion sôma*), along with various phosphorescent bodies, as a source of illumination.

382. [43,11] On light not being a body, Arist. *DA* 2.7, 418b13-15; Alex. *Mant.* 124,9-10; 132,37;138,3-139,28; *in Sens.* 31,13-17; 33,13. See also n. 375 on 42,19-22 above.

On illumination as instantaneous (*akhronôs*), see Alex. *in Sens.* 135,13-14. Although it is often translated as 'atemporally', the Greek *akhronôs* does not imply that something occurs timelessly or outside of time, since the events in question can be dated. The word indicates rather that, unlike events which require an extended duration (*deisthai khronikou diastêmatos, Mant.* 143,31-4), these events are *without duration* and so instantaneous: in fr. 16 Giannakis, Alex. explicitly compares them to the 'now' and to points, which begin or cease to exist without any process of generation or destruction (1995/96, 169 and 177). Illumination occurs throughout the medium 'all at once' (*athroôs, Mant.* 143,19-23.26-8; 145,2-5; *in Sens.* 132,8-16; 135,16-17; cf. *Mant.* 139,17-19; 142,13-16): as soon as a source of illumination is present, so is light, and as soon as it disappears so does the light (see n. 376 on 42,22-43,4 above). Alex. further argues that seeing itself and indeed perceiving in general occurs instantaneously and so 'apart from time' (*khôris khronou*) in the sense of duration. Nonetheless, colours are the only perceptibles which are *transmitted* through a medium instantaneously: *in Sens.* 135,13-17; *in Meteor.* 129,3-14; fr. 16 Giannakis (1995/96, 169 and 177); cf. *Mant.* 143,29-33. For Alex.'s view on these issues, see de Groot 1983, 180-2 and 1991, 37-8, cf. 52-3. For Arist.'s views on the temporal character of illumination, see *DA* 2.7, 418b20-6; *Sens.* 6, 446a20-447a11 (446b9-13, 447a9-10).

According to Alex. the fact that these events are instantaneous shows that they are not changes (*kinêseis*) in the primary sense, since all such change is 'in time' in the sense that it has duration: *Mant.* 143,23-8; *Quaest.* 1.22, 35,19-21; *in Sens.*

59,25; 124,9-10; *in Meteor.* 129,3-9; cf. *Mant.* 139,22; 143,6-7; *in Sens.* 30,1-2; 135,9-11. For discussion, see Sharples 1998, 78-9.

383. [43,11-16] Alex. recapitulates here the causal story of how vision is produced by visible objects through a medium, first outlined at 42,7-12, but without adding any of the qualifications he often adds (see n. 375 on 42,19-22). He speaks here simply of colours being able to affect the medium (*kinêtikon*, 43,12.14; cf. 42,6-7) and of the medium's being modified (*paskhein*) by the colour and the eye by the medium (43,13-14). He likewise fails to mention the stimulation in the eyes being relayed or transmitted to a primary or central sense, as he had before (39,18-21), although nothing he says here precludes such a process either. More interesting, though, is the opening inference, which makes fully explicit the causal assumptions underlying Alex.'s general approach: a colour can be seen in the light *only if* it can affect the light in some way, since it is by doing this that seeing comes about: compare Arist. *Sens.* 2, 438b2-5. In speaking of colour affecting light, as he does earlier at 42,11-12, Alex. is thinking of light in effect as the actively transparent medium (43,7-8), which colour is equally said to affect (42,6-7.9-10): cf. *in Sens.* 35,6-12.

Although Alex. standardly uses the Greek *opsis* for the power of sight, as opposed to the body which has this power, the *opthalmos* or *omma* – for the contrast, see e.g. 44,9-11 below and 57,13-14 (or indeed Arist. *DA* 2.1, 412b18-20) – it is clear that *opsis* here must signify the eye, as it can in Greek, since otherwise the reference to its transparency at 43,15 and the plural *opsesin* at 43,20 would not make sense (see also 62,4). It is relevant, as AD rightly point out (184), that Arist. himself uses *opsis* in this way at *DA* 2.7, 419a13, in departure from his more common usage of the term for the power; see also *Sens.* 2, 438a13 and Alex. *in Sens.* 26,10.

For Alex.'s reference to 'inquiries into how we see', see n. 384 on 43,16-18 below.

384. [43,16-18] On phosphorescent objects, see 42,4-7 above, with corresponding note. In the present passage, Alex. refers twice (43,16.18) to writings on sight, which examine 'How We See', and he refers to them again at *in Meteor.* 141,11-12 together with *On the Soul*. Both Rose (1863, 374-5) and Moraux (2001, 365 n. 216) construe these as references to a work of Alex.'s and so are forced to take a phrase in the *in Meteor.* passage, 'which *he* also recalls in *On the Soul*' (*hôn kai autos emnêmoneuse*, 141,12), to be a gloss inserted by a scholiast. But Moraux also argues against identifying it with *Mant.* 141,29-147,25, since this passage does not discuss phosphorescent objects at any length (although it does mention them at 144,21-3; see Sharples 2004, 88-9 esp. n. 284). So we would then have to posit a lost work of Alex.'s.

There is an alternative, though, if (as BD have argued, 282) it is not a scholiast who says 'which he also recalls in *On the Soul*' at *in Meteor.* 141,12, referring to Alex., but rather Alex. himself referring to Arist. This reading is far more natural and economical. And we need not take it to refer to another possibly lost work of Arist.'s either, as BD seem to, on the basis of Arist.'s remark at *DA* 2.7, 419a6-7 that phosophoresent objects are the subject of 'another discussion' (*allos logos*), a phrase which may just indicate that it is a topic 'for another day'. Consider a passage from Alex.'s *in Sens.*, where he describes how visible objects situated along the line of sight affect the medium and thereby the eyes, in terms much like those above at 43,18-44,2, something he claims that Arist. 'said when he spoke *about how we see* in *On the Soul*' (*eirêken hote elegen en tois Peri psukhês peri tou pôs horômen*, *in Sens.* 25,21-6). All of these references, that is, may be to nothing more than Arist. *DA* 2.7. It is striking that Themistius (*in DA* 61,21-4), who takes Arist.'s remark that phosphorescent objects are the topic of 'another discussion' to refer to another treatise, can only cite Arist.'s *Sens.* (which speaks about these objects only in passing at 2, 437b5) and the third book of *On Sight* by Alex.'s teacher, Sosigenes (see n. 370 on 42,4-5 above). He is not aware of a separate treatise *How We See* by either Arist. or Alex. On Sosigenes' book, see Moraux 1984,358-60. Moraux conjectures that Themistius is entirely dependent here on Alex.'s lost commentary on the *DA* for his references. But this is just a guess on Moraux's part, offered without argument or evidence.

385. [43,18-44,1] *Mant.* 146,20-8; *in Sens.* 25,21-6; cf. *in Meteor.* 141,12-16.23-9. Alex.'s language here suggests that in some sense 'tingeing' (*anakekhrôsmenon*, 43,19; cf. *hôsper khrôseôs*, Mant. 146,17-18) is indicative of a *general* phenomenon and that a colour affects the transparent medium in this way not only when the effect on the medium is itself visible, as in the cases described at 42,12-19, but also in quite ordinary cases when it is not visible, unlike the distal object: see discussion in n. 375 on 42,19-22. Tingeing does not in any event involve the medium's being modified or altered except in a qualified sense: see again n. 375 on 42,19-22. Later Alex. will explicitly deny that the illuminated medium receives colours as matter does when they are relayed to sight (62,3-7).

For the line of sight, see Arist. *PA* 2.10, 656b29-31, which he also uses to explain the location of afterimages at *Insomn.* 2, 459b13-18; Alex. points out that the line of sight is not deflected even by strong winds: *Mant.* 129,21-4; *in Sens.* 28,27-8.

The 'exclusive modification' (*idion pathos*) Alex. refers to here is presumably a transferred epithet: it is the modification due to a *perceptible* exclusive to sight, namely, colour: see 40,21-41,5.

386. [44,1-2] The reflection one sees in another's eyes might seem irrelevant here and likewise for the parallel passage at *Mant.* 146,20-8. But it is explicitly part of the dialectical context for the parallel passage at *in Sens.* 25,21-6, which criticises Democritus for in some way identifying sight with the reflection of an object in the eye (Arist. *Sens.* 2, 438a5-6). In the course of elaborating Arist.'s rejection of this theory (438a7-12), Alex. states what he thinks is the correct explanation of vision and of the reflection seen in another's eyes (*in Sens.* 24,14-26,7), as he also does in the passage above and at *Mant.* 146,20-8. Both take the reflection to be due to the fact that the eye's contents, which they call the *korê* (see n. 392 on 44,7 below), are not only transparent, but smooth and bright, especially at the aperture we refer to as the 'pupil', in which the reflection appears. On the difference between transparent materials generally and those which are reflective, see *Mant.* 142,21-31; cf. *in Sens.* 26,21-5; 36,2; also Sorabji 1991, 230 n. 14.

387. [44,2-3] cf. 44,10 below. Alex.'s claim about sight being due to the reception of colour and a kind of likening is just a particular instance of the general characterisation he offered at 38,21-39,2 above. He again makes it clear that it is the organ rather than the power which receives a perceptible quality like colour, and that there is some sense in which the organ takes on the colour (whether this is 'literal' colouration or not). On the notion of 'likening', see 39,10-18 above with corresponding note.

388. [44,3-4] 59,12-20; *Mant.* 106,30-107,1; *Quaest.* 1.2, 7,12-13; Arist. *DA* 2.7, 418b26-9; cf. 2.11, 424a7-9; *Sens.* 3, 439b6-10. This claim appears to be an instance of a more general principle, namely, that something cannot become F unless it is not F to begin with. But if (as Arist. assumes) we are able to see every colour, then the organ must be able to receive every colour; therefore, it cannot have any colour of its own. An analogous claim can be made for every sense except touch, which must have tangible qualities of its own, as no organ can be intangible (2.11,

423b31-424a10). An even stronger claim will be made for the understanding, which Arist. thinks is capable of understanding everything whatsoever and so cannot be anything in actuality at all (beyond the ability to understand), and so *a fortiori* cannot have any organ (3.4, 429a18-27). Alex. discusses the contrast between touch and the other senses at 59,1-20 below and *Mant.* 106,30-107,7 and the case of understanding at 84,10-85,5; *Mant.* 106,24-9 and 107,7-20.

389. [44,4-5] See esp. 46,6-12 below; also 44,23-45,1; 45,7; *in Sens.* 47,3-8; 48,17; *Quaest.* 1.2, 5,10-19; 7,12-13; Arist. *Sens.* 3, 439a26-7 (cf. b1-5). As we shall see below, coloured bodies also contain transparent material, even though they have a definite shape of their own (*hôrismena,* 44,18-23; 45,5-46,6; 46,12-19). Those that lack a definite shape (*ahorista*) not only get their boundaries from surrounding objects, but get their colour from them as well (46,6-12). Alex. explains that these sorts of bodies receive, but do not retain, colours because of their moisture and lack of definite shape: *in Sens.* 47,3-8; *Quaest.* 1.2, 6,7-8. He adds at *Quaest.* 1.2, 5,10-19 that it is precisely because such materials are capable of receiving colour, while lacking one of their own, that they are apt for relaying the colours of things truly, precisely because there is no admixture with a colour of their own.

390. [44,5] 42,7; 52,18-19; *Mant.* 147,27-9; *in Sens.* 26,13.22; 44,4; 50,8-9; 52,19-20; 89,2-3.9. Arist. *Sens.* 2, 438a14-15.

391. [44,6] Arist. *Sens.* 2, 438a13-15, b5-8. The perceptual organ Alex. has in mind here is clearly the eye. But notice that he only says that the eyes are that *through which* (*di' hou*) the awareness of colours occurs, rather than that *in* which it occurs. Elsewhere he is clear that this awareness occurs in the heart, which is the primary perceptual organ, and *not* in the eyes. But he does not make this denial explicitly in the *DA*: see n. 353 on 39,21-40,3.

Alex. discusses in great detail at *in Sens.* 26,10-27,6 why the eyes consist of water rather than air, as he goes on to claim just below at 44,7.

392. [44,7] 59,14; *Quaest.* 3.6, 91,13-14; *in Sens.* 26,10-11; 27,6.7; 31,4; 35,17-36,4. Arist. *DA* 3.1, 425a4; *Sens.* 2, 438a16-22, b5-11, b19; *HA* 1.9, 491b20-1; *GA* 5.1, 780b23.

The Greek *korê* is often translated as 'pupil', due no doubt to the derivation of the English 'pupil' from the Latin *pupilla*. But these are false friends. The Greek *korê,* like the Latin, can be used for dolls or figurines (lit. a 'little girl') and so by extension for the part of the eye where one sees a tiny reflection of oneself, as Plato explains at *Alc. I* 133A. But where precisely does one sees the image? It is not unnatural to think of the doll-like figure as *inside* the eye, rather than at the aperture, much as we instinctively think of a mirror image as being at some distance behind the surface of the mirror; and it is surely the geometry of appearances that is relevant here, not whether there is an actual figurine at either of these locations (since there isn't any).

In fact, neither Arist. nor Alex. uses *korê* for the aperture in the iris, as we do, but for the interior contents of the eye that are visible through this aperture. This is clearly how Alex. understands Empedocles' famous lantern fragment (DK 31 B84.10-11): see *in Sens.* 34,13-15. Arist. explicitly identifies the *korê* as 'the moist [material] inside of the eye, by which we see' (*to d' entos tou ophthalmou, to men hugron, hôi blepei*) at *HA* 1.9, 491b20-2, in contrast with the 'dark' part of the eye (*to melan,* the iris and pupil, properly speaking) and the white of the eye (*to leukon,* the sclera). See also *HA* 3.18, 520b3-5; 4.8, 533a8-9; *DA* 2.8, 420a14; *Sens.* 2, 438b5-16; *GA* 5.1, 780b22-9 (cf. a25-36). On this point, see Sorabji [1974] 1979, 49 n. 22; Johansen 1998, 56. For references to uses of *korê* in other ancient authors, see Mugler 1964, 226-8. Although Mugler regards the aperture as the primary meaning, which is extended *pars pro toto* to the whole eye, none of his texts decisively support this, while many explicitly support the meaning I have argued for here.

For Alex., Sharples appeals to Arist.'s usage (2005*b*, 348 n. 12) in generally translating *korê* as 'eye jelly'. But he thinks that sometimes it must be rendered 'pupil' (2004, 130 n. 441), even alternately within the same passage: see his translations of *Mant.* 128,25 and 129,2.5.10.21; 142,17.21.31; for 'pupil', cf. also 136,14.16.18; 146,19.25. But it is possible to take virtually all of the term's occurrences, both in these passages and in the rest of Alex.'s corpus, as consistently referring to the interior contents of the eye. This includes references to the vertex of a visual 'cone' being at the centre of the *korê*, which should be construed as the centre of the eyeball rather than the centre of the aperture at or near the surface (*Mant.* 130,15; 146,19.31-3; *in Meteor.* 149,28) – this understanding of the geometry is made explicit in Damian *Opt.* 2,19-21 and 12,12-16 Schöne (even though he himself uses *korê* for what we call the pupil). It might be thought that Alex. *Mant.* 128,25 is an exception and must refer to the pupil. But it can refer here to the interior of the eye as well: on the theory under consideration, the interior of the eye *as a whole* would constitute a passageway from the optic nerve to the pupil for the body that sees. A more plausible exception is *Mant.* 135,6-10, which concerns the relative sizes of the *korê* and the incoming Epicurean simulacra of the object, since presumably the simulacra will have to be small enough to fit through the aperture of the pupil. But the wording of Alex.'s objection looks garbled, and if what he means is that the *korê* can be no *smaller* than the simulacra, then it will be true *a fortiori* of the interior of the eye no less than the pupil, and so does not constitute a clear exception to the rule.

393. [44,6-9] *Mant.* 142,26-32; *in Sens.* 26,15-27,6; 35,25-36,4. BD claim (283) that Alex.'s appeal to the 'density and consistency' (*pakhutêta te kai sustasin*, 44,8-9) of the vitreous jelly has no parallel in Arist.'s work. But in fact Arist. claims at *Sens.* 2, 438a15-16 that water is 'more easily retained *and more condensed*' than air (*euphulaktoteron* kai eupilêtoteron), if at any rate we follow the reading in MSS EMY, with most modern editions. Ironically, the last term does not occur in the text Alex. used for his commentary, which has 'more easily contained' (*euhupolêp-toteron*) instead. But Alex.'s develops his explanation along much the same lines: he refers to water's superior consistency (*mallon sunestanai, in Sens.* 26,19; *sustasin mallon ekhei*, 26,21) and goes on to explain that water is a mean between the sparseness of air and the solidity of glass and other transparent bodies, making it ideal for perception (26,26-27,6). The idea that the density of the vitreous jelly keeps it inside the eyeball is not peculiar to Arist. either. Plato suggests at *Tim.* 45BC, using similar terms, that the denser material in the eye is kept in (*to men allo hoson pakhuteron stegein pan*) because of the way the eyes are compacted (*sumpilêsantes*).

More generally, Arist. explains different animals' different sensitivity to light and colours in terms of the amount of moisture in their eyes: *GA* 5.1, 780a1-5.

394. [44,9-13] Alex. recapitulates here (44,9-11) what he said earlier about the activity of seeing (44,2-3), which provided the basis for his conclusions about the eye, the organ of sight, in the preceding argument (44,3-9; cf. 43,14-15). He then extends those comments by elaborating briefly on the power of sight, which underlies this activity (44,11-13), before returning again to questions about light and colour. As AD 185 point out, there is little that can be said about the power itself beyond defining it in terms of its activity. Alex. preserves here the distinction between the alteration (*alloiôsis*) produced by visible things and the activity (*energeia*) by which we have awareness and cognition of them, even though he does not emphasise it: for more on this distinction, see n. 344 on 38,21-39,2.

395. [44,13-14] 44,23-5; 89,1-2; *Mant.* 148,23; 149,32-5; *in Sens.* 43,13-15; 46,21-47,3; 47,12-13; *in Metaph.* 142,13-16. Alex. also says such things about *sources* of illumination such as fire, at *DA* 46,1-4; *in Sens.* 45,26-46,3; cf. *Quaest.* 1.2, 6,33-7,1. But there is no genuine inconsistency here, as AD 185-6 seem to allege: both light and the sources of illumination can be visible in the highest degree without contradiction. Superlatives do not in general preclude ties.

Alex.'s statement here seems to go beyond Arist. in several ways, for which he was vigorously criticised by Moraux (1942, 89-92), first for characterising light as 'visible in the highest degree' (*malista horaton*) and second for the underlying causal principle that seems to be presupposed here. Both will play a critical role later in the treatise in Alex.'s discussion of the productive understanding (*nous poiêtikos*), where he enunciates a fully general version of the principle: for any attribute *F*, whatever is *F* in the highest degree is responsible (*aition*) for anything else's being *F* (88,23-89,11). This principle has seemed to many to be fundamentally Platonic and non-Aristotelian – Merlan declares, in fact, that it is 'as close to what causality is in Neoplatonism as possible.' (1969, §§14-15, 38-40 at 39; see also Donini 1974, 42-8.) For detailed discussion of the principle, including its relation to Platonism, see the notes on 88,23-89,11 below. The present note is concerned with Alex.'s claims only in so far as they concern light.

Moraux's objection that light is not visible for Arist., because the transparent is colourless, is simply mistaken. As AD rightly point out (185-6), colours are not the only things which are visible on Arist.'s view: phosphorescent objects also are, despite not having colour of their own (*DA* 2.7, 419a1-6; cf. 418a26-8), a point Alex. also makes above (42,4-7; cf. 43,16-18). AD suggest (186) that Alex. is here assimilating light to its source, fire, which Arist. already recognises as visible (*DA* 2.7, 419a23); and given that fire and other illuminants are responsible for the visibility of colours, they might themselves be regarded as having this quality themselves in the highest degree, based on the general causal principle Arist. enunciates at *Metaph.* 2.1, 993b24-6 (see also *An. Post.* 1.2, 72a29-32).

This response does not go to the heart of the matter, though, since an objection similar to the original one can easily be constructed. Light, as Alex. immediately goes on to say (44,15; cf. 43,7-8), is the activity of the transparent medium, in so far as it is transparent, that is, of the transparent medium when it is illuminated. The medium in this condition, however, is something that one *can see through* (*diopton*) – *in Sens.* 45,11-21 (cf. 43,20-2) and also *Mant.* 148,7-10 (though the text here requires supplementation, either with Bruns or Bessarion, see Sharples 2004, 144 n. 485; 2008, 204 ad loc.); cf. *Quaest.* 1.2, 5,15-19. – in which case light might not seem to be the sort of thing that can be *seen itself*. As Arist. says himself, the transparent material is 'not visible on its own, to put it simply' (*ou kath' hauto de horaton hôs haplôs eipein, DA* 2.7, 418b5). So we still need an explanation of why light, as the activity of the transparent medium, is visible and indeed to the highest degree. AD's interpretation, moreover, poses an additional difficulty. If correct, it would invert Alex.'s explanatory strategy: his conclusions about light would merely be an *application* of the general causal principle stated later, rather than a case he regards as intuitive on its own, which can then be offered as *evidence* for the general principle (as seems to be his strategy at the crucial juncture, 88,26-89,2).

In fact, Alex. has entirely orthodox grounds within Arist.'s philosophy for thinking that light is visible in the highest degree. Later in the present passage and elsewhere, he systematically elaborates Arist.'s claim at *Sens.* 3, 439b11-12 that colour is the limit of transparent material in a body with a definite shape (see 44,18-19 below with corresponding note). On this view, *all* bodies are transparent to a greater or lesser extent, not simply those we can see through (see 44,20-1 with corresponding note); and their colour is due precisely to the amount of transparency present in each, in so far as it is transparent. So a body which has transparency in the highest degree, such as air or water, thereby has the basis of visibility within itself to the highest degree (*Mant.* 149,34-5; *in Sens.* 45,16; 46,1-2). It is rather coloured bodies which are imperfect in this regard: they are not fully transparent, due to the presence of earth in their composition, and so opaque (see 45,7-11 below with corresponding note) – even flame is not fully transparent due to the admixture of earth in smoke (*Mant.* 149,24-6; *in Sens.* 46,17-18). Colour thus ranges between white or, better, 'bright' (*leukon*), which is the most 'luminous' (*phôtoeides*) colour, and black or 'dark' (*melan*), which is the privation of light (see 45,10-19 with corresponding note). At *Quaest.* 1.2, 6,26-30 Alex. explains that those solid bodies are bright which have 'the most transparent body' present in them, which he later identifies with fire (7,1), and he characterises white or bright in terms much like light in the present passage: it is 'colour in the highest degree and visible in the highest degree' (*malista gar touto khrôma kai malista horaton*) and 'responsible for bodies being more coloured and being more visible' (*tou te mallon kekhrôsthai tois sômasin aitia kai tou mallon horatois einai*). The exceptional visibility of light and bright colour is thus due to the same cause, namely, the high degree of transparency of the body which exhibits them.

Arist. himself also seems to regard light as not only visible, but visible in the highest degree. The transparent medium may not be visible *in itself*, but it is nonetheless visible – it is just visible through an *extraneous* colour (*ho esti men horaton ... di' allotrion khrôma*, *DA* 2.7, 418b4-6), that is, its colour is due to something else, such as the presence of an illuminant. It is thus no contradiction to claim that its activity, light, is itself highly visible: the glare (*augê*) in air and sheen on water are offered as clear evidence that both mediums are coloured in some way (*Sens.* 3, 439b1-2) and light is even spoken of as 'like a colour' (*hoion khrôma*) of the transparent medium (*DA* 2.7, 418b11), that is, as the kind of thing that we ordinarily see. However we interpret these passages (for further discussion, see n. 397 on 44,16 below), they suggest that light is visible in some way. More strongly still, light seems to be the kind of 'extreme' or 'intense' perceptible (*tôn aisthêtôn hai huperbolai, sphodra aisthêta*) which Arist. often speaks of as damaging to our perceptual organs precisely *because of* the superlative degree of its perceptible quality. For the general point, see *DA* 2.12, 424a28-32; 3.2, 426a29-b8; 3.4, 429a31-b3; 3.13, 435b7-9. For what is excessively bright (*lian lamprou*) in particular, see 2.10, 422a21-8; *GA* 5.1, 780a7-14. On other extreme perceptibles, cf. also 2.9, 421b23-5; 2.10, 422a29-32; 2.11, 424a10-15.

    396. [44,15] 43,7-8 with corresponding note.

    397. [44,16] Arist. himself nowhere says that light is a colour without qualification. The closest he comes to is to say that it is '*like* a colour of the transparent' (*hoion khroma tou diaphanous*) at *DA* 2.7, 418b11 and that the glare in air and sheen on water show that these mediums are coloured or 'tinged' (*khrômatizomena*, *Sens.* 3, 439b1-2). But when he speaks more precisely, he says that light is only an *extrinsic* colour of the transparent medium (*khrôma tou diaphanous kata sumbebêkos*, *Sens.* 3. 439a18-19) – the transparent is not visible on its own (*ou kath' hauto horaton*), but only through an *extraneous* colour (*di' allotrion khrôma*), that is, it is visible due to *something else's* colour (*DA* 2.7, 418b4-6). Richard Sorabji adds (in his editorial comments) that there are good reasons to distinguish light from colour. Colour, glare, and sheen are all surface phenomena; illumination is not, but suffuses an entire volume. Unlike colour, furthermore, light is not seen, but rather *seen through* (Sorabji 2004*b*, 134).

Alex. vacillates on whether light is a colour. Immediately below at 45,1 and elsewhere he qualifies the claim. Light is 'like a colour, not simply as such, but extrinsically, because the transparent does not receive light in a way that modifies it' (*hôsper khrôma tou diaphanous, oukh haplôs, alla kata sumbebêkos, hoti mê pathêtikôs anadekhetai to diaphanes to phôs, in Sens.* 42,26). The transparent receives light as if it were its own colour (*oikeion khrôma*), although in fact it is not (*Quaest.* 1.2, 6,16-17; cf. 5,12-19; *Mant.* 144,16; 150,2; *DA* 42,7-8). It is colour only 'in a way' (*khrôma pôs on, in Sens.* 52,9) or 'analogous' (*analogon*) to it (*Quaest.* 1.21, 35,14-15). Illuminants 'colour it in a way' (*khrônnusin tropon tina*) and light is 'like a colour' of the transparent medium (*Mant.* 144,5-6).

In other passages, though, he makes the stronger, unqualified claim he makes here. At *in Sens.* 43,12-17 he insists that light, because it is a colour (*khrôma on*), is visible in the highest degree and pre-eminently, and that the 'other colours' (*tôn allôn khrômatôn*) are perceived because of it, a phrase which recurs again at 47,2-3 and below at *DA* 46,3. Sharples believes (2004, 134 n. 453; 2008, 200 ad 144,6) that Alex. goes further and claims that light is the transparent medium's '*own* colour' at *Mant.* 144,16 and 150,2. But these last remarks are both qualified with *hôsper*: each should be rendered '*as though* it were the transparent medium's own colour', as in his fuller statement at *Quaest.* 1.2, 6,16-17 (with Sharples' note).

398. [44,16-19] Arist. *Sens.* 3, 439a26-30, b10-18. Alex. *DA* 45,5-46,6; 46,12-19; *Mant.* 148,2-6 (cf. 150,13-18); *Quaest.* 1.2, 5,2-3.21-2; *in Sens.* 49,4-8; 51,21-4; cf. 44,20-1; 47,24-5. Alex. is aware that this is a counterintuitive view and that we typically only speak of substances we can see through as 'transparent' (*in Sens.* 45,11-21)

Bruns' suggested emendation at 44,17-18 is extravagant and unnecessary. AD (187) suggest that Alex.'s back reference ('in the way just mentioned') is to light's being the activity of the transparent (44,15). But in any case colour is nowhere described as an activity of the body to which it belongs. Alex. might be taken more plausibly to be referring to the fact that colour, like light, is *in* transparent material and, more importantly, that it is responsible (*aition*) for things in general *being seen* (44,14).

399. [44,20-1] Arist. describes transparency as 'a kind of common nature and power' (*tis koinê phusis kai dunamis*) at *Sens.* 3, 439a23; more generally, see 439a21-5; b8-10. Alex. follows suit: *Mant.* 147,27-30; 148,1-2.9-12; 149,1-3; *in Sens.* 44,4-9; 45,9-11; 45,21-47,20; *Quaest* 1.2, 6,1-3 (though compare 5,22-3). By taking both light and colour to be due ultimately to the same underlying cause, the Aristotelian reconceives the notion of what is 'transparent' along the lines of its etymology, in Greek as in English – it is that *through which* things *appear* (see *DA* 43,5-8 above; cf. 44,23-5 below) – rather than that which is *seen through*, for which he uses the term *diopton*. See also n. 400 on 44,21-3 below.

400. [44,21-3] Arist. *Sens.* 3, 439a26-8, b7. Alex. *Mant.* 147,30-148,2; 148,29-149,3; *Quaest.* 1.2, 5,30-6,1; *in Sens.* 44,22-45,3. If the claim here about matter is applied to the transparent medium, then it seems to contradict 42,21-2, as BD point out (285), and so needs to be understood in some broader sense of reception that does not imply literal alteration; cf. also AD 187. Both sets of commentators appeal to the notion of the material intellect at 81,24-5 as an example of such a sense.

The lines above (44,20-3) give us the underlying rationale for the Aristotelian conception of transparency (see n. 399 on 44,20-1): every body is transparent in so far as it can in some sense 'receive' colour, that is, in so far as it is susceptible in some way to colour as such (cf. Arist. *Sens.* 3, 439b7). The transparent medium may not be genuinely modified or changed by colour and so does not acquire a colour of its own (see n. 375 on 42,19-22 above; also 62,5-7 below). But it is such that it can relay whatever effect colour has on it to the visual organs of animals, which are sensitive to it (42,8-11; 43,11-16; 43,18-44,1). The transparent nature mixed with earth in solid bodies, in contrast, is able to possess and manifest colour and in turn affect the medium surrounding it. See 42,5-7 and 43,12 above and 45,5-46,6 below.

401. [**44,23-5**] *in Sens.* 45,11-16. On the etymology of 'transparent', with further references, see n. 378 on 43,5-8 above. Notice the implicit qualification in Alex.'s remark: the transparent medium, which we can see through, is just something that is transparent *in the highest degree*. As we have just seen (44,20-1), *all* bodies are transparent to some degree, including those we cannot see through. Cf. *Mant.* 148,7-9.

For the claim that the transparent medium is coloured or tinged by something outside it, see esp. *in Sens.* 49,8-50,5 (cf. 50,7-13); *Mant.* 144,5-6; as well as 42,11-19 and 43,18-20 above. The contrast between extraneous colours and a colour of one's own is implicit at Arist. *Sens.* 3, 439a31-b6.

402. [**45,1**] 44,16, with accompanying note.

403. [**45,2-3**] 43,8-11, with accompanying note; cf. 43,2.

404. [**45,3-5**] 42,22-43,4, with accompanying note.

405. [**45,5-6**] cf. Arist. *Sens.* 3, 439a33-b1. Alex. *DA* 45,18-19; *in Sens.* 50,5-7; 51,25-7. The contrast here is with the transparent medium, which has colour only extrinsically and from an extraneous source: see n. 397 on 44,16. BD (286) seem to think mistakenly that this passage concerns translucent solids like gems and so contradicts 42,7-8. But those are solids that *lack* a colour of their own, whereas the present passage is more plausibly about solids that *have* a colour of their own (see 45,17-19 below and n. 372 on 42,7-8 above).

If we take Alex.'s words here in their most straightforward sense, as claiming that the *interior of bodies* is coloured, he may be departing from Arist., who says only that colour is *on the surface* of things which are intrinsically visible (*to epi tôn kath' hauto horatôn*, *DA* 2.7, 418a29-30). In *Sens.* 3, Arist. does insist that 'one must think that the same [nature] that is coloured outside is *also within*' (*alla tên autên phusin dei nomizein, hêper kai exô, tautên kai entos*, 439a33-b1); and Alex. might conceivably have taken this to mean that this nature is *coloured* within: in his commentary on the passage, Alex. in fact claims that Arist. *says* that these objects are coloured inside (*entos kekhrôsthai legei*, *in Sens.* 50,6). But strictly Arist.'s actual words need only mean that this nature, transparency, *is present* within. And this strict reading may well be all that is justified: as Richard Sorabji points out (in his editorial comments), the interior of a solid object might be the same colour as its surface, a different colour, or even colourless.

In saying that the colour is 'inside', however, Alex. may have meant only that colour is *intrinsic* to the solid: it is due to the material composition of the body itself rather than borrowed from surrounding bodies, as the tingeing of a transparent medium is. This, in fact, is how Alex. goes on to explain the claim from his commentary on *Sens.*: 'Arist. says things that have a colour of their own from themselves are coloured inside because (*dihoti*) they have a colour of their own and what is responsible for colour (*to aition tou khrômatos*) within themselves' (*in Sens.* 50,5-7). If so, then Alex.'s position might be compatible with a 'surface only' reading of Arist. after all. The colour of a solid will, as Arist. says, be present '*in* the boundary' (*Sens*. 3, 439a31-2). But the interior 'depths' of bodies (*ta en bathei tôn sômatôn*) will have colour at most potentially, through their power, instead (*dunamei khrôma ekhein*, 51,25-6).

406. [45,6-7] cf. Arist. *Sens*. 3, 439b1-6. On the impermanence of light in the medium, see n. 376 on 42,22-43,4 above. For a similar contrast between how transparent materials, with and without a definite shape, look from different distances and positions, see *in Sens*. 50,16-26; compare Arist. *Sens*. 3, 439b3-5 with 440b16-18.

407. [45,7-10] *Mant*. 148,11-14; 149,15-32; 149,36-150,6; *in Sens*. 45,23-6; 46,6.12-19; 47,8-15; *Quaest*. 1.2, 7,4-7. Cf. also *DA* 46,4-6; *Quaest*. 1.2, 6,26-33.

408. [45,10-19] cf. Arist. *Sens*. 3, 440b14-23; 442a12-16; Alex. *Quaest*. 1.2, 6,26-7,7; *in Sens*. 53,5-8. Alex. draws an even more fine-grained distinction at both *Mant*. 150,7-9 and *in Sens*. 47,15-20, where he sets apart those bodies which are more transparent and truly 'luminous', from those which are just 'close' (*engus*) to these and so merely bright. As BD 287 rightly point out, the objects in the passage above are not in any case phosphorescent: they still need light in order to be seen (46,19).

AD argue (188) that the earlier explanation above at 45,5-10 is more limited than the present one, applying only to solid, sublunary bodies, on the grounds that earth is not part of transparent mediums like air and water, or the heavenly body at all, whereas the explanation here (45,10-11) applies to all bodies. But there is no fundamental conflict here. The earlier explanation does in fact apply to sublunary bodies of air and water, since Arist. holds that *every* sublunary body (or those 'near the middle' anyway) contains each of the four elements, including earth – he is explicit on this last point, *GC* 2.8, 334b31-3 (see also 335a22-3 and 2.3, 330b21-5) – ordinary bodies of air and water are not pure samples of the corresponding elements (*GC* 2.8 passim; for brief comments, see Sorabji 1988, 70 nn. 38 and 40). The heavenly body is still an exception, but it is a marginal one, since anywhere fire can be invoked, earth can too and *vice versa*. The two explanations are not in competition with each other, moreover, since the underlying principle turns on the proportion of *several* ingredients to each other in a mixture: Arist. *Sens*. 3, 440b14-23. If it is the proportion of earth to fire, as Alex. explicitly states at *Quaest*. 1.2, 6,26-7,7 (and as AD later argue themselves, 189), or even of earth possibly to all three remaining elements, which are all transparent in varying degrees (as Sorabji 2004*b*, 130 argues; cf. 1972, 293), then both of the explanations offered above could be in play.

AD also worry that fire will not be involved in all cases, especially the heavens. But Alex. offers fire as just an example of something bright (as BD 287 rightly note). This broader characterisation allows him to extend the second explanation to the case of the heavenly body, which may be a reason why he does not mention either sublunary element at 46,4-6.

409. [45,20] 45,25-46,1; Arist. *Sens*. 3, 439b11-18 (cf. a27-32). For further references to Alex., see n. 398 on 44,16-19 above.

410. [45,21-2] 46,12-17; *Quaest*. 1.2, 5,3-8; 7,13-17; *in Sens*. 44,18-20. A given body and the transparent material that makes it up are, in Arist.'s terminology, 'one and the same in number'. But they differ 'in being' or 'in account' – what it is to be a body is not the same as what it is to be transparent. Consequently, what it is to be the boundary of one is not the same as what it is to be the boundary of the other either. See n. 416 on 46,12-17 below.

411. **[45,22-4]** *Mant.* 148,4-5; *Quaest.* 1.2, 6,3-7. For 'appearance' (*phantasia*) used in this way, see *Sens.* 3, 439b5-6.

412. **[45,24-46,1]** 45,20; *Mant.* 150,13-19; *in Sens.* 48,10-13; 51, 21-4. This sentence amplifies the reason underlying the previous one: things are visible to us in virtue of their surfaces facing us, and these are visible because they have the power to affect the intervening medium so as to be seen. This power, which in the central cases just is the colour, must therefore reside in the surface. The subsequent move to identify this with the surface of the body in so far as it is transparent still requires further justification.

413. **[46,1-6]** AD 191 not unreasonably describe these lines (46,1-6) as 'the summary and foundation of Alex.'s entire theory of light and colour'. On fire as something visible in the highest degree, see 44,13-14 above (with accompanying note for further references). On fire as a source of light, 45,2-5. On light as contrasted with the 'other colours', see n. 397 on 44,16. On colour as belonging to transparent material with a definite shape, see 44,17-19; 45,20; cf. 46,6-7. On colour as due to the proportion of mixture (whether of earth, fire, or what is 'bright'), see 45,7-19.

The most striking feature of this passage, though, is how full and explicit its causal claims are. In saying that fire and other illuminants are such as to produce (*poiêtikois*) light and thereby make (*poiei*) other things visible and so become responsible (*aitia*) for their being seen (cf. 44,13-14), Alex. does more than just elaborate Arist.'s summary remark at *Sens.* 6, 447a11, that light produces seeing (*to phôs poiei to horan*; though compare *DA* 3.5,430a16-17). It makes clear that in Alex.'s mind these are not merely sufficient conditions, but explanatory ones as well.

414. **[46,6-11]** For the argument here, see also *Quaest.* 1.2, 5,11-15; *in Sens.* 48,22-49,4. On the transparent medium as only being coloured in a way, by something extraneous to it, see 44,23-45,1 with accompanying notes; on its not having a colour of its own, see 44,3-4 and n. 397 on 44,16.

415. **[46,11-13]** *Quaest.* 1.2, 5,19-23; *in Sens.* 49,4-8. AD 192 rightly reject Bruns' emendation here (following the Hebrew translation) as making nonsense of the passage: the successive sentences beginning *hôn gar* and *hôn de* are links in a continuous argument concerning coloured solids, as the parallel passage from the *Quaestiones* makes clear, not a contrast between transparent mediums and solids.

416. **[46,12-17]** 45,21-2, with accompanying note. At *in Sens.* 47,25-48,10, Alex. argues that bodies do not differ in degree as to whether they are bodies, but they do differ in how transparent they are; therefore, even if the boundary of the body and the transparent are 'one and the same in number', they will still differ 'in account' (48,5). At *in Sens.* 49,15-21 he adds a further battery of arguments to show that colour is not the boundary of the body as a body: colour is a quality, surface a quantity (15-16); every body has a surface, but not every body is coloured (17); a single surface may have many colours (17-19) and a single colour might be on many surfaces (20-1).

417. **[46,17-19]** The second half of this claim is surprising: for while it is true that the colour of a solid could not be *seen* unless it were illuminated, there is no reason to think that it would not still *have* its colour even when it was not illuminated, esp. given Arist.'s own realism about colours: objects still have their colours even when they are not seen in *DA* 3.2, 426a20-7.

Bibliography

Accattino, Paolo. 1988. 'Alessandro di Afrodisia e la trasmissione della forma nella riproduzione animale'. *Atti della Accademia delle Scienze di Torino*, Classe di scienze morali, storiche e filologiche, 122: 79-94.

Accattino, Paolo. 1992. 'Alessandro di Afrodisia e gli astri: l'anima e la luce'. *Atti della Accademia delle Scienze di Torino*, Classe di scienze morali, storiche e filologiche, 126: 39-62.

Accattino, Paolo. 1993. 'Ps. Hippocr. in Alex. Aphr. *De anima*', in F. Berger, C. Brockmann, G. de Gregorio et al. (eds), *Symbolae Berolinenses für Dieter Harlfinger*, 169-73. Amsterdam: Verlag Adolf M. Hakkert.

Accattino, Paolo. 1995. 'Generazione dell'anima in Alessandro di Afrodisia, *De anima* 2.10-11.13?' *Phronesis* 40: 182-201.

Accattino, Paolo and Pier Luigi Donini. 1996. *Alessandro di Afrodisia: L'anima*. Traduzione, introduzione e commento. (= Biblioteca Universale Laterza, v. 447.) Rome: Laterza.

Ackrill, J.L. 1972/73. 'Aristotle's Definitions of *psuchê*'. *Proceedings of the Aristotelian Society* 73: 119-33.

Algra, Keimpe. 1995. *Concepts of Space in Greek Thought*. Leiden: E.J. Brill.

Annas, Julia. 1992. *Hellenistic Philosophy of Mind*. Berkeley: University of California Press.

Asmis, Elizabeth. 1984. *Epicurus' Scientific Method*. Ithaca: Cornell University Press.

Barnes, Jonathan. [1971/72] 1979. 'Aristotle's Concept of Mind'. *Proceedings of the Aristotelian Society* 72 (1971/72): 101-14. Reprinted in Barnes, Schofield, and Sorabji 1979, 32-41.

Barnes, Jonathan, Susanne Bobzien, Kevin Flannery, and Katerina Ierodiakonou. 1991. *Alexander of Aphrodisias: On Aristotle's Prior Analytics 1.1-7*. Ancient Commentators on Aristotle. London: Duckworth.

Barnes, J., M. Schofield, and R. Sorabji (eds). 1979. *Articles on Aristotle*, 4 vols, vol. 4: *Psychology and Aesthetics*. London: Duckworth.

Bergeron, Martin and Richard Dufour. 2008. *Alexandre d'Aphrodise: De l'âme*. Texte grec introduit, traduit et annoté. Paris: Librairie Philosophique J. Vrin.

Berryman, Sylvia. 2002. 'The Sweetness of Honey: Philoponus against the Doctors on Supervening Qualities, in C. Leijenhorst, C. Lüthy, and J.M.M.H. Thijssen (eds), *The Dynamics of Aristotelian Natural Philosophy from Antiquity to the Seventeenth Century*, 65-79. (= Medieval and Early Modern Science, vol. 5.) Leiden: Brill.

Bonitz, Hermann. [1870] 1955. *Index Aristotelicus*. Graz: Akademische Druck- u. Verlagsanstalt. (Originally published as vol. 5 of I. Bekker (ed.), *Aristotelis Opera*.)

Caston, Victor. 1996. 'Why Aristotle Needs Imagination'. *Phronesis* 41: 20-55.

Caston, Victor. 1997. 'Epiphenomenalisms, Ancient and Modern'. *Philosophical Review* 106: 309-63.

Caston, Victor. 1998. 'Aristotle and the Problem of Intentionality'. *Philosophy and Phenomenological Research* 58: 249-98.

Caston, Victor. 1999. 'Aristotle's Two Intellects: A Modest Proposal'. *Phronesis* 44:199-227.

Caston, Victor. 2005. 'The Spirit and the Letter: Aristotle on Perception', in R. Salles (ed.), *Metaphysics, Soul, and Ethics: Themes from the work of Richard Sorabji*, 245-320. Oxford: Oxford University Press.

Caston, Victor. 2006. 'Aristotle's Psychology', in M.L. Gill and P. Pellegrin (eds), *The Blackwell Companion to Ancient Philosophy*, 316-46. Oxford: Blackwell Publishing.

Chaniotis, Angelos. 2004a. 'New Inscriptions from Aphrodisias (1995-2001)'. *American Journal of Archaeology* 108: 377-416.

Chaniotis, Angelos. 2004b. 'Epigraphic Evidence for the Philosopher Alexander of Aphrodisias', *Bulletin of the Institute of Classical Studies* 47: 79-81.

Charlton, William. [1970] 1983. *Aristotle's* Physics, *Books I and II*. Translated with Introduction and Notes. Oxford: Clarendon Press, 1970. Reprinted, with corrections, 1983.

Close, A.J. 1969. 'Commonplace Theories of Art and Nature in Classical Antiquity and in the Renaissance'. *Journal of the History of Ideas* 30: 467-86.

Courcelle, Pierre. 1974-75. *Connais-toi toi-même: De Socrate à Saint Bernard*. 3 vols. Paris: Études Augustiniennes.

Crivelli, Paolo. 2004. *Aristotle on Truth*. Cambridge: Cambridge University Press.

Davies, Malcolm and Jeyaraney Kathirithamby. 1986. *Greek Insects*. London: Duckworth.

de Groot, Jean Christensen. 1983. 'Philoponus on *De anima* II.5, *Physics* III.3, and the Propagation of Light'. *Phronesis* 28:177-96.

de Groot, Jean Christensen. 1991. *Aristotle and Philoponus on Light*. New York: Garland Publishing.

Dillon, John. [1977] 1996. *The Middle Platonists*. Revised edition with a new afterword. Ithaca: Cornell University Press, 1996. (1st edn, 1977.)

Donini, Pier Luigi. 1971. 'L'anima e gli elementi nel *de anima* di Alessandro di Afrodisia'. *Atti della Accademia delle Scienze di Torino*, Classe di scienze morali, storiche e filologiche, 105: 61-107.

Donini, Pier Luigi. 1974. *Tre studi sull'Aristotelismo nel II secolo d. C.* (= Historica, politica, philosophica: Il pensiero antico, studi e testi, vol. 7.) Turin: G.B. Paravia & Co.

Ebert, Theodor. 1983. 'Aristotle on What is Done in Perceiving'. *Zeitschrift für philosophische Forschung* 37: 181-98.

Ehnmark, Erland. 1957. 'Transmigration in Plato'. *Harvard Theological Review* 50: 1-20.

Eichholz, D.E. 1949. 'Aristotle's Theory of the Formation of Metals and Minerals'. *Classical Quarterly* 43: 141-6.

Ellis, John. 1994. 'Alexander's Defense of Aristotle's *Categories*'. *Phronesis* 39: 69-89.

Emilsson, Eyjólfur Kjalar. 1988. *Plotinus on Sense-Perception: A Philosophical Study*. Cambridge: Cambridge University Press.

Everson, Stephen. 1997. *Aristotle on Perception*. Oxford: Clarendon Press.

Fontenrose, Joseph Eddy. 1959. *Python: A Study of Delphic Myth and its Origins*. Berkeley: University of California Press.

Frede, Dorothea and Burkhard Reis (eds). 2009. *Body and Soul in Ancient Philosophy*. Berlin: Walter de Gruyter.

Frede, Michael and Günther Patzig. 1988. *Aristoteles 'Metaphysik Z'*. Text, Übersetzung und Kommentar. 2 Bände. Munich: Verlag C.H. Beck.

Geach, Peter. 1969. *God and the Soul*. London: Routledge & Kegan Paul.

Giannakis, Elias. 1995/96. 'Fragments from Alexander's Lost Commentary on Aristotle's *Physics*'. *Zeitschrift für Geschichte der arabisch-islamischen Wissenschaften* 10: 157-87.

Gill, Mary Louise. 1989. *Aristotle on Substance: The Paradox of Unity*. Princeton: Princeton University Press.

Glucker, John. 1978. *Antiochus and the Late Academy*. (= Hypomnemata, Heft 56.) Göttingen: Vandenhoeck & Ruprecht.

Gottschalk, H.B. 1986. 'Boethus' Psychology and the Neoplatonists'. *Phronesis* 31: 243-57.

Gottschalk, H.B. 1987. 'Aristotelian Philosophy in the Roman World from the Time of Cicero to the End of the Second Century AD', in *Aufstieg und Niedergang der römischen Welt*, ed. Wolfgang Haase, 2.36.2: 1079-1174. Berlin: Walter de Gruyter.

Graf, Fritz. 2009. *Apollo*. London: Routledge.

Hahm, David E. 1977. *The Origins of Stoic Cosmology*. Columbus: Ohio State University Press.

Hahn, Johannes. 1989. *Der Philosoph und die Gesellschaft: Selbstverständnis, öffentliches Auftreten und populäre Erwartungen in der hohen Kaiserzeit*. (= Heidelberger Althistorische Beiträge und Epigraphische Studien, Band 7.) Stuttgart: Franz Steiner Verlag.

Henry, P. 1960. 'Une comparaison chez Aristote, Alexandre et Plotin', in *Les Sources de Plotin*, 429-49. (= Entretiens sur l'Antiquité Classique, vol. 5.) Vandoeuvres-Genève: Fondation Hardt.

Hicks, R.D. 1907. *Aristotle, De anima*. With translation, introduction and notes. Cambridge: Cambridge University Press.

Huffman, Carl. [2005] 2009. 'Pythagoras'. Revised version. *Stanford Encyclopedia of Philosophy*. http://plato.stanford.edu/entries/pythagoras/ (First version, 2005.)

Huffman, Carl. 2009. 'The Pythagorean Conception of the Soul from Pythagoras to Philolaus', in Frede and Reis 2009, 21-43.

Inwood, Brad. 1985. *Ethics and Human Action in Early Stoicism*. Oxford: Clarendon Press.

Inwood, Brad. [1992] 2001. *The Poem of Empedocles*. A Text and Translation with an Introduction. Revised edition. (= *Phoenix*, suppl. vol. 39) Toronto: University of Toronto Press, 2001. (1st edn, 1992.)

Inwood, Brad. 2009. 'Empedocles and *metempsychôsis*', in Frede and Reis 2009, 71-86.

Joachim, Harold H. 1903. 'Aristotle's Conception of Chemical Combination'. *Journal of Philology* 29: 72-86.

Johansen, T.K. 1998. *Aristotle on the Sense-Organs*. Cambridge: Cambridge University Press.

Johnston, Sarah Iles. 2008. *Ancient Greek Divination*. Malden, MA: Wiley-Blackwell.

Kahn, Charles H. 1985. 'Democritus and the Origins of Moral Psychology'. *American Journal of Philology* 106: 1-31.

Katayama, Errol G. 1999. *Aristotle on Artifacts: A Metaphysical Puzzle*. Albany, NY: State University of New York Press.

Kerferd, G.B. 1971. 'Epicurus' Doctrine of the Soul'. *Phronesis* 16: 80-96.

Kim, Jaegwon. 1993. 'The Nonreductivist's Troubles with Mental Causation', in J. Heil and A. Mele (eds), *Mental Causation*, 189-210. Oxford: Oxford University Press, 1993. Reprinted in Jaegwon Kim, *Supervenience and Mind: Selected Philosophical Essays*, 336-57. Cambridge: Cambridge University Press, 1993.

Kupreeva, Inna Veniaminovna. 2003. 'Qualities and Bodies: Alexander against the Stoics'. *Oxford Studies in Ancient Philosophy* 25: 297-44.

Lennox, James G. [1997] 2001. 'Nature does Nothing in Vain ...', in H.-C. Guenther and A. Rengakos (eds), *Beiträge zur antiken Philosophie: Festschrift für Wolfgang Kullmann*, 199-214. Stuttgart: Franz Steiner Verlag, 1997. Reprinted in Lennox 2001, 205-23.

Lennox, James G. 2001. *Aristotle's Philosophy of Biology: Studies in the Origins of Life Science*. Cambridge: Cambridge University Press.

Lewis, Eric. 1988. 'Diogenes Laertius and the Stoic Theory of Mixture'. *Bulletin of the Institute of Classical Studies* 35: 84-90.

Lewis, Frank A. 2008. ' "What's the Matter with Prime Matter" '. *Oxford Studies in Ancient Philosophy* 34: 123-46.

Lloyd, A.C. 1962. 'Genus, Species, and Ordered Series in Aristotle'. *Phronesis* 7: 67-90.

Lloyd, G.E.R. 1966. *Polarity and Analogy: Two Types of Argumentation in Early Greek Thought*. Cambridge: Cambridge University Press.

Lloyd, G.E.R. 1987. *The Revolutions of Wisdom: Studies in the Claims and Practice of Ancient Greek Science*. (= Sather Classical Lectures, vol. 52.) Berkeley: University of California Press.

Lloyd, G.E.R. 2006. 'The Master Cook', in his *Aristotelian Explorations*, 83-103. Cambridge: Cambridge University Press.

Lloyd, G.E.R. and G.E.L. Owen (eds). 1978. *Aristotle on Mind and the Senses*. Proceedings of the Seventh Symposium Aristotelicum, Cambridge 1975. Cambridge: Cambridge University Press.

Long, A.A. and D.N. Sedley. 1987. *The Hellenistic Philosophers*. 2 vols. Cambridge: Cambridge University Press.

Lynch, John Patrick. 1972. *Aristotle's School: A Study of a Greek Educational Institution*. Berkeley: University of California Press.

Mansfeld, Jaap. 1990. 'Doxography and Dialectic: The *Sitz im Leben* of the "Placita"'. *Aufstieg und Niedergang der römischen Welt* 2.36.4, 3056-3229. Berlin: Walter de Gruyter.

McLaughlin, Brian. 1992. 'The Rise and Fall of British Emergentism', in Ansgar Beckermann, Hans Flohr, and Jaegwon Kim (eds), *Emergence or Reduction? Essays on the Prospects of Nonreductive Physicalism*, 49-93. Berlin: Walter de Gruyter.

Menn, Stephen. 2002. 'Aristotle's Definition of the Soul and the Programme of the *De anima*'. *Oxford Studies in Ancient Philosophy* 22: 83-139.

Merlan, Philip. 1969. *Monopsychism, Mysticism, Metaconsciousness: Problems of the Soul in the Neoaristotelian and Neoplatonic Tradition*. (= Archives internationales d'histoire des idées, vol. 2.) The Hague: M. Nijhoff.

Moraux, Paul. 1942. *Alexandre d'Aphrodise: Exégète de la noétique d'Aristote*. (= Bibliothèque de la Faculté de Philosophie et Lettres de l'Université de Liège, fasc. 99.) Liège: Faculté de Philosophie et Lettres.

Moraux, Paul. 1967. 'Aristoteles, der Lehrer Alexanders von Aphrodisias'. *Archiv für Geschichte der Philosophie* 49: 169-82.

Moraux, Paul. 1973. *Der Aristotelismus bei den Griechen: Von Andronikos bis*

Alexander von Aphrodisias. Band I: Die Renaissance des Aristotelismus im 1. Jh. v. Chr. Berlin: Walter de Gruyter.

Moraux, Paul. 1984. *Der Aristotelismus bei den Griechen: Von Andronikos bis Alexander von Aphrodisias*. Band II: Der Aristotelismus im I. und II. Jh. n. Chr. Berlin: Walter de Gruyter.

Moraux, Paul. 2001. *Der Aristotelismus bei den Griechen: Von Andronikos bis Alexander von Aphrodisias*. Band III: Alexander von Aphrodisias. Ed. von Jürgen Wiesner. Berlin: Walter de Gruyter.

Morison, Benjamin. 2002. *On Location: Aristotle's Concept of Place*. Oxford: Oxford University Press.

Mugler, Charles. 1964. *Dictionnaire historique de la terminologie optique des Grecs: Douze siècles de dialogues avec la lumière*. (= Études et Commentaires, vol. 53.) Paris: Librairie C. Klincksieck.

Nussbaum, Martha C. 1978. *Aristotle's De motu animalium*. Text with translation, commentary and interpretive essays. Princeton: Princeton University Press.

Oliver, James H. 1970. *Marcus Aurelius: Aspects of Civic and Cultural Policy in the East*. (= *Hesperia*, Suppl. 13.) Princeton: American School of Classical Studies at Athens.

Oliver, James H. 1977. 'The *diadochê* at Athens under the Humanistic Emperors'. *American Journal of Philology* 98: 160-78.

Oliver, James H. 1981. 'Marcus Aurelius and the Philosophical Schools at Athens'. *American Journal of Philology* 102: 213-25.

Opsomer, Jan and R.W. Sharples. 2000. 'Alexander of Aphrodisias, *De intellectu* 110.4: "I heard this from Aristotle." A Modest Proposal'. *Classical Quarterly* 50: 252-6.

Rashed, Marwan. [1997] 2007. 'A "New" Text of Alexander on the Soul's Motion', in R. Sorabji (ed.), *Aristotle and After*, 181-95. (= *Bulletin of the Institute of Classical Studies* 68 (1997), supplement.) Reprinted in Rashed 2007b, 143-57.

Rashed, Marwan. 2005. *Aristote, De la génération et la corruption*. Texte établi et traduit. Nouvelle édition. Paris: Les Belles Lettres.

Rashed, Marwan. 2007a. *Essentialisme: Alexandre d'Aphrodise entre logique, physique et cosmologie*. (= Commentaria in Aristotelem Graeca et Byzantina: Quellen und Studien, Band 2.) Berlin: Walter de Gruyter.

Rashed, Marwan. 2007b. *L'héritage aristotélicien: Textes inédits de l'Antiquité*. Paris: Les Belles Lettres.

Rescher, Nicholas and Michael E. Marmura. 1965. *The Refutation by Alexander of Aphrodisias of Galen's Treatise on the Theory of Motion*. Translated from the medieval Arabic version, with an introduction, notes, and an edition of the Arabic text. Islamabad: Islamic Research Institute.

Rose, Valentin. 1863. *Aristoteles Pseudepigraphus*. Leipzig: B.G. Teubner.

Ross, W.D. 1961. *Aristotle De anima*. Edited, with Introduction and Commentary. Oxford: Clarendon Press.

Ryle, Gilbert. 1949. *The Concept of Mind*. New York: Barnes & Noble, Inc.

Salles, Ricardo. 2001. 'Compatibilism, Ancient and Modern'. *Archiv für Geschichte der Philosophie* 83: 1-23.

Sandbach, F.H. 1985. *Aristotle and the Stoics*. (= *Proceedings of the Cambridge Philological Society*, suppl. vol. 10.) Cambridge: Cambridge Philological Society.

Schroeder, Frederic M. 1981. 'The Analogy of the Active Intellect to Light in the "De Anima" of Alexander of Aphrodisias'. *Hermes* 59: 215-25.

Sharples, R.W. 1975. 'Aristotelian and Stoic Conceptions of Necessity in the *De fato* of Alexander of Aphrodisias'. *Phronesis* 20: 247-74.

Sharples, R.W. 1983. *Alexander of Aphrodisias on Fate*. Text, Translation and Commentary. London: Duckworth.

Sharples, R.W. 1987. 'Alexander of Aphrodisias: Scholasticism and Innovation'. *Aufstieg und Niedergang der römischen Welt*, 2.36.2, 1176-1243. Berlin: Walter de Gruyter.

Sharples, R.W. 1990. 'The School of Alexander?" in Richard Sorabji (ed.), *Aristotle Transformed: The Ancient Commentators and their Influence*, 83-111. London: Duckworth.

Sharples, R.W. 1994*a*. *Alexander of Aphrodisias, Quaestiones 2.16-3.15*. Ancient Commentators on Aristotle. London: Duckworth.

Sharples, R.W. 1994*b*. 'On Body, Soul, and Generation in Alexander of Aphrodisias'. *Apeiron* 27: 163-70.

Sharples, R.W. 1998. *Theophrastus of Eresus: Sources for his Life, Writings, Thought, and Influence*. Commentary vol. 3.1: Sources on Physics (Texts 137-223). With contributions on the Arabic material by Dimitri Gutas. (= Philosophia Antiqua, vol. 79.) Leiden: Brill.

Sharples, R.W. 1999. 'On being a *tode ti* in Aristotle and Alexander'. *Méthexis* 12: 77-87.

Sharples, R.W. 2004. *Alexander of Aphrodisias, Supplement to 'On the Soul'*. Ancient Commentators on Aristotle. London: Duckworth.

Sharples, R.W. 2005*a*. 'Implications of the New Alexander of Aphrodisias Inscription'. *Bulletin of the Institute of Classical Studies* 48: 47-56.

Sharples, R.W. 2005*b*. 'Alexander of Aphrodisias on the Nature and Location of Vision', in Ricardo Salles (ed.), *Metaphysics, Soul, and Ethics in Ancient Thought: Themes from the Work of Richard Sorabji*, 345-62.

Sharples, R.W. 2008. *Alexander Aphrodisiensis, De anima libri mantissa*. A New Edition of the Greek Text with Introduction and Commentary. (= Peripatoi: Philologisch-historische Studien zum Aristotelismus, Band 21.) Berlin: Walter de Gruyter.

Shields, Christopher. 2007. 'The Peculiar Motion of Aristotelian Souls'. *Proceedings of the Aristotelian Society*, suppl. vol. 81: 139-61.

Siegel, Rudolph E. 1968. *Galen's System of Physiology and Medicine: An Analysis of his Doctrines and Observations on Bloodflow, Respiration, Humors and Internal Diseases*. Basel: S. Karger.

Siegel, Rudolph E. 1970. *Galen on Sense Perception: His Doctrines, Observations and Experiments on Vision, Hearing, Smell, Taste, Touch and Pain, and their Historical Sources*. Basel: S. Karger.

Sorabji, Richard. [1971] 1979. 'Aristotle on Demarcating the Five Senses'. *Philosophical Review* 80 (1971): 55-79. Reprinted in Barnes, Schofield and Sorabji 1979, 76-92.

Sorabji, Richard. 1972. 'Aristotle, Mathematics, and Colour'. *Classical Quarterly* 22: 293-308.

Sorabji, Richard. [1974] 1979. 'Body and Soul in Aristotle'. *Philosophy* 49 (1974): 63-89. Reprinted in Barnes, Schofield, and Sorabji 1979, 42-64.

Sorabji, Richard. [1987] 2010. *Philoponus and the Rejection of Aristotelian Science*. 2nd edn. (= Bulletin of the Institute of Classical Studies, Suppl. 103.) London: Institute of Classical Studies, 2010. (1st edn, 1987.)

Sorabji, Richard. 1988. *Matter, Space, and Motion: Theories in Antiquity and their Sequel*. London: Duckworth.

Sorabji, Richard. 1991. 'From Aristotle to Brentano: The Development of the Concept of Intentionality', in Henry Blumenthal and Howard Robinson (eds), *Aristotle and the Later Tradition*, 227-59. (= *Oxford Studies in Ancient Philosophy*, suppl. vol.)

Sorabji, Richard. 2003. 'The Mind-Body Relation in the Wake of Plato's *Timaeus*', in Gretchen J. Reydams-Schils (ed.), *Plato's* Timaeus *as Cultural Icon*, 152-62. Notre Dame: University of Notre Dame Press.

Sorabji, Richard. 2004a. *The Philosophy of the Commentators, 200-600 AD: A Sourcebook*. 3 vols. London: Duckworth.

Sorabji, Richard. 2004b. 'Aristotle on Colour, Light, and Imperceptibles'. *Bulletin of the Institute of Classical Studies* 47: 129-40.

Sprague, Rosamond Kent. 1989. 'Aristotle and Divided Insects'. *Méthexis* 2: 29-40.

Striker, Gisela. [1983] 1996. 'The Role of *oikeiôsis* in Stoic Ethics'. *Oxford Studies in Ancient Philosophy* 1 (1983): 145-67. Reprinted in her 1996, 281-97.

Striker, Gisela. [1991] 1996. 'Following Nature: A Study in Stoic Ethics'. *Oxford Studies in Ancient Philosophy* 9 (1991): 1-73. Reprinted in her 1996, 221-80.

Striker, Gisela. 1996. *Essays on Hellenistic Epistemology and Ethics*. Cambridge: Cambridge University Press.

Thillet, Pierre. 1984. *Alexandre d'Aphrodise: Traité du destin*. Paris: Les Belles Lettres.

Todd, R.B. 1972. '*Epitêdeiotês* in Philosophical Literature: Towards an Analysis'. *Acta Classica* 15: 25-36.

Todd, R.B. 1974. 'Lexicographical Notes on Alexander of Aphrodisias' Philosophical Terminology'. *Glotta* 52: 207-15.

Todd, R.B. 1976. *Alexander of Aphrodisias on Stoic Physics: A Study of the* De mixtione *with Preliminary Essays, Text, Translation and Commentary*. Leiden: Brill.

Tracy, Theodore. 1969. *Physiological Theory and the Doctrine of the Mean in Plato and Aristotle*. Chicago: Loyola University Press.

Tracy, Theodore. 1982. 'The Soul/Boatman Analogy in Aristotle's *De anima*'. *Classical Philology* 77: 98-112.

Tracy, Theodore. 1983. 'Heart and Soul in Aristotle', in John P. Anton and Anthony Preus (eds), *Essays in Ancient Greek Philosophy*, vol. II, 321-39. Albany, NY: State University of New York Press.

Wardy, Robert. 1990. *The Chain of Change: A Study of Aristotle's* Physics *VII*. Cambridge: Cambridge University Press.

Watts, Edward J. 2006. *City and School in Late Antique Athens and Alexandria*. Berkeley: University of California Press.

West, M.L. 1992. *Ancient Greek Music*. Oxford: Clarendon Press.

Westerink, L.G. 1959. *Damascius, Lectures on the* Philebus, *wrongly attributed to* Olympiodorus. Text, translation, notes and indices. Amsterdam: North-Holland Publishing Company.

Whittaker, John. 1990. *Alcinoos: Enseignement des doctrines de Platon*. Introduction, texte établi et commenté par John Whittaker et traduit par Pierre Louis. Paris: Les Belles Lettres.

White, Michael J. 2003. 'Stoic Natural Philosophy (Physics and Cosmology)', in B. Inwood (ed.), *The Cambridge Companion to the Stoics*, 124-52. Cambridge: Cambridge University Press.

White, Nicholas. 1979. 'The Basis of Stoic Ethics'. *Harvard Studies in Classical Philology* 83: 143-78.

White, Nicholas. 1985. 'The Role of Physics in Stoic Ethics', in Ronald H. Epp (ed.),

Recovering the Stoics, 57-74. (= *The Southern Journal of Philosophy* 23, Supplement.)

Wilberding, J. 2011. *Porphyry: To Gaurus On How Embryos are Ensouled and On What is in Our Power*. Ancient Commentators on Aristotle. London: Bristol Classical Press.

Wilkins, Eliza Gregory. 1917. *'Know Thyself' in Greek and Latin Literature*. Ph.D. diss., University of Chicago.

Williams, C.J.F. 1982. *Aristotle's* De Generatione et Corruptione. Translated with notes. Oxford: Clarendon Press.

Zeller, Eduard. 1923. *Die Philosophie der Griechen in ihrer geschichtlichen Entwicklung*. Teil 3.1: Die nacharistotelische Philosophie. 5. Auflage. Leipzig: O.R. Reisland.

English-Greek Glossary

This Glossary lists key terms in the English translation for both Parts I and II and the Greek words which they standardly represent. It can thus also serve as an aid to locating terms in the Greek-English Index. In some cases a family of cognate terms is represented by one or two leading members.

absence: *apousia, sterêsis*
abstractions: *ta ex aphaireseôs*
absurd: *atopos*
absurdity: *atopia*
abundance: *euporia, plêthos*
accept: *suntithesthai*
acidic: *oxus*
acidity: *oxutês*
active: *drastikos*
activity: *energeia, ergon*
accompany: *sunhodeuein*
accomplished: *spoudaios*
accrue: *prosginesthai*
accumulated: *athroos*
accurate: *akribês*
accurately: *akribôs*
achieve: *epitelein*
acquire: *lambanein, proslambanein*
acquired: *epiktêtos*
acquiring: *lêpsis*
acquisition: *lêpsis*
acrid: *drimus*
act: *poiein, prattein*
action: *praxis*
action, capable of: *praktikos*
activate: *energein*
active: *drastikos*
actively: *kat' energeian*
activity: *energeia*
actuality, in: *energeiai*
add: *proslambanein*
added, be: *prosginesthai, prostithesthai*
adding: *sunteleia*
admit: *paradekhesthai*
advanced: *teleios*
advanced, less: *atelesteros*
affect (n.): *pathos*
affected, be: *paskhein*
affected first, be: *propaskhein*
affected, by being: *pathêtikôs*
affirmation, make a: *kataphanai*
affirmative: *kataphatikos*
age: *gêraskein*

agree: *homologein, sumphônein*
agreement: *sumphônia*
aim: *prothesis*
aim at: *stokhazesthai*
air: *aêr*
aligned: *kat' euthuôrian*
alive, be: *zên*
alone: *monos, exhairetos*
alter: *alloiousthai*
alter, able to: *alloiôtikos*
alteration: *alloiôsis*
amorphous: *amorphos*
amputation: *aphairesis*
analogous: *analogon*
analogously: *analogôs*
analogy: *analogia*
analyse: *dialambanein*
ancient: *arkhaios*
anger: *orgê*
angry, become: *orgizesthai*
animal: *zôion*
animate: *empsukhos*
apparatus: *hupêresia*
apparent: *phaneros*
appear: *phainesthai*
appear through: *diaphainesthai*
appearance: *phantasia*
appetite: *epithumia*
apple: *mêlos*
apply: *prosginesthai, epharmozein*
appreciate: *manthanein*
apprehending, for: *gnôstikos*
apprehension: *gnôsis*
approach: *prosienai, proshiesthai*
appropriate: *oikeion*
appropriately: *oikeiôs, prosêkontôs*
apt: *epitêdeios*
aptitude: *epitêdeiotês*
aquatic: *enhudros*
arbitrariness: *apoklêrôsis*
argument: *logos, sullogismos*
army: *stratopedon*
arrange: *paraskeuazein*

arrangement: *thesis*
art: *tekhnê*
artefact: *to kata technên ginomenon*
artificial: *tekhnikos*
artisan: *tekhnitês*
ascent: *anhodos*
ascertaining: *heurêsis*
asleep, be: *koimasthai*
assemble: *athroizein*
assimilated to, become: *exhomoiousthai*
assistant: *epikouros*
assistance: *boêtheia*
assume: *hupolambanein*
assumption: *lambanomenon*
attached to, naturally: *prosphuesthai*
attribute (v.): *katêgorein, anatithenai*
audible: *akoustos*
auditory: *akoustikos*
augmentative: *auxêtikos*
authoritative: *kurios*
avoid: *phugein, ekklinein, apostrephein*
avoided, to be: *pheuktos*
avoiding: *phugê*
awake, be: *egrêgorthai*
aware, being: *antilambanesthai*
aware, capable of being: *antilêptikos*
aware conjointly: *sunaisthanesthai*
awareness: *antilêpsis*
awareness, accompanying: *sunaisthêsis*

backwards: *opisô*
bad: *kakos*
balance: *summetria, mesotês*
balance, appropriate: *to summetron*
ball: *sphaira*
basic: *prôtos*
basis: *hupobathra*
be together: *sunhuparkhein*
becoming: *genesis*
being: *to einai, on*
belief: *doxa*
belief, have a: *doxazein*
believe: *doxazein*
believed, can be: *doxastos*
believing, for *or* capable of: *doxastikos*
bench: *bathron*
between: *metaxu*
bile: *kholê*
bitter: *austêros*
black: *melan*
blade: *sidêros*
blanching: *ôkhrotês*
blank: *agraphos*
blend (n.): *krasis, krama*
blend (v.): *kerannunai*
blend, good: *eukrasia*
blood: *haima*

blood, containing: *enhaimos*
blood vessel: *phleps*
bloodless: *anhaimos*
blushing: *eruthêma*
body: *sôma*
body of: *athroos*
bodily: *sômatikos*
bone: *osteon*
born, be: *apotiktesthai*
bound (v.): *peratoun, horizein*
boundary: *peras*
bow: *prôra*
brain: *enkephalos*
breath: *pneuma*
brick: *plinthos*
bright: *leukos*
bring together: *sullegein*
broader sense, in a: *koinoteron*
bronze: *khalkos*
build in: *enkatoikodomein*

calm: *hêsukhia*
cannot be heard: *anêkoustos*
cannot be seen: *ahoratos*
cannot be smelled: *anosphrêtos*
carry: *okhein, pherein*
carry along with: *summetapherein,
    sunanapherein*
cart: *hamaxa*
carve: *temnein*
cease: *sumpauesthai, pauein,
    methistasthai*
centre: *kentron*
chameleon: *khamaileôn*
change: *kinêsis, metabolê*
change, able to produce: *kinêtikos*
change, produce: *kinein*
change first: *prokinein*
change jointly: *sunkinein*
change place: *methistasthai*
changing place: *metastasis*
character: *poion*
characteristic: *oikeion*
characterisation: *logos*
characterise: *katêgoreisthai*
choice: *prohairesis*
choice, worthy of: *hairetos*
choosing: *hairesis*
chosen, be: *krinein*
circle: *kuklos*
circumference: *periphereia*
circumscribe: *apokrinein*
circumstance: *peristasis*
cithara: *kithara*
class (v.): *perilambanein*
cleanse, able to: *rhuptikos*
clear: *saphês, phaneros*

clear, able to make: *dêlôtikos*
clear, make: *dêloun*
clear, making: *dêlôsis*
clearly: *saphôs*
cloak: *himation*
close: *engus*
close shut: *muein*
clothing: *skepasma*
cognition: *krisis*
coincide: *sunhaptein, epharmozein*
cold: *psukhros*
cold, grow: *apopsukhesthai*
coldness: *psukhrotês*
collide with: *prospiptein*
colour (n.): *khrôma*
colour (v.): *khrômatizein, khrôizein*
colour, of the same: *homokhroos*
combination: *parathesis*
combined: *koinos*
come together: *sunhodos*
coming into being: *genesis*
coming-to-be: *genesis*
co-mingle: *mignunai*
command: *prostassein*
commensurateness: *summetria*
common: *koinos*
common sense: *koinê aisthêsis*
communicate: *mênuein*
communicate, able to: *mênutikos*
communication: *mênusis*
community: *koinônia*
completion: *entelekheia*
complex: *poikilos*
compose: *sunkeisthai*
composite: *sunamphoteros, to sunkeimenon*
composition: *sunthesis*
compound (adj.): *sunthetos*
compound (n.): *sunthesis*
compound (v.): *sunkeisthai*
comprehend: *perilambanein*
comprehension: *perilêpsis*
compresent with: *suneinai*
conceive: *lambanein, ennoein*
concept: *noêma*
conception: *ennoia, epinoia*
conclusion: *sumperasma*
concur: *suntrekhein*
confine: *eneilein*
conflate: *sunhaptein*
conflict: *makhê*
conformity: *oikeiotês*
confused, be: *planan*
congenital: *sumphutos, sumphuês*
connect by passages: *suntetrainein*
consequence: *akolouthos, hepomenon*
consequence, be a: *hepesthai, akolouthein*

consider: *lambanein*
consistency: *sustasis*
constitution: *sustasis*
construct: *kataskeuazein*
construction: *kataskeuê*
contain: *periekhein*
contact: *haphê*
continuity: *sunekheia*
continuous: *sunekhês*
contour: *morphê*
contract: *sustellein*
contraction: *sustolê*
contradistinguish: *antidihairein*
contrariety: *enantiôsis*
contrary: *enantios*
contrast: *antitithenai*
contribute, make a contribution: *suntelein, sunergein*
contribution: *sunteleia*
control: one who is in control of himself, *enkratês*; one who is not in control of himself, *akratês*
converse: *antistrophê*
convert: *antistrephein, methistanai*
conviction: *pistis*
convinced, be: *pisteuein*
cook: *pessein*
cooking: *pepsis*
cool down: *katapsukhein*
cooling: *empsuxis, psuxis*
cooling down: *katapsuxis*
correspond: *hupokeisthai*
corresponding: *antikeimenos, kata*
cough: *bêttein*
cover up: *epikaluptein*
culmination: *teleiotês*
cultivation: *exergasia*
cure: *hugiazein*
cut: *temnein*
cut across: *enallattein*

damage: *apôleia*
dancer: *orkhêstês*
dancing, for: *orkhêstikos*
dark: *skotos*
darkness: *skotos*
death: *thanatos*
decay: *anesis*
declare: *proagoreuein*
decree: *prokêruttein*
deficient, be: *apoleipesthai*
define: *horizein*
definition: *horismos, logos*
definition to, give: *horizein*
deliberate: *bouleuesthai*
deliberation, for *or* capable of: *bouleutikos*

delirium: *paraphrosunê*
deliver: *parapempein*
delivery: *parapompê*
demonstrative: *apodeiktikos*
density: *pakhutês*
denial, make a: *apophanai*
deny: *anteipein*
depend: *êrtêsthai*
depth: *eisokhê*
derivatively: *deuterôs*
desirable: *orektos*
desire (n.): *orexis*
desire (v.): *oregesthai*
desiring, for: *orektikos*
destroy: *phtheirein*
destruction: *phthora*
destructive: *phthartikos*
detach: *apoluein, aphairein*
detail, in: *prosekhôs*
detail, lack: *epipolaios*
detect: *phôran*
determinate: *aphôrismenos, hôrismenos*
develop: *teleioun*
developed, highly *or* fully: *teleios*
development: *epidosis, teleiôsis*
deviate: *parallattein*
diagonal: *diametros*
die: *apothnêskein*
differ: *diapherein*
difference: *diaphora, heterotês*
differentiate: *diarthroun*
digest: *kateirgnunai*
digestion: *katergasia*
dilate: *aneurunein*
directed towards: *anaphora*
direction: *diastasis*
directly: *ep' eutheias, ex eutheias*
discern: *krinein*
discernible: *gnôrimos*
discriminate: *diakrinein*
discriminating: *diakrisis, epikrisis*
disparity: *parallagê*
disperse: *thruptein*
dispersion: *thrupsis*
disposed in a certain way: *pôs ekhein*
disposition: *hexis*
dispositional: *kath' hexin, en hexei*
dispute (n.): *amphisbêtêsis*
dispute (v.): *amphisbêtein*
dissection: *anatomê*
dissimilar in genus: *anhomogenês*
dissimilar types, belonging to: *anhomoeidês*
distance: *diastêma, apostêma*
distance, be at a: *aphistasthai*
distinct: *kekhôrismenos*
distinct, be: *kekhôristhai*

distinctive: *diaphoros*
distinctly: *enargesteron, tranôs*
distinctively: *diapherontôs*
distinguish: *khôrizein*
distribute: *paraspeirein*
distrust: *apistein*
disturb: *enokhlein*
disturbed, not easily: *duspathês*
diversified: *polutropos*
diversity: *parallagê*
divide: *dihairein, skhizein*
divine: *theios*
divisible into parts: *meristos*
division: *dihairesis*
do: *prattein*
done, ought to be: *prakteos*
done, can be: *praktos*
downwards: *katô*
drawing: *graphê*
drug: *pharmakon*
drunk, to be: *methuein*
dry: *xêros*
dryness: *xêrotês*
duality: *to ditton*
dye, murex: *halourgês*

ear: *ous*
earth: *gê*
earthy: *geôdês*
echo (n.): *êkhô*
echo (v.): *êkhein*
effect: *pathos*
effluence: *aporrhoia*
element: *stoikheion*
eliminate: *aposkeuazesthai*
emerge above: *gennasthai epi*
emission: *anathumiasis*
emit: *prohiesthai*
empty: *kenos*
enable: *paraskeuazein*
enclose: *periekhein, enapolambanein*
encounter: *peripiptein*
end: *telos*
end product: *perittôma*
endorse: *sunkatatithenai*
endorsement: *sunkatathesis*
endorsement, for: *sunkatathetikos*
endpoint: *peras*
engages in activity: *energein*
enlarge: *sunauxein*
enmattered: *enhulos*
ennumeration: *katarithmêsis*
enquire further: *epizêtein*
entailed by: *hepesthai*
enter: *eiseinai, epeisienai*
entrance: *eishodos*
error: *dihamartia, planê*

error, be in: *diapseudesthai*
essence: *ousia, logos, to ti ên einai*
esteem, hold in the highest: *presbeuein*
eternal: *aidios*
eunuch: *eunouchos*
evidence: *sêmeion, marturion*
evident: *enargês, dêlos*
evident, be: *dêloun*
examine in detail: *parakolouthein*
exceed: *huperballein*
excess: *huperbolê, pleonasmos*
excess, be in: *pleonazein*
excited, be: *organ*
exclusively: *idiôs*
exhale: *ekpnein*
exhibit: *emphainesthai*
exist: *huphistasthai*
exist in conjunction with: *parhuphistanai*
exist prior: *prohuphistasthai*
existence: *hupostasis*
expansion: *auxêsis*
experience (n.): *empeiria*
experience (v.): *paskhein*
explanation: *paramuthia*
expound: *ektithenai*
express: *diasêmainein, sêmainein*
expressing oneself: *hermêneia*
extend: *diatenein, metapherein*
extend through: *diienai, dierkhomai, diaphuein*
extended sense, in an: *kata metaphoran*
extension: *diastêma*
extension *or* something extended: *megethos*
exterior: *peras*
external: *ektos*
extraneous: *allotrios*
extraordinary: *amêkhanos*
extreme: *akros*
extrinsic characteristic: *sumbebêkos*
extrinsically: *kata sumbebêkos*
eye: *ophthalmos, omma, opsis*
eye's interior: *korê*
eyelid: *blepharon*
exiting: *khusis*

facilitate: *paraskeuazein*
fall: *piptein*
fall short: *elleipein*
fall under: *hupopiptein*
false: *pseudês*
falsehood: *pseudos*
falsehood, possess: *pseudesthai*
far away: *porrô*
fear: *phobos*
fill: *plêroun*
filled: *mestos*

fire: *pur*
fire, set on: *proskaiein*
first: *prôtos*
fit: *epharmozein*
fitness: *epitêdeiotês*
flavour: *khumos*
flavoured: *enkhumos*
flavourless: *akhumos*
flee: *phugein*
flesh: *sarx*
flow: *rhein*
foam: *aphros*
foggy, be: *epikaluptein*
foliage: *khlôra*
follow: *akolouthein, akolouthos, hepesthai, epakolouthein*
foot: *pous*
foot-long: *podaios*
footed: *pezos*
force: *bia*
forced: *biaios*
forceful: *biaios*
forcibly: *biaiôs*
foreknow: *progignôskein*
fork: *ektropê*
form (n.): *eidos*
form (v.): *sunhistanai*
formation: *sustasis*
formless: *aneideos*
forwards: *prosô*
foundation: *arkhê*
fragrance: *euôdia*
frog: *batrakhos*
fruit: *karpos*
fulfil: *plêroun*
fulfilment: *eudaimonia*
full: *plêrês*
fully: *holoklêrôs*
function: *ergon, skopos*
fundamental sense, in the: *kuriôs*

general (adj.): *koinos*
general (n.): *stratêgos*
generally: *katholou*
generate: *gennan*
generation: *genesis*
gentle: *êremaios*
genus: *genos*
go against: *antiprassein*
go away: *aperkhesthai*
god: *theos*
gold: *khrusos*
goldish: *krusoeidês*
good: *agathos*
govern: *dioikein*
governing part: *hêgemonikon*
grace: *euskhêmosunê*

grafted onto, be: *prosgignesthai*
grant: *keisthai*
grasp (n.): *gnôsis*
grasp (v.): *lambanein, gnôrizein*
grasping: *lêpsis*
greenish: *poôdês*
ground: *edaphos*
grow, able to: *auxêtikos*
grow, cause to: *auxein*
growing: *auxêsis*
growing, capable of: *auxêtikos*
growth: *auxêsis*
guide: *hodêgein*
guided by smell: *huposmos*

habit: *ethos*
hair: *thrix*
hand: *kheir*
hard-eyed: *sklêrophthalmos*
hardness: *sklêrotês*
harm: *blabê*
harmonise: *epharmozein*
harmony: *harmonia*
harmony, be in: *harmozein*
hate: *misein*
head: *kephalê*
health: *hugieia*
healthy: *hugiainein*
hear: *akouein*
heard, cannot be: *anêkoustos*
hearing: *akoê*
heart: *kardia*
heat (n.): *thermotês, to thermon*
heat (v.): *thermainein*
heaviness: *barutês*
heavy: *barus*
help (n.): *boêtheia*
help (v.): *boêthein*
high-pitched: *oxus*
highest: *teleutaios, kuriôtatos*
hit: *plêssein*
hold: *pisteuein*
hold in: *katekhein*
hold together: *sunekhein*
hollow (adj.): *koilos*
hollow (n.): *koilotês*
homogeneous: *homoiomerês*
homonymously: *homônumôs*
honey: *meli*
honey water: *melikraton*
honeyed wine: *oinomeli*
hot: *thermos*
house: *oikia*
human (being): *anthrôpos*
humour: *khumos*

I: *egô*

idea: *noêma*
ill, be: *nosein*
illness: *nosos*
illuminate: *phôtizein*
imagination: *anazôgraphêsis*
imitate: *mimeisthai*
immediately: *euthus*
immortality: *athanasia*
impact: *plêgê*
impact, make a: *plêssein*
impede: *empodizein*
imperceptible: *anaisthêtos*
imperishable: *aphthartos*
impinge: *prospiptein*
impression: *tupôsis*
impression, make: *tupoun*
imprint: *tupos*
in many ways: *pleonakhôs*
inactive: *anenergêtos*
inactivity: *anenergêsia*
inanimate: *apsukhos*
incapable of coming-to-be: *agenêtos*
incapable of perishing: *aphthartos*
include: *periekhein*
incommensurable: *asummetros*
incorporate: *proskrinein*
increase (n.): *epidosis*
increase (v.): *epiteinein*
incredible: *paradoxos*
incredibly: *paradoxôs*
indemonstrable: *anapodeiktos*
indication: *sêmeion*
indistinctly: *amauroteron, amaurôs*
individually: *idiai*
inferior to, be: *apoleipesthai*
infinitely many: *apeiros*
infinity: *apeiria*
inform: *eidopoiein*
ingest: *prospheresthai*
inhalation: *anapnoê*
inhale: *anapnein*
inherence: *huparxis*
initially: *prôtôs*
inner organs: *splankhnon*
inquiry: *zêtêsis*
insane, be: *parakoptein*
inscribe: *engraphein*
insecure: *akataleptos*
insensitive: *anaisthêtos*
inseparable: *akhôristos*
inside: *endon*
instantaneously: *akhronôs*
instruction: *didaskalia*
instrumental: *organikos*
intelligible: *gnôrimos*
intend: *boulesthai*
intense: *sphodros*

intention: *boulêsis*
intention, for: *boulêtikos*
intermediate: *metaxu*
internal: *entos*
intervening: *metaxu*
interweave: *sumplekein*
intrinsically: *kath' hauto*
investigate: *historein, zêtein*
involve: *khrêsthai*
irrationally: *alogôs*
itself just on its own: *auto kath' hauto*

join: *sunagein, epharmozein,
     epizeugnunai*
judgement: *hupolêpsis*
juxtaposition: *parathesis*

keep: *phulassein*
know: *ginôskein, epistasthai, eidenai*
know, not: *agnoein*
knower: *epistêmôn*
knowing: *gnôsis*
knowledge: *gnôsis, epistêmê*
known, what is: *epistêtos*

lack (n.): *sterêsis, aporia*
lack (v.): *sterein*
language: *logos*
largeness: *megethos*
last: *eskhatos*
lead: *prohêgeisthai*
learn: *manthanein*
leave along with: *sunaperkhesthai*
leave behind: *kataleipein*
left, on the: *aristeros*
leg: *skelos*
less clear: *asaphesteros*
life: *bios, zôê, to zên*
light: *phôs*
lightness: *kouphotês*
like: *homoios*
like, become: *homoiousthai*
likeness: *homoiotês*
likening: *homoiôsis*
limit (n.): *peras, horos*
limit (v.): *perainein*
line: *grammê*
lingering: *paramonos*
link: *suzeugnumi*
live: *zên*
liver: *êpar*
located in: *hidrusthai*
long for: *ephiesthai*
longed for: *ephetos*
longing: *ephesis*
look: *blepein*
lose: *sterein*

loss: *apobolê*
love (v.): *philein, eran*
love, object of: *erômenos*
lover: *erastês*
low-pitched: *barus*
lower: *katô*
luminous: *phôtoeidês*
lungs: *pleumôn*
lustre: *eukhroia*
lyre: *lura*

magnificent: *perittos*
magnificently: *perittôs*
maim: *pêroun*
maimed (n.): *pêrôma*
main: *kephalaios*
maintain: *phulassein*
make: *kataskeuazein*
make up: *anaplêroun*
management: *oikonomia*
manifest in addition: *paremphainein*
marketplace: *agora*
marvel: *thauma*
material: *hulikos*
mathematical: *mathêmatikos*
matter: *hulê*
mature (n.): *teleios*
mature (v.): *teleioun*
measure: *metrein*
medical: *iatrikos*
medium: to *metaxu*
melody: *melos*
melted, can be: *têktos*
membrane: *humên, khitôn*
memory: *mnêmê*
message: *prosangellia*
metal: *metalleutos*
metempsychosis: *metempsukhôsis*
middle, in the: mesos
mirror: *katoptron*
missing: *leipein*
mistake: *apatê*
mistakes, make: *apatasthai*
mix: *mignunai*
mix in: *enkatamignunai*
mixed, can be: *miktos*
mixture: *mixis*
modified, be: *paskhein*
modification: *diathesis*
modify: *diatithenai*
moist: *hugros*
moisten: *hugrainein*
moisture: to *hugron, hugrotês*
moment, for just a: *akariaios*
mortal: *thnêtos*
motion: *phora*
mould further: *prosanatupoun*

move: *kinein, pherein*
multiply: *pleonazein*
murex dye: *halourgês*
muscle: *mus*
mutual: *koinos*

nail: *onux*
name (n.): *onoma*
name (v.): *onomazein*
name, call by: *onomazein*
narrowing: *stenotês*
natural: *phusikos*
natural endowment, good: *euphuia*
naturally: *kata phusin*
naturally less gifted: *aphuesteros*
naturally more gifted: *euphuesteros*
nature: *phusis*
nature, be by: *phuein*
nature, in accordance with: *kata phusin*
necessary: *anankaion*
neck: *trakhêlos*
needle: *belonê*
negative: *apophatikos*
non-bodily: *asômatos*
non-bodily entities: *ta asômata*
non-evident: *adêlos*
non-homogeneous: *anhomoiomerês*
non-rational: *alogos*
nose: *rhis*
nourish: *trephein*
nourished, capable of being: *threptikos*
nourishing: *trophimos*
nourishment: *trophê*
now: *nun*
number: *arithmos, plêthos*
number, in: *kat' arithmon*
numerically: *kat' arithmon*

obey: *peithesthai*
object: *pragma*
oboe: *aulos*
oboe, for playing: *aulêtikos*
oboe, play: *aulein*
occur first: *prohêgeisthai*
odorous: *osmôdês*
odour: *osmê*
odourless: *aosmos*
oesophagus: *stomakhos*
ointment: *emplastos*
old age: *gêras*
on its own: *kath' hauto*
opposed to, be: *diaballesthai*
opposition: *antithesis*
order (n.): *taxis*
order (v.): *tassein*
organ: *organon*
origin: *arkhê*

outline: *tupos*
outside: *exô*
outside, from: *exôthen*
overflow: *huperballein*
own, its: *oikeios*
oyster: *ostreon*
oysters, similar to: *ostreôdês*
ox: *bous*

pain, feel: *lupeisthai*
painful: *lupêros*
painter: *grapheus*
pairing: *sunduo*
palpitation: *pêdêsis*
part: *meros, morion*
particular: *kathekaston*
pass: *khôrein*
passing: *parhodos*
passion: *thumos*
patent: *phaneros*
path: *hodos*
perceive: *aisthanesthai*
perceive, what can: *to aisthêtikon*
perceived, able to be: *aisthêtos*
perceiver: *ho aisthanomenos*
perceiving, capable of: *aisthêtikos*
perceptible: *aisthêtos*
perception: *aisthêsis*
perceptive: *aisthêtikos*
perceptual organ: *aisthêtêrion*
percolation: *diêthêsis*
pericardium: *perikardios*
perish: *phtheiresthai, diaphtheiresthai*
perish along with: *sumphtheiresthai*
perishable: *phthartos*
perishing: *phthora*
persist: *menein, summenein,*
 hupomenein, sôzesthai
perspicuous: *saphês*
persuade: *peithein*
phrase: *logos*
picture: *anazôgraphêma*
pile: *sôros*
pilot: *kubernêtês*
piloting, of or for: *kubernêtikê*
piper: *aulêtês*
place: *topos*
place directly on: *epitithesthai*
placing: *thesis*
plainly: *phanerôs*
planning: *boulê*
plant: *phuton*
plausibility: *pithanotês*
pleasant: *hêdus*
pleasure, feel: *hêdesthai*
porous: *araios*
portrait: *eikôn*

position: *thesis*
position, change in: *metabasis*
power: *dunamis, exousia*
power, in its: *dunamei*
practical: *praktikos*
practise: *askein*
precede: *progignesthai*
predispose against: *prodiaballein*
pre-eminently: *prôtôs*
prefer: *prokrinai*
premiss: *protasis*
prepared: *hetoimos*
preponderant, become: *pleonazein*
presence: *parousia*
present (v.): *phantazesthai*
present, be: *pareinai*
preservation: *sôteria, têrêsis*
preserve: *sôzein, têrein*
preserve, able to: *sôstikos, têrêtikos*
prevent: *kôluein*
prime: *paraskeuazein*
primarily: *prohêgoumenos*
primary: *prôtos*
primary perceptive part: *to aisthêtikon*
principle: *arkhê*
principle of change or movement: *arkhê tês kinêseôs*
probative: *deiktikos*
probe: *psêlaphoun*
proclaim: *prolegein*
produce: *poiein, empoiein*
produced, be: *gignesthai*
production: *genesis*
productive: *poiêtikos*
progress (v.): *proienai*
progression: *prohodos*
proof: *deixis*
proper: *oikeion*
proportion: *analogia, logos*
proportional: *analogon*
protect against: *phulassesthai*
protrusion: *exokhê*
prove: *deiknunai*
provide: *khorêgein*
provider: *khorêgos*
proximate: *prosekhês*
proximately: *prosekhôs*
pull: *helkein*
pure: *katharos*
purplish: *porphuroeidês*
pursue: *metadiôkein*
pursued, to be: *diôktos*
push: *ôthein*
put together: *parakeisthai*
puzzle: *aporia*
puzzling: *aporos*
puzzled, be: *aporein*

Pythian god: *Puthios*

qualify: *proskeisthai*
quality: *poiotês*
qualityless: *apoios*
query (v.): *zêtein*
quick: *takhus*

rage: *orgê*
rational: *logikos*
ready: *epidektikos*
reason (n.): *logos, aition, aitia*
reason (v.): *logizesthai*
reasoning, capable of: *logistikos*
rebound (v.): *anaklan*
rebound (n.): *anaklasis*
receive: *dekhesthai, lambanein*
received, to be: *dektos*
receptacle: *hupodokhê*
receptive: *epidektikos, dektikos*
recollect: *anamimnêskein*
recollection: *anamnêsis*
recovered: *episkeuastos*
recovery: *apokatastasis*
reference, can make: *endeiktikos*
reflect: *ephistanai*
reflect: *emphainesthai*
reflected image: *emphasis*
refute: *elenkhein*
regard: *phronein*
regulation: *oikonomia*
reinvigorated: *episkeuastos*
reject: *apostrephein*
relation: *skhesis*
relative: *pros ti*
relax: *anhienai*
relay (n.): *diadosis*
relay (v.): *diadidonai*
release: *analuein*
remain: *menein, summenein*
remember: *mnêmoneuein*
remove: *exhairein*
repel: *apôthein*
repelled, be: *apostrephesthai*
replacement: *antiperistasis*
report: *diangellein, eisangellein*
represent: *phantasiousthai*
represented, what is: *to phainomenon*
representation: *phantasia, phantasma*
representing, for or capable of: *phantastikos*
reproduce: *gennan homoion hautôi*
reproducing, for or capable of: *gennêtikos*
reproduction: *gennêsis*
resist: *antitupein*
resistance: *antereisis, antitupia*
resolution, come to a: *suntithesthai*

resources: *khorêgia*
responsible: *aitios*
responsible, what is: *aitia*
responsible factor: *to aition*
responsive: *sumpathês*
responsiveness: *sumpatheia*
rest: *êremia, argia*
rest, be at: *êremein*
rest, bring to: *êremizein*
retain: *sôzein, stegein*
return: *anastrephein*
return back again: *palindromein*
reveal: *dêloun*
revenge, take: *timôreisthai*
reverence, have great: *presbeuein*
rhythm: *rhuthmos*
right, in its own: *kath' hauto*
right, on the: *dexios*
root: *rhiza*
rot: *sêpesthai*
roughness: *trakhutês*
rower: *eretês*
rudder: *oiax*

safe: *asphalês*
salty: *halmuros*
same in form: *homoeidês*
sand: *ammos*
savoury: *liparos*
say: *legein*
sea: *thalatta*
sea creature: *thalassios*
seat, have one's: *kathidrusthai*
second: *deuteros*
secure: *katalêptikos*
secure grasp, attain a: *katalambanesthai*
securing: *katalêpsis*
see: *horan*
seed (n.): *sperma*
seed (adj.): *spermatikos*
seeing: *horasis*
seen, cannot be: *ahoratos*
sense: *aisthêsis*
sensible: *eulogos*
sensibly: *eulogôs*
sensitivity, greater: *euaisthêsia*
separable: *khôristos*
separate (adj.): *khôristos*
separate (v.): *khôrizein*
separated: *kekhôrismenos*
separation: *khôrismos*
sequence: *hodos, taxis*
sequester: *diaspan*
serially: *kata meros*
set out: *ektithenai*
shakes: *tromos*
shape (n.): *skhêma*

shape (v.): *skhêmatizein*
shape, with a definite: *hôrismenos, horistos*
shape, without a definite: *ahoristos*
shapeless: *askhêmatistos*
share in, have a: *koinônein, metekhein, metalambanein*
shift (n.): *metastasis*
shift (v.): *methistasthai*
shine: *stilbein*
ship: *naus*
shortage: *endeia*
shortfall: *endeia*
show: *deiknunai*
shrink: *meiousthai*
shudder (n.): *phrixis*
shudder (v.): *phrittein*
side: *pleura*
sight: *opsis*
signet ring: *sphragis*
similar: *homoios*
similar kind, of a: *sungenês*
simple: *haplous*
simply as such: *haplôs*
simultaneously: *hama*
sinew: *neuron*
size: *poson*
slate: *pinakis*
slight, make a: *oligôrein*
smallness: *mikrotês*
smell: *osphrêsis*
smell, perceive: *osmasthai*
smellable: *osphrantos, osphrêtos*
smelling, capable of: *osphrantikos*
smelling, for: *osphrêtikos*
smith: *khalkeus*
smithing, for: *khalkeutikos*
smooth: *leios*
smoothness: *leiotês*
soak: *dihugrainein*
sober, to be: *nêphein*
softness: *malakotês*
solid: *stereos*
solidity: *pêxis, stereotês*
song: *melos*
soul (n.): *psukhê*
soul (adj.): *psukhikos*
sound (n.): *psophos*
sound (v.): *êkhein*
sound, emit a: *psophein*
sound, capable of emitting: *psophêtikos*
sour: *struphnos*
source: *pêgê*
sow: *kataballein*
sow seed: *speirein*
spatially: *metabatikôs*
speak: *legein*

specific: *aphôrismenos*
specific thing: *tode ti*
speech: *dialektos*
speed: *takhos, takhutês*
spicy: *pikros*
spin: *dinein*
spontaneous: *automatos*
spot: *sunhoran*
sprouting: *blastêsis*
star: *astêr*
start: *arkhein*
state: *legein*
statue: *andrias*
stay: *menein, diamenein*
steep: *enapoplunein*
stem (n.): *kaulos*
stem (v.): *ekphuein*
stew: *pessein*
stick: *baktêria*
stone: *lithos*
stored away: *apokeisthai*
strength: *sphodrotês*
stretch over: *periteinein*
stretching: *ektasis*
strike: *empiptein, tuptein*
string: *khordê*
striving: *hormê*
striving, for or capable of: *hormêtikos*
structure: *kataskeuê*
studied, can be: *theôrêtos*
study, engage in: *theorein*
study: *theôria*
study, for engaging in: *theôretikos*
subject: *hupokeimenos, pragma*
submit: *hupotassesthai*
subsequent: *deuteros*
subsequent, be: *hepesthai*
subserve: *hupêretein*
subservient: *hupêretikos*
substance: *ousia*
'such', a: *toionde*
suffice: *arkein*
sufficient: *hikanos*
suitable: *epitêdeios*
suitable condition: *epitêdeiotês*
summary, in: *suntomôs*
sun: *hêlios*
superficial: *epipolaios*
supervene: *epigignesthai*
surface: *epiphaneia, epipedon*
surpass: *pleonektein*
superfluously: *matên*
superior: *timiôteros*
supplement: *prostithenai*
supplementation: *prosthêkê*
suppose: *hupolambanein*
surprised, be: *thaumazein*

surround: *perilambanein, perikeisthai*
survive: *sôzesthai*
sustaining: *sôstikos*
sweet: *glukos*
synopsis, give a: *sullabein*

tactile: *haptikos*
take on in addition: *proslambanein*
take up: *analambanein*
take to be the case: *hupolambanein*
tangible: *haptos*
task: *ergon, hupêresia*
tastable: *geustos*
taste (n.): *geusis*
taste (v.): *geuesthai*
taste, what can: *geustikos*
temperate: *eukratos*
temple: *neôs*
tend: *apoklinein*
tendency: *rhopê*
term: *onoma*
terminate: *teleutan*
testify against: *antimarturein*
theory: *dogma*
things there are: *ta onta*
think: *dianoeisthai, phronein*
thinking, for or capable of: *dianoêtikos*
'this', a: *tode*
thought: *epinoia, noêsis, phronêsis*
tinge: *khrônnunai*
tinge anew: *anakhrônnunai*
time: *khronos*
time, at the same: *hama*
total: *holoklêros*
tongue: *glôtta*
tool: *organon*
tortoise: *khelonê*
touch: *haphê*
touch, able to: *haptikos*
trace: *enkataleimma*
trace back: *anagein*
train: *progumnazein*
transfer: *metapherein*
transform: *metaballein*
transformation: *metabolê*
transition: *metabasis*
translate: *metapherein*
transmit: *diakoneisthai*
transmit, able to: *diakonêtikos*
transmitter: *diakonos*
transmitting, for: *diakonikos*
transodorant: *diosmos*
transonant: *diêkhês*
transparency: *diaphaneia*
transparent: *diaphanês*
trap: *apolambanein*
treat: *therapeuein*

treatise: *logos, pragmateia*
tree: *dendron*
trigger, able to: *metablêtikos*
true: *alêthês*
trumpet: *salpinx*
trunk: *thôrax*
truth: *to alethes*
truth, possess: *alêtheuein*
turn back: *anakamptein*
twofold: *dittos*
type: *eidos*

unclear: *asaphês*
uncooked: *apeptos*
uncover: *apokaluptein*
uncovered: *askepês*
undergo a modification: *paskhein*
underlying (subject): (*to*) *hupokeimon*
undermine: *anhairein*
understand: *noein, manthanein, akouein*
understand, able to: *noêtikos*
understandable: *noêtos*
understanding: *nous, to noein*
understanding, act of: *noêsis*
undeveloped: *atelês*
undigested: *akatergastos*
undispersed: *athruptos*
undivided: *adihairetos, askhistos*
unenmattered: *ahulos*
unify: *henoun*
unity: *henôsis*
universal: *katholou*
universe: *kosmos*
unlike: *anhomoios*
unmixed: *amigês*
unmodifiable: *apathês*
unnamed: *anônumos*
unpleasantness: *duskhereia*
untransformed: *ametablêtos*
up to us: *eph' hêmin*
upwards: *anô*
use (v.): *proskhrêsthai, katakhrêsthai, khrêsthai*
used to, become: *ethizesthai*
useful: *khrêsimos*

vain, in: *matên*
vaporous: *atmidôdês*
variation: *tropê*
vegetable: *lakhanon*
vegetative: *phutikos*
vessel: *angeion*
vestige: *ikhnos*

view: *doxa*
view, come into: *hupopiptein*
virtue of, in: *kata*
visible: *horatos*
visual: *horatikos*
vital: *zôtikos*
vividly: *sphodros*
vocal: *phônêtikos*
voice: *phônê*
voice, have a: *phônein*

walk: *badizein*
walk, take a: *peripatein*
walking, capable of: *poreutikos*
wall: *toikhos*
wash, able to: *pluntikos*
water: *hudôr*
wax: *kêros*
weak: *amudros*
weave: *huphainein*
weaver: *huphantês*
weaving, for: *huphantikos*
well-being: *to eu einai, to eu*
well-blended: *eukratos*
wet dream: *oneirôgmos*
what is: *to on*
what is not: *to mê on*
whip: *mastix*
whole: *holos*
wide: *eurus*
wind-pipe: *artêria*
wine: *oinos*
wing: *pterux*
winged: *ptênos*
wish: *boulesthai*
withdraw: *hupokhôrein*
womb: *gastêr*
wood: *xulos*
wool: *erion*
work: *erga*
workings: *erga*
worm: *skôlêx*
wrestle: *palaiein*
wrestler: *palaistês*
wrestling, for: *palastikos*
write: *graphein*
write down: *antigraphein*
writing tablet: *grammateion*

yielding: *eiktikos*
you: *su*
youth: *neotês*

Greek-English Index

The present index lists occurrences of Greek terms of interest, together with their English translations, for both Parts I and II. Although it is meant to be fairly complete, it should not be assumed to be exhaustive: for a full listing and accurate count of the occurrences of a term, the reader should use a computer search on the *TLG*. Note also that the general listing at the beginning of an entry in particular is not complete: if a citation is given under a more specific sub-entry within an entry, or is cross-listed as being under another entry, the citations are *given only under that specific sub-entry or cross-listed entry*. The entries and sub-entries are alphabetised by their English transliteration, not the Greek alphabet. If an occurrence crests over a line, only the first line number is given. A range of lines indicates that there are at least two occurrences of the term within two lines of each other throughout the range.

aer, air, 6,24; 8,21; 19,22.27.35; 26,17; 42,7; 44,5.9; 47,1-2.7.11.15.18.22.25; 48,1.4.8-12; 49,10-12.16; 50,12-14.20.24; 52,18; 53,5.8.14; 57,3; 58,21-2; 59,15; 62,5

adêlos, non-evident, 72,20

adihairetos, undivided, 48,13; 61,20; 63,19.27

agathos, good, 89,3-4; *to malista kai prôtôs agathon*, what is good pre-eminently and to the highest degree, 89,2

agenêtos, incapable of coming-to-be, 6,14

agnoein, not know, 33,7

agora, marketplace, 13,19

agraphos, blank, 84,25-8

ahoratos, cannot be seen, 52,14

ahoristos, lacking a definite shape, 44,15; 46,8. For *ahoriston diaphanes*, see under *diaphanês*

ahulos, immaterial. For *ahulon eidos*, see under *eidos*

aidios, eternal, 6,14; 81,7; 82,18

aisthanesthai, perceive 12,13; 16,15; 32,26; 39,13; 40,26; 51,10; 52,21; 54,24-55,1; 56,21; 57,1; 58,14.18; 59,6; 60,20.26; 61,1-2.11-12.18-19; 62,5; 63,3.21-2; 64,10; 65,3-6.9-10; 66,28; 67,6-7; 78,6.10; 79,9.16; 83,4.20; 84,6-7; 87,2-3; 91,21; 92,11; 93,11-15.23; 96,19-20; *ho aisthanomenos*, the perceiver, 29,6; 58,6; 65,9; cf. 57,1; 60,26; 65,4; *to aisthanesthai*, perceiving, 29,7; 40,19; 65,10; 84,5; *to aisthanomenon*, what

is perceived, 84,7; *to kat' energeian aisthesthai*, to perceive actively, 69,4

aisthêsis, perception, perceiving, 30,13; 32,26; 38,20; 39,6-9; 40,4.9; 41,12; 43,15; 55,2; 56,18-20; 57,7-9.13-16.19; 58,2.19; 61,6.22; 62,17; 64,3; 66,11-13.23-7; 67,2-5.8-9.23-6; 68,18.21-3.27-9; 69,12-14; 70,1.7.10; 71,6; 72,3.16-17; 73,3.9; 74,3-5.22; 75,17.20-3; 76,10; 77,3.11; 78,10.13-14.18; 83,9.16.19-21; 84,4.12; 86,16; 87,4-5.12.19; 91,12.22-4; 92,23; 93,2; 97,3.11; sense, 18,28; 19,1; 39,11.17; 40,13-14.21.26; 41,2-4.11; 51,9.25; 52,16; 54,5; 55,3.15.18-19.26-7; 56,5; 57,6.12.18; 58,7-8; 59,8.20.23; 60,1.3.8-10.14-15.19-20.23; 61,8.25-6; 62,1; 65,4-6.12.20-1; 66,3-5; 68,20; 73,4-6; 74,26-7; 81,4; 83,2-6; 86,7.10; 93,18.22-4; *kat' energeian aisthêsis*, perception in activity, 12,18; 39,14; 68,27.31; 69,2.16; 70,2-3.19; 83,13; 87,1; 91,8; *koinê aisthêsis*, common sense, 62,20; 63,6.13; 65,3.9.17; 78,10.12; 97,13; *kuria aisthêsis*, principal perception, 65,8; *prôtê aisthêsis*, primary perception, 65,8. For *geustikê aisthêsis*, see under *geustikos*; for *haptikê aisthêsis*, see under *haptikos*

aisthêtêrion, perceptual organ, 12,14; 19,1; 24,10; 41,4.16-20; 44,2-6; 55,3; 57,4.7; 58,3-4.9-12; 59,1.13; 60,4.15; 62,2.14.17; 63,14-18.22-4; 64,2-4.10.21-2; 65,1; 66,2-3; 69,12;

enhulos, enmattered, 18,10; 83,19; 87,23; 88,11; 90,5; cf. *hôs en hulêi* under *hulê*. For *enhulon eidos*, see under *eidos*

enkatoikodomein, build in, 49,1; 50,13

enkataleimma, trace, 38,10; 63,3; 68,7.10.27; 69,1-2.16; 70,4-5.9.12.15.19.23; 72,8.11; 97,13

enkatamignunai, mix in, 54,16

enkephalos, brain, 99,31; 100,5

enkhumos, flavoured, 53,7.11.25; 54,10. For *enkhumos xêrotês*, see under *xêrotês*; for *enkhumos hugrotês*, see under *hugrotês*

enkratês, one who is in control of himself, 27,8

ennoein, conceive, 80,12.14

ennoia, conception, 77,3; 85,23

enokhlein, disturb, 42,2

entelekheia, completion, 16,1.6-10; 17,12; 24,1-2; 52,2; 78,25-6; 81,26; *entelekheiai*, in actuality, 54,20; *prôtê entelekheia*, first completion, 16,7-10; 21,5

entos, internal, inside, 45,5; 49,20; 56,16; 69,1. For *entos meros*, see under *meros*; for *entos aisthêton*, see under *aisthêton*

epakolouthein, follow, 80,6

êpar, liver, 95,2; 97,7

epeisienai, enter, 50,13

epharmozein, harmonise, 2,17; fit, 28,19; coincide, 63,10-12.24; apply, 86,26

ephesis, longing, 36,7; 79,7

ephetos, longed for, 79,6

eph' hêmin, up to us, 67,1; 73,11.12; *ouk eph' hêmin*, not up to us, 66,28; 73,8

ephiesthai, long for, 32,15

ephistanai, reflect, 6,7

epidektikos, receptive, can receive, 5,8; 10,26; 15,1; 81,19

epidosis, development, 30,6; 94,15; increase, 35,17; 36,20

epigignesthai, supervene, 25,2; 26,22; 79,26; *gignesthai + epi*, 10,25; 24,19

epikaluptein, cover up, 52,24; (perf. pass.) be foggy, 71,25

Epikouros, Epicurus, 26,17

epikouros, assistant, 98,16

epikrisis, discriminating, 71,27

epinoia, thought, 6,17.20; conception, 14,9

epiktêtos, acquired. For *epiktêtos nous*, see under *nous*

epipedon, surface, 50,27

epiphaneia, surface, 18,11-12; 45,21-2; 46,15-16

epipolaios, superficial, 13,3; lack detail, 71,6

episkeuastos, reinvigorated, 36,8

epistasthai, know, 78,15; 99,5-6; *epistêmôn*, knower, person who knows, 39,8; 86,1-4

epistêmê, knowledge, (pl.) branches of knowledge, 39,7; 66,12.16.23; 67,9-11.25; 72,25; 82,3.6.9; 86,2-3; 89,23; 90,1

epistêmonikos, for *or* capable of knowing, 82,19. For *epistêmonikê dunamis*, see under *dunamis*; for *epistêmonikos nous*, see under *nous*

epistêtos, what is known, 66,17; 81,8

epitêdeios, apt, suitable, fit, 13,5; 36,23; 41,20; 98,14

epitêdeiotês, aptitude, 12,25; suitable condition, 37,1; fitness, 81,14; 84,24.28; 85,3

epiteinein, increase, 26,10

epitelein, achieve, 99,29

epithumia, appetite, 12,16; 13,2; 74,2-3; 78,23

epitithesthai, place directly upon, 57,16.19; 58,1.10

epizêtein, enquire further, 60,22

epizeugnunai, join, 63,9

eran, love (v.); *erômenos*, object of love, 79,6

erastês, lover, 79,6

êremaios, gentle, 50,22-3

êremein, be at rest, 22,25-6; 23,2-7; 86,6

êremia, rest, 22,24; 23,1; 41,5; 65,13; 83,21

êremizein, bring to rest, 22,26

eretês, rower, 79,20

ergon, function, task, 2,26; 22,27; 23,3; 32,12; 36,21; 49,12.18; 65,17; 83,12; 97,12; (in pl.) workings, activities, work, 2,14.16; 32,10; 69,3

erion, wool, 47,5

êrtêsthai, depend, 12,18

eruthêma, blushing, 77,14

eskhatos, last, ultimate, 29,22; 94,4; 94,28; 99,12; (pl.) extremities, 95,11. For *eskhaton aisthêstêrion*, see under *aisthêstêrion*

ethizesthai, become used to, 83,5

ethos, habit, 81,25

eu, well; *to eu einai*, well-being, 49,19; 81,18-19; 93,20; *to eu*, well-being, 49,23; wellness, 81,20

euaisthêsia, greater sensitivity, 52,6

eukhroia, lustre, 31,4

shape, 44,19; 45,20; 46,1.5. For
hôrismenê kinêsis, see under *kinêsis*
horman, strive, 72,21.26; 73,2.29; 79,14
hormê, striving, 12,19; 49,5; 50,8;
72,14-16.21-3; 73,1.21; 75,22-3; 77,16;
78,23; 79,9.23.26; 80,5; 97,15. For
kath' hormên energeia, see under
energeia
hormêtikos, able to strive *or* enable
striving; *to hormêtikon*, the part for
striving, 73,27; 75,10; 76,2-3.6.15;
99,8.22; *to koinon hormêtikon te kai
orektikon*, the common part for
striving and desiring, 78,22. For
hormêtikê dunamis, see under
dunamis; for *hormêtikê psukhê*, see
under *psukhê*
horos, limit, 35,7
hothen, that from which (= the principle
of change or efficient cause), 73,25
hou heneka, that for which (= the end
or final cause), 24,14 (cf. 24,16, 28,8);
73,26; see also *telos*
hudôr, water, 3,17; 6,24; 8,21; 11,18;
34,11; 42,7; 44,5; 47,2; 51,17; 52,18;
53,5.8.12-14.17-18; 54,6-7; 57,3;
58,20-2; 59,15; 62,14
hugiainein, be healthy, 16,16;
31,15-20; 41,15
hugiazein, cure, 100,7
hugieia, health, 25,4-9; 31,15-20
hugrainein, moisten, make moist,
54,20; 55,2
hugros, moist, moisture, 26,8; 40,1-3;
44,5; 53,2; 54,4-10.14.18-20;
54,23-55,1; *to hugron*, moisture,
3,18-19; 51,19; 53,25; 54,4
hugrotês, moisture, 8,19; 19,35; 40,25;
54,7.16.24; 55,22; 58,26; 94,19;
enkhumos hugrotês, 53,19
hulê, matter, 2,26-5.1; 5,6.19-22;
6,2.5.17.22.28; 7,7; 8,1.18; 9,6;
10,3.4.12; 11,20; 12,7; 13,24; 14,3;
15,12.23.26; 17,16-18,10; 18,14.18;
19,4.5.23.24; 26,28; 31,13.18.24;
36,23; 54,6; 66,14; 81,25; 84,1-3.20;
85,17; 87,7.10; 88,13.18-22; 89,15-16;
94,19; *akhôristos tês hulê*,
inseparable from matter, 4,28; 6,1;
aneu (tês) hulês, without (the) matter,
83,14; 91,15; see also *khôris (tês)
hulês* below; *apo tês hulês khôrizein*,
separate from the matter, 85,13 (*apo
tês hulês khôrismos*, separation from
the matter, 18,23; 89,14); *en (têi)
hulêi*, in matter, 4,21; 88,16; see *hôs
en hulêi* below; *haplôs hulê*, matter

simply as such, 4,5-7.24; *hôs (ontôn)
en hulêi*, as being in matter, 83,17.22;
87,3.12 (cf. *enhulos*); *hôs
kekhôrismenon hulês*, as separated
from matter, 88,13; *hôs hulê*, as
matter, 83,23; 84,6; see *oukh / mê hôs
hulê* below; *hôs meta hulês*, as
accompanied by matter, 84,7; *khôris
(tês) hulês*, separate from (the)
matter, 60,5; 66,13; 78,8; 83,15;
85,14.19; 86,29; 87,21.26; 88,15.25;
89,12.17.21; 90,5; 91,8; 92,22; cf.
khôris tôn hulikôn peristaseôn,
separate from material material
conditions, 85,15; see also *aneu (tês)
hulês* and *apo tês hulês khôrismos*,
above; also *khôrizein tês hulês*, under
khôrizein; *kuriôs hulê*, matter in the
fundamental sense, 4,4.7.16.22; 7,15;
mê memigmenos hulêi, not mixed
with matter, 89,16; *meta (tês) hulês*,
in conjunction with, 8,9; 18,6;
91,14-15; *oukh / mê hôs hulê*, not as
matter, 62,2-3.13; 83,16.22; 84,6;
87,4; see *hôs hulê* above; *oukh hôs en
hulêi*, not as in matter, 83,22;
oukh / mê hôs meth' hulês, not as
conjoined with matter, 83,23; 84,7;
91,15; *prosekhês hulê*, proximate
matter, 4,23; 10,24; 44,21 (cf.
prosekhôs hupokeimenon,
proximately underlying subject,
7,21); *sun (têi) hulêi*, conjoined with
matter, 18,1; 89,21; 91,15
hulikos, material; *hulikê peristasis*,
material condition, 84,8; 85,15. For
hulikos nous, see under *nous*
humên, membrane, 56,19-22
huparxis, inherence, 90,4
huperballein, to exceed, overflow, 13,4;
59,7
huperbolê, excess, 59,19; 60,9
huperesia, task, 77,23; apparatus, 86,8;
99,28
huperetein, subserve, 16,12; 75,29;
76,17
huperetikos, subservient, 76,9.14;
99,27; 100,14
huphanein, weave, 23,21
huphantês, weaver, 23,21
huphantikos, for weaving, 23,21
huphistasthai, exist, 4,17.26; 5,1.21;
18,4.17; 19,7; 29,13; *kath' hauto
huphistasthai*, existing on its own,
4,8.20.24-6 (cf. 23); 17,11.14; 19,7.20
(cf. 19)
hupnos, sleep, 71,1.26; 74,26-7

ous, ear, 49,1; 50,13.17.21.24; 57,4
ousia, essence, 1,3; 2,11; 4,14; 15,22;
  16,18; 19,12.15-17; 22,27; 27,1; 28,16;
  30,20; 32,7; 35,15; 61,7; 92,6;
  substance, 5,2-3.10; 6,2-6; 12,8; 14,25;
  15,1; 20,27; 26,19; 59,13; 59,13;
  aisthêtê ousia, perceptible substance,
  2,27; *meros tês ousias*, part of
  substance, 6,3; *sômatikê ousia*, bodily
  substance, 2,27
oxus, high-pitched, 34,2; 55,28; acidic,
  51,24; 55,21
oxutês, acidity, 53,22

pakhutês, density, 44,8
palaiein, wrestle, 23,18-19
palaistês, wrestler, 23,18-19
palastikos, for wrestling, 23,19
palindromein, return back again, 95,11
paradekhesthai, admit, 25,10
paradoxos, incredible, 2,14.23;
  11,6.10-11; *paradoxôs*, incredibly, 2.24
parakeisthai, put together, 25,17
parakolouthein, examine in detail, 2,10
parakoptein, be insane, 70,18
parallagê, diversity, 8,14.16; disparity,
  10,22
parallattein, deviate, 75,12
paramonos, lingering, 86,11
paramuthia, explanation, 2,9
parapempein, deliver, 50,16
paraphrosunê, delirium, 100,6
parapompê, delivery, 95,3
paraskeuazein, prime, 13,5; enable,
  36,21; arrange, 50,28; facilitate, 51,1
paraspeirein, distribute, 37,12
parathesis, juxtaposition, 12,2;
  combination, 13,6
pareinai, be present, 40,14; 43,1; 44,4;
  45,6; 58,13-18; 63,2-4; 66,25;
  69,8.11-13; 70,16; 71,1-2; 77,4; *ou/mê
  pareinai*, not present, 39,5; 62,16;
  66,26-8; 67,1; 68,8; 69,10.15.26;
  70,16; 71,1; 73,1. See also *parousia*
paremphainein, manifest in addition,
  84,15
parhuphistanai, exist in conjunction
  with, 65,18
parodos, passing, 62,18
parousia, presence, 29,5.9; 31,7.28;
  35,27; 36,26; 38,1; 43,2.9; 45,2.11;
  92,17. See also *pareinai*
paskhein, be modified, undergo,
  7,10-14; 16,15; 39,17.20-1; 41,9.11;
  42,18; 43,13.20; 54,7.24; 57,7-11.15;
  59,3.7; 61,30; 63,22; 64,6-11.19-21;
  66,12; 75,23; 84,2.6; 85,2-4; 86,7;

89,15.20; 98,21; be affected, 13,2;
  experience, 71,18
pathêtikôs, by being modified, 62,13
pathos, modification, 39,18.21; 41,13;
  43,20; 44,8; 51,17-19.21; 53,25; 54,17;
  57,12-14; 62,2-3.17; 63,22; 64,2.5-8;
  76,18; 77,1.12.21; 84,1-3; 86,11;
  100,5; effect, 50,27; affect, 13,2-5;
  71,25; 97,2; state, 98,24; *sômatikon
  pathos*, bodily affection, 84,5
pauein, cease, 4,3; 7,1-2; 86,25
pêdêsis, palpitation, 98,18
pêgê, source, 40,2
peithein, persuade, 2,13; *peithesthai*,
  obey, 1,5; 2,2; 74,10
pepsis, cooking, 33,19.25-6; 35,1; 51,18;
  53,17; 54,10-11; 95,3; see *pessein*
  below
perainein, limit; *peperasmenon*, limited
  (in number), 27,4; 28,7.14
peras, boundary, 14,20; 45,20-46,1;
  46,8-13.18; limit, 17,13-14; endpoint,
  63,9-12.15-17.23-4; 64,1; 97,28
peratoun, bound (v.), 46,10
periekhein, include, contain, enclose,
  14,20; 18,7; 32,29; 47,12; 48,2; 50,15;
  80,18; 98,10
perikardios, pericardium, 98,11
perikeisthai, surround, 98,19
perilambanein, comprehend, 16,19;
  class, 56,12; surround, 98,11
perilêpsis, comprehension,
  comprehending, 82,13; 83,11; 85,12;
  92,14
peripatein, take a walk, 80,12-13;
  82,5-7
peripiptein, encounter, 93,5; incur,
  98,20
periphereia, circumference, 63,8
peristasis, circumstance, 41,12. For
  hulikê peristasis, see under *hulikos*
periteinein, stretch over, 56,19
perittôma, end product, 36,4; 92,20;
  95,18
perittos, magnificent, 2,12; *perittôs*,
  magnificently, 2,24
pêrôma, maimed, 32,12
pêroun, maim, 32,18; 35,20; 81,26; 82,11
pessein, cook, 33,27; 53,12; 95,2
pêxis, solidity, 3,19
pezos, footed, 13,14
phainesthai, appear, 44,25; 45,24;
  50,26; 67,7; *to phainomenon*, what is
  represented, 71,3
phaneros, obvious, clear, 27,8; 35,25;
  99,30; apparent, 45,23-4; *phanerôs*,
  plainly, 8,14; 12,15

psuxis, cooling, 77,15.18-19
ptênos, winged, 13,14
pterux, wing, 96,4
Puthios, the Pythian god (= Apollo), 1,6
pur, fire, 5,4-12; 6,21.23; 8,21; 11,7;
    16,4; 19,22.35; 20,3; 26,17; 34,12;
    35,8; 43,9; 45,2.12; 46,1; 53,8; 79,2

rhein, flow, 54,9
rhis, nose, 57,5
rhiza, root, 37,18; 94,22
rhopê, tendency, 12,10
rhuptikos, able to cleanse, 51,20; 53,6
rhuthmos, rhythm, 26,6

salpinx, trumpet, 49,8
saphês, perspicuous, 17,2; clear,
    32,24-5; *saphôs*, clearly, 2,8; 3,3
sarx, flesh, 56,15-23;
    57,2-4.8-9.12-14.17; 58,3.7.24; 93,17;
    98,6.10.13-14; 100,15
sêmainein, signify, 13,11; 40,7;
    sêmainomenon, sense, 13,11
sêmeion, indication, evidence, 46,7;
    52,5; 56,17.23; 94,27; 95,7-9; 96,22
sêpesthai, rot, 53,21
sidêros, blade, 98,11
skelos, leg, 18,20
skepasma, clothing, 80,14-15
skhêma, shape (n.), 3,8; 4,11-15; 6,19;
    11,21; 14,1-2; 18,21; 20,22; 21,2.8;
    31,4; 41,5; 50,16; 65,13; 70,21;
    72,7-10; 83,20; 84,9; 98,5-6
skhêmatizein, shape (v.), 3,1.6; 19,25-6;
    34,3; 46,10; 48,13.16.19; 50,14
skhesis, relation, 43,3.10; 45,3; 56,9; 71,5
skhizein, divide, 95,5
sklêrophthalmos, hard-eyed, 53,1
sklêrotês, hardness, 55,22
skôlêx, worm, 67,3; 74,5
skopos, function, 35,10.13
skotos, dark, darkness, 42,5; 43,17;
    52,14; 56,14
Sôkratês, Socrates, 72,25
sôma, body, 1,3, 2,20.24; 3,11.13; 4,5.8;
    5,9.14-22; 6,7.12-21; 7,3.11-14.17;
    8,16.24; 10,2-3.11.27-8;
    11,2-4.7-9.12.22; 12,2-3.7-25;
    13,5.8-12.16.18.21; 14,5-19.25;
    15,4-5.8-9.12.15-20.27; 16,2; 17,10-11;
    17,15-19,8; 19,20-2; 20,2;
    21,11.14-18.22-4; 22,6.10-12.15-19.26;
    23,5.26; 24,2.20-2; 25,3.9; 26,18;
    28,1.7; 31,6.16-18.21-4; 34,7; 35,1;
    36,1.12.20; 37,6; 43,11; 44,20; 45,9.24;
    46,15; 47,10; 48,8; 52,2.5; 54,2; 57,5;
    58,9.19.23-7; 59,5; 60,7.10.15; 62,18;

68,6; 69,10; 75,28; 76,17; 77,1.4.14.21;
    92,4.19; 93,6; 94,7.25.29; 95,3.22.26;
    96,1; 98,5.10-13; 100,2-3.12-14;
    apsukhon sôma, inanimate body,
    63,5; *empsukhon sôma*, animate body,
    11,8; 14,21; 63,5; 75,27-9; *haploun* vs
    suntheton sôma, simple vs compound
    body, 3,21-4,9; *haploun sôma*, simple
    body, 3,22.25.28; 4,10.16.19.27;
    5,4.8.19; 7,16; 8,3-8; 8,26; 9,14;
    10,13.16; 11,9; 16,3; 19,29-20,6 (cf.
    19,21-3); 20,20.23-6; 26,22; 31,27;
    34,9; 54,12; 58,20; 93,11.14; *meros tou
    sômatos*, part of the body, 18,15-27;
    24,7-9; 94,29 (cf. 95,7); 100,14;
    organikon sôma, organic body,
    16,4.10-14; 24,11; 27,17; *phusikon
    sôma*, natural body, 3,14.16.22-4;
    4,16; 5,4; 7,15; 8,2.5.13.26; 9,8; 10,1;
    16,3.10; 19,16; *prôta sômata*, basic
    bodies, 7,16; 10,14; 24,4; 26,27; 58,27;
    suntheton sôma, compound body,
    3,22-5; 4,5.23.27; 7,22-8,8; 8,26;
    9,9.23; 16,4; *tekhnikon sôma*, 16,3;
    theion sôma, divine body, 43,9; 45,3.
    For *sôma dia sômatos dierkhesthai*,
    see under *dierkhesthai*
sômatikos, bodily; 21,15.27; 86,8;
    sômatikon morion, bodily part, 78,1.
    For *sômatikê dunamis*, see under
    dunamis; for *sômatikê kinêsis*, see
    under *kinêsis*; for *sômatikê ousia*,
    bodily substance, see under *ousia*; for
    sômatikon organon, see under
    organon; for *sômatikon pathos*, see
    under *pathos*
sôros, pile, 47,22
sôstikos, able to preserve, sustaining,
    35,26; 93,6.8
sôteria, preservation, preserving, 35,14;
    36,5; 75,31; 93,4; 95,15
sôzein, preserve, retain, 10,15;
    11,13.16.19; 15,6.7; 20,19; 37,9; 63,1;
    67,27; 68,9-10.16.20; 70,6.12; (pass.)
    persist, survive, 18,23-4; 19,8; 98,23
speirein, to sow seed, 32,11
sperma, seed (n.), 32,2-4; 36,3.23;
    37,10.14; 38,4; 92,20
spermatikos, seed (adj.), 37,17
sphaira, ball, 48,18
sphodros, strong, intense, vivid,
    50,20.23; 60,13; 63,3; 71,9. For
    sphodra aisthêton, see under
    aisthêtos; for *sphodra phantasia*, see
    under *phantasia*; for *sphodra noêton*,
    see under *noêtos*
sphodrotês, strength, 50,19

Index of Passages Cited

The passages of ancient authors cited are listed by the abbreviations used above, together with the full title, with passages from these sources cited in bold italics. If the passage is mentioned in a note to the translation, the reference is to the page and line numbers of Alexander's text to which the note corresponds (e.g. 5,5-6); if the passage is mentioned in the introduction, the reference is to the page and note numbers of the introduction (with an 'i' appended to the page number of the present volume (e.g. 12i or 15i n.40)). Passages that only partially overlap are listed as separate entries, so in searching for a passage, the reader is advised to glance at neighbouring entries as well.

Subject Index

In the index below, the numerals generally indicate page and line numbers in *Alexander's* text (which appear in the margins of the translation). References to the Introduction are indicated by appending an '*i*' to the page number of the present volume (e.g. 12*i* or 15*i* n.40). References to the translator's notes are indicated by appending '*n*' to the page and line numbers of the passage to which the note belongs. If a citation is given under a more specific sub-entry within an entry, or is cross-listed as being under another entry, the citations are given only under that specific sub-entry or cross-listed entry. Discussions of ancient authors by Alexander are included in the subject index below, as well as any I have mentioned in the notes (apart from Alexander and Aristotle). Citations from ancient works are listed in the Index of Passages.

abortion, 38,4-8*n*; cf. 14*i*
Academy (Old), 1,9*n*; 1,4-2,4*n*; 3,28-4,4*n*
accident, *see* extrinsic characteristic
accompanying awareness (*sunaisthêsis*), 15,15-17; Stoic view, 15,15-17*n*
acting (*poiein*): in virtue of form, 7,9-13
activity (*energeia*): *vs* change (*kinêsis*), 12,9-13,8*n*; *vs* power, 8*i*; 9,20-6; 16,8-10.16-18; 32,25-7; 32,30-33,5
Aetius, 3,28-4,4*n*
affect (*pathos*), 13,2-5; *see also* modification
afterimages, 43,18-44,1*n*
air, 6,24; 8,21; 19,21.27.35; 26,17; 42,7; transparent, moist, and without a definite shape, 44,4-5
akrasia, see under loss of control
Alcinous, 3,28-4,4*n*; 27,15-28,2*n*
Alexander: 'The Commentator', 18-19*i* n.1; *How We See*, 43,16-18*n*
alive, 29,4-10; *see also under* life
alteration (*alloiôsis*), 12,17; *vs* growth, 33,28-34,8*n*; illumination and tingeing are an alteration only 'in a way' (*pôs*), 42,19-22*n*; 42,22-43,4*n*; perception occurs through a kind of alteration, 14*i*, 39,1-2; perception not an alteration, though it involves them, 15*i*, 38,21-39,2*n*; 44,9-13*n*
analogy, 10,12-14; 20,19-22; 24,26-7
Andronicus, 25,2-4*n*
anger, 12,16; 13,1.6-8; 23,15
animal: a natural, compound body, 10,1-2; compound of matter & form, 10,1-8; 12,6-7; compound of soul and body, 10,1-8; 11,14-12,7; defined by perception, 10,8-10; 29,14-15;

30,12-13; 38,18-19; initial formation of, 14*i*, 36,19-37,3; non-rational, 30,9-15; rational, 30,9-15; sense of touch is necessary, 40,14-15; what it is to be an animal is located in what is hot and moist, 40,1-2
animate (*empsukhon*), 16,16; 20,7; 21,4.10; 23,22; 24,11; 27,20; 29,3-10; body, 12,2-3; 14,7-8.21-2; 15,19; 19,6-9; distinguished from inanimate by power for nourishing oneself, 29,3-10
Antiochus of Ascalon, 1,9*n*; 1,4-2,4*n*; 3,28-4,4*n*; 41,13-42,3*n*
appetite (*epithumia*), 12,15; 13,2; involves bodily changes, 12,15
Apollo, *see under* Pythian god
Apollodorus, 18,10-14*n*; 18,25-19,1*n*
Arcesilaus, 20,8-19*n*
Aristotle of Mytilene, 19,21*n*
Aristotle of Stagira, 2,4-9; 16,5; 19,21*n*; his authority, 2*i*; 2,4-9*n*; *How We See*, 43,16-18*n*; *On the Soul*, 2,6
Arius Didymus, 7,9-13*n*
arkhê, see under origin and principle
art (*tekhnê*), 2,13*n*; 3,8-13; 23,26-8*n*; 24,8-9; analogy with nature, *see under* nature; imitates nature, not vice versa, 3,15-16.
artefacts, 5*i*; 3,2-13; 4,25-5,1; 16,3; 20,21; forms not substantial, 5,1-2; qualities in virtue of their form, 6,4-6; substances in virtue of their matter, 6,4-6
assimilation, *see under* likening
Atticus, 2,17-18*n*
aulos, see under oboe

www.ingramcontent.com/pod-product-compliance
Lightning Source LLC
Chambersburg PA
CBHW071513110726
47908CB00003B/820

* 9 781472 557988 *